# Getting To The Next Level

## A Blueprint For Taking You And Your Business To The Top

### Manuel Palachuk

Great Little Book Publishing, Inc.
Sacramento, CA

**GLB**

http://www.grealittlebook.com

Great Little Book Publishing Co., Inc.
Sacramento, CA

Getting To The Next Level
A Blueprint For Taking You And Your Business To The Top

http://www.greatlittlebook.com

Developmental Editor: Laura Napolitano
Copy Editor: Kathryn de Grasse
Graphics Artist: Chathuranga Gammanpila
Graphics Designer: Manuel Palachuk
Cover Artist: Sally Galli
Layout Designer: Yvonne Betancourt

ISBN Paperback - 978-1-942115-39-7
ISBN PDF - 978-1-942115-40-3

# DEDICATION

To my parents, Frank and Ramona Palachuk.

"One will weave the canvas; another will fell a tree by the light of his ax. Yet another will forge nails, and there will be others who observe the stars to learn how to navigate. And yet all will be as one. Building a boat isn't about weaving canvas, forging nails, or reading the sky. It's about giving a shared taste for the sea, by the light of which you will see nothing contradictory but rather a community of love."

From *Citadelle* by Antoine de Saint-Exupéry

Modern extrapolated version:
"If you want to build a ship, don't drum up people together to collect wood and don't assign them tasks and work, but rather teach them to long for the endless immensity of the sea."

Dear Mom and Dad,

Thank you Dad for telling me I could do anything I was willing to learn how to do or be anything I was willing to learn how to be. I believe it actually made my life harder because I found so many things to be excited about, enjoy, and throw myself into. So many things I wish I could have shared with you but you died so young. So many things I've shared with my son who you never knew and who never knew you.

Thank you Mom for allowing and helping me to pursue everything I wanted to, and for allowing me to be anything I wanted to be. I know it made my life harder because my unsettled mind found so many things to do, while all I wanted to do was be someone my father would be proud of. I knew you were proud of me because you told me so.

Thank you both for teaching me to long for the endless immensity of the sea.

I miss you both dearly every day of my life.

Manuel Palachuk

# TABLE OF CONTENTS

# LIST OF FIGURES

# Preface

In my life, I have never been fond of work simply for the sake of work; it's just not for me. I'm referring to holding a job just to collect a paycheck and going home with no concern for the quality of the actual work I do, the products we create, or the services we provide. At a very early age, I learned to recognize it and how to avoid it at all costs. I quickly formulated a dislike for companies that have no concern for the culture that exists in their business or no real compass direction for their business other than to make money.

Everywhere along my path, I have paid very close attention to the culture and compass of the businesses I worked in and the teams I worked with or on. Early on when I decided to build my first real business with employees and a storefront, I already had a good idea of what I wanted the company to stand for, how we would position and present ourselves, and where we were going. I was careful to protect those who came onto the team and how we together behaved as a business because it mattered to me. It mattered very much to me because I already saw firsthand how the culture and compass of a business, left to the influence of the ground level people in the company, can go completely awry. With no clear influence or guidance from the top, these organizations were not highly successful and some easily ended up becoming horrible places to work.

I have been in the service industry in one fashion or another for over forty years. It's not because I'm sixty some years old, but rather because I cut my teeth on service delivery as a newspaper boy before I was ten years old. My brothers all had newspaper routes, and I helped them not only deliver papers but also sign up new subscriptions and even walk the route collecting the monthly subscription fees. Of course I eventually moved into having my own routes and recruited my friends to help me run multiple routes.

Due to the nature of my education and career paths, I've been lucky enough to have worked in or been exposed to the inside of various industries and areas of work such as demolition and construction, food service, retail, printing and binding, manufacturing, and production. I've even had the opportunity to work in the U.S. Department of Energy as a contractor for several years. My assignments and positions have put me inside of manufacturing and production operations from Mexico to Canada and nearly every single state of the U.S. in businesses as small as one man shops to as large as Weyerhaeuser and Alcoa.

I can definitively state that I love and respect small businesses and the people who work in and with them. All hail the small business entrepreneurs and those who believe in them enough to provide them with capital, work for them, partner with them, or support them in any way. And don't forget the patrons who also prefer small and local businesses when there are more logical and viable choices. I can also state that although I liked working for large organizations, I really do prefer working with small and medium-sized businesses (SMBs) much more.

Now I don't want anyone to misunderstand somehow that I do not think there is a use for big business or that I am bent on their destruction or have some agenda or anything like that. Without big business we certainly could not do some of the things people in general and the world at large needs desperately to advance our society and species. But it really comes down to what I believe is the individual contribution potential of small businesses and the freedom of control the small business owner has over the business compared to larger companies. Add to this preference the fact that there are tens of millions of small and medium size businesses around the world that are, in fact, the backbone of the world. Without them, the world we have built today stops dead.

To this point, I have owned my own successful computer and IT service business. I have served as the Chief Operations Officer of a managed service provider company and President of another. I have also coached with many companies and mentored entrepreneurs around the world. I've turned businesses around and saved them from disappearing in the largest economic downturn (so far) in a generation.

In nearly every single small and medium-sized business I have worked in or with, there has been one common thread that threatens these businesses' existence and future. It exists not necessarily by failure and certainly not by design, but in my opinion, usually by either neglect or hubris. What is this thing that threatens the success and wellbeing of so many perfectly viable businesses? The complete and total lack of understanding that for your business to succeed, there must be a solid business roadmap and strategy that is the result of a well-thought-out business model.

What I have witnessed is that most entrepreneurs start a business using the basics of a simple business model but don't pay attention to the next level of business knowledge that is required to go further when the time comes. To put it in the simplest of terms, when most people go into business, they have or quickly pick up the basics of business finance and then human resources, then sales, then marketing, and so on. But when the business gets in trouble or stalls, they find they have not mastered the tools necessary to understand what's really going on in the business versus what they had planned.

Business owners and managers need the ability to dismantle their model and clearly identify what's broken or in need and then fix it. However, they instead rely on the business basics they do understand which usually are as simple as stop spending, cut costs, sell more, sell cheaper, and sell faster. The next level of business knowledge I refer to above is what's required for a business to get turned around, become a market leader, or to get to the next level.

And it's not enough to have a solid business roadmap and strategy based on a solid business model. You must actually follow the roadmap, execute on the strategy, and actively build the model. Further, if you want to have more than just a mediocre business where you employ a few folks and make an okay profit, where you actually grow the business and get to the next level, you have to actively cultivate your roadmap and strategy and check on the model you're building.

Here is where I will tell you quite plainly that you do not need a degree in business management to thrive or succeed. By all means, it should certainly help you significantly, but in fact there is no guarantee that even with a nice college degree you're going to go stratospheric. I have seen plenty of smart people with MBAs run perfectly good businesses into the ground. How? Why? This is where the hubris comes in. They thought they did not need to use those powerful tools they were shown when they were in school. And on the other side, people with much less education than I have run successful businesses for many years without a problem. How? They had a business model they intended to build and a solid roadmap and strategy, and they stuck to it.

This book is a culmination of the relevant business concepts, methods, tools, and best practices that I have put together from my experience in running my own successful businesses as well as helping others run or elevate theirs. There is no magic and no special sauce. However, I do include some of my own trademark ideas and tools devised to help convey important business concepts that are the foundation of a solid business roadmap, strategy, and model.

This book is not a numbers book. That is, it is not all about crunching the numbers and poring over financial reports, although I do go over some basic accounting and numbers. It is about building a solid business roadmap and strategy based on a solid business model. It will give you the roster of tools, the breakdown on how to use them, and even a few case studies. The scope of this book is obviously limited to a certain level of business management knowledge and I will always try to be as clear as I can when I have reached the edge of those points.

I wrote this book because I want to give a blueprint for success that any small business owner or entrepreneur can follow without having a degree in economics or business. One that would be the "next level" guide I referred to previously, intended to get you beyond the basic economics of the business. This book is in no way intended to substitute or replace any degree or course offered on Business Management. I believe it can be considered a layman's guide to building a great business roadmap and strategy based on a solid business model using internationally understood and accepted business concepts, methods, tools, and best practices.

Throughout this book I will be making specific references to several authors and excellent works usually relating to specific subjects as I discuss them. I'm not referring to the appropriate crediting of quotes or ideas to the original author just for writing purposes, but also because many of these mindsets, ideas, and viewpoints are some of the most innovative thinking I've ever come across. I firmly believe that reading these additional relevant works will build and solidify the concepts I have taken particular hold of myself. For this purpose, I have also included what I consider to be an extensive bibliography.

In closing, I would like to take a minute to give proper credit where credit is due. That is, to all those entrepreneurs and business owners who have trusted me with their businesses over the years, most particularly my brother Karl Palachuk. He trusted me with his business while he branched out into publishing and full-time authoring. He always asked important questions and gave the most valuable feedback but never questioned my decisions.

# ACKNOWLEDGEMENTS

A big thanks to my brother Karl Palachuk for his content review of this book and the many conversations on the content; they helped me greatly in the innovation of my original concepts. Also, thank you for advising me along the way and, of course, for publishing this book. But more than that, a very special thank you for explicitly trusting me with his business for all those years. It was a lot of fun working with him and I enjoy that we are still collaborating so many years later. You've been a source of inspiration all along the way.

Thank you to my life adventure partner Laura Napolitano for editing every single sentence of this book in true Virgo fashion (Fear the red pen!) and for her content review. Thank you for all the years' worth of listening to me drone on about my ideas and concepts and especially for helping me flesh them out. And thank you for supporting me in the endeavor that is my coaching business and the endeavor that was this book. This book has been in the making for nearly five years and in all that time, she has listened to me and provided invaluable feedback and input. You are my truest pal and confidant.

Thank you to my dear departed friend Scott Mallet who also trusted me with his business so many years ago. Allowing me to help his business provided me with the final rays of insight that inspired me to write this book and inspired some of my innovative concepts. I think of him all the time and I always wish he could have spent another lifetime's worth in the business he loved so much. How great it would be to chat with you now.

I must also thank my best friend Stephen H. Watkins Jr. for always talking shop with me and for helping me ruminate on processes and flesh out ideas. I don't know that he actually realizes he was part and parcel of this book. We've shared our nefarious plans and ideas of personal and business affairs for over 25 years. This was just another of so many.

Thank you to my brother Robin Palachuk for the many conversations over the years that he may not quite be aware were about my business concepts for this book as well as those conversations he certainly knew were about this book. He was a big contributor to the rounding out of the Human Element and its placement in the pyramid.

A giant thank you to Kathryn de Grasse for her superb editing work. Also, a hero's thank you to the pre-readers of the book. These folks, although bribed with free copies of the book and free coffee, were willing to read it because of genuine interest. Bet you'll never do that again! Thank you for taking the time and for your excellent feedback. Your input is what helped me fine-tune things and smooth out the wrinkles in the flow. Pre-reader heroes (in no particular order): James Riley, Brian Glover, Mike Ita, Rory Breen, Schyler Jones, William Lanier, Don Bentz, Alex Rodriguez, and Josh Liberman.

Thank you to my graphics wizard Chathuranga Gammanpila for being so helpful and receptive to the MANY changes and for his outstanding design work on most of the figure graphics.

Thank you to Sally Galli who did the book cover layout and created the exact image I had in mind for the two business people getting to the next level. I spent more time worrying about getting that graphic just right than I did about the book content overall. Dinner will always be on me.

A really big thank you to Yvonne Betancourt for doing the book layout and making my work look sharp. You are certainly the magician behind the curtain in this show.

Thank you to the Small and Medium-sized Business (SMB) and Small and Medium-sized Enterprise (SME) communities for helping me crowdsource information and for allowing me to share my ideas with you. And lastly, thank you to all of my clients as you are the source of so much content, data, and especially inspiration. Allowing me to help each of your businesses did much more than provide me with a proving ground of concepts and innovations. It allowed me to do something I am passionate about—helping you get to the next level! Among these I must especially thank the early adopters and first group of GTTNL clients: Patrick Eloi, Jon J. Sastre, Philipp Baumann, and David Moadab. One final honorable mention goes out to my friend John Vighetto; thanks for lunch.

# Introduction

According to the 2013 U.S. Census there are nearly 6 million businesses in operation in the United Sates. If you consider Small and Medium-sized Businesses (SMBs) to be less than 500 employees, then SMBs represent over 99.7% of all U.S. businesses. If you consider, as I do, a SMB to be fewer than 100 employees, then SMBs represent 98.2% of all U.S. businesses. These very same Small and Medium-sized Businesses employ more than 40 million people and have a total payroll of more than 1.5 billion dollars.

The statistics I present here are only for the United States, the third largest country in the world by population. Conversely, China and India have more than four times the population of the U.S. Larger or smaller, the ratio of big businesses to SMBs is going to be relatively similar knowing that no other country cultivates big corporations like the good ole' U.S. (yet). And the next closest seven—Indonesia, Brazil, Pakistan, Nigeria, Bangladesh, Russia, and Japan—what is their percentage of SMBs to big businesses? Again, not far off enough from the U.S. to skew the ratio too much.

There is a business relationship model called the Value Chain that was introduced by a man named Michael Porter. He had the insight to recognize and detail how businesses interact with each other on all levels. He presented that in your business, your customers are looking for value in the products and services they receive from you. If you provide it, this helps them in turn create great products and services of high value to their own customers. This applies to your relationship with your vendors as well. You no doubt expect the highest value products and services you can get for your money. This is in its simplest terms the Value Chain.

If this is true you must also be able to see that your competitors, your associates, every business you can name are part of the Value Chain. And because of the intricacies of who actually does business with whom, the Value Chain binds businesses across sectors and across industries. And thanks to the explosion of the global economy in the Information Age, this relationship described by the Value Chain is more globally intertwined than ever before in history. And it's only becoming more intricate and extended.

If you look at the North American Industry Classification System (the standard used by federal statistical agencies to classify businesses) you will see that the overwhelming majority of small businesses are classified with the word Service in their title. From Agriculture to Cultivating, Food, Health, Mining, Professional, Technical, Transportation, and the list goes on. If you consider the relationship businesses have with each other through the Value Chain, it's not hard to see that small businesses are both the bread and butter and supplier for other small businesses all over the world. I see the relationship of Small and Medium-sized Businesses as a fabric that covers the whole world.

To my point: I believe that small business is the backbone of the world and the service industry in particular is the heart. All hail the entrepreneur! And as an entrepreneur and business coach I want to see to it that the world has a strong back and a good heart. My business vision is a solid fabric of small businesses around the world, woven of strong culture and compass with a dedication to quality products and services.

In this book I lay out the best tools and methods I know of for defining your business roadmap and executing on your business strategy. I intend to lay a complete blueprint for building or even rebuilding your organization, and I will show you the tools that can help you create a significant competitive advantage in your industry, something that is actually quite rare in the SMB space.

I fear there are too many business owners and operators who are trying to swing for the fences with every deal and every product or service. Too many have the mindset of, "I'll just go right to it and deal with the details and metrics later." No discovery, warm up, or planning, just hang a sign out and plug in the cash drawer and start doing business. That's all fine and dandy, but at some point you have to take time to plan your success and detail the metrics by which you will gauge it. If you do not, I promise you, you will NEVER get to the next level. You will become part of the statistic of millions of businesses that never saw the light of day after the (insert name of most recent economic downturn here).

If you feel you will never get ahead and never have the time to go back and do it the way it needs to be done so you can get to the next level, I will share with you one of my favorite sayings: When you're up to your ass in alligators, don't forget you're here to drain the swamp!

Read everything I present in this book and start your roadmap to success. Learn success as a habit and master continuous incremental improvement of your business. You can do this! I know because many others before you have done it. And nothing in this book requires magic, voodoo, or prayer. Not that these can't help you in the right situation, but why rely on these when you have a solid plan and the right tools? My mission is to take you and your business to the next level and this is the blueprint to do it.

This book is laid out carefully and intentionally to present and discuss ideas, concepts, methods, and tools as building blocks and then to give context and if possible examples for implementation. The scope of what this book can and does cover must of course have boundaries and I will try to be clear when I have reached those points. I will however spend sufficient time on innovations, ideas, and tools that I have personally created or conceived, as this book represents their official release to the wild, and therefore to the world.

In Chapter 1, I start with a view of the future, specifically: What does the next level look like? I present concepts and ideas to set the stage for all future discussions and try to impress the idea that whatever you come up with, you must be able to effectively convey it to others in order to attract the talent and resources you need to realize your planned success. Along the way I will try to illicit specific thinking on your part about where you are, where you're going, how you'll get there, and all that will be required. In this chapter I also briefly introduce the most important tools you will use for architecting you success.

In Chapter 2, I do a quick review of what I call the tenets of business and management. Knowing that the vast majority of SMB owners and entrepreneurs may have never taken a single formal business class or may just need a little review, I make sure there is a clear understanding of the specific terminology and long-standing practices common to any business. I also share some of my favorite business mentors' philosophies and insights. I close with the rally to a shared vision and cause that will fuel your business rocket and help you set the trajectory for the stratospheric success you are after.

In Chapter 3, I begin to introduce the tools and methods for defining your business. All of the tools outlined here are handpicked, industry accepted, and time proven. I start with what many may consider basics, but you must have them in your toolbox or you won't be building anything.

In Chapter 4, I continue with tools that are more associated with analyzing your business operations in various levels of detail. Several of the tools I cover may give you the feeling that you're in over your head but you must remember, you are on your way to the next level and these tools will be required. They are what help you analyze and tune your competitive advantage.

Chapter 5 outlines additional handpicked, industry accepted, and time proven tools that are more appropriate for refining your business once it's off the ground. Once again, you may see many familiar tools but you will also be introduced to two tools that are my own innovation. These two special tools were developed specifically for gauging your business maturity and for executing on business strategy.

Chapter 6 is all about the Pyramid of Purpose and Value, specifically the top segment of the pyramid which I refer to as the organization's Culture. This segment is all about the organization's Vision, Mission, Values, and the ever important Human Element.

In Chapter 7, the discussion continues with the middle segment of the Pyramid of Purpose and Value I refer to as the organization's Compass. It discusses the Products, Services, Target Market, and the selected Operating Systems employed by the organization. I will also discuss Competitive Advantage and how important it is to having a chance at stratospheric success.

In Chapter 8, I round out the Pyramid of Purpose and Value with the lower segment I refer to as the organization's Blueprint for Success. I will detail the critical elements of an organization (Resources, Performance Measures, Roadmap, and Strategy) and show how these elements interrelate to formulate your Blueprint for Success.

In Chapter 9, I will introduce and fully detail the Business Maturity Index (BMI) which will be used to gauge your organization's long-term success and maturity. The BMI is at the heart of Getting To The Next Level as it is the tool used to measure your organization and to compare it to other organizations of a similar makeup.

In Chapter 10, I provide the prerequisite information for Chapter 11 with a primer of Agile Project Management methodology. It includes a brief comparison to the legacy Waterfall methodology of project management and some example of Agile in action. If you think this chapter is not relevant to you, please reconsider and please do not skip it. It is key to the entire Getting To The Next Level system and it is the linchpin for leveraging the most powerful method I have yet to share with you.

Chapter 11 is what every preceding chapter has been carefully crafted to build up to. It is where I use the tools at hand and put all the pieces together to architect the example business Roadmap & Strategy for success. I will use examples and threads of previous content to run through a full simulation of breaking a business down, laying out the pieces, and writing up the Blueprint for Success. I will conclude with a brief look at how using an Agile project board can significantly help you manage your grand roadmap and strategy.

Chapter 12 is the complete case study of the example subject business, The Goober Group. They are an IT company that has decided it's time to go from IT Schmos to Managed Service Pros and I have laid out their entire Business Analysis and Roadmap & Strategy for review. You will note that this is the example company used in discussions within Chapters 6, 7, 8, and 11.

And finally, Chapter 13 takes a look at what the Next Level looks like. I touch on more than a dozen business facets that cannot go undiscussed including formulating a possible end game, protecting your organization from financial losses and other potential catastrophes, and getting help when it's time. I also include a brief discussion on Continuous Incremental Improvement and Discipline and Execution as Core Competencies. I wrap up with a brief look at how to put everything that has been presented together for application and reapplication.

A few final notes before I actually launch into the book. Both in writing and in conversation, my favorite analogies usually tend toward sailing, not only because it is my oldest love in life but also because as humans, it represents some of the greatest examples of perseverance and need for structure, order, and procedure in our human history. It also happens to just be my style.

You are going to read the words Culture and Value in this book perhaps more times than in any ten other books combined. This book is about building the culture of your organization around value and the value of building that culture. It was suggested by several pre-reviewers that I warn readers who notice the frequent use of these two words in case they, for whatever reason, become inclined to start a drinking game based on either or both words. So here it is: Important safety tip—don't do that. You could go blind or destroy your liver. Seriously. Plus you would also miss out on the entire message of the book because you drank heavily for almost every chapter.

Also, as you read this book please believe me when I tell you that you are, in fact, for all intents and purposes building a machine. One that must be well-designed, well-built, well-documented, well-staffed, and well-cared-for. If you are missing a key part, it will not perform as you want, need, or intend it to and it will be inefficient at best. You must realize, believe, and buy into the fact that there must be a process for everything and these processes must be followed.

If you take this to heart and endear to the methods and message I have poured into this book, I'm willing to guarantee you great if not stratospheric success.

Good luck in all your endeavors.

*No matter how dramatic the end result, the good-to-great transformations never happened in one fell swoop. There was no single defining action, no grand program, no one killer innovation, no solitary lucky break, no miracle moment.*

– Jim Collins

# 1.0

## WHAT DOES THE NEXT LEVEL LOOK LIKE?

There is what I believe to be a universal axiom which I will call the Axiom of Business Competition, and it states: No matter when you start your business or how long you've been running it, as of today, you are in the most competitive economy that the world has ever seen. If the economy is running strong, you're fighting to keep your market share and the competition is fierce. If the market is feeling weak and run down, you're fighting to keep your market share and the competition is fierce.

This might seem like a redundant statement but it points out what too many businesses do not see: Every single day, you should be running your business as if you were on your way somewhere and there is another business on your heels, because there is. What I present is that for you to just keep up—for you to keep the market share you have, the clients you have, and the profit margin you have—you must be constantly innovating and marketing for your business. But if you want to get ahead—if you want to get a larger market share, if you want to take a bigger piece of the pie, if you really want to get to the next level—you must also have a significant competitive advantage.

A competitive advantage is at hand when you or your organization have something the others do not, something in your favor. It can be as simple as keen business acumen or as powerful as cash flow. We all know that a keen business acumen and about $2.50 will get you a cup of coffee anywhere in town. But if you have cash flow, you have true agility that is not always abundantly available to the majority of small businesses. Now this is not just a competitive advantage, it is a significant competitive advantage. Cash is king is another well-known universal axiom of business. And cash flow coupled with solid profit directly translates to agility and options for everything you do in your business. And this is a very good advantage to have.

However, the most important and powerful significant competitive advantage in business is a clearly defined roadmap and strategy for getting to the next level. You can argue that there are more powerful advantages to be had, and I would certainly entertain each of them and I would easily classify and prioritize each of those somewhere below a solid roadmap and strategy. I stand on the simple fact that no business has experienced systematic sustainable success by accident, by simply selling a product and taking in the cash and nothing else. They had a plan of some kind for success and they made choices for their future based on the results of executing on those plans.

What about those Cinderella story startups or other such fairytale stories about stratospheric success overnight? If you examine nearly every one of these stories that you come across, you will see there is a perfect intersect of supply, demand, and timing. They didn't get to the next level. They were single or dual stage rockets that were lit, fired off, and made a pretty pattern in the sky for folks to gawk at and swoon over. What I'm talking about is systematic and sustainable success where you get to the next level and stay there. Your organization has truly made it to the next level and aside from poor judgement or mishandling of affairs, you will never go back to the lower level you used to operate at. It is systematic because it's the direct result of the execution of a specific plan. And I'm not saying you can't go stratospheric. It is still possible to go stratospheric, but it must be a controlled flight.

Running your business without a roadmap and strategy is simply maintaining a business. You are providing some jobs to the local economy (and yourself), moving cash around, and providing services or products that are needed. Success might come along in the form of opportunity and if the timing is right, you could make some big progress. But your business is maintaining, not producing. You are performing the everyday tactics that keep the doors open, paying yourself and your employees, and doing some kind of marketing for whatever you're selling.

To get to the next level, you must have a roadmap and strategy that shows the clear path your business will need to follow in order to get there, a plan that is complete with well thought-out strategies for execution. With this kind of roadmap and strategy in hand, you truly have a significant competitive advantage. You must also have the potential for creating sustainable success for your organization. And sustainable success directly translates into performance.

Direct translation: Roadmap and Strategy = Significant Competitive Advantage = Sustainable Success.

*Figure 1-1. Getting To The Next Level*

What is the next level anyway and what does it look like? The next level for your organization does not need to be relative or translatable to any other organization nor does it need to be a grand and lofty future vision. But it does in fact need to be a future vision. It needs to be a direct translation of at least one step in the right direction toward realizing the ultimate vision for your business. Although we can break down and represent businesses relative to their maturity, market share, size, revenue, and many other metrics, we cannot really compare their business vision or what the next level looks like for each. For most small businesses the next level is often very personal and very simple. The next level is this beautiful new version of your business that you have imagined and fully set your mind and soul to seeing come true. You define the next level.

## Start With the End in Mind

As is always true with self-study, you must ask the right questions in the right way at the right time to illicit the response you need (not want, but need) at any given point in time. To clearly see what the next level looks like for you or your organization, you must first ask yourself and answer with all clarity and honesty: Based on where we are at today, knowing what we know, left to our own devices, what do we need to do to get to where we are going? And not to make things harder or add layers of mystique, but this means you at least must have formulated a vision for your business. Everyone in business sets out to do something and even though they have not put the vision into words or drawn a nice picture to share with anyone, they had a motivating idea that compelled them to act.

If you were to ask yourself what the vision for your business is or was, could you even answer the question in just a few sentences and have the same answer if asked again in a week? Could you, if pressed, put the vision into words or draw a nice picture to share with others? I ask this because so many small businesses start with a big fantastic idea but in very short order find themselves, as I mentioned earlier, just plugging along trying to see if they can even make payroll 24 times in a row for one entire year and have a few dollars left over. But if you have a vision and you can covey it to others, it means you can also remind yourself that you are out to accomplish something, to build something, and that you are in fact on your way somewhere.

Sometimes the vision really is just to stay small, profitable, and successful by being the best you can be at what you do, with no interest in growing the business and no grand plans for taking over the entire market segment you're in. This simple vision is not to be underestimated because if you can do that much, you are ahead of so many other companies out there. As the old saying goes: You must change to remain the same and change comes at a price. The price may come as missed opportunities because you're not tooled correctly to offer the new services potential clients are asking for or build those products. It may also be at the cost of quality talent because the services you provide, although changing with the times, are not cutting edge and do not offer the challenges that keep the best people on board with your organization.

But what if the vision is to be the best in a market segment? What if you do in fact want to grow a business, expand, and be the number one name people say when they discuss your front line product or service? The answer is that now, you had better put this vision into words and draw a nice picture to share with everyone you know and meet. If you don't, no one will buy in and no one will get on board, and worst of all, when you are trudging through the worst days a business can experience, you may just forget why you even started this endeavor to begin with. But put it into words, draw the picture of what you are out to accomplish and I assure you people will follow, they will buy in, and when things get hard and times get rough, you will have a beacon of light for your team to collect around and follow.

Your shared vision really is the heart of the business, even more so than what you sell or supply. Imagine if you will the explorers of long ago setting sail to find fame and fortune with maps of the new lands in hand. Kings and queens and entrepreneurs of the day would certainly not have bought in to these endeavors had someone not painted a very clear and enticing picture and told a very compelling story of how the future would look if the business ventures were successful. And they were in fact business ventures, complete with bonuses for productivity and penalties for falling short or not delivering. Very few sailors would have ever stepped aboard a ship headed to the edge of the world if the captain could not convince them of this vision of promised lands and riches. And getting paid to go to sea was one thing, but getting paid to not come back was not something even the most illiterate men of the time would have bought into.

Now imagine they're at sea in the worst storm you can imagine, when things are at their worst, seemingly lost and at the will of the sea, wandering aimlessly, and the crew is about to commit mutiny. The captain would then pull out his vision of the future, this map of the new lands, and he would show it to everyone and tell them the story again. Of course we know from history what happened when the crew simply stopped believing in the vision no matter how convincing the captain was in his telling of the story. And we also know from history what happened when the captain kept the vision clear and the crew together—nothing less than some of the most fantastic adventures and discoveries the world has ever known.

Your business and your vision for it are no different. If you have a valid business vision and you can rally people to your cause, the rewards are exactly as promised. And when things are at their lowest, you will have something pinned to the wall that you can point at and re-tell your story that reminds everyone why they got on board in the first place. And if you tell a compelling story and they still believe in the vision, you keep moving toward your destination and goals. But you must have a very clear picture of how you see the future of this business and you must be able to tell a compelling story. Do this and you have the makings of more than just adventures and discoveries; you have the guiding light that people will rally around in the dark and maybe even help carry on when you're gone.

## Startup, Turnaround, Merger, Acquisition, Cruising

If you are starting up a new business venture, it is likely reminiscent of one of a few very common scenarios. You are ready to leave your job (or you have just quit) and you want to strike out on your own doing something you know how to do well, that you believe you can make money at. It is highly likely that in this new venture you will have the very same job you have now. Of course you are striking out on your own because you feel you can run a business better than the people you have worked for in the past. And who better to show them all how it's done than you? Another possibility is that you've somehow come up with capital to fund your big idea and it's time to strike out on your own, hoist your sails, and make way.

In either scenario your startup is in the fledgling stage and unless you inherited some great process documentation and a well laid out business structure, you are going to spend a significant amount of time getting the basic processes documented, defining and refining your products and services, identifying and clarifying your target market, and so on. You are trying to get the business basics hammered out and prove your business concept can in fact make money consistently and reliably. Accomplish this and you are at the next level.

If your business is in trouble for whatever reason and you have come to the realization that it needs an intervention, you are about to embark on what is called a turnaround. The most tenuous part about a turnaround is the commitment level of the principals and stakeholders to do what is truly required to get this business seaworthy and on an even keel. One part of the business turnaround that hurts the heads and the hearts of the owners is the fact that the next level may end up being a step back to a bit of solid ground they've stood on before, a step backwards and down. But relative to where you are now and considering your options should you choose to continue on this course, it is what the next level looks like. You mend your sails, plug the holes in the hull, re-step the mast, and then get back on course. You've lost valuable time and headway in your journey but you're not fully sunk, and you can recover all lost headway given time.

When two organizations or entities come to the conclusion that combining forces makes good sense, it is called a merger. It is most commonly done to overcome some shortcoming both businesses have or to create a competitive advantage neither currently has. It's a great idea but in practice, a merger in small businesses is always an extremely hard thing to pull off successfully. The problems start when the principals and stakeholders find their respective visions for the organization don't quite line up as they believed they had before committing to this relationship. If the merger goes bad, separation of the two entities and all that has been merged and created since the merger becomes just like a divorce. But pull it off successfully and the next level for you should be a bigger, more refined, stronger version of the individual companies. Ideally with more resources, more core competencies, and a focused plan to actuate, you are positioned to make a move on the market in some way.

Acquisitions are simply one business purchasing the clients, talent, core competencies, and equipment from another company. Often the acquired business is stripped down to its useful components, and that which does not clearly and directly add to the acquiring business's value or the value provided to its clients is scrapped or discarded. I'm sorry to make it sound so cut and dry but no matter how cleanly it is performed and how politically correct you try to say everything related to an acquisition, it is a business decision with a purpose. This is where the term "hostile takeover" comes from. It doesn't have to be hostile but it never really is a pretty thing either.

Getting to the next level for an acquisition means successfully slip streaming the new processes you gain into your systems, assimilating the desired clients and culling the rest, actuating the newly realized core competencies, and finding homes (or not) for the new talent in your pool. An acquisition should be smoother than a merger for the simple fact that there is only one business vision and it is the vision of the acquiring organization. But most of the same criteria apply in that when you've made it to the next level you have more resources, more core competencies, and you are ready to formulate a grand new plan and make a move on the market in some way.

What about a business that's just cruising along fine and sustaining, making a modest profit, with no grand plans to expand or progress? What does the next level look like for them? I could simply say there is no next level, not until you decide you want to grow your client base, expand your operation, or make some move. What I choose to say is that the next level is whatever you decide it is. Where do you want to go and what do you want to do? If you say your little business is fine doing what it's doing and you're not interested in changing anything, that's perfectly fine. I know there are businesses out there that have that luxury but they are not involved in technology in any way. If they are involved in technology, as I mentioned earlier, you must change to remain the same. Stand still and you will be driven over.

Even a business that does not intend to expand or grow must constantly be marketing their products and services. They must be innovating new things to add to the line card of offered products and services. They must constantly be refining their core competencies just to keep up. They must be rejuvenating operating systems and equipment. They must continue to be profitable, maintaining cash flow and retaining business value for the organization. And they must always have clear sights set on their target market knowing who they will take on as a client when a slot opens. They need to know when they will be replacing talent due to normal attrition, skills required, or performance. For these organizations the next level looks like a leaner, meaner, more fit version of themselves.

And if your business is on the move and absolutely knows they have somewhere to be, for your organization the next level looks like one step, large or small, square in the direction of your business vision. One step closer to the vision you've drawn up, one more solid step in your mission to accomplish what you've built your business to do.

## Your Business Identity

Your business identity is the boiled down and condensed version of your story conveyed in the simplest way possible. It's who you are, what you are trying to do in the world. While it covers everything from your business vision and mission to the company name and logo and on to your business strategy and roadmap for success, it is also how your organization interacts with the world. This is not as simple as donating to local charities, or aligning with a political party; it is much more. To borrow some appropriate terminology from the author Daniel Goleman in his book *Focus: The Hidden Driver of Excellence*, it includes:
  "Inner Focus: The Culture and Climate in the company."
  "Other Focus: Competitive landscape we are in."
  "Outer Focus: The larger realities that shape the environment the outfit operates in."

There are plenty of great tools to help you define and convey your organization's business identity, but you must be aware that there are many aspects that will never be committed to paper. Among the most important and often illusive are ethics and integrity. You can state organizational values, but as the saying goes, you are who you are every day. Your business has to look, smell, and taste like the company you want it to be and to be seen as. And it is more than just the suit or dress you wear and how you present in the light of day. It is also how the people and organization operate after hours and in the shadows of night.

There is also a lot to be said for a company that looks like it's on its way somewhere. You can see the momentum of a company as it rolls along collecting steam. If you have been around long enough, look at how Microsoft caught our eyes, or Intel, Apple, and Google. What matters is that there is sincerity in what your organization says and does and that it matches what people hear and see. When the two are aligned and true, when the culture and the compass of your business are coupled together, you will know it and feel it throughout your organization. I promise. But it all starts with your business identity being well defined, documented, and shared.

## The Pyramid of Purpose and Value

Strategy planning and execution on the planned strategy are what will ultimately determine the success of any business. An essential component of execution is the ability to effectively convey the structure of the organization and the planned strategy. For if the structure and the strategy do not make sense, or are not properly communicated to everyone involved regardless of what level of the organization they are on, they won't know where the organization is going or how they can help it get there.

Failure to convey your structure and strategy will leave the people inside your organization frustrated or just plain confused. Those whom you wish to buy into your plans and maybe even fund them will not see what you see. And the end result value you should be creating for your clients and customers will not be the result of focused intent but rather that of happenstance.

The Pyramid of Purpose and Value is a simple graphical depiction of an organization's structure, strategy, and business identity. It is quite common to use the shape of a pyramid for communicating an organization's strategy as both are layered structures with specific requirements for optimal strength and longevity. But by depicting all the key elements of your organization's structure, strategy, and identity in a pyramid form, it becomes very easy to see the relationship of the layers and how they support each other.

The power of the pyramid is that if it is built correctly it can clearly convey your organization's structure, strategy, and identity in a way that everyone involved can understand with little extraneous explanation. But you must get this big picture, this big grand plan out of your head and onto the wall so that others can see it, fall in love with it, and come participate in the construction. To borrow a line from *Field of Dreams*, "If you build it, they will come."

For my purposes I developed a pyramid that is a culmination of all the best elements I have found in other pyramids, infused with elements of my own perspective on business structure, strategy, and identity (see Figure 1-2). I will be going into detail about each section and each level of the pyramid in the following chapters. For now I'm going to give you a quick rundown to show how simply and clearly it conveys the elements of your business identity that can be easily and clearly conveyed.

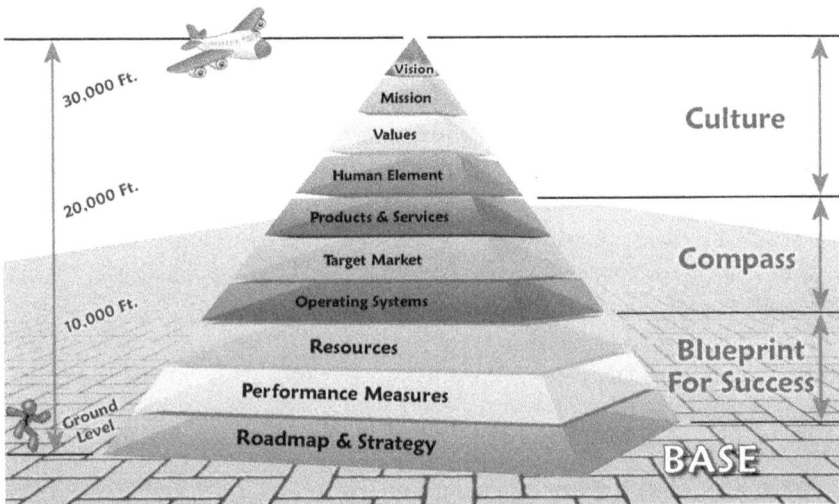

*Figure 1-2. The Pyramid of Purpose and Value*

The Pyramid of Purpose and Value includes elements of your business that are high level and esoteric such as the Business Vison and Mission.

These higher level elements are easily conveyed but not always easily translated into actions. The pyramid also includes elements that are as specific and detailed as the strategies and tactics you focus on every single day. These low level elements are hard to convey in simple terms but if properly laid out, they are easily translated into actions. Specific levels of the pyramid are grouped together into three segments that represent the outward facing definition of your business. These segments are: your organization's Culture, Compass, and Blueprint for Success.

The top segment of the pyramid defines your organization's Culture. It is the essence of what your organization is at its heart. It is the answer to the question of "Who are we?" You will notice it includes a special level called Human Element. The Human Element is not the Human Resources aspect of your organization; it is much more. It is an expression of how you feel about the human element of your organization and it is the clear parameters of what you want to cultivate for talent in the organization. It is strategically placed here because you must have the right people caring for and conveying the Vision, Mission, and Values of the organization.

The middle segment of the pyramid defines the organization's Compass. It is the clear and well defined direction the organization and business is headed. It is the needle that points you toward the horizon and it is the course you steer your ship along. It calls out not only what you will and will not offer for products and services, it also very specifically details who is and who is not in your target market in addition to defining your ideal customer. And finally, it specifies the tools and systems you will rely on to accomplish your ultimate goals, execute on strategy, and bring to life your vision.

The lower segment of the pyramid defines your Blueprint for Success. As you will see, each successive lower layer of the pyramid is more detailed than the one above it but none so specifically as the layers in this segment. This segment is where the strategically directed actions of the organization are translated into measurable results. Every level of your pyramid must be carefully thought out and detailed but these levels more directly determine your success than any others. There is one element missing from the pyramid as depicted here and it is simply that your pyramid must be built on a solid BASE. The details and discussion of the solid BASE will also be covered in Chapter 8.

## Your Business Success and Maturity

Gauging the success of a business can be subjective or objective depending on who you are and where you're standing when you perform the evaluation. Subjective generally being those things we think and feel emotions about (Opinion) and objective being those things we can see, touch, and tangibly feel (Fact). If you are the owner or principal of the company you will likely want to be subjective and optimistically say, "We are doing well, making money, and growing."

However, you must also keep a firm grip on the objective side of things and look at the numbers, the key performance indicators and metrics that tell the only truly measurable side of the story. If you are on the outside of the organization your evaluation is likely first prone to the objective, looking only at the numbers. From the outside you may not even care about the subjective side because you are not endeared in any way to the endeavor or the players.

You must also be able to gauge and share the overall maturity of your business. The maturity of your organization is a direct reflection of its retained knowledge and process refinement among other things. From the management systems to the production operations, your organization can only see and show that it is getting to the next level if it can somehow reliably gauge the overall business maturity. The level of business maturity your organization represents is an important factor in its overall business strategy because organizations of significantly different levels of maturity rarely do continued business as close business partners.

You may find that you are the customer of a remarkably mature business but you will not likely become a strategic business partner to them (for more than a short stint anyway) simply because your organizational maturity precludes you from performing on the same level. Likewise, you may find you have clients whose business maturity is immature enough that it significantly hinders their ability to recognize and therefore take advantage of the product and service offerings you present.

Gauging the overall maturity of your organization can be harder than gauging its success simply because identifying valid metrics and Key Performance Indicators (KPIs) for a business's maturity can be very elusive and, well, subjective. Nonetheless, you must have ways of gauging and presenting both your business success and overall maturity in both subjective and objective terms to those inside and outside your organization.

The easier side of gauging and presenting your organization's success and business maturity will be the objective side. Raw numbers can be collected and displayed easily assuming you have selected KPIs correctly. Charts and graphs are easily constructed with current levels and goals and put on display and shared with everyone. The subjective side of your business success and maturity will be a little harder to gauge and convey and even harder to compare to other organizations of similar size and makeup without the right tools.

As we progress I will delve deeper into the subject of gauging your business success and overall maturity, and I will detail and use specific tools to gauge and share them. All of the tools we will be looking at can be effectively utilized by organizations of any size from micro-sized to large corporations. While many of the tools presented in upcoming chapters have been around for many years and can be found in various forms, there is one special tool devised specifically to address your organization's overall maturity. It is the Business Maturity Index and because of its importance, it will be fully detailed in a chapter of its own.

## The Way of the Turtle

I believe that instantaneous, Cinderella story-type success is overrated. I also happen to know that many great stories of instantaneous success may seem to have happened overnight but in fact did not. Many books have been written with the focus of peeling back the layers to look inside these success stories with hopes of revealing what really happened and how we all might duplicate this kind of success for ourselves. They all reveal four simple truths: There was a long term vision; No success ever happens by itself; No successful person succeeds solely based on their own efforts; and Success does not happen overnight.

There is a noted story about the Oakland Athletics baseball team that put up a twenty consecutive game winning streak which turned their seemingly lost season around. They were the first team in 100 plus years of American League baseball to win 20 consecutive games. The first two-thirds of the season the team had been in a real slump with a terrible record of 20 wins to 26 losses. The Athletics' coach, Billy Beane, focused on several aspects of the team and the way they played to create a significant competitive advantage.

His budget for top level baseball players was severely limited compared to nearly every other Major League Baseball team. However, he managed to sign players with specific key skills that would be leveraged by the way his team trained to play the game. He trained the team to not just swing for a home run at every chance they had at bat. Instead he made them work for the base hits that load the bases one at a time and lead to runs batted in.

His strategy was simple: Get fast runners with good batting averages and then play the odds well. He told the team that if they wanted to win the pennant and have a chance at the World Series, they just had to focus on the ultimate goal. Play the game as a team, as perfect as they can, and they would have the odds in their favor. And he was right. That season they went on to win their division and did in fact have a spot in the post season playoffs. For the Athletics, this winning streak was a culmination of many things coming together for that season, but their regular season record under Coach Billy Beane was consistently one of the best in baseball.

The Athletics' coach knew that by identifying the inefficiencies in the game and negating them as much as possible by putting the right talent in the right place, he could literally play the odds of the game. But he needed to have the team on board and they needed to believe it would work. He told a compelling story and he had a very specific strategy for repeatable and reproducible success. And most importantly, he was able to effectively convey it to others.

In 1983, two men made a bet about whether a great stock market trader was simply born to be great or if they could be taught to be great. To prove their theory, noted financial market gurus Richard Dennis and William Eckhardt selected a group of people from various backgrounds, ages, and knowledge to participate in their experiment. They would become known as Turtles, named after the trading method Dennis and Eckhardt developed over the years.

Dennis and Eckhardt very clearly documented their recipe for trading stocks. The recipe was clear about market signs to look for and how to read them, when to buy in, and when to sell out. The recipe was not overly aggressive or risky, in fact it was exactly the opposite. Their trading recipe relied on long-term statistics and played the odds of success to realize the greatest gains with the least possible risk.

Each student in the class was given the same training and a starting balance to work with. Each member of the class created their own path as they attempted to follow the training they were given in hopes of parlaying their bankroll into hundreds of thousands if not millions of dollars. Each class participant's story is of interest, but one student in particular managed to become far and away the top trader in the class, one who reportedly amassed over 30 million dollars in the next four years. This student was Curtis Faith, a 19-year-old high school graduate. How did he do it? He followed the plan and the process he was taught, he did not let sentiment or emotion get the better of him, and above all, he was patient in allowing every trade to develop as planned.

The way of the turtle is to devise a strategy and plan and then execute on that plan without falter. This means stacking the odds in your favor by eliminating inefficiencies and removing uncertainty wherever possible, and not allowing outside people or outside elements to change your plans and goals. The tactics and strategy or even the timeline may be altered, but not the ultimate destination. You must believe in your own vision of this thing you are building when cash is drawn down just as you do when cash is flowing. You must set aside sentiment and emotion and know that every day that you make measurable progress, you are in fact on your way and you will get to the next level.

## The Reality of What is Required

Whether you're a startup, turnaround, merger, acquisition, or just cruising along doing business and trying to get to the next level, you must have the same intent in your actions. That intent is to take action and execute on your well laid out business strategy which moves you along your roadmap for success. I've recognized that when I consult to individuals and companies, once we have completed the business analysis, I always end up starting with the one thing they have most avoided and just did not want to do. I start with this not because I want to torture them or exert control, but simply because it is usually the one thing that is and has been their biggest roadblock in getting to the next level.

I often think of people who are not driving their business forward simply because of these things they just do not want to do as being afraid to do business. You have to actively participate in the well-being of your own company and if you cannot, maybe you should not be attempting this endeavor. I know it sounds harsh but if this is not what you really want to be doing, stop now. Along the same lines, I often wonder how someone can read a book or listen to a speech and hear the words they need to hear, believe what they have heard, but then not take any action. Things such as: generating the reports that will actually show you your true profitability, documenting a critical process, firing the toxic employee, or dropping a mean client.

It's fine to just sell some products or services, have a set customer base and roster of employees, and run a simple functional business. Very few businesses have this luxury and most businesses will die a slow death if they attempt this for long. As the saying goes, you must change to remain the same, but intentional stagnancy may actually be harder to maintain than planned growth. Any business that intends to grow and be truly competitive cannot operate this way. Will the business run the owner or will the owner run the business? Will your business be maintaining or will it be producing? I hope it will be growing and producing as it gets to the next level.

I believe there is a litmus test to tell if you should continue to pursue a given endeavor or if you should stop, close up shop, and find something else to do. First you must know and believe that humans tend to do what they really want to do in their hearts. We tend to put off the thing we simply do not want to do or just do not want to deal with. Also, most people do not start endeavors that they do not at some point think they can be successful at. We start little things with big plans and big things with little plans but they are all the same. We believe in this thing and we believe in ourselves.

The litmus test is this: You must believe in the idea, the plan, and the vision enough that all negatives will be outweighed by the desire to see this thing come true. No matter what is thrown at you and no matter what must be done for the survival and progress of the vision, you feel it is worth it and it drives you to do whatever is necessary. When you stop feeling this—not just for a day or when you're in a slump, but every day—you are done, get out. No one can build a dream they do not believe can come true.

My advice is that you must run your business like it will be taken over if you don't do it right. You may run out of capital or even worse, someone will lure your customers or your quality talent away. And this type of employee will likely take your standards, processes, and lessons learned along with them to your competition. You must also be prepared to the best of your ability for the next economic downturn or catastrophic event. You must have a solid plan and strategy and you must follow the way of the turtle. You must plan for success and then create it.

To sum it up, you must be able to withstand not only the drawdowns to your finances and other resources when things get rough, but also the drawdowns to your emotions. Running a successful business is not for the faint of heart and at times it will take nothing less than everything you have. But this is why the smartest and most successful entrepreneurs collect the best talent they can for their team, the best people to have in their circle of council, and they reach out for help when they need it. They do what it takes and they just do not give up.

## Success as a Habit

To be successful, first you have to show up. Opportunities present themselves to those who are present and receptive. Those who do not show up will never see them and will likely never realize what they've missed. We create our own success. I know from my own experience that you will be successful at what you focus your energy on, both in business and in life. I hold firmly to the belief that you are who you say you are every day, or as I like to say, we create our own success every day in what we choose to do and how we choose to do it.

You must incorporate things in your life that give you inspiration, make you feel good about your endeavor, and make you want to do great things. They may be physical, mental, or spiritual but they must be part of your mix, and you must do them every day. These habits are what make you successful because to the extent you follow and endear to these habits, you will be successful. There are books filled with successful habits and preachings but in my opinion, the top three habits that contribute to success are integrity, discipline, and execution.

Integrity is revealed in your intentions and in what you actually do. If your vision is enticing to people and they believe your intentions are just, they will buy in and get on board. But if your integrity is misaligned or false, the vision is soon seen for the smoke and mirrors it is and people will not only walk away, they will never come back. Integrity is also one of the most powerful internal motivators. If you believe in what you are doing, you tell a heartfelt and honest narrative of what you are trying to accomplish and people can genuinely feel it. If everyone in the organization feels it, then this will echo throughout the organization and it will bind the organization together.

Discipline is that thing that makes us do what we need to do when we need to do it, regardless of objections or obstacles. Discipline is what holds you and your team to a plan, process, or procedure that everyone agrees is right. Discipline, especially the discipline to follow a set strategy—sometimes over extremely long timelines—is what sets the most successful entrepreneurs apart from all others. It is also what sets leading businesses apart from their competitors when it is deeply engrained into the organization.

Execution itself is a discipline, the discipline of producing measurable results. The master management consultant Peter Drucker once said, "Strategy is a commodity, execution is an art." Those who know how to execute on strategy lead teams and lead industries. You learn from your mistakes and you build on your successes. For those who have an execution mentality and who drive their organization to adopt it, learning from mistakes and building on success is in their DNA. The few people who consistently exhibit the highest level of integrity, demonstrate the greatest discipline, and execute like clockwork have in fact made success a habit.

*If you don't understand how to run an efficient operation, new machinery will just give you new problems of operation and maintenance. The sure way to increase productivity is to better administrate man and machine.*

– W. Edwards Deming

# 2.0

# THE TENETS OF BUSINESS & MANAGEMENT

If you ask one hundred business managers to break down the modern-day business into an easily understandable framework, you will likely get one hundred similar but unique answers. Each will break a business down according to their own preference or viewpoint. Some will break it down by department, role, responsibility, and function. Others will start with the organization chart and then the business units and so on. However, I do believe that most would agree that there is a certain minimum of required components of a feasible business, and that there are also minimum required core competencies related to running that business in order to keep it healthy.

How we view or break down a business depends on the purpose of the conversation we are about to have. And because a business can and often does become a complex thing, we must have several ways of breaking it down for examination and discussion. If we want to talk about feasibility, we usually want to see the business broken down into dimensions like value proposition, target market, sales strategy, and so on. If we are going to talk about the finances of an organization, we will want to break it down into the various aspects of accounting such as cost and revenue centers and so on. Likewise if we want to discuss management, we will look at the organization chart and the lines of responsibility that lead all the way from the worker to the top of the chart as these are the functions of management.

This chapter is in no way intended to be a MBA in a day or some all-encompassing business manager's reference. It is however intended as an introduction or review of the generally accepted dimensions, aspects, and functions of any healthy business. I use the term healthy business because, as you may see in your own organization or those of others, many businesses are not truly balanced which is unhealthy. They are not balanced because they are focusing on what they believe are the most important aspects of the business to the mutual exclusion of other aspects that are just as critical, which is ironic given these neglected aspects would in fact balance the business out.

For the primary purpose of this book and the conversation we are about to have, we must share a simple construct of a business that is easy to understand, share, manage, and balance. The construct should be universally acceptable and be drawn from long-standing business principles. This chapter details that construct of the business starting with the required components for a viable business and the core competencies required to run it. It will clearly identify what is known as the value chain and introduce the business value aspects of every business. It will clarify the primary functions of management, aspects of accounting, and dimensions of the business overall. It will also detail the primary objectives that drive performance and are at the heart of the business roadmap and strategy.

## The Purpose of a Business

For any for-profit organization, earning a profit is a requirement and an imperative. Money is the lifeblood of any business (for-profit or non-profit) and that is exactly why the first question asked whenever someone says, "I'm going to start a new endeavor," is, "How will you fund this grand plan of yours?" It must be noted that both for-profit and non-profit organizations also share a primary objective of conserving capital. That is to say even if turning a profit is not required by your organization, as in a non-profit, you are not excused from doing everything possible to conserve capital by running an efficient business. However, contrary to popular belief, the purpose of a business is not to make money. Let me explain.

The purpose of a business is to attract customers with your offerings and to endear them to you and your organization as the preferred provider of the things they want, need, and find valuable. Value being the key word, and if you look at the complete breakdown and functions of a well-run business, you will see that there is a life cycle of value in play. There are two types of value involved: the value you put into the products and services, and the perceived value to the client of these products and services. The two are not the same and if the two are misunderstood, you will end up creating high value products and services that no one wants.

But when you have successfully created a product or service of high enough value to the client and you effectively market it, it will be consumed. And if you do this really well, people will want more or they will tell all their friends. That is the free market at its best. But you must also keep your offerings desirable and in demand by constantly adding or reaffirming the value as an ingredient and as perceived by the intended customer. If you do this it means you can continue to provide the right products and services that perfectly match the wants and desires of those who you are marketing them to.

Once again, the purpose of a business is to create and deliver products and services of high enough value that those in your target audience not only become your customers, they remain your customers as well. The business is here to support the purpose, not the other way around. Remove the need for a system of attracting customers and cultivating repeat business and you are reduced to just a peddler of things, selling whatever you can to whoever passes by or happens upon your stand. This is not to say that the peddler is not a valid business by definition but it asks the important question: Is this endeavor maintaining or producing?

## Business Basics Review

The most basic definition of a business from the Merriam Webster Dictionary is: The activity of making, buying, or selling goods, or providing services in exchange for money. If you wish to start (or re-evaluate) a business you should responsibly take a pragmatic look at your plan for creating products and services and making money to see if the plan is in fact feasible. When analyzing your business for feasibility there are components that must all exist and must be scrutinized in depth before setting out (or continuing) to do business.

The minimum required dimensions to be evaluated for the feasibility of a business are as follows:
- Value Proposition – A product or service that has perceived utility and therefore value to a potential customer.
- Target Market – A group of potential customers to offer your Value Proposition.
- Competition – At least a rudimentary understanding of what

your competition looks like and where the holes are in the market that you intend to fill.

- Marketing Strategy – A plan for how you will get the attention of your potential customer so you may present your Value Proposition.
- Sales Strategy – The methods and processes for exchanging the Value Proposition for revenue.
- Production Model – The tools and methods employed to create your products and services.
- Distribution Model – The tools and methods employed to get the products and services to the customer once they have taken you up on the Value Proposition.
- Cash Flow –The funds to operate the organization every day.

Note that this is not a complete list of dimensions that are evaluated in a complete business feasibility study. The term feasible means that the business model works and nothing more, no assumptions beyond that it is practical and workable. No real consideration for risk, sustainability, competition, regulations, or several other significant factors. With the above noted component, assuming you have the right talent on board to do the work, you have a feasible business. This describes the business model of the vast majority of small businesses run by the sole proprietors and individual entrepreneurs.

Many entrepreneurs when they strike out on their own quickly discover these basic requirements must exist and must all be in some form of balance or else the ship sinks. And when they are trying to get to the next level they also find that the above list is missing very important considerations which then blocks their progress. Many more businesses do not find out until after they have already failed that the lack of understanding and consideration for these dimensions was the primary cause.

The basic business, however feasible, is a particularly fragile and often considerably risky venture. If even one of these components gets off track and the balance is upset, you could lose your business in very short order. I use the term feasible business because anything less is an incomplete business venture that is destined to fail for lack of basic structure. If you cannot consistently deliver products you will fail. If you cannot follow through on sales of products and services, even though your customers are asking for them, your business is not feasible. And even cash flow can only hold off the sinking for so long.

If you want to remove much of the fragility and risk in your business venture, the most powerful thing you can do is to gain access to working capital. You also seek working capital when you are trying to expand your offerings, operations, or generally grow your business. Working capital gives you agility in what you do and how you do it as you get to the next level. Capital buys time, energy, and resources and is the essence of agility. It provides that ever precious lifeblood of any business – cash flow. This is when the small business must actually make a formal Business Plan.

The formal Business Plan includes a complete Feasibility Study among other components. It paints the robust and enticing picture that tells the compelling story that investors and entrepreneurs will buy into. When the time comes it doesn't matter if the investor is a big bank or your in-law, both will need answers to important questions about your business model. Your potential investors will not want to hear your sales pitch and they will not want to get into a discussion of how much money you think you're going to make or how many customers you expect to attract. They will want to know more specifics about your business model. This means a formal Business Plan and a complete Feasibility Study, not just the minimum required dimensions indicated above. I will detail the complete Business Feasibility Study and the Business Plan in the next chapters.

Now I will cover the minimum required core competencies to run any feasible business and keep it healthy. These core competencies are the building blocks of your business and are based on the long-standing concept that an organization is simply a series of functions. When performing a business analysis, these competencies or functions are the specific aspects that are focused on to provide the crucial insight.

The required core competencies of running a feasible business and keeping it healthy (in no particular order) are:
- Marketing – Identifying potential customers and advertising you products to them
- Sales – Filling the requests for products and services in exchange for revenue
- Finance – Managing money and accounting for income and expenses
- Production – Creating the products and services you offer
- Distribution – Getting your products or services to the market
- Research & Development – Innovation of new and refinement of existing offerings

- Regulations – Complying with laws and regulations applicable to your business
- Human Resources – Cultivating the talent for your organization
- Management – The activities related to controlling each aspect of the business

It should be noted that if your business is primarily Service Delivery, you will find that Production competency is represented largely by projects such as new installations, retrofits, or upgrades. Also your Distribution competency will largely be the Service Coordination function required to manage the actual delivery of service.

These are the basic core competencies that every organization should possess in one fashion or another to properly operate a feasible business and keep it healthy. To be a healthy business, your organization must be both a valid business by the definition here and it must be able to consistently execute on all the core competencies defined here. If your business is feasible and healthy, it has a chance at being sustainable and thus around for a while. It has a chance of accomplishing something in the world if it were to be so inclined.

But note that there are no inherent performance expectations attached to these competencies beyond the assumption that you do these things as required or as needed. There are also no implied drivers of the business such as the inclination of the owners or stakeholders to accomplish something in the world, a clear Vision for the world if their endeavor were to be successful. These performance expectations and drivers are not required in order to have or run a simple business. To have and run a simple business, with the hope of being sustainable, the business only needs to be valid and healthy.

Performance of a business means that it is effectively doing exactly what it was created to do—generate revenue and retain value for the business. Performance of the business implies expectations such as Distribution must get the products to market in a timely fashion, or Finance must see that you are profitable. The performance expectations are derived from the objectives of the business and they are called out in the business roadmap and strategy.

Drivers are what make the difference between a simple business and a business that is on its way somewhere. A business that is intent on getting to the next level does not simply call out maintaining performance as a business strategy. It brandishes innovative marketing and product ideas and calls out performance expectations. And drivers steer that performance. People who have an inclination or motivation to accomplish something are driven, and drivers are the product of those people's imaginations, wants, needs, and desires. Whether it is to release a new offering, generate more revenue to fund a new endeavor, or get to the next level, it doesn't happen without drivers.

The most powerful drivers are extracted from the most overlooked elements of an organization: the vision, mission, and values. This is coincidentally why so many businesses are simply maintaining at best and not producing. They have failed to effectively derive these very important drivers from the organization's vison, mission, and values. In their absence there may be performance requirements for the organization that will produce results, but they are just metrics for a given component of the business. These placeholder metrics are not tied to accomplishing the mission or attaining the vision, and they are certainly not about upholding the values. Drivers are revealed throughout the development of the business roadmap and strategy.

Sustainability of an organization means that it has proven it can stand on its own and perform. Performance implies the organization has protected its strategies from imitation by competition. This infers that the business is capable of remaining both feasible and healthy over time. This is why remaining feasible and healthy must be an ongoing discussion within the long-term planning for the organization. It is at the core and is given the highest consideration when mapping out the business roadmap and strategy.

## Management & Leading Functions

The general categories of management that any feasible and healthy business must master are known as the five functions of management. These five functions along with fourteen underlying principles of management were conceived of and detailed by Henri Fayol in his 1916 book *Administration Industrielle*. Today's dynamic businesses are learning and developing more modern and organic methods of motivating, inspiring, and effecting work product. It's now safe to say they are also moving more and more toward the mindset and associated principles of leadership in place of Fayol's age-old principles of management.

This then presents the issue of whether you should cling to the old management principles of the past or rally to a new set more clearly aligned with the preferred leadership mindset. My stance is that you should certainly move to a leadership mindset versus a management mindset; however, it does not really change the core functions of what must be performed to realize the work product. These core management functions will be ever present regardless of the selected mindset. I will have my say on the subject of leadership versus management in a later chapter, but for the current conversation on the tenets of business and management, let's look past these age-old principles of management and focus only on the functions of management.

It is valid to say that there are day-to-day functions that are always at the top of the list for anyone who is charged with effecting results toward obtaining specific objectives, be they manager or leader. Even if your organization model is as flat as a crepe, the people responsible for direct results have routine functions they must perform to produce work product effectively and efficiently. Management and leadership by design are about problem solving, scheduling, cheerleading, following up, verifying, directing, and many other activities that can be categorized into one of five basic management and leadership functions.

The five functions of management and leadership are as follows:
- Planning – The cultivation and adjustment of tactics and strategies for everything from day-to-day to the bigger long-term business roadmap and strategy.
- Organizing – The structure of the company and its components coupled with the designation of resources to tasks and projects involving timelines and deadlines.
- Commanding (Leading) – The activities affecting the efficient and timely work product through clear goals, instruction, expectations, and feedback.
- Coordinating – The activities affecting the efficient and timely allocation of resources coupled with the communications necessary to support operations.
- Controlling – The verification of policy, standards, procedures, and performance with expectations, objectives, and guidelines.

I do personally prefer the term Leading vs. Commanding as it implies some level of a bidirectional communications path and therefore a relationship. Also, Commanding carries a connotation that there is no participation by the talent hired in the well-being of the organization when in fact there is more and more an expectation of it in today's world. However your management methods manifest themselves in your organization, at least these five functions are ever present.

# The Value Chain

The concept of the Value Chain was introduced by the management professor Michael E. Porter in his book *Competitive Advantage: Creating and Sustaining Superior Performance*. The value chain has a key significance in much of what is presented in this book and it is detailed more in an upcoming chapter, but for our current and upcoming discussion we must take a sneak peek at it. We are going to take a look at the overall concept and layout of a basic value chain and its components. The value chain presented here is what should be considered the general all-purpose or base value chain. It represents the most common activities for a typical business–small, medium, or large (see Figure 2-1).

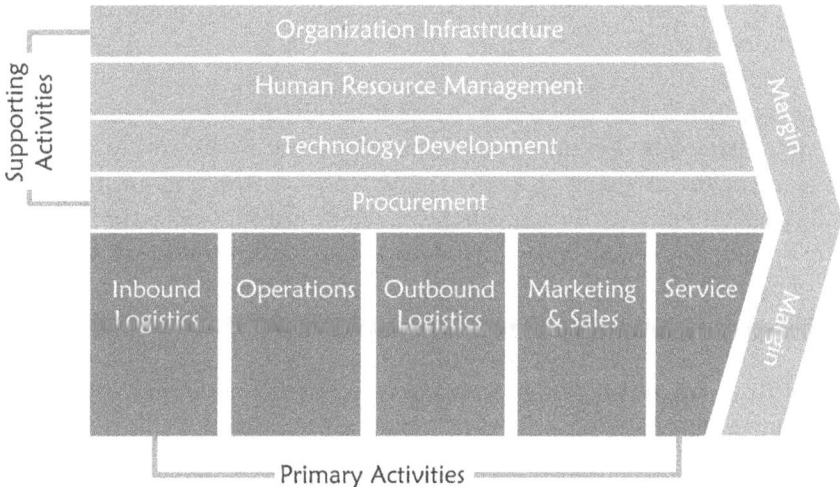

*Figure 2-1. The Value Chain*

The value chain is the concept that every organization can be broken down into the activities that are preformed to design, produce, market, deliver, and maintain a product or service. Once broken down, the value chain allows for systematic evaluation of the strategic and relevant activities of the organization and their interaction with each other. The goal is to fully understand the behavior of costs and the existing and potential sources of differentiation in the business.

Managing cost is of course a primary objective in any business and if done well can lead to a solid position of cost leadership in the market. Differentiation in any aspect of what you do to create or deliver your products leads to that very precious uniqueness I mentioned earlier. A focus on these two, Cost Leadership and Product Differentiation, plus a third aspect, Market Focus (the focus on your selected market), are the three generic business strategies that can result in a solid competitive advantage for any business. I will discuss the generic business strategies in the next chapter.

The value chain displays total value of the organization and consists of value activities and margin. Value activities are the distinct activities an organization performs in creating products and services. Margin is the difference between the total value and the cost of the value activities performed. There are five generic categories for primary activities in your organization: Inbound Logistics, Operations, Outbound Logistics, Marketing & Sales, and Service. There are four generic categories for supporting activities of your organization: Organization Infrastructure, Human Resource Management, Technology Development, and Procurement.

The concept Porter lays out states that competitive advantage cannot be understood by looking at the organization as a whole but rather by looking at the strategic and relevant activities of the organization and how they interact with each other. Products and services pass through the activities of your value chain in some semblance of order, and at each activity the product or service should gain some value. True value should directly translate into margin or profit. This margin then can be used any way you wish within the organization. You may pour it into human resources, product development, marketing, customer incentives and kickbacks, or even pay it out in bonuses.

The value chain is only part of what Porter defined as the larger Value System. The Value System shows how any business and their respective value chain has links to Upstream Value from suppliers and a link of Downstream Value to their customers. When your customer is also a business creating products and services, there is then a Channel Value. This Channel Value Chain is created as each of these organizations link together, passing value through links.

## Basic Functions of Any Business

To this point I have covered the critical dimensions to be addressed when validating your business, the core competencies required to actually run the business, the most prominent functions of managing the organization, and the most common activities you must effect for strategic advantage when creating value in your business. Of all the core competencies, activities, and functions I've covered to this point, there are two and only two that must be held as core and primary above all others. The first is marketing and the second is innovation. Innovation is not simply just research and development. However, successful research and development almost always translates into innovation. As a side note, although innovation is not specifically called out as a dimension for evaluation in determining the feasibility of your business, you can be certain that innovation is required to create a value proposition, the most critical element of a feasible business.

I've heard these two aspects of business—marketing and innovation—alluded to as more than essential in many different ways in numerous books from different authors spanning the last one hundred years. But none have stated it so eloquently and concisely as the professor and management consultant Peter F. Drucker in his book *The Practice of Management*. He states, "Because the purpose of business is to create a customer, the business enterprise has two—and only two—basic functions: marketing and innovation. Marketing and innovation produce results; all the rest are costs. Marketing is the distinguishing, unique function of the business." I call specific attention to these two functions because more than any others I could focus on, these go directly to the heart of the business, yet they are simultaneously the most neglected activities of the majority of small organizations, much to their detriment of those organizations.

Recall that the value chain indicates Marketing as a primary activity and Technology Development (Innovation) as a supporting activity. Recall also that these two are at the top of the list when evaluating a business for feasibility. They are both required and they have a symbiotic relationship. If you have not created anything new, if you are not innovating, you have no new message for your potential customers. If you are not actively marketing on a regular basis, you do not have your finger on the pulse of the market desires and sentiment. More so today than ever, the message you send gets stale fast in the light of new, more interesting products and services that are constantly moving in. That's innovation and marketing in action.

So many small and medium-sized organizations are not innovating or marketing, and there are a myriad of common and easily understood reasons. Not always valid, but easily understood. Among the most common are cash flow and revenue. "We're strapped right now. We just can't afford it. Besides, we don't have the resources." Right behind this excuse is the organizational maturity and size. "We're just a small company; we don't need to do all that fancy marketing and we don't need to innovate anything." Innovation and marketing are like training for an athlete—if you want to get to the next level, you get yourself to the gym and make training your focus, and if you need help you get a trainer or a coach.

The biggest excuse that tops them all is, "We're doing fine without putting any efforts into marketing and innovation. We've got plenty of business." But this one stems from a false sense of security that will absolutely put organizations out of business while they are napping. A false sense of security brought on by just enough market response to existing products and services to lull the business executives into believing they are producing when they are really only maintaining. And a thriving economy only veils the reality more. During an up economy you usually have more than you can handle for business, making you think you're booming. Well look around, everyone is booming. When the economy pulls back or turns down will you make it through on your stores? Will you be able to spin up the innovation and marketing fast enough to keep your market share and customer interest in your products and services?

An organization that does not actively innovate or market is neither balanced nor sustainable. In fact I would also state that you could not prove your business is truly feasible or healthy if you are not innovating and actively marketing. The purpose of the business is to attract and endear the customer to you and your organization as the preferred provider of those things they want, need, and find valuable. How can you possibly be competitive on any level if you are not innovating in the simplest of ways to keep the things your customer wants, needs, and finds valuable, fresh, and the best available at top value? And how can you endear the customer to you let alone attract them in the first place if you are not actively marketing?

## Organizational Environments

Not to get too technical but I do need to have a few specific terms to use throughout the book regarding the environments inside your organization, those you interact with, and those you operate within. The environments of your organization can be defined in fairly simple terms. There are three concentric levels and each level has its own environment (see Figure 2-2).

Your organization is of course at the center of everything and this is where we start. This is the Organizational Level and it contains the Micro Environment, which is the internal environment of organization itself. Within this environment you will find all the forces of your organization such as vision, mission, values, your product and service offerings, the roadmap and strategy, and so on. It is represented by the Pyramid of Purpose and Value.

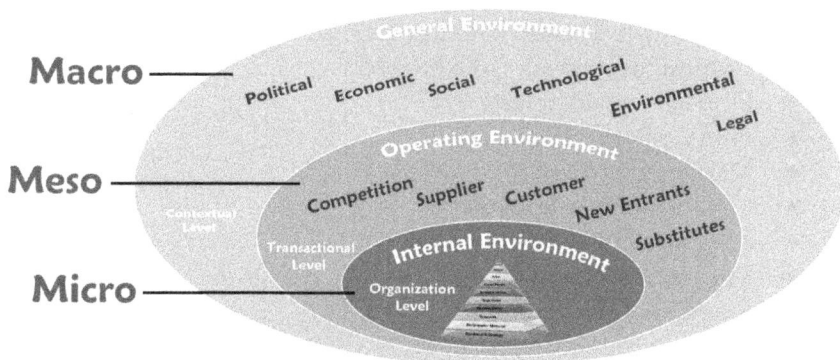

*Figure 2-2. Organizational Environments*

Next is the Transactional Level which contains the Meso Environment, which is the environment your organization interacts with. Within this environment you will find all the industry and market forces that your organization interacts with such as customers, suppliers, distribution, and competitors.

And last is the Contextual Level which contains the Macro Environment. Within this environment you will find all the forces of a more global nature including political, economic, social, technological, environmental, and legal.

Much of the discussion on evaluating and analyzing the business and formulating strategies will rely on this basic environment model to clarify interactions within the environment under discussion. Don't think too hard on it; just know that there is order in the universe of your organization.

## Business Value Aspects

Before I begin discussing Business Roadmap & Strategy, I would like to introduce the concise list of persistent aspects of any business that will be referenced throughout the remainder of this text. These aspects are persistent because they are derived from the common and ever present activities and functions of any valid and healthy business. In fact I have already discussed each of them to this point with only one exception, Communications & Collaboration. I refer to this concise list of persistent aspects simply as the business Value Aspects (see Figure 2-3).

There are exactly ten business Value Aspects:
- Communications & Collaboration
- Finance & Accounting
- Human Resources
- Marketing
- Organization Infrastructure
- Procurement & Logistics
- Production Operations
- Research & Development
- Sales
- Service Delivery

*Figure 2-3. Business Value Aspects*

You may ask yourself: If the list is derived from the many activities and functions that have been introduced to this point, why not just use the term Value Activities or Value Functions? I choose to use the term Aspect over Function or Activity as it is a more accurate term to describe the fluid and symbiotic working of a business and the value created versus the strict segmentation of processes that are performed. Aspect is a more robust word that implies more than just function or activity. It implies that you will be examining and considering from multiple angles. It infers you will be scrutinizing the nature, quality, and character of your subject matter.

You will likely see a close correlation of these Value Aspects with the activities listed in Porter's Value Chain. This is no coincidence because as indicated, the Value Aspects are derived from common business activities and Porter's Value Chain relies on many of these very same common activities. However, Porter was not the lone influence. The ten Value Aspects were in fact carefully culminated through evaluation of the business functions and activities consistently used by several leading business management masters over the last fifty-plus years.

There is however a major difference between the Value Chain and the Value Aspects. Porter's Value Chain is an important tool for discerning the elements of an activity that add value to and have a direct relationship to the end product or service provided to the client. It is a tool for evaluating and defining strategic advantage in an organization. The ten business Value Aspects on the other hand are the specific perspectives of the organization that all have a hand in and responsibility to create value in your products and services. They will be the specific views you consider when analyzing your business overall and building your all-encompassing business roadmap and strategy.

These will also be the aspects to evaluate when measuring your overall organizational maturity. To summarize: The Value Chain is a tool specific to defining or refining strategy while the Value Aspects are the perspectives of your organization to be addressed when defining and refining your business. You build up your strategy using the Value Chain and when it comes time to execute, you break it down into Value Aspects. Don't be concerned if the distinction between the two is not crystal clear just yet. I assure you it will be before you are expected to implement and execute.

These Value Aspects have, to the extent possible, a symbiotic relationship in that they are each essential to the organization and each can both support and benefit the others, or they can weaken and hinder the others. Each of these ten Value Aspects has been selected because each is ever present in the organization regardless of their significance. That is, even if your business does not intentionally innovate through active research and development, this aspect of your business exists and it can have a profound effect on the other aspects of your business. For example: Failure to recognize that the ingredients you have been using to make your Super Tuscan wine have been slowly getting sweeter due to rainfall in the region they grow which will certainly change the flavor of your wine and therefore the value proposition to your customers.

These ten Value Aspects clearly define the framework of small and medium-sized businesses more than any others I can find. Each and every one of these aspects must be in balance for your organization to remain healthy and have a chance at performing and sustaining. They also must be in balance for your business to truly get to the next level. An organization that focuses on only a few aspects of the business and neglects the others will not have a sustainable model. You cannot excel at marketing and sales but lag in inbound logistics (the delivery of your products and services). If you do, the customers will scream for their money back and when they do, the wheels fall off your wagon. You cannot be great at building products and services but have poor human resources processes. If you do, you will never find or retain the best talent to run the production or deliver the services consistently.

A business really is a machine. You put resources in one end and turn the handle. The customer puts money into the machine and lays their hands under the chute to collect and consume the output. If a component of the machine is not working on par with all the others, you have a faulty machine that is inefficient at best. It cannot go faster if you try to increase output. If your machine is missing a component altogether, you just have a broken machine. Your output is not likely to be what you intended nor what the customer thought they would be getting.

Some may propose that not every business has each of these aspects to evaluate or cultivate. They may propose that one or two of these aspects are not considered significant in their organization. It is a rare case that an organization does not have each and every one of these Value Aspects in play to some extent. The business Value Aspects are the components of the machine. Each one has a part in your organization, no matter how grand or simple. Each is required and each must be on par with the others for your machine to be able to run at its most efficient over the course of time.

The one Value Aspect that has not been covered is Communications and Collaborations. It is the one specific Value Aspect of any organization that is significantly overlooked in modern-day business. Communications today is basically free. Anywhere you go in the world you can communicate with anyone else; all you need is access to the internet or a satellite phone. We do business more differently than ever before in today's interconnected world. We do business by communicating and collaborating with suppliers, partners, and clients all over the world as if they were right next door, twenty-four hours a day. But we are horrible at communications and collaboration because we don't realize it's not enough to just get connected, we need to get connected with the right resources and use them.

This Value Aspect—Communications and Collaboration—is not directly about the tools used such as the phone system, forums board on your website, or the white board in the conference room. It's about the methods and culture around the practice of communications and collaboration. It deals more with the advancement of team skills, practices, and utilization of the previously mentioned tools. It is the most esoteric (least tangible) of all the business Value Aspects. It is in fact the glue that holds all the other aspects together. Only through the best possible communications and collaboration can you have a fully balanced business capable of getting to the next level. Cultivate and improve this aspect of your organization in any appreciable way and you will see a tenfold return on your investment. For many organizations, that may be just enough to get up to par.

## Developing Your Business Roadmap & Strategy

What follows next is the hard work of developing your business roadmap and strategy. The task at hand, although straightforward, will not be easy and it is not for the faint-hearted. But if you complete this task without long delays and in earnest, you will be far ahead of the greatest percentage of small and medium-sized organizations in business today. Why? Because the vast majority of businesses in operation today have no stated vision or mission beyond simply making money let alone a roadmap and strategy for getting to the next level.

If you manage to discover and address the most important elements related to the value proposition you offer your customers, you may very well have a significant competitive advantage in your market. Not just because you followed through to completion the building out of your Pyramid of Purpose and Value or your roadmap and strategy, but because you will have thoroughly examined your business's inner workings and constructed a complete and concise plan for success. A well-developed and balanced strategic plan that focuses on realizing the vision of the organization, delivering on value to the customer, and seeing far enough forward to be prepared for what may come.

Again, there is no magic involved, just hard work and many hard decisions. Hard decisions are baked into nearly every step of the process and show up at every turn. What is your vision and mission? Who is your customer? What does the customer value? What is your plan? These are but a few of the hard decisions. You must know exactly where you are now and how you got here as well as where you are going and how you will get there. And you do indeed need to be going somewhere. This entire process is pointless unless you are trying to get somewhere, to get to the next level, or even to just get off the ground.

At this point, because of the groundwork I have laid, the process for developing your Business Roadmap & Strategy can be described in one simple statement: design your Pyramid of Purpose and Value from the top down. Then you will have a well-developed and balanced business roadmap and strategy for success. From there you will be ready to build (or rebuild) your business from the ground up accordingly by executing on a well-developed and balanced strategic plan. The process will be the same for entrepreneurs wishing to define a new business venture and those wishing to refine an existing venture. These are typically the new startups and the turnarounds.

The process will largely be the same for organizations looking to merge, acquire, or be acquired. These endeavors will follow the exact same steps but with more of an evaluate-and-document mindset. However, once the merger or acquisition is complete, there will be a need to run through everything again with the same view as if you were performing a turnaround. For those organizations that are running fine but are looking to get to the next level, they must be excruciatingly detailed in every step. A significant competitive advantage belongs to those who can build a clear and concise plan that allows them to tell a compelling story that gets people on board and behind them. But the pyramid must be complete from the top to the bottom. Vision, Mission, Values, and every level below must be designed to support all the levels above it.

I have mentioned balance many times in the discussions about the business health, the Value Aspects, the roadmap and strategy, and the organizational maturity. Balance is an imperative throughout this entire process and in every aspect of your business. Once you have built out your Pyramid of Purpose and Value including your business roadmap and strategy, the greatest challenges you will face will be in executing on the strategy and implementing the changes required in a well-balanced way.

Execution on strategy means focusing on operations, performance, and results. It is highly objective in that it is not influenced by emotions, opinions, or personal feelings. It is a body in motion. Implementing change is about defining vision and mission, organizational culture, focusing on target markets, strengths and weaknesses, and strategies. It is very subjective in that it is open to greater interpretation based on personal feelings, emotion, and aesthetics. It is a mind in motion.

In martial arts we have a special symbol we look to for inspiration—the symbol of yin and yang. It is a constant reminder of the need for balance between things such as study and practice or between mind and body. Yin is the quiet mind and active body (practice) while Yang is the quiet body and active mind (study). Both are ever present, and the decision to develop them is left to the free will of the individual. The ever elusive intent is to have perfect balance.

Yin and Yang are not opposing forces but rather complimentary in that together, they form a system in which the unit is greater than the sum of its components. So it is with executing on strategy and implementing change in your organization. Executing on strategy is the Yin, quiet mind and active body—practice. Implementing change is the Yang, quite body and active mind—study. And the unit that you wish to be greater than the sum of its components is your organization, the business, where study and practice meet.

Many extremely smart entrepreneurs and managers believe they can circumvent the process of building their Pyramid of Purpose and Value and the business roadmap and strategy. They try to design (not build) the pyramid from the ground up, stopping at the middle levels, leaving the Culture completely unaddressed and the Compass largely undetermined. They are effectively glossing over the important subjective elements of the organization that define the most critical changes required to create success. These organizations have been seduced by the ease of defining a standard set of metrics and then simply applying generic strategies and tactics.

The easy metrics and simple strategy are given priority over the tedium and pains involved in defining the top levels of the pyramid. This leaves strategy as nothing more than financial prediction and tracking. If you have no defined vision, mission, and values, you have no Culture. If you have a poorly defined value proposition (products and service) or target market and you have not solidified the tools you will use to produce, you have no Compass. You effectively have a ship and a map but no crew, no financial backing, and no idea where you're headed.

You also cannot build (not design) your pyramid from the top down and stop at the middle levels, focusing on only the subjective or esoteric elements of your organization. Of course you must have a well-defined vision, mission, values, people process, and so on, but not at the cost of a stifled roadmap and strategy. When the pyramid is built from the top down, the well intending management and leadership are hyper-focused on creating a fertile culture for creativity but have neglected to balance out with execution on strategy.

You effectively have a really nice ship—well manned and well-funded but no map and no plan for how you're going to get where you want to go. The management and leadership must have the patience and persistence necessary to properly focus on and fully develop a solid foundation for their pyramid. This means thorough analysis without paralysis combined with determining a well-developed and balanced strategy with attainable goals. It means knowing that there is a potential for failure in pursuing difficult challenges but that the reward is active learning and a new level of experience.

If your organization and every aspect cannot slow down to do things right, nothing will change. Culture must be shifted and you must act your way into a new way of thinking. You must execute on strategy and you must implement change as if they were a martial art discipline or a super power. This requirement is tied closely to the lower levels of business maturity and to organizations that have stalled at middle or higher levels.

A level one organization, a fledgling or immature business, is purely reactive. A level two organization is moving away from reactive toward proactive and one day even higher. Level one organizations and organizations that have stalled tell themselves, "We're fine right here, we don't really need to change," or, "We don't really need to change that much." But when your organization is reactive, it is the biggest lie you perpetuate which traps your organization there, unable to break out and get to the next level. This spells the demise for so many organizations before they ever get off the ground and also for those faced with stiff challenges at higher levels. But those who stop the lie and break out of the old ways are able to get to the next level and never look back. Let's get to the next level!

*You've got to eat while you dream. You've got to deliver on short-range commitments, while you develop a long-range strategy and vision and implement it. The success of doing both. Walking and chewing gum if you will. Getting it done in the short-range, and delivering a long-range plan, and executing on that.*

– Jack Welch

# 3.0

## Tools & Methods for Defining Your Business

There is an old saying that a carpenter is only as good as his tools. What we set out to do here is nothing less than architect our ideal business from the top down and build it from the ground up. We must have all the right tools for the job and we must have the best tools for the application. What I have selected for inclusion in the next several chapters are the tools I believe are the basics required for the task at hand. You will no doubt find alternate versions of many of these tools that are preferred to those presented here, and that's fine. I also fully expect you will have or find additional tools to add to the tool box and even substitute different favored versions. Again this is fine; just don't get too caught up on finding the ultimate perfect tools to use to design, build, refine, and drive your project or it will never get off the ground.

For each tool introduced I will provide a brief history where applicable, a basic understanding of how it works, and some guidance on where and when it might be used as necessary. In Chapters 3, 4, and 5, I will not be introducing tools that cannot readily be found and researched in the general and common knowledge of business management. Some tools will be detailed more than others. Although I will be introducing tools that I have developed and tailored specifically for my Getting To The Next Level coaching program, each is simply my innovative application of existing concepts.

For the sake of reference and clarity, the tools I have developed specifically for the Getting To The Next Level methodology are each detailed in full in their own chapters in this book. You've already been introduced to the Ten Value Aspects in Chapter 2. You were also introduced to the Pyramid of Purpose and Value in Chapter 2; it will be detailed further in Chapters 6–8. And I will introduce the Business Maturity Index and Business Agile Strategy Execution (BASE) at the end of Chapter 5.

The tools I introduce here are not just for big companies or giant organizations. Each of them can be right-sized for even a single-person operation when it is applicable to the business model being cultivated. For example, one intimidating-sounding tool named the McKinsey 7-S Framework is a tool for evaluating the balance of many aspects of the organization relative to the shared values of the organization. In a one-person operation this may not be directly applicable when the "organization" is comprised of you, your dog, and your spouse (part-time). But it certainly comes into use when you're looking to get to the next level and your fledgling organization of even a small handful of employees finds itself at odds in ways you cannot quite get a handle on. This tool forces you to ask the questions you may not think to ask or address as you should and is therefore very appropriate for this size of an organization.

The tools introduced in this and in the following chapters are building blocks. They are introduced in a specific order so that, as each is defined and explained and where possible, the following tool may rely on the previous tool. They also follow the natural progression of an entrepreneurial endeavor, from venture concept through normal operations to full business rework. Following this order allows a continued conversation without need for repetitive explanation or discussion. Some tools may point to or call out tools that have not yet been defined but will be. I rely on your ability to see the relationship and the path and navigate accordingly.

## Critical Thinking

Two tools must be introduced early on to address imperative skills required by every entrepreneur and every organization in day-to-day operations and long-term strategy cultivation. These two tools are the models for Critical Thinking and Process Control. These two tools are grouped together because they are closely related to the core competency of decision making and strategy development. I will cover Critical Thinking first and then Process Control. There are several tools you can skip over or do without but these two are required for getting to the next level. If you cannot address complex problems and control processes, you will not make it very far.

It may seem like it is unnecessary to call out Critical Thinking as a tool but it is absolutely critical, no pun intended. All too often truly smart people come to what they believe are solid conclusions, but these conclusions are actually based on limited information or formulated in a vacuum. They simply have not cultivated the core skills of Critical Thinking and adopted a solid process. What I offer here is a basic model that can fulfill the important need for some sort of process with a solid structure. This model will serve you well until you formulate your own or adopt another, as long as you have one on hand. This tool goes a long way toward setting a standard of how your organization chooses to address important problems, questions, and issues. And there will be important problems, questions, and issues at every turn as you build out every level of your pyramid.

In his book *An Experiment in the Development of Critical Thinking*, Edward M. Glaser states, "Critical thinking calls for a persistent effort to examine any belief or supposed form of knowledge in the light of the evidence that supports it and the further conclusions to which it tends." Glaser's model requires three things:

1) The Attitude of being open, receptive, and willing to think carefully about problems within your current experience.
2) The Knowledge of basic methods for logical inquiry and reasoning.
3) The Skills required for applying those methods.

You and your team must learn that when they recognize a problem, come up with an important question, or discover an issue, this is the time to immediately begin searching for a workable means of addressing it effectively, and this is where the Critical Thinking model comes in (see Figure 3-1).

The Phases of Critical Thinking are:
**Discover** – Gather all information possible from all relevant reliable sources.
**Analyze** – Comprehend assumptions, arguments, evidence, and key points to assimilate how they interconnect and relate to each other.
**Synthesize** – Appraise the similarities and differences, existence, and non-existence of logical relationships. Make logical connections, draw conclusions, and develop generalizations.
**Apply** – Test the conclusions and generalizations by applying them to the initiating problems, questions, and issues.
**Justify** – Re-establish new beliefs, values, and patterns of beliefs based on the new experiences. Develop accurate conclusions, make inferences, clarify implications, and render effective judgments.

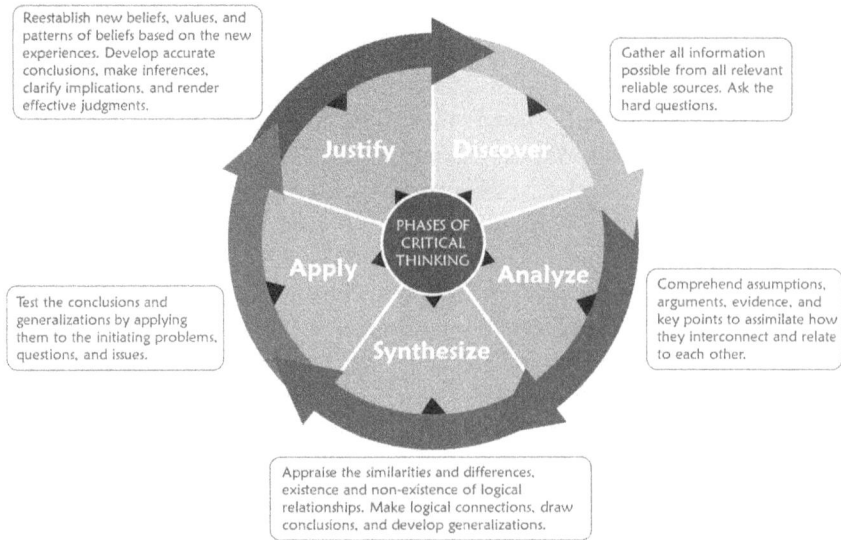

Reestablish new beliefs, values, and patterns of beliefs based on the new experiences. Develop accurate conclusions, make inferences, clarify implications, and render effective judgments.

Gather all information possible from all relevant reliable sources. Ask the hard questions.

Test the conclusions and generalizations by applying them to the initiating problems, questions, and issues.

Comprehend assumptions, arguments, evidence, and key points to assimilate how they interconnect and relate to each other.

Appraise the similarities and differences, existence and non-existence of logical relationships. Make logical connections, draw conclusions, and develop generalizations.

*Figure 3-1. Phases of Critical Thinking*

## Process Control

A companion skill to Critical Thinking is basic Process Control. You could actually think of it as a subset or streamlined version of the Critical Thinking process. It comes into play when the application just isn't that complex. Process Control tools come in all sizes and shapes for a myriad of applications, but what I offer here is the four-stage model for continuous improvement for business process management. The PDCA Cycle (Plan-Do-Check-Act) is the four-stage closed loop sequential model originally introduced and popularized by W. Edwards Deming. Deming is considered by many to be the father of modern quality control as his theories are the basis for the discipline known as Total Quality Management (TQM) and the foundation elements of the ISO 9001 quality standards.

This model has been adopted and endeared by the Agile, Six Sigma, and LEAN methodology movements. Each has coupled with this model as it so clearly represents the Japanese Kaizen philosophy of Continuous Improvement (CI) which is deeply embedded in each of these disciplines. I have made it a point to clarify the associations of PDCA to Agile, Six Sigma, LEAN, and CI because I will continue to refer to these terms throughout this text. Feel free to refer to the Glossary for a brief definition of each of these terms if you are not already familiar with them but rest assured, each will be detailed as I progress. The model proposes to guide the individual or team through improving the effectiveness and overall quality of critical processes throughout the organization. Although most commonly associated with Product Lifecycle Management, this tool can assist in basic project management, human resource, logistics, and every other aspect of the business. This process control model will be employed in the overall project of building out every level of your pyramid and in the execution of the strategies that will get you and your organization to the next level (see Figure 3-2).

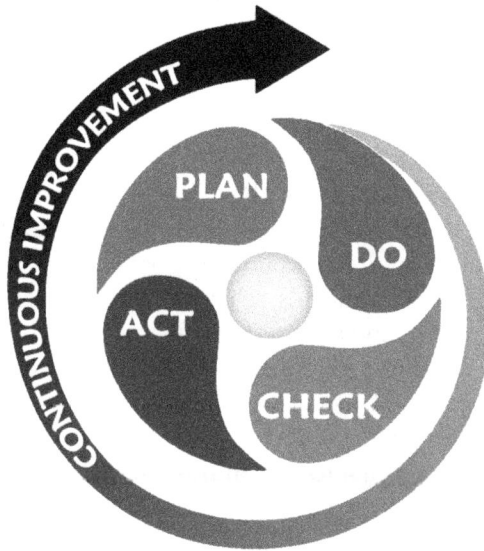

*Figure 3-2. Four Stages of the PDCA Cycle*

The Four Stages of the PDCA Cycle are:
- Plan – Discovery and analysis or reevaluation of the root cause of the problem or issue at hand.
- Do – Develop or refine the actionable strategy and tactics. Clearly define or refine metrics for measuring effectiveness, progress, and success.
- Check – Measure actual results and compare to the defined metrics for the desired results and any available data from previous cycles.
- Act – Solidify the changes into the process. Document results, formally change the processes or procedures, and inform everyone about the changes.
- Repeat as necessary until the desired output is realized.

Notice that if the problem or issue still remains in any way, you continue the cycle until you have either completely eliminated it or ground it down to a tolerable level. This is Continuous Improvement (CI) in action.

## GOST Strategy Planning

The greatest majority of the tools you will employ in defining and refining your organization are designed to reveal important strengths, weaknesses, opportunities, threats, problems, holdups, issues, and so on within the many aspects of the organization. You will then be tasked with sorting, organizing, prioritizing, and translating this mass of data into coherent and actionable bullet or line items on what I refer to as your organization's big laundry list.

Taking an individual item from the big laundry list as the next and most important thing you must do for the organization, you now have a simple single goal. To attain this goal you must have a set and logical method for breaking this selected item or goal down into line or action items. These line or action items must also be translated into understandable components capable of being conveyed to everyone involved and capable of being executed upon. The GOST Strategy Planning model is your tool and it dictates that you answer specific questions for each of its four components in order to effectively formulate your plan for attaining this goal.

These four components of the GOST Strategy Planning model are:
- Goals – The very specific purpose to which a given endeavor is directed.
  What will be achieved or accomplished if we are successful?
- Objectives – The specific tangible and measurable time-bound landmarks of the goal.
  What measurable metrics will have changed and within what time frame?
- Strategies – The detailed plan and methods for accomplishing the desired Goal.
  What approach will we employ in utilizing our resources to achieve our Goal?
- Tactics – The actions that put resources and methods to use according to the plans.
  What are the specific actions that must be executed upon and how?

To further clarify the relationship of the four components, see Figure 3-3. Objectives and Goals are the What of your endeavor while Tactics and Strategy are the How. Objectives are the short-term measurable landmarks that incrementally move you closer and closer to achieving your ultimate goal over time. Tactics are the day-to-day actions that put resources into play according to the methods and plan called out in the long-term strategy. For the tactics to work you must focus on objectives, variables, and assumptions that the overall strategy for success relies upon. Objectives and Tactics are the broken down into the more tangible pieces of the Goals and Strategy, respectively.

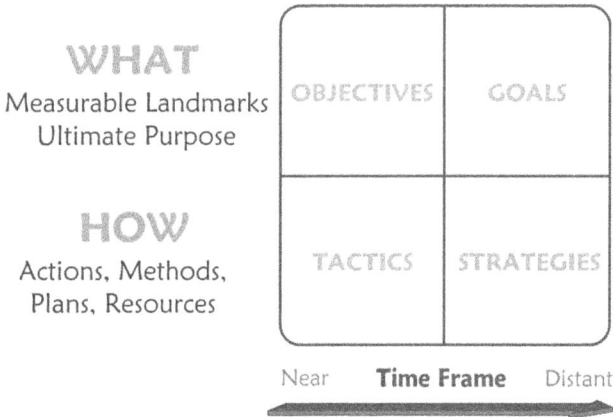

WHAT
Measurable Landmarks
Ultimate Purpose

HOW
Actions, Methods,
Plans, Resources

| | OBJECTIVES | GOALS |
|---|---|---|
| | TACTICS | STRATEGIES |

Near **Time Frame** Distant

*Figure 3-3. Relationship of GOST Strategy Planning Tool*

To complete the detail of this tool, let's look at the GOST Strategy Plan with clear examples (see Figure 3-4).

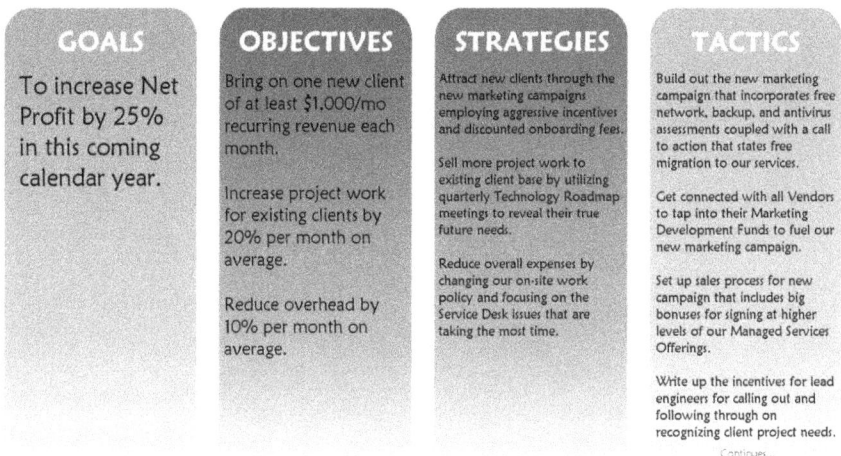

| GOALS | OBJECTIVES | STRATEGIES | TACTICS |
|---|---|---|---|
| To increase Net Profit by 25% in this coming calendar year. | Bring on one new client of at least $1,000/mo recurring revenue each month. | Attract new clients through the new marketing campaigns employing aggressive incentives and discounted onboarding fees. | Build out the new marketing campaign that incorporates free network, backup, and antivirus assessments coupled with a call to action that states free migration to our services. |
| | Increase project work for existing clients by 20% per month on average. | Sell more project work to existing client base by utilizing quarterly Technology Roadmap meetings to reveal their true future needs. | Get connected with all Vendors to tap into their Marketing Development Funds to fuel our new marketing campaign. |
| | Reduce overhead by 10% per month on average. | Reduce overall expenses by changing our on-site work policy and focusing on the Service Desk issues that are taking the most time. | Set up sales process for new campaign that includes big bonuses for signing at higher levels of our Managed Services Offerings. |
| | | | Write up the incentives for lead engineers for calling out and following through on recognizing client project needs. |

Continues...

*Figure 3-4. GOST Strategy Planning Tool Example*

Please take note that as we move from the ultimate Goal down through the structure to the ground level Tactics, the more detailed and specific things become. This is the simplest version of what is known as a Strategy Map. The level of detail will be directly proportional not only to the proximity (in time) of the goal to your current situation but also to the grandeur of the goal. To put it another way: When you first think of a goal you typically do not get too deep into the planning until you are sure it is the right thing to do, as it is going to become the focus of your or your team's efforts. Likewise, if the goal is relatively small it tends to be treated as an Objective, i.e. weigh it, measure it, and then just get it done.

The GOST Strategy Planning model should be seen as both a standalone tool for planning simple, single-goal success strategies you or your team have focused on, or as a building block for planning complex strategies. I will discuss complex strategies in later chapters but for now, the GOST Strategy Planning model is introduced here to provide you with the basic elements of any solid strategy plan.

## SMARTER Goals and Projects

The concept of SMARTER Goals and Projects is really just a litmus test for whether your goal or your project has actually been properly thought out. It also provides you with the answers to the most likely questions you will need to answer when defending this proposed endeavor (see Figure 3-5).

**S** | **Specific:** What exactly are we intending to accomplish? This is the Who, What, When, Where, Why, and How we use to define a Goal or construct a Project Description and Scope.

**M** | **Measurable:** How will we evaluate and demonstrate the progress of our endeavor? We must have specific metrics and criteria we will rely on to indicate our ultimate success.

**A** | **Achievable:** Can we actually attain this goal or outcome with the resources we have? We must possess or retain the capacity and capability to accomplish this endeavor.

**R** | **Relevant:** How does this Goal or Project tie into and support the overall organizational roadmap and strategy? We must be creating Value for us or for our clients with this endeavor.

**T** | **Time-bound:** Are there realistic timelines and deadlines for this endeavor? Each landmark and the endeavor overall must have specific target times, dates, and frequencies called out in order to realize a timely completion.

**E** | **Execution:** Will we commit to execution on this plan once laid out? The foresight and ability to take action on the task and objectives to accomplish success as planned.

**R** | **Retrospective:** How well did we plan, perform and execute? The review of everything related to the planning and execution of this Goal or Project so that we may continually improve on our processes and methods.

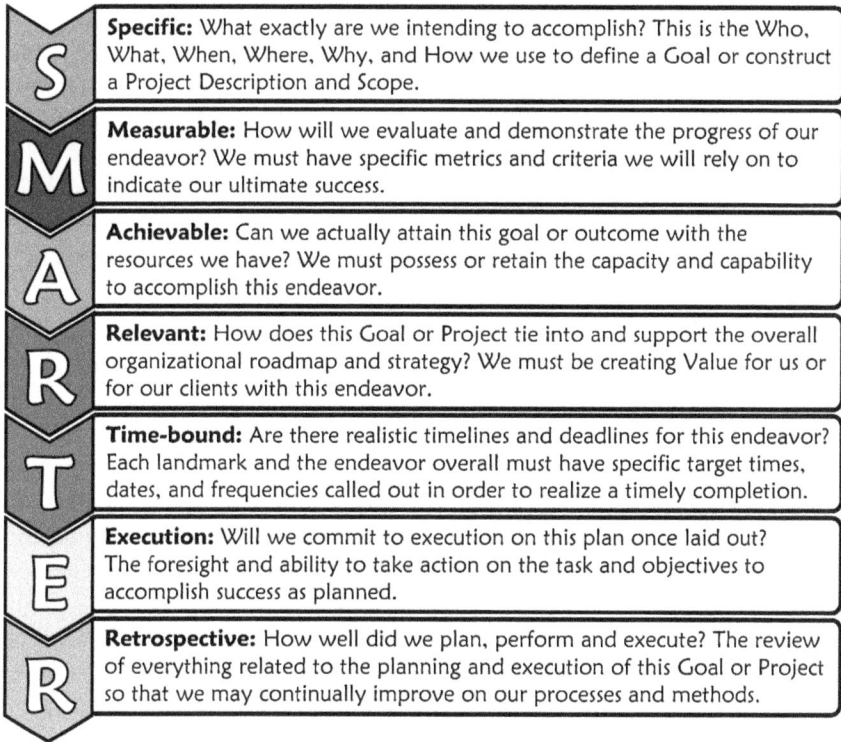

*Figure 3 5. SMARTER Goals and Projects*

Notice that Achievable asks whether you possess or can obtain the resources to make this happen while Execution demands commitment to the endeavor. Too many excellent plans are laid out but simply get scrapped because no one executes on them. One smart fellow I know would always say he was willing to share or give away his best ideas and even the plans themselves without fear of his competitors scalping his success. He knew that even with the perfect recipe for success, it is only the rare entrepreneur that, if they recognize the opportunity, has what it takes to execute on the plan. Use this tool as a pair of goggles you put on just before you release your big project, plan, or roadmap to the wild. This could save you millions one day.

## Core Competency Matrix

Core Competencies are a synergy of resources and skills that allow an organization to establish a competitive advantage in their market. Every organization should be aware of what Core Competencies are required to run the business itself and to provide the products and services they offer to their customers with the greatest value and the greatest efficiency. An organization typically does not magically possess Core Competencies. An organization cultivates the Core Competencies they need by acquiring quality talent and building key processes. It is a never-ending process of refining processes and training talent. The organization must also know which Core Competencies they should insource and maintain and which they should outsource. You must focus on the Core Competencies of your core business and outsource the rest.

While it's true that the processes of Market Analysis, Competitive Analysis, and Business Analysis help you identify what Core Competencies are needed to be highly profitable and to create a competitive advantage, it does not mean you need to directly possess these competencies. On the other hand, if the opportunity presents itself and it makes business sense to bring that competency into the organization and own it, then that is what you should do. However it cannot be the norm to change Core Competencies with the tides. Only when there is a break-over of all relevant considerations should an organization change its stand. It's also true that opportunities present themselves and if the time and other considerations are favorable they should be capitalized upon.

There are several categories of Core Competency for an organization but there are only two primary categories: Key Technologies and Key Processes. If you are a service-based organization you must also know, track, and cultivate the Core Competencies required to service your customers. This may mean adopting a new Core Competency for your client's primary software application or manufacturing process. Think of the relationship of Core Competencies similar to the relationship of the Vale Chain. You may outsource a Core Competency to a vendor just as you may insource a Core Competency for a client.

When it comes to the importance of a quality people process this tool is, in my opinion, one of the most important in that process, second only to how you select and hire talented people. Once you hire this wonderful, talented person, you must have clear, concise, and well-defined roles and responsibilities for this new person. You must also have a clear path for their growth within your company. This tool will help you map out each and every one of those paths right from the beginning, and it will continue to map out these paths as your people grow, mature, and thrive. If you happen to be a one-man shop and you are planning to someday expand, this tool will be instrumental in helping you figure out exactly how many hats you currently wear and give you satisfaction in knowing you have all the bases covered. You can then begin cloning yourself.

Many companies know what their offerings are but they don't take the time to detail the Key Technologies and Key Processes required to deliver those products and services. These would include everything from the Customer Relations Management (CRM) and accounting packages to product production processes, client training procedures, vendor management tools, and so on. Any technology or process that, if it were to fail or be compromised, would cause you to produce a less-than-quality product or deliver a less-than-desired service is a key one. This includes the Key Technologies and Key Processes insourced for your clients. It should not be hard to see that these tie back directly to the roles and responsibilities of the individuals who make up your company.

When you combine each of the aspects laid out here, the ultimate goal in any company regardless of size is to have coverage of all key technologies and processes evenly distributed across your company. The best way to accomplish this is to list all of these core competencies and all of the talented people you have in your company and then match them up. The result is what I refer to as a Core Competency Matrix (see Figure 3-6).

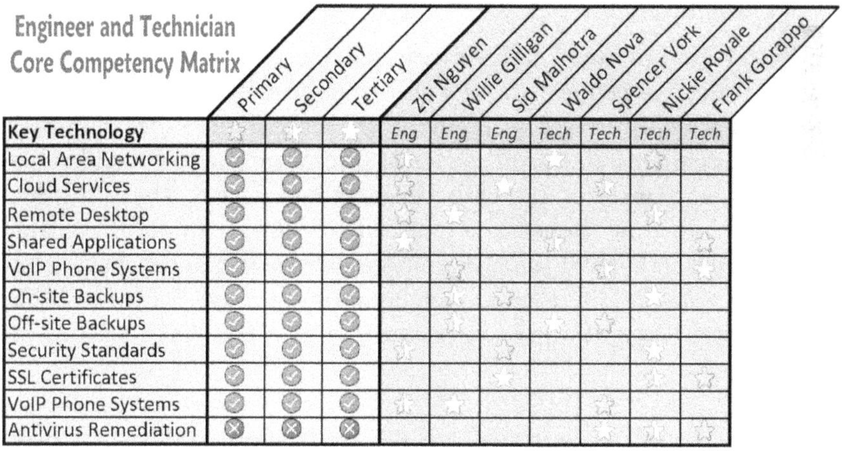

**Engineer and Technician Core Competency Matrix**

| Key Technology | Primary | Secondary | Tertiary | Zhi Nguyen | Willie Gilligan | Sid Malhotra | Waldo Nova | Spencer Vork | Nickie Royale | Frank Gorappo |
|---|---|---|---|---|---|---|---|---|---|---|
| | | | | Eng | Eng | Eng | Tech | Tech | Tech | Tech |
| Local Area Networking | ✓ | ✓ | ✓ | | | | | | | |
| Cloud Services | ✓ | ✓ | ✓ | | | | | | | |
| Remote Desktop | ✓ | ✓ | ✓ | | | | | | | |
| Shared Applications | ✓ | ✓ | ✓ | | | | | | | |
| VoIP Phone Systems | ✓ | ✓ | ✓ | | | | | | | |
| On-site Backups | ✓ | ✓ | ✓ | | | | | | | |
| Off-site Backups | ✓ | ✓ | ✓ | | | | | | | |
| Security Standards | ✓ | ✓ | ✓ | | | | | | | |
| SSL Certificates | ✓ | ✓ | ✓ | | | | | | | |
| VoIP Phone Systems | ✓ | ✓ | ✓ | | | | | | | |
| Antivirus Remediation | ✗ | ✗ | ✗ | | | | | | | |

*Figure 3-6. Core Competency Matrix for an IT Company*

If you have identified your core competencies and successfully matched them up with the right talent, then you can set clear and concise training paths for everyone involved and begin progress toward your goal. Regardless of the size of your company, in order to have true redundancy, you must have a primary and a secondary and, if at all possible, a tertiary coverage for each competency on the list.

The Core Competency Matrix should be used to target and drive training for existing employees and to target the talents of potential new employees. If you have a robust quality people process, this means you have regular employee evaluations to see to it that everyone on the team has clear goals for their progress in their career and more specifically within the company. The Core Competency Matrix is what should drive those goals based on the company needs and the employee desires, tempered by seniority.

## DiSC Profile

When selecting the quality talent to fill the needs of your organization, you must enlist some help in narrowing the field of candidates. Since you should be heavily focused on getting the right people, this also means making sure they will thrive in the environment you are building. You will no doubt have clear and concise roles and responsibilities laid out and you should even have some form of skills assessment tests. But you certainly should have at least one tool to help you identify an individual's behavior styles for the purpose of melding together the best team you can.

Believe it or not these assessments and profiles can be extremely accurate and revealing in how well someone will fit into a team or group with respect to the assessments of each of the other members. These assessments and profiles can of course also help the individual understand themselves better because they reveal to the individual their own interactive behavioral traits. There are a lot of tools available for assessing individual skills, cognition, personality, and behavior but I am only going to discuss one such iteration—the DiSC Profile. It has the broadest range of applications and can be used by any business to great benefit.

The DiSC Profile is derived from the foundation works of William Moulton Marston, a psychologist. Marston published his book *Emotions of Normal People* in 1928 and in it, he describes four critical behavioral traits exhibited by every human. They are Dominance (D), Inducement (I), Submission (S), and Compliance (C). Fast forward to today and what you have is a series of questions that present a finite list of specific adjectives to the subject. How an individual answers these questions about themselves helps determine the extent to which each of these four forces—now more commonly termed Dominance (D), Influence (I), Steadiness (S), and Conscientiousness (C)—are likely to be exhibited in their natural behavior (see Figure 3-7).

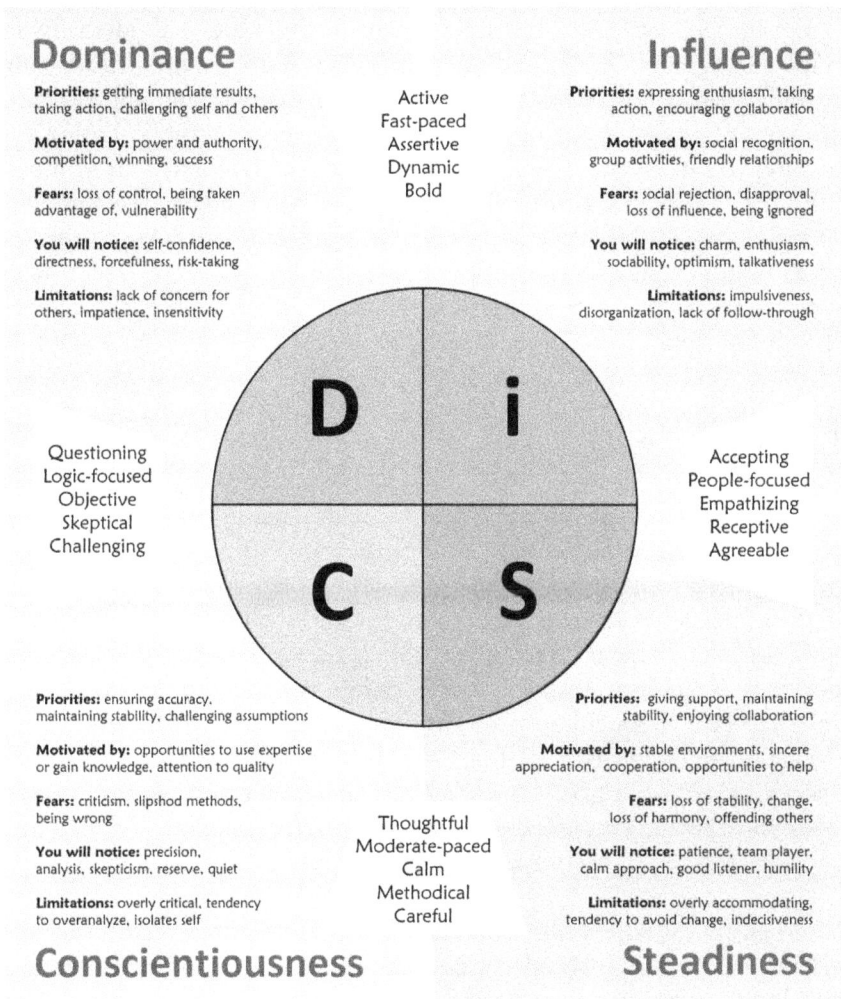

## Dominance

**Priorities:** getting immediate results, taking action, challenging self and others

**Motivated by:** power and authority, competition, winning, success

**Fears:** loss of control, being taken advantage of, vulnerability

**You will notice:** self-confidence, directness, forcefulness, risk-taking

**Limitations:** lack of concern for others, impatience, insensitivity

## Influence

**Priorities:** expressing enthusiasm, taking action, encouraging collaboration

**Motivated by:** social recognition, group activities, friendly relationships

**Fears:** social rejection, disapproval, loss of influence, being ignored

**You will notice:** charm, enthusiasm, sociability, optimism, talkativeness

**Limitations:** impulsiveness, disorganization, lack of follow-through

Active
Fast-paced
Assertive
Dynamic
Bold

D    i

Questioning
Logic-focused
Objective
Skeptical
Challenging

Accepting
People-focused
Empathizing
Receptive
Agreeable

C    S

**Priorities:** ensuring accuracy, maintaining stability, challenging assumptions

**Motivated by:** opportunities to use expertise or gain knowledge, attention to quality

**Fears:** criticism, slipshod methods, being wrong

**You will notice:** precision, analysis, skepticism, reserve, quiet

**Limitations:** overly critical, tendency to overanalyze, isolates self

Thoughtful
Moderate-paced
Calm
Methodical
Careful

**Priorities:** giving support, maintaining stability, enjoying collaboration

**Motivated by:** stable environments, sincere appreciation, cooperation, opportunities to help

**Fears:** loss of stability, change, loss of harmony, offending others

**You will notice:** patience, team player, calm approach, good listener, humility

**Limitations:** overly accommodating, tendency to avoid change, indecisiveness

## Conscientiousness

## Steadiness

*Figure 3-7. DiSC Profile Behavioral Traits*

The standard DiSC Profile as administered will be a series of approximately eighty questions and will take about fifteen minutes. The profiles come in several varieties including Workplace, Sales, Leadership, and Management. For nearly any work role, my preference is the DiSC Workplace Profile. It gives both the employer and the tester a great amount of insight into how best to communicate and work effectively with this personality type. In tight knit and even small organizations it is quite common for employers to have potential talent go through a DiSC Assessment as part of the pre-employment screening.

There are definable human traits for top sales people, exceptionally effective leaders, and top level managers. There are identifiable traits for nearly every significant role you can come up with in your organization. Those who are building these assessments and profiles are investing heavily with both time and money with the intention of helping you build the best team you can. It does not matter if you use the DiSC Profile or some other chosen assessment type for building or refining your teams. What matters is that you recognize the value of assessments like these for how they can influence who you let onto your team and how they can positively influence where you place them within the team.

## Feasibility Study

This is the first real business tool, and though it may be the most boring one, it is in fact the most important one. Before you begin any new business venture, or when reevaluating one, you must determine if the endeavor is feasible. You must answer in all honesty several key questions in order to draw your conclusion and make an educated decision. Your investors and stakeholders will demand that you do. In Chapter 2, I touched on the minimum required dimensions to be evaluated for determining if a given business is feasible. That short list was more of a go/no-go checklist in comparison to a complete Feasibility Study. You will need a much more detailed, quality narrative supported by evidence which is backed by real data.

The Feasibility Study is the entrepreneur's in-depth evaluation to see if the idea will work and if they should proceed with the venture and build a Business Plan. It answers the question: Will it work? The Business Plan is what you share with potential investors, stakeholders, and executives which explains specifically how the business will work. It answers the question: How will it work? The Feasibility Study by nature depends on market research data that can be less than perfect depending on the source or availability of that data. This is always taken into consideration when evaluating the study as the weight of this data is balanced against the weight of the overall proposition and its supporting documentation.

Here you will lay out the complete list of requirements for your study which will result in a detailed multipage report. Each dimension listed below will have its own section in the report. You can then share and discuss this report with your circle of council, other entrepreneurs, your business coach, and even potential backers. They will help you test and tweak the feasibility. They will give you their valuable input so that you are able to make a well-informed decision about whether you should proceed with building a Business Plan. Keep in mind that you are using these tools as building blocks. The Feasibility Study calls on the support of several individual tools, the most important of which I will cover in the next two chapters.

## Executive Summary

The result of your in-depth analysis should be compiled into a formal report starting with an Executive Summary and closing with Final Recommendations. The Executive Summary is actually written up after the analysis is complete; it is a summary of the key dimensions under scrutiny. It is often presented as a standalone document that potential investors or stakeholders would review to decide if they are interested in looking at the full report. It is not worded as a sales pitch but rather as indicated, a summary of the findings tempered with the optimism realized from its evaluation.

## Value Proposition

Describe in detail the products and services (offerings) that you believe will have perceived utility and therefore value to a potential Customer. Most investors will want you to tell them how your products and services are unique. They do not need to be new inventions. Note that your products and services do not need to be the unique part of your business that gets it rolling. It may be how you deliver the same products and services that others do that is unique.

You will have to describe how your customers will acquire and use your products and services, where you will get the materials and components used to create your products and services, and how they will be tested. You will also need to give some idea of the lifecycle of the products and services.

Tool Tip: *Target Market Analysis, Product Lifecycle Analysis*

## Research & Development
This is where you will provide any technical information about the products and services as necessary. You will want to describe any ongoing research that may be required to drive the innovation or lifecycle of the products and services.

Tool Tip: *Target Market Analysis, Product Lifecycle Analysis*

## Target Market
This is a clear description of who you believe your customers and end users of your products and services are. Describe how they will buy your products and services and how frequently they will need to resupply or re-engage. You will need to provide as much relevant detail about the demographics of your market as possible: age, gender, career, position, income, education, ethnicity, location, language, habits, interests, concerns, needs, desires, mood, and so on. You will also need to discuss current market and economic mood or sentiment. Are they favorable or unfavorable? Will they change or continue and for how long?

You may have no choice but to start with a broad demographic but when it comes to the Business Plan, it will need to be narrowed. You should try to break your demographics into primary and secondary markets. Describe how large your primary and secondary markets are (market share) and how it is expected to grow or shrink in the short and long term.

Tool Tip: *Target Market Analysis, Product Lifecycle Analysis*

## Competition
Describe who you believe your direct competition will be in your target market, whether direct or indirect. If you can identify and research them well enough, describe their products and services, market share, strategies, and even strengths and weaknesses if known. Next describe how your offerings compare to those of your competition with an emphasis on any uniqueness of your offerings. If your offerings are new to the market, indicate so and then state how difficult it will be for your competition to copy your offerings and how long it will take if they do attempt it.

Tool Tip: *Ansoff Matrix, Porter's Five Competitive Forces, Porter's Generic*

*Strategies, Bowman's Strategy Clock*

## Industry

This is where you describe the intended industry your business will operate within. You should know and describe the segment within the industry that your organization fits. You need to research your intended industries well enough to describe its size, growth rate, supply and demand trends, and the forces that drive it. Drivers are things such as innovation, politics, culture, economy, change, and regulation.

Tool Tip: *Industry Study*

## Business Model

This is where you will describe the business model your organization will follow and how you will generate revenue. Indicate if you will sell products or deliver services or both. Perhaps you will sell only licenses or access passes. Will you have recurring revenue, repeat customers, or one-time patrons?

Tool Tip: *Pyramid of Purpose and Value*

## Partnerships

Describe who your partners are expected to be including vendors and any key clients. Describe the relationship in terms of how they fit into your organization's value chain and how you fit into theirs. What will you rely on these partners for and what will they rely on you for? How will you vet potential partners so as to protect your brand and secrets?

Tool Tip: *Value Chain*

## Marketing Strategy

This is where you will describe your basic marketing strategy for how you will get the attention of your potential Customer so that you may present your Value Proposition. It does not need to be quite as detailed here as it will be in the Business Plan but it should indicate the expected one, three, and five-year marketing budgets. This budget must include spin-up costs for initial branding and logos. These will be line items in your Capital Requirements. Will you have sales, discount coupons, offers, incentives, and so on?

Tool Tip: *Ansoff Matrix, Porter's Five Competitive Forces, Bowman's Strategy Clock*

## Sales Strategy

This is where you will describe your basic sales strategy and process for how you will sell or deliver your Value Proposition in exchange for revenue. Will you be selling and delivering as a retailer, wholesaler, business to business, or direct to the end consumers themselves? Will you sell or offer from a brick and mortar storefront or a website? Describe your pricing structure and expected profit margins. What will be your payment terms and method of payment? Will you have warranties, returns, rebates, discounts, and so on?

Tool Tip: *Target Market Analysis, Industry Study*

## Production Model

Describe the basics of how the organization will source and create products or organize services including outsourcing. What tools and methods are employed to create your products and services and how intricate is the process? Discuss quality control and protection of proprietary processes. You will need to indicate if physical space is required and estimate the costs of acquiring, leasing, or building.

Tool Tip: *Critical Thinking*

## Distribution Model

Describe the basics of how you will get your products and services to customers once they have taken you up on the Value Proposition. These are the methods and process you will employ to deliver the products and services such as online digital delivery, self-service, in person, on-site, third-party supplier, and so on. Discuss use or leverage of partnerships and other channels. Indicate the estimated associated costs per unit delivered.

Tool Tip: *Critical Thinking*

## Management and Personnel

This is where you briefly describe the core competencies your people will need to possess as a whole. Discuss the required or desired qualifications, background, experience, and skills. They can be broken down by position and title or roles and responsibilities as desired. You must estimate the cost for finding and retaining the quality talent you will need.

Tool Tip: *Pyramid of Purpose and Value, Core Competency Matrix*

## Intellectual Property

Describe any desire or requirements for patents, copyrights, and trade or service marks. Indicate if they are already in possession or if they will need to be obtained. If they are already in possession, indicate each in brief. If they are in discovery, indicate status and any existing results of searches or applications.

Tool Tip: *Pyramid of Purpose and Value*

## Regulation Concerns

Describe any regulations or restrictions that may affect your organization's operations in any relevant or significant way. This would include local, state, and federal government for any location you wish to do business. Consider trade or industry regulations and restrictions as well (political concerns when relevant fall into this category). Do not wait for the Business Plan to first mention them.

Tool Tip: *PESTEL Analysis*

## Environmental Issues

Describe any known environmental problems related to the property you intend to occupy or any possible issues related to your products and services. Discuss any impact your organization will have on the environment in any way. If the impact will be a cost center, discuss it here and now. Do not wait for the Business Plan to first mention them.

Tool Tip: *PESTEL Analysis*

## Critical Risk

Describe here any relevant critical risk the organization may face before startup, during and after. Indicate resources, methods, or strategies that are either creating risk or will be at risk.

Include discussion of perceived or realized market or economic sentiment and mood.

Tool Tip: *Critical Thinking, Porter's Five Competitive Forces, PESTEL Analysis, Ansoff Matrix, SWOT Analysis*

## Entrance Strategy

This is where you describe the general strategy for getting into the market and spinning up the business. Discuss timelines, deadlines, landmarks, and milestones include the triggering events and how they relate. Discuss resource and financial requirements for each point on the timeline.

Tool Tip: *Critical Thinking, GOST Strategy Planning, SMARTER Goal and Projects*

## Exit Strategy

This is where you describe the major stop indicators that signal a failure of the strategy. It will look similar to the Entrance Strategy but it will have events and triggers that show burndown thresholds for resources and/or cash. It will briefly discuss the systematic dismantling of the existing structure for the greatest preservation of capital.

Do not skip this section. You can and must gracefully spin down a venture that is going sideways. Driving the endeavor into the ground burns down significantly more valuable resources than just capital; it also destroys opportunities and relationships.

Tool Tip: *Critical Thinking, GOST Strategy Planning*

## Financial Projections

Describe the funds required to get this venture off the ground and keep it running until it is self-sufficient and producing regular revenue. Include proposed sources of funding, stages of financing, projections for cash flow, and uses of the capital. You will want to include a brief discussion of your credit and debt in addition to any skin you will be putting into the game, i.e. equity. You will need the following financial documents:
- Balance Sheet Projections – Income, Liability, Capital
- Income Projections – Revenue, COGS, Profit, Expenses,

Income
- Cash Flow Projections – Cash In, Cash Out
- Break-Even Analysis – ROI Prediction
- Cost Benefit Analysis – Investment Justification

Tool Tip: *Financial Statements*

### Final Recommendations

The Final Recommendations will be the last page of the report and should be a short and to-the-point argument and narrative that either supports or opposes the venture. The narrative should ideally indicate the likelihood of success, potential for returns, and address any known or potential significant risk. If the venture is supported you move forward, and if it is not you either go back to the top to re-work it or you scrap it.

The arguments for or against are not usually simple Yes or No answers but rather stipulations such as "Yes if …" or "No unless …" It is acceptable to have multiple potential recommendations or alternative approaches called out as well. For example there may be options for implementation based on initial funding. The Final Recommendation should also call out any limitations to the proposition elements or the reliability of data that the recommendations are based upon.

The Final Recommendation must be based on factual information and as accurate of data as can be acquired. Gut feeling and sentiment have no place in the construction of the recommendation. Those are for the investors to rely on when reviewing your proposal and for you in making it all happen. You must start with a recommendation based on real numbers and reliable data.

## Business Plan

One you have completed your Feasibility Study and come to the conclusion that you do in fact intend to pursue venture capital for your endeavor, you must write a formal Business Plan. The formal Business Plan is typically constructed for one of three reasons: as a blueprint for operation, when reorganizing the business, or when seeking investors or funding. For our purposes, the Pyramid of Purpose and Value is much more suitable for presenting the business blueprint for operations or when reorganizing the business—it was specifically designed for these purposes. But the formal Business Plan is required when approaching investors and seeking funding. It presents only the relevant and required information in a specific layout and format that venture capital and lending institutions will expect to see. They may be very impressed with your pyramid but it will be overkill.

The Business Plan calls for much of the same research to be performed as the Feasibility Study but the results are compiled and presented in a different format. The Feasibility Study is presented as the results of a study intended to evaluate a proposition—the endeavor. The Business Plan is the endeavor presented as a proposition. It paints a clear and enticing picture of the business venture. It tells a compelling story of how the future would look if the business venture were successful. The story is told against the backdrop of the value potential offered and the market it is offered to. It is painted with solid data, concise plans, and specific requirements for the success of the endeavor.

The layout and components of the Business Plan can vary greatly depending on the endeavor being undertaken and the target audience. It is not uncommon to have a lending institution provide a specific format that all submissions must be presented in. The best thing to do is to prepare a standard format Business Plan and then be prepared to tailor the version you present to the audience. The data will always be the same but there may be more detail requested for various sections. To this point, if you have built out your Pyramid of Purpose and Value and you have performed your due diligence in a Feasibility Study, you really only need to grab the required components from these and lay them in place within the business plan.

Please remember the following is not intended to be a complete Business Plan layout but a generic layout and brief description of the most important components. There are no Tool Tips called out in this section. Once again, if you've completed your Pyramid of Purpose and Value and a detailed Feasibility Study, you can include either in the Appendix and then refer to them throughout the plan as needed. Provided your plan is in fact solid, any investor would welcome the detail to which you have planned the success of your business.

## Executive Summary

The Executive Summary is without question the most important section of a business plan from a narrative viewpoint. It is where you tell potential investors where you and your company are, where you are going, and how you intend to get there. It is your opportunity to get the attention of investors with your compelling story. Just as with the Feasibility Study, the Executive Summary is written last. It can only be written after all supporting and compelling evidence has been completely compiled. It too is often presented as a standalone document that potential investors or stakeholders would review to decide if they are interested in looking at the plan.

The Executive Summary must stand on its own in that it summarizes all of what is found in the report without introducing information or speculation on content that is not contained in the full report. Key elements of the Executive Summary include but are not limited to:

- Vision and Mission statement – Always start with this
- Company information and background – Very brief
- Track Record to date – For existing businesses
- Problem – What need of the market is not being met and why?
- Consequences – What will be the results if this problem is not solved?
- Analysis – What the market study tells you about the problem
- Approach – Your unique method of addressing this need
  This is your Value Proposition, i.e. Products and Services and their uniqueness
- Recommendations – A summary of your future plans for success
- Outcome – Financial projections based on success – The ROI
- Conclusion –Where you state the financial needs to launch and grow this venture

## Company Description

The short and to-the-point narrative of the business including any relevant information about the founders, current stakeholders, key talent, physical presences, primary products and service, industries, initial target markets, market share, and even the exit strategy of principals. Provide enough information for the reader to understand who and what the business is, where it's going, and how it intends to get there. This is where you give the potential investors something or someone to root for.

## Market Analysis

This is where you will detail to the extent necessary the results of several of the Analyses performed for the Feasibility Study. You will start with the description and details of the Target Market for perspective. You will then describe the results of your Product Life Cycle Analysis. Next you will detail the relevant results of the Competitive Analysis and the PESTEL Analysis. And last you will share your pricing models, margin projections, and expected market share growth.

## Organization and Personnel

This is a combination of the information pulled from the Pyramid of Purpose and Value and the Feasibility Study and expanded upon significantly. It must be very detailed in nature as this is actually the underlying entity the venture capital providers will be writing the check to. They will want to know who you are and how you operate as an entity. They must be able to see that there is a solid structure under this organization providing them with a reasonable expectation of success. It will be directly related to the make-up, history, and track record of the organization. Expect to spend a significant amount of time collecting and presenting this information.

## Products and Services

This is where you detail the products and services you intend to offer and the Value Proposition they represent to your target market. This includes expanding on the Problem, Consequences, and Approach narrative. Focus on the utility and warranty of the offerings and how they present a solution to the customers' problem of filling their needs. Be certain to include the product life cycle so as to demonstrate potential for ongoing growth of the product or service line. You can and should pull a large amount of information directly from the Feasibility Study. Look to the sections on Value Proposition, Research & Development, and Intellectual Property. All of this information supports the product or service line as a solid package of value offering versus just another mediocre competitor pressing into the market with just another mediocre offering. Make your Value Proposition shine as a well thought-out and researched innovation.

## Marketing and Sales

Marketing and Sales are where you create a customer by systematically presenting that Value Proposition and delivering on it. This is where you will detail the Problem, Consequences, and Approach strategy, not just the narrative. Focus on the market positioning of the offerings by discussing how it will penetrate and gain your business a larger market share based on its lifecycle and uniqueness. Discuss the use of Partnerships and channels for distribution and reach. Discuss communications methods and strategies for reaching your customers. This would include things like advertising, promotions, incentives, public and community interactions, and direct and outside selling. You should even have examples and samples of the printed materials detailing your products and services in the appendix.

Next you will discuss the specifics of your sales processes and strategies. Start with the basics of how you intend to sell. Indicate if you will be utilizing an internal sales force or leveraging independent representatives or even outsourcing to a sales force service. Indicate what the beginning force looks like and how it will progress as a product and service as market share increases. Discuss in detail the compensation, incentives, and bonus programs and levels.

Describe your prospects and the breakdown of where they were developed from and how they are broken out into first approach (hot), second approach (warm), and third approach (cold). Describe in detail the breakdown of the sales metrics from calls or touches per day or week resulting in x number of sales and of what average size. You must be able to show how the money will flow based on how you will drive sales.

## Funding Request
Now comes the part where you must present your specific venture capital needs. Provide a simple and concise narrative of what your financial needs are and generally how they will help you get to the next level. Be specific about your current financial position and your short-term funding requirements. Indicate why you need them and what they will do for you. Don't get too specific about where the dollars go in the chart of accounts, but do indicate the cost center they will flow to. Example: The initial $50,000 will allow us to ramp up our R&D to get the product from beta to release in less than six months including patent applications.

Proceed to discuss future funding requirements over the next three to five years in the same fashion. Provide your narrative and strategy about how you see things playing out. Discuss how you will buy out a competitor, buy the patent rights for a product, pay down existing debt, buy out a partner, ramp up marketing, and so on. You will need to be very specific about the amounts being requested. State the timelines for disbursement, desired terms, desired interest, and repayment plan contingencies. If you have painted a compelling picture, this is part of the compelling story you tell to get people on board. And if you see the means to an end, tell that story too. If you intend to sell the business once it is right-side up or flush and ripe for acquisition, say so.

## Financial Projections

Here is where you will provide excruciating detail of all financials related to the venture. You will start with the historical financial information about the organization, then you will discuss specifically what you intend to do with the venture capital you are requesting and how it will get you to the next level. If the Business Plan is for an existing business looking to get to the next level, you will need to produce relevant financial history demonstrating past performance. You will need to produce no less than the Income, Expense, Balance Sheets, and Cash Flow Statements. The reports should be for no less than a year but are typically for the past three to five years. These numbers must be verifiable and they will likely also be checked against what you have reported on your state and federal taxes.

One of the most important components of the plan is what your business intends to do with the venture capital it is requesting. You must be able to demonstrate that you understand where this cash flow can most help your business and it must be realistic. You will need to put together quarterly projections for the first year and annual for the next two to five years. You are basically extrapolating your financial data from your past history through present day to a point forward in time. This means the Income, Expense, Balance Sheets, and Cash Flow projections that will provide the required historic and future view of the business finances.

Your projections must include and properly represent your previous Funding Request. This is to say that the numbers must add up all the way down the line. When requesting large amounts of venture capital it may be required that your projections and history are validated by an external accounting entity. It is always recommended to present your projections on a graph and provide specifics about return ratios, burn rates for cash flow, expected landmarks, launch points, and turning points.

## Appendix

The Appendix is simply the organized landing place for all relevant and required supporting documents. Do not use it as a dumpster for content and data you have compiled but are not sure where to put. If the content does not specifically support your proposition or provide relevant detail, leave it out unless requested.

- Resumes of Key Management
- Letters of Reference
- Copies of Patents and Trademarks
- Visual References of Products and Service
- Promotional Material Examples
- Personal and Business Credit History
- Feasibility Study
- Details of Target Market Analysis
- Financial Reports
- Private Placement Disclaimers

Take special notice of a document called the Private Placement Disclaimer. The Private Placement Disclaimer is a document discussing the potential for downsides in the venture. While the Business Plan brings into focus the vision of the entrepreneur and the endeavor and the potential upsides of the business, this is the disclaimer of possible risk involved. If you intend to raise capital, it is what makes clear that the Business Plan is a venture, not a guarantee for success.

Tool Tip: *Every Tool in the Box*

*Innovation is the specific tool of entrepreneurs, the means by which they exploit change as an opportunity for a different business or a different service.*

– Peter F. Drucker

# 4.0

## Tools & Methods for Analyzing Your Business

### Product Life Cycle Analysis

The Product Life Cycle Analysis is a tool used to approximate and assess the potential for cost, sales, profit, and longevity of a given product or service. You can also plot the life cycle of existing and past products to study their behavior in order to learn from their performance. All products go through five stages in their life cycle. The stages are: Development, Introduction, Growth, Maturity, and Decline. Many products and services see their life cycle extended beyond their planned or expected lifetime. It's not uncommon for a product or service to be revised and then re-introduced as a new version or even revamped and considered an entirely new product.

The Product Life Cycle Analysis is one of the major drivers in the innovation, marketing, and sales aspects of your organization. It dictates when to look to lenders for research and development funding, when to push money into marketing, and what sales expectations and metrics to assign. And it dictates the planned obsolescence of those products and services in favor of more relevant and profitable offerings.

You should know the life cycle of every product and service your organization offers and you should be plotting the demonstrated performance over the graph of the predicted performance for each of them. They should also be reviewed and revised periodically to ensure you are optimizing value offerings for your customers and profit for your business (see Figure 4-1).

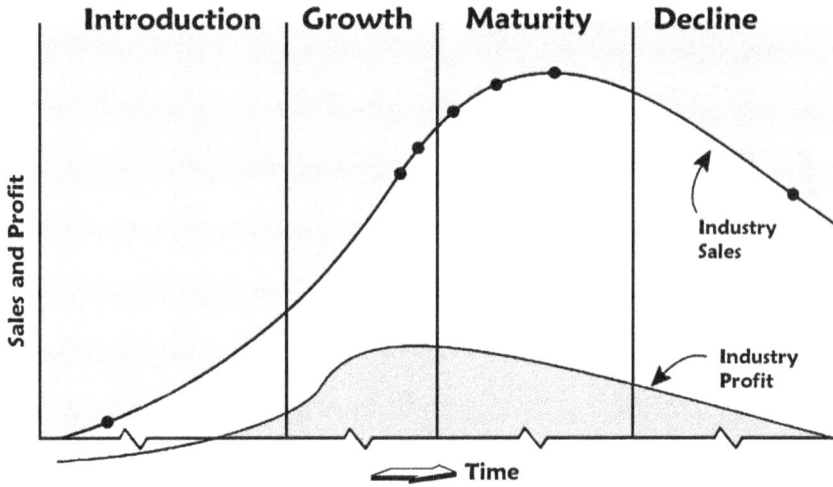

*Figure 4-1. Stages in the Product Life Cycle*

### Development

During the innovation and development stage the focus will primarily be on defining and testing the utility and value to potential clients. Much of the research and development will be technical research and market studies with the smaller balance on development. Financial strategies will be focused on projecting required resources if the product or service is released as well as budgeting for R&D and marketing funds for the next stage. Once the product or service has been developed sufficiently to where it is believed it will create a value proposition to the customer, it then moves to Introduction.

### Introduction

Marketing strategies will shift from market study to market introduction. The focus will be on strategic positioning of the new offerings to establish a competitive advantage. Advertising, promotions, and sales will be focused on developing awareness and establishing market share. Human resources strategies will be addressing resource needs based on the predictions for demand and sales. The research and development efforts will shift from research to full development, correcting design issues, and implementing features.

### Growth

Marketing is focused on establishing a niche for the product or service as a preferred brand. Advertising efforts will leverage media channels, sample programs, and promotions. Communications channels are established for everyone in the Value Chain to strengthen partnerships for the immense competition that will likely occur in the Maturity stage.

Research and development and production operations must maintain focus on quality. It is common for offerings in this stage to have the quality sacrificed for the false belief that it is part of the cost of rapid growth. This is risky and it should be avoided at all costs. The reputation of the organization is at stake. The people process will be focused on retaining the core competency that supports these products and services.

## Maturity

As the product or service matures, the competition shows up from all angles and the focus becomes efficiency and profit generation. Only those organizations that run a tight ship and have firmly established vertical market share will realize any longevity through this stage. Marketing efforts are focused on customer loyalty and repeat or recurring sales.

Production operation strategies will be focused on timely delivery in tune with driving efficiency, repeatability, and reproducibility to keep overhead to a minimum. Metrics will be established for costs, efficiency, defects, rework, etc. The people process will be focused on maintaining optimal management and team leadership. Those who can produce results and operate within budgets and other constraints will be promoted, shifted, or hired.

## Decline

At this stage, the market is so saturated that only the revision or rework of the product will allow its life to be either extended or revived. Regardless of the efforts, if sales cannot be revived and the offering is in full decline, the decision must be made to drop it or milk it dry of all profit. If it is dropped, all funds and efforts are quickly and swiftly switched to other products. Even if it is to be milked dry, the majority of resources are redirected and only a skeleton crew is left to produce or support it. There are other strategies for end-of-life products including concentrating on a small market with minimal effort, buying similar offerings to increase market share and profit, selling it off, and liquidating it.

Tool Tip: *Critical Thinking, Process Control, Gap Analysis, Ansoff Matrix, Porter's Five Competitive Forces, Porter's Generic Strategies, Bowman's Strategy Clock, PESTEL Analysis*

## Target Market Analysis

The Target Market Analysis is performed to identify your target market and to identify what share of that market you can reasonably expect to gain with your offering of products and services. It forces you to analyze your competition and their products and services versus yours. It asks several important questions and requires you to draw specific conclusions.

The Target Market Analysis is critical to any venture, new or existing. It should be performed annually if not more frequently depending on the products and services your business offers. It is the most influential component in defining who you sell to and how you sell to them. It is a behavioral study of your customers in the Meso Environment you share with them.

### Prerequisites

Before you can begin your market analysis there are three things you must know or have in hand. First, you must have identified the specific industry your organization operates within. You should also have researched the size and historic growth rate of the industry, and you should be aware of current trends and characteristics of the industry. It is common for businesses to operate in multiple industries because of the products they offer.

Next, you must know what you intend to sell or offer as products and services to your target market. You can only identify a target market if you know everything possible about what it is you are offering and what the perceived utility or value is to the end user or customer. Each product or service line will require its own analysis.

Last, you must have access to market research data to analyze or you must know where to find it. This is market research data from government or private industry which tells you everything from how many people live in a given country to what the average shoe size is of every household in the south corner of Mobile, Alabama to how Native Americans feel about global warming.

It's all out there and it costs anywhere from $0 to millions of dollars depending on what you want and how accurate you need it to be. And if it's not out there already someone will get it for you for a price. Sources of this data are beyond the scope of this book but you should certainly start with the numerous censuses for your country, region, etc. Then move to other free data you can find online. Only after you have narrowed your market sufficiently should you spend money on more specific or granular data and only to the extent needed.

**Target Market**

You must first establish how big the overall realistic market is for your specific product or service in the industry you operate within. To identify the Total Available Market (TAM), begin by filtering the industry market data down based on the most realistic and obvious realities such as geographical location, political boundaries, and language. Example: Within the entire world market of this industry, which regions of the world can you do business in? Which countries? Which languages?

The TAM could realistically be the entire world in today's economy and with the right resources. However your organization is not likely able to produce enough products or provide services for the TAM so you must narrow it further (see Figure 4-2).

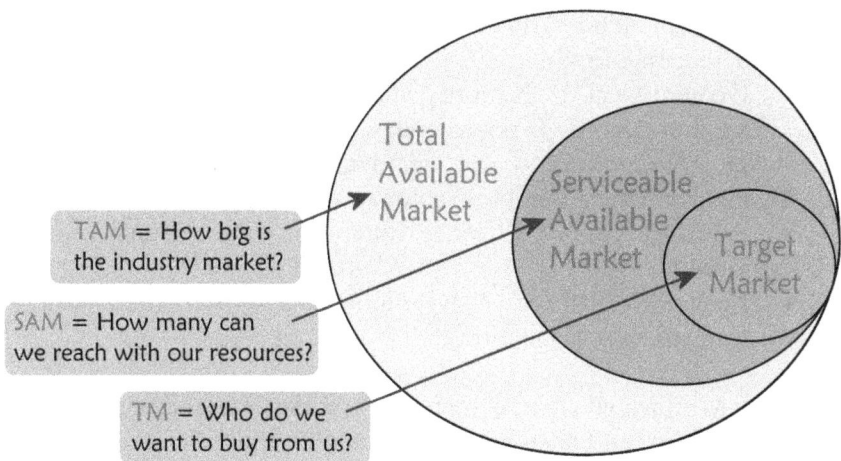

Figure 4-2. Market Perspective

To narrow the TAM you need identify the Serviceable Available Market (SAM). This is the realistic market opportunity of your organization based on its core competencies, resources, and production or service capability. If you're looking into a new venture or expanding an existing market, you may choose to draw a larger circle in the SAM based on projections and expectations.

To establish the SAM you apply further filters to the market data such as physical, financial, and competency limits of your organization's capability. Example: How far are you capable or willing to travel to service a client? Even if you are doing business online selling digital downloads, there are realistic limits to which operating systems your application will run on or that you will service. Again, you must know your product or service and you must be realistic in evaluating your organization's limitations.

From the Serviceable Available Market you will identify your Target Market. To identify your target market you apply more filtering and this time, it is more about where you can make the biggest splash and gain greatest penetration based on how your product or service fits into the wants, needs, and desires of your potential customer. You simply ask questions about the target market relative to the product or service. What age range of people will likely use more of your services? What are the lifestyles of people that will be most attracted to this product?

## Market Segmentation

The SAM can be filtered down to your target market by segmenting it within these categories:

- Geographical – Nations, states, regions, countries, cities, neighborhoods, or postal codes.
- Demographically – Age, gender, marital status, family size, income, education level, occupation, race, and religion.
- Psychographic – Lifestyle, interests, values, opinions, and attitudes.
- Behavior – Tracked behavior indicating knowledge of, attitude towards, and usage rate.

The level to which you can segment your market data is directly related to the granularity and detail of the market data you have access to. The hardest data to come by and the most expensive is also the most valuable. What are the needs of the customer and are they being fulfilled? How often does the customer buy a new one of these products per year? What are they willing to spend on them?

## Market Share

You must estimate how much of the target market share you can gain from entry into that market with your products and services. What percentages of share will you be able to maintain and for how long before competition pushes back? What is the potential or forecasted growth over the next several years for this market? What is the expected annual revenue from purchases or use of services your target market will make? Once again, look to the resources mentioned earlier. Be prepared to explain the logic behind your calculations and estimations.

## Primary Target Market

Now that you have identified your target market and you know the size of it, you need to break it into primary and secondary. The primary market is where you will put the primary focus of your efforts and the bulk of your marketing funds. The secondary market will be advertised to and cultivated but to a lesser extent. Defining primary and secondary can be extrapolated from estimated revenue you came up with when evaluating your market share. You primary market may also be defined by simply asking who you can afford to effectively advertise to right now within the constraints of your existing or near-future budget.

## Competitive Analysis

This is where the actual analysis comes in. You must identify the competition in the target market for those products and services you intend to offer. This is another behavioral study but this time it is of the competition you share the Meso Environment with.

You must assess your competition on no less than these characteristics:
- Who has the market share and how big is it?
- What are their strengths and weaknesses?
- How important is their market share to them?
- What are the barriers to entry into this market?
- Is there a window of opportunity for entry into this market?

Tool Tip: *Ansoff Matrix, Porter's Five Competitive Forces, Porter's Generic Strategies, Bowman's Strategy Clock*

The process of Competitive Analysis is not as simple as merely answering the questions above. Your ultimate goal is to identify the strategy that will bring you success in entering the market, gaining your market share, and holding it for as long as possible throughout the product life cycle. This requires that you perform the Competitive Analysis and that you circle back with the findings to adjust the proposed offering in order to optimize your penetration into the target market. You may end up adjusting the price, size, color, variations, frequency, inclusions, etc. And you may even find that adjusting your target market will yield better, more desired results.

**Summary**
Target Market Analysis is not easy due to the need for timely, relevant, and useful data. As your organization matures you will find a growing budget for market studies and market tests. Having quality market studies and market tests at hand won't get you out of doing the work outlined above; it will just lead to more fruitful results.

It is worth noting that it is not unrealistic or uncommon for an organization to adjust their products and services to match their target market. You may have heard the saying that it's easier to develop a new product than it is to find a new customer. If you have a niche and established relationships with your customers, you may find yourself pouring money into innovation of an existing product or service line versus advertising to a new demographic.

# Ansoff Matrix

One of the best tools for identifying and evaluating business growth opportunities is the Ansoff Matrix. It was developed by business manager and mathematician Igor Ansoff in the late 1950s. The matrix shows the relationship of existing and new products relative to existing and new markets. The idea is that a business can pursue various strategies depending on relevant criteria about the products and services, organization's core competencies, risk, desired growth direction, etc. (see Figure 4-3).

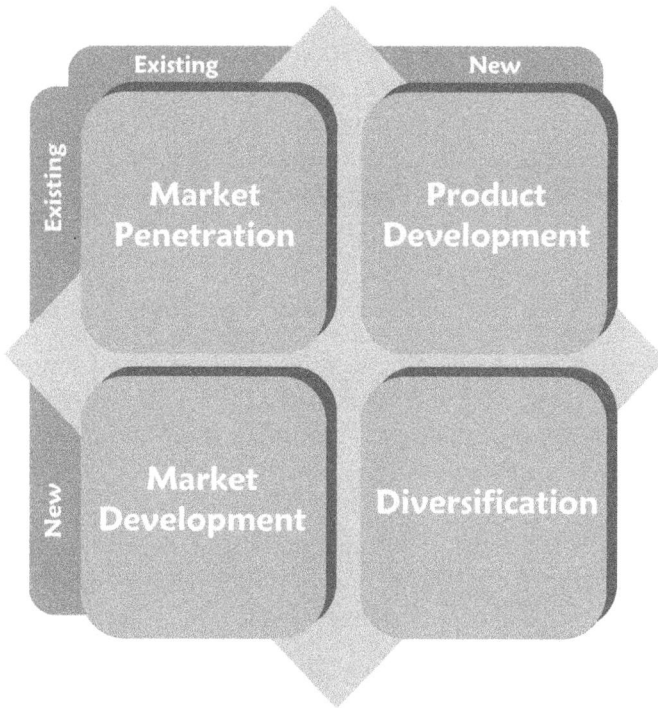

*Figure 4-3. Ansoff Matrix*

## Market Penetration

This strategy is to grow market share with existing products in the existing markets. This strategy is considered the least risky as the organization is not becoming a new threat in a new market. They need only an increased advertising budget, expanding sales pipeline, and increased production capability.

## Market Development

This strategy is to grow market share by presenting existing products to new markets. This strategy is considered more risky because it requires the organization to enter into a new market. This means they will be seen as a new threat and they may be blocked or limited by the various competitive strategies of the existing market shareholders. The organization will need to perform a market analysis and develop competitive strategies for the new market.

**Product Development**
This strategy is to develop new products for existing markets. This strategy is also considered more risky. It requires the organization to go through the entire innovation process of creating new products and services. Innovation requires financial commitment and risk is inherent. Once developed, presenting these new offerings to an existing market will not be as difficult as attempting to present to new markets.

**Diversification**
This strategy is for developing new products for new markets. This strategy is the most risky as it combines all the issues of moving into a new market coupled with all those related to innovating new products and services. The Diversification strategy is inherently higher risk but if successful, it also provides higher returns.

Tool Tip: *Gap Analysis, SWOT Analysis, McKinsey 7S Model*

# Porter's Five Competitive Forces

There are two tools that are closely related and of great value to any business intending to get to the next level. The first is Porter's Five Competitive Forces and the second is Porter's Generic Strategies. Both were developed by the professor and economist Michael Porter and were detailed in his 1985 book *Competitive Advantage*. Here, I discuss the first of the two tools.

Porter states that the first fundamental determinant of a business's profitability in a given industry (and therefore the markets within it) is how attractive it is to the organization. How attractive an industry or market is depends on how competitive it is. A highly competitive market is not as attractive simply because you will not be as profitable. Porter calls out the five specific forces that together determine the overall competitive intensity of a given industry and therefore determine how attractive and profitable it would be (see Figure 4-4).

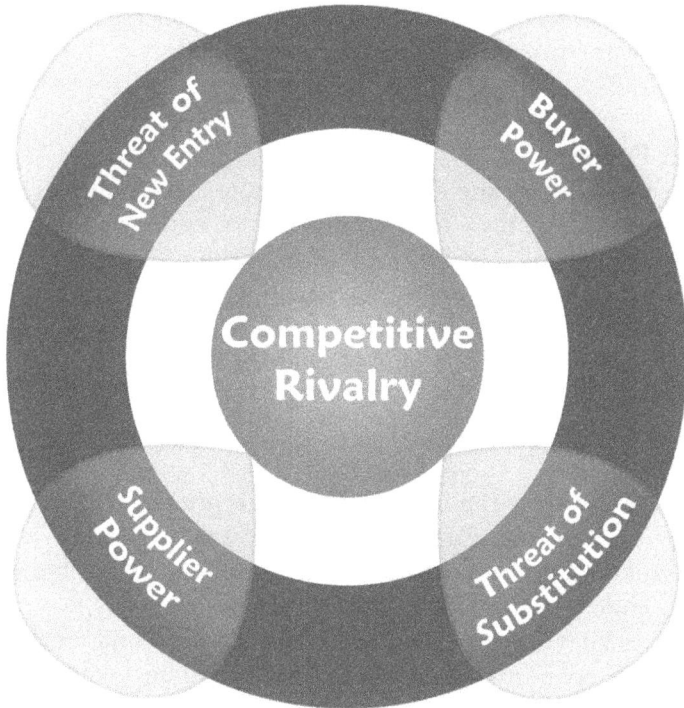

*Figure 4-4. Porter's Five Competitive Forces*

Porter states that the organization's ultimate goal is to select a strategy that allows them to at least cope with these forces if not turn them to their favor. If an organization cannot understand and manage these forces, they will not be profitable. And if they cannot influence them, they will not realize maximum profitability in their target market.

## Competitive Rivalry

The forces of existing competition in the industry all pressing against each other. This is considered the central force as it is the major factor in the overall competitiveness of the industry. Your organization's ability to withstand these forces will directly determine its ability to move into a new market or withstand the pressure from trying to take more space.

## The Threat of Substitution

The force exerted by the possibility of different products and services being offered that can be used in place of existing ones. Your organization must be able to protect the uniqueness and other traits of its products and services from being copied, mimicked, or even stolen. Doing so maintains market share and margin.

## Supplier Power

The force exerted by the supplier's ability to control prices of your required resources. This is the overall ability of suppliers to this market to control pricing as a function of their position in the market. Your organization's ability to freely choose suppliers allows you agility and options which all translates into control of your margin. Lack of choice restricts you and your ability to effect margin.

## Buyer Power

The force exerted by the customer to drive prices down. This is the ability of the buyer to force your prices lower because of how they interact and respond to your products and services. Your organization's ability to endear customers to your organization or to your products and services allows you to maintain relative pricing and market share. Inability to do so means the client can easily switching to other offerings resulting in a loss in market share and margin.

## Threat of New Entry

The force exerted by the new competitors entering or attempting to enter into the market. This is natural and most common when an industry and market have become highly profitable. Creating and maintaining barriers to entry is the best way to protect the market from becoming saturated with competition. The strongest barriers are Patents, Trademarks, Copyrights, and product or service uniqueness.

## Summary

By identifying and considering the strength and direction of each of these forces, you can assess the strength of your position and your ability to make a sustained profit in a given industry and its markets. The business strategy and the marketing strategy you select will be largely based on the evaluation of the market using this model. Porter indicates that the strength of these forces varies depending on the industry and that it can change over time as an industry evolves.

Tool Tip: *Gap Analysis, SWOT Analysis, McKinsey 7S Model*

## Porter's Generic Strategies

In his 1985 book *Competitive Advantage*, Michael Porter also states that whether an organization experiences above or below average performance is a result of its relative position within the industry or market. He indicates that to experience above-average performance you must have a long run with a sustainable competitive advantage. There are two basic types of competitive advantage: lower cost of production (Cost Leadership) and high differentiation in products and services (Differentiation). Cost Leadership and Differentiation are direct results of an organization's ability to navigate within an industry or market and to deal with the Five Competitive Forces.

An organization must define the scope of where they will establish and assert (focus) either a Cost Leadership or Differentiation. With the addition of the scope dimensions, we have what Porter referred to as the three generic strategies: Cost Leadership, Differentiation, and Focus. He notes that the Focus strategy has two variants, Cost Focus and Differentiation Focus (see Figure 4-5).

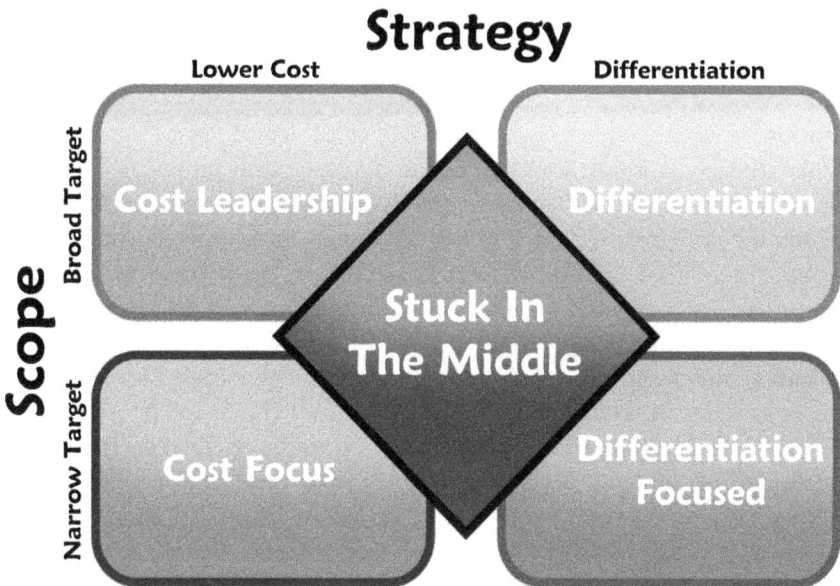

*Figure 4-5. Porter's Generic Strategies*

The source of the competitive advantage is either through Cost Leadership or product and service Differentiation. The scope is either a narrow target market or a broad target market. The broad target market may even be multiple markets in an industry or multiple industries.

## Cost Leadership

This strategy is about focusing on efficiency of production and delivery for higher margins, allowing for highly competitive pricing. This strategy works best when there is a diverse range of markets and industries being covered by the offered products or services. This allows for sourcing in large quantities and cost averaging. One of many significant competitive advantages arises from locking in supplier pricing while blocking access to those resources by competitors. This strategy relies heavily on process as a core competency among others.

## Differentiation

This strategy is about focus on uniqueness of the product or services offered or some aspect of creating, marketing, and delivering the offering. The strongest differentiation advantages come from the uniqueness of the products or services its self. Uniqueness can be about the production, delivery system, or anything considered of value to the buyer. Significant competitive advantage arises when there is a long term uniqueness associated with a strong brand across many industries and markets. This strategy requires innovation as a key competency among others.

## Focus

This strategy is about creating niche markets with pinpoint focus on specific customers with specific products and services. The strongest focus advantages come when an organization is able to service the unique needs of a small specific market, or they have production and delivery methods unlike any other in similar segments. Cost Focus and Differentiation Focus are represented in their own cells because although Cost and Differentiation are variations of focus, an organization would not pursue both with the same product line. That would be an ineffective contradiction to that variant of the Focus strategy.

## Summary

Exactly how each of these strategies will be applied is going to be significantly different depending on the industry and market it's applied to. Selecting the right strategy will not necessarily be easy just because they have been defined. You must perform your due diligence and properly analyze your desired market and study both your competition and the products and services being offered by all. Remember that the ultimate goal is to create a competitive advantage by adopting one of the three generic strategies and applying it as best suites your organization, market, and offerings.

To provide the most effective closing statement, I believe it is best to share a direct quote from Porter: "Being all things to all people is a recipe for strategic mediocrity and below-average performance, because it often means that a firm has no competitive advantage at all." An organization that attempts to employ each of the three strategies across their target markets but fails to accomplish this for even one of these strategies ends up stuck in the middle. Being stuck in the middle is a competitive disadvantage, one realized by too many small organizations in business today.

Tool Tip: *Gap Analysis, SWOT Analysis, McKinsey 7S Model*

## Bowman's Strategy Clock

Another tool to help you define your strategy and create a competitive advantage is the Stragety Clock. It was developed by Cliff Bowman and David Faulkne and detailed in their 1996 book *Competitive and Corporate Strategy*. Bowman's Strategy Clock expands on Porter's Generic Strategies by establishing eight unique directions an organization can move when deciding how to position their products and services in an industry and market (see Figure 4-6).

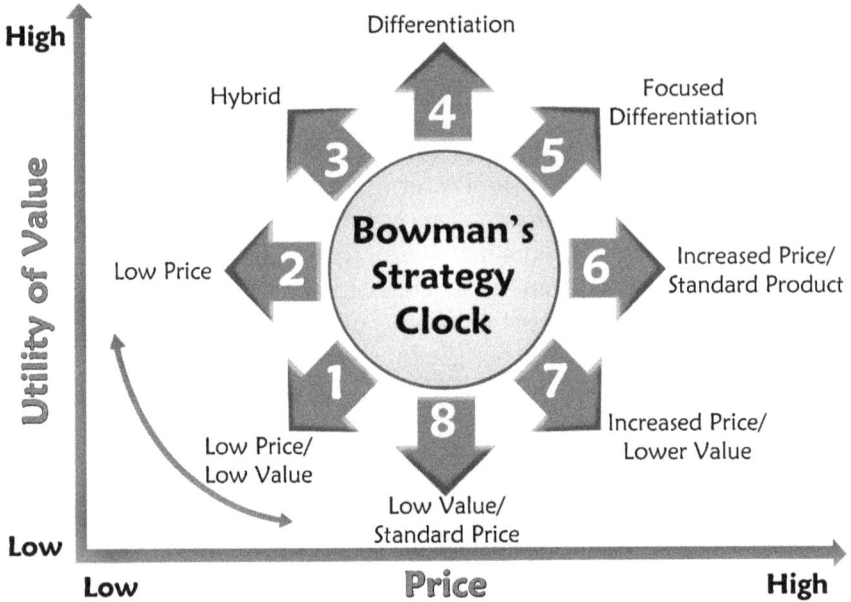

*Figure 4-6. Bowman's Strategy Clock*

Note that Bowman and Faulkne correlate their eight strategies to perceived value to the customer and delivered price of the product or service. Porter's model correlates the generic strategies to market relative size. I point this out so there is no misunderstanding that these two models cannot simply be laid one over the other to see a direct correlation of one to the other.

I believe that much of Bowman's Strategy Clock is self-explanatory so I will only provide a summary description and touch on certain relevant points.

Point 1 on the clock is the bargain basement and representative of the stereotypical "Made in" insert name of country willing to produce or provide at this level. This strategy will only work when the market is massive in size—global sized. In our time it would not be accurate to say no one operates here because they do. And if they can do so while making a profit where no one else is willing to operate, that is a significant competitive advantage no matter who you are.

As you move around the clock to higher numbers you see products and services representative of everyday things with everyday labels. At point 5 you are seeing products that are unique and high priced, meaning a small, specific target market focus. As you get to point 6 you are at products and services that, although they are of average quality, they have fancy branding and marketing and somehow sell for a higher price. This is the long-time brand leadership area.

It is my preference to refer to Bowman's Strategy Clock when generating the initial idea of what your strategy will be as you perform your Feasibility Study. Will you be price driven or quality driven, or something in between? Once you start actually writing a proper Business Plan, I believe you should clarify much more specifically which of the three generic strategies you will adopt and develop from Porter's Competitive Advantage model.

Tool Tip: *Gap Analysis, SWOT Analysis, McKinsey 7S Model*

## PESTEL Analysis

The PESTEL Analysis is a behavioral study of the Contextual Level or Macro Environment I discussed in Chapter 2. PESTEL is an acronym for the Political, Economic, Social, Technological, Environmental, and Legal forces and influences of the Macro Environment on your Meso Environment and into your Micro Environment (see Figure 4-7). These external forces and influences are usually beyond the organization's control and often present themselves as threats. You have a responsibility to the organization, stakeholders, and customers to know and understand all the forces and effects of all the elements of your environment on all levels.

The PESTEL Analysis model is obviously nothing more than a framework and prescribed process for systematically evaluating those elements outside the industry and markets you operate within. It is a necessary analysis for any organization to at least consider when evaluating markets and developing strategies. These elements of the Macro Environment can have a significant effect on the Meso and Micro Environments. To think that your organization is so small as to not be affected would be unwise at best.

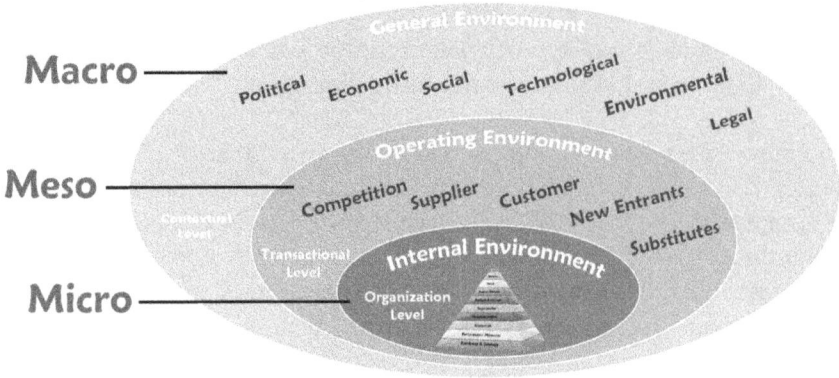

*Figure 4-7. Organizational Environments*

When the economy as a whole dips down significantly, every part of your organization's environment is affected. Think about the 2008 U.S. subprime mortgage issue and the following recession. If you were a shrimp farmer running a small operation almost anywhere in the Gulf of Mexico when the Deepwater Horizon caught fire and collapsed, you were affected and not just by the environmental impact. Political, economic, social, technological, and legal forces came into play regardless of your business size.

**Political Analysis**
These are the forces, factors, and influences from government at any level, local to global. They include elements such as: political policy, political stability, taxation, trade regulations and tariffs, and social policies. There should always a balance between political forces and factors and the free markets but depending on where you're located, this is clearly not always the case. At a minimum an organization must consider all the forces, factors, and influences of politics when analyzing markets and competition for any given region they intend to expand in or into.

**Economic Analysis**
These are the forces, factors, and influences of a market economy on any level, local to global. They include elements such as: efficiency of financial markets, disposable income, access to credit, employment rates, interest rates, inflation, recession, recovery or prosperity, skill level of workforce, and labor costs. Economic factors of a region directly determine the overall health of that region. In today's global

economy the health of one region can have a significant effect on others around the globe. The economic forecast of the region an organization intends to expand or establish a market share in must be studied and should include forecasts looking several years forward.

## Social Analysis

These are the forces, factors, and influences of a society on any level, local to global. They include elements such as: population demographics, distribution of wealth, class structure, changes in lifestyles, lifestyle trends, education levels, culture, and sentiment. The mindset and mentality of your target market is largely revealed in how they behave. Understanding these forces, factors, and influences are the key to understanding what drives your potential customers' selection and consumption of products and services. This is the most elusive and therefore the most valuable data you can get your hands on provided it is accurate.

## Technological Analysis

These are the forces, factors, and influences of technological changes on any level, local to global. They include elements such as: innovations and discoveries, rate of development and advances, rate of technological obsolescence, and new platforms. Depending on your organization's industry, this analysis may be one of the most difficult to perform because of the shear speed of technology in the world today. As the role of technology in business is ever-increasing, research and development is key. The organization's overall strategy must be to continuously track relevant technology in order to minimize threats and capitalize on opportunities.

## Environmental Factors

These are the forces, factors, and influences from the custodianship of the environment at any level, local to global. They include elements such as: waste disposal, environmental protection, energy consumption and regulation, and attitude toward the environment. The global impact on the environment is a growing concern and how it is perceived is affecting consumers more and more. Governments all over the world are beginning to levy significant fines for leaving footprints on the environment. And consumers are becoming more willing to switch brands when they see the results of that behavior.

**Legal Factors**
These are the forces, factors, and influences from legislation at any level, local to global. They include elements such as: health and safety, employment regulations, equal opportunities, advertising standards, consumer rights and laws, product labeling and product safety, antitrust laws, and patent infringements. You must have at least a rudimentary understanding of the laws and regulations in your local region. Failure to do so can create unnecessary legal costs. Conservation of capital dictates that you should always remain within the established regulations, and basic ethics indicate so as well.

There are obviously many more external forces but these are the primary ones that you must consider in your analysis of markets and competition. The organization must identify, prioritize, and be vigilant of these forces and effects in order to stay healthy and to maintain competitive advantage.

Tool Tip: *Critical Thinking, Process Control, Pyramid of Purpose and Value*

## McKinsey 7S Framework

In their book *In Search of Excellence: Lessons from America's Best-Run Companies*, Tom Peters and Robert Waterman briefly discuss their innovative multi-variable framework for analysis of the organization's hard and soft elements. It was born of their research into the development of tools that could expand the common business problem-solving methods. They were keen to take note that in addition to what are considered hard elements of the business—organizational Structure and Strategy—there were definable soft elements. They also recognized the need for an organization to endear to the people of the organization as more than just staff or workers. They devised what they refer to as "A watershed model that addresses the critical role of coordination, rather than structure in organizational effectiveness" (see Figure 4-8).

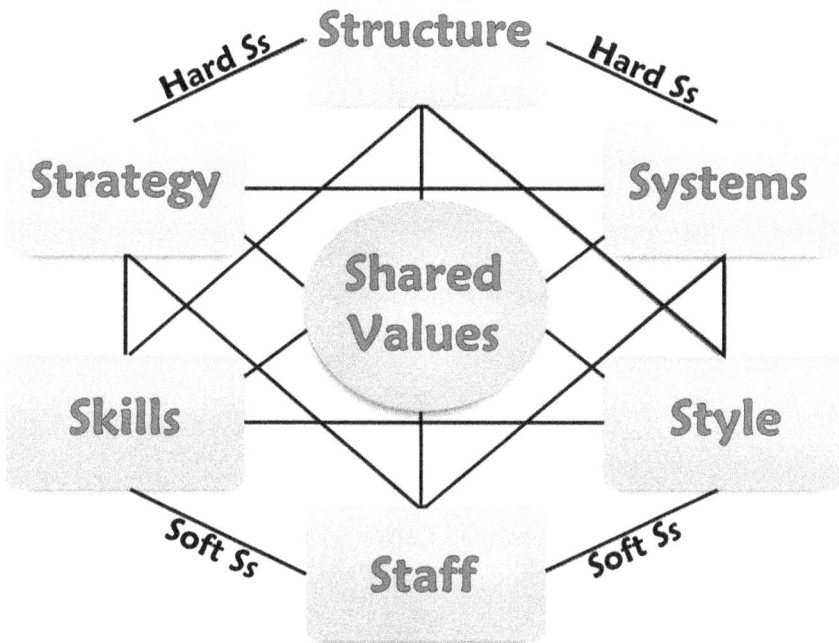

*Figure 4-8. McKinsey 7S Framework*

Their goal was to define a tool that would help management understand the relationship of these elements in hopes that they could effectively manage more than just the hard elements. Only after they had developed and released it to the wild did they fully realize the utility of this tool they had handed to professional managers—a way to manage elements previously dismissed as out of the control or influence of management. They created a tool that would allow an organization to, as they put it, "pinpoint the causes of organizational malaise" but also "to determine what was working despite the structure and ought to be left alone." The 7S Framework is an organizational evaluation tool and it is also a change management tool.

The 7S Framework allows an organization to develop core competencies and capabilities of the individual and the organization in a way that is in balance with both the hard and soft elements of the business. The framework states that all elements are interdependent and dictates that all elements must be in balance at all times. Changes to one element must take into consideration the effects on all other elements. What Peters and Waterman propose is that the elements of the 7S Framework together form the overall culture of the organization and that it is a symbiotic relationship which must be protected and cared for. My preference is to view the Soft Elements as the Culture of the organization and the Hard Elements as the Compass.

## Hard Elements

Hard Elements are by nature more tangible and therefore much easier to manage compared to Soft Elements. Relative to the Pyramid of Purpose and Value these represent the significant factors of the organization's Compass and Blueprint for Success.

- Strategy - These are the many plans the organization employs in its long-term endeavor to create value and maintain competitive advantage.
- Structure - The way the organization is structured, including departments, roles, responsibilities, accountability, relationships, and who reports to whom.
- Systems - These are the processes and procedures that govern everyday activity, including management information systems, customer relations systems, retail systems, call center systems, online systems, etc.

## Soft Elements

Soft Elements are by their nature harder to manage. Soft Elements are the foundation of the organization and are more likely to create the sustained competitive advantage. Relative to the Pyramid of Purpose and Value these represent the significant factors of the organization's Culture.

- Shared Values - These are the core values of the organization, not only as stated but as evident in the business culture and the general work ethic.
- Style - This is the style of leadership adopted by top management and their overall approach.
- Staff - This is the quality talent of the organization, including the People Process that dictates how they are developed, trained, and motivated.
- Skills - These are the core competencies and capabilities that exist within the organization.

To use the model you simply need to adhere to the principle that for any organization to perform at its best, the seven elements must be in alignment. If one element is causing undue stress on others there is a misalignment and inconsistencies. You can use the model to evaluate specific components of the organization, such as teams and roles, or to evaluate specific Value Aspects, such as Communication or Service Delivery. You simply need to ask the right questions about their alignment relative to the organization's decided culture and the seven elements. If you're asking the right questions, misalignments, and inconsistencies will be revealed. Use the 7S Framework as a checklist when considering strategy and change. Consider it a mirror to hold up which will enable you to see blind spots and other issues that may not normally be in your view.

Start with the Share Values and evaluate Soft Elements first. Ask questions like: Does our method of communications with our clients (Style) convey our Shared Values? Next, address Hard Elements. Ask questions like: Does our organization Structure have the flexibility to support this Strategy? And lastly, look at the Hard-to-Soft Element supports and vice versa. Does this Strategy support the other elements or will it cause undue stress on Staff? How will the Structure of the organizational changes we are proposing affect the Skills and Staff required to operate? Remember that there are no wrong answers, there are just unasked questions. The more you ask the more that will be revealed.

Tool Tip: *Pyramid of Purpose and Value, DiSC Profile*

## Gap Analysis

There countless analyses you can perform on your business as a whole and countless tools to help you to focus on the key answers you need depending on what exactly you are trying to get answers to. I have carefully selected tools that fit specific needs and have intentionally kept the range of tools relatively narrow. When it comes to the actual analysis of the organization overall or just aspects of it, I have chosen to only present the Gap Analysis and the SWOT Analysis tools. I believe these two tools, when properly applied, will cover the vast majority of common business analysis needs.

My preference is to use the Gap Analysis as a lighter weight tool for focusing on specific aspects and the SWOT as a heavier weight tool for broader considerations. In practice, I would always start with the SWOT Analysis for an overall Business Analysis and once the majority of the issues are discovered, I would focus on each using the Gap Analysis. Likewise, when addressing issues that present themselves in the day-to-day running of the business, I would follow the simple rule to never use a bigger hammer than required. This means when addressing these one-off or as they come along issues, you would start with the Gap and only move to the SWOT if it's apparent more details and information are needed. Do not be bound by this; consider it a guideline for application. Each of these tools has a specific purpose and place and I intend to further clarify as we move along.

You are likely already familiar with the principles of the Gap Analysis as it is one of the most basic tools we come across and use all the time. Whenever you have asked the question, "What is it we are trying to accomplish here?" you have in fact begun a Gap Analysis. The Gap Analysis seeks to identify very simply where you are now, how you got here, and where you are going. From there, it helps you define how you will get there. This last component is what makes this analysis tool a problem resolution tool when used properly. See Figure 4-9 for the proper and preferred phases of a Gap Analysis.

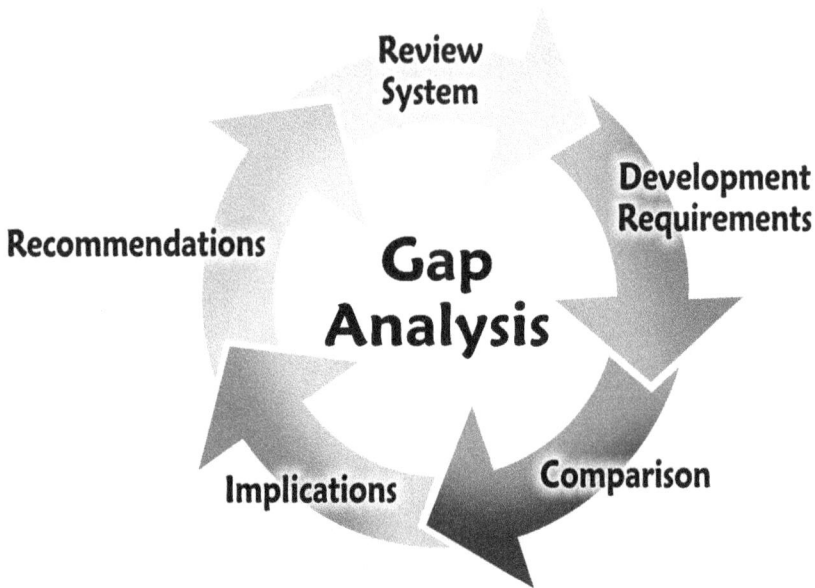

*Figure 4-9. Gap Analysis Process*

### Review System
Every well laid-out process or system should have a built-in method for gauging progress and measuring results. Even a well laid-out strategy will call out landmarks, turning points, and goals to show progress has been made and indicate when decisions must be made along the

way. The review process is simply the collection of the results being exhibited in preparation for analysis. This is the "Where are we at?" phase. If this is a new endeavor, you may be recording the starting point state and status.

## Develop Requirements

Developing requirements means defining or redefining the ideal results, targets, goals, landmarks, etc. They must be specific and realistic. Consider applying the GOST or SMARTER tools here. These requirements should address time, energy, inclination, and resources. This is the "Where are we going?" phase. If this is the first pass at this phase, you are simply setting the goals and identifying the metrics for the next level.

## Comparison

With a clear picture of where you are and measurable metrics for comparison you can determine if you are making headway. The evaluation is to determine if you can clearly see direction and measurable progress. This phase should be about the numbers, not about the effort and inclination. Did we meet our goals for sales? Did we finish on time or late and if so by how much? This is the actual Gap Analysis phase. If this is the first pass at this phase, you will be using this analysis for the launch of the endeavor.

## Implications

This is the phase that addresses the effort and inclination of the endeavor. Did we have the right people on the task? Did we have the right training for key people? Was the success properly tied to our Vision or Mission so that people would see to it that it was accomplished? This is the "How did we get here?" phase. If this is the first pass at this phase, you will be asking similar questions but in a different tense. Do we have the right people on task? Do they have the right training for key people? For success, how do we properly tie expectations to our Vision or Mission so that people will see to it that it is accomplished?

## Recommendations

The complete retrospective allows for the drawing of conclusions and development of recommendations for how to proceed. This is where you set goals, objectives, strategies, and tactics. This will involve timelines, deadlines, resources, expectations, and metrics. This is the "How will we get there?" phase. If this is the first pass, you are simply creating the initial criteria for execution.

The Gap Analysis is a powerful tool for continuous incremental improvement. It allows for a closed-loop process for problem solving and for developing system strategy. It is the foundation for measuring investment of time, energy, inclination, and resources to reach a goal or succeed at an endeavor. It can help you answer important questions about nearly every aspect of your business like:

- Knowing what we know now, if we were not already doing this today, would we ever embark on this endeavor?
- Is the mission of this endeavor still valid? If so, how could or should it best be taken to the next level?

The Gap Analysis can also help an organization understand and resolve knowledge gaps when addressing core competency requirements. And it can help identify gaps in strategy when evaluating execution plans (see Figure 4-10).

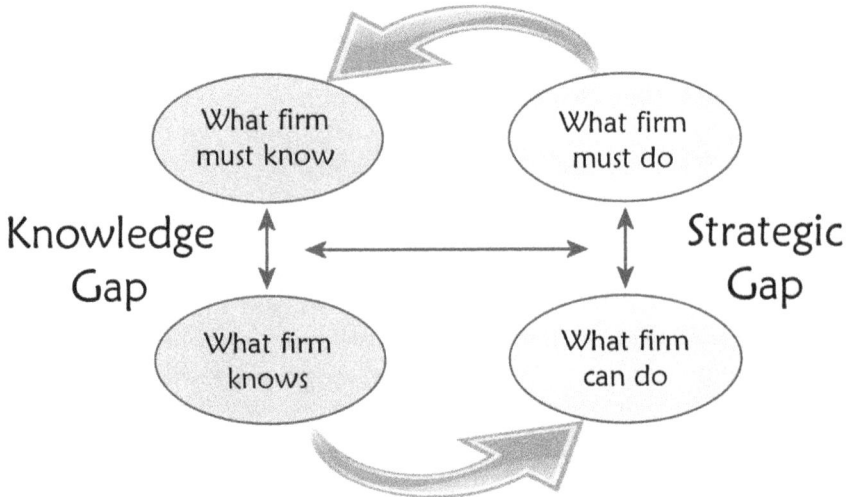

*Figure 4-10. Knowledge and Strategy Gap*

The Gap Analysis tool can serve you well in almost every decision possible for your business. It creates open dialogue and promotes ideas and critical thinking on many levels. You must simply learn to ask the right questions in the right way to elicit the response you need. I suggest you always start with: Where are we now? How did we get here? Where are we going? How will we get there?

## SWOT Analysis

Now we come to what may very well be the most powerful tool for the analysis of your organization as a whole or your business as an endeavor. Much of my philosophy in Getting To The Next Level relies on obtaining the most accurate and detailed information possible about every aspect or element of the organization. This highly valuable information is the fodder for all discussions and planning of the business roadmap and strategy. When properly executed, the SWOT Analysis is exactly what will yield the most valuable information you need to get to the next level.

I will offer only a quick note on the origin and history of the SWOT Analysis. I don't believe there is a definitive origin for this tool and I admittedly did not spend much time looking. What matters to me is that it is internationally recognized and its history can easily be traced back to the 1950s. It is still highly utilized today and for our purposes, it is the definitive tool for kicking off your overall Business Strategy development campaign.

SWOT is an acronym for Strengths, Weaknesses, Opportunities, and Threats. The analysis process seeks to identify and categorize the forces and factors of each of the SWOT attributes into Positive or Negative force and either Internal or External factors. Like any other analysis framework or model, it requires you to ask the right questions to illicit useful responses. The analysis will only be as good as the questions posed and the answers received. One of the features that make this model so easy to apply is that the questions and the reasonable expectations of possible answers to those questions are conveniently embedded in the model itself (see Figure 4-11).

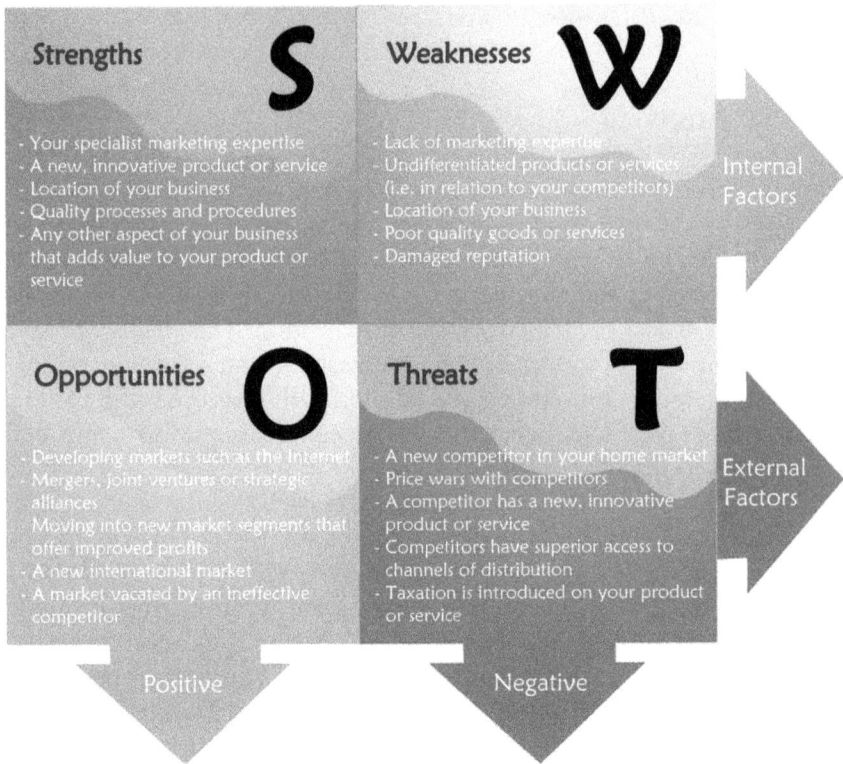

| Strengths **S** | Weaknesses **W** | |
|---|---|---|
| - Your specialist marketing expertise<br>- A new, innovative product or service<br>- Location of your business<br>- Quality processes and procedures<br>- Any other aspect of your business that adds value to your product or service | - Lack of marketing expertise<br>- Undifferentiated products or services (i.e. in relation to your competitors)<br>- Location of your business<br>- Poor quality goods or services<br>- Damaged reputation | Internal Factors |
| Opportunities **O** | Threats **T** | |
| - Developing markets such as the Internet<br>- Mergers, joint ventures or strategic alliances<br>- Moving into new market segments that offer improved profits<br>- A new international market<br>- A market vacated by an ineffective competitor | - A new competitor in your home market<br>- Price wars with competitors<br>- A competitor has a new, innovative product or service<br>- Competitors have superior access to channels of distribution<br>- Taxation is introduced on your product or service | External Factors |
| Positive | Negative | |

*Figure 4-11. SWOT Analysis Model*

## Strengths

For the organization, these are the Internal Factors throughout all business functions across all business aspects which directly or indirectly have potential to add value to your products and services, thereby establishing or strengthening your competitive advantage. These are what you capitalize on when developing your Business Strategy. When applying the analysis to other subjects, consider what internal factors and characteristics, tangible or intangible, are to be evaluated. Look for competencies and capabilities of the specific subject.

## Weaknesses

For the organization, these are the Internal Factors throughout all business functions across all business aspects which directly or indirectly have potential to decrease value of your products and services, thereby diminishing or weakening your competitive advantage. These are what you seek to negate, eliminate, or possibly strengthen when developing your Business Strategy. When applying the analysis to other subjects, consider what internal factors and characteristics, tangible or intangible, are to be evaluated. Look for competencies and capabilities of the specific subject.

## Opportunities

For the organization, these are the External Factors throughout the entire Environment, Industry, and Market which, if capitalized on, directly or indirectly have potential to add value to your products and services, thereby establishing or strengthening your competitive advantage. These are what you seek to capitalize on when developing your Business Strategy. When applying the analysis to other subjects, consider what external characteristics and factors, tangible or intangible, are to be evaluated. Look at position, finance, time, energy, inclination, and resource requirements of the specific subject.

## Threats

For the organization, these are the External Factors throughout the entire Environment, Industry, and Market which, if not protected against, directly or indirectly have potential to decrease value to your products and services, thereby diminishing or weakening your competitive advantage. These are what you seek to negate, eliminate, or possibly weaken when developing your Business Strategy. When applying the analysis to other subjects, consider what external characteristics and factors, tangible or intangible, are to be evaluated. Look at position, finance, time, energy, inclination, and resource requirements of the specific subject.

## Internal and External

The Factor of Internal versus External is always relative to the subject of the analysis. You have control over your Internal Factors but not over your External Factors. An organization would have Strengths and Weaknesses because of its structure, core competencies, or financial situation. The organization would seek to protect itself from Threats and capitalize on Opportunities in the industry or market it operates within. An individual would likewise have Strengths and Weaknesses as a result of their education, training, and retained knowledge. They would also seek to capitalize on Opportunities presented and threats realized in the work market or the organization itself.

You would not attempt to apply these Factors to the wrong perspective. That is to say, even though you see the new employee as Strength because of their potential if properly trained, this does not create an Opportunity on your part. The Opportunity is their Opportunity realized as External to themselves. Likewise you would not consider a disgruntled employee as a Threat inside the company to be dealt with in a long-term strategy. They themselves are a Weakness inside the organization and would be dealt with in a short-term HR strategy. Be careful not to create new dimensions and increase the depth of complexity by pointing Internal Factors to the outside or External Factors to the inside.

### Positive (Favorable) and Negative (Unfavorable)

The Forces of Positive and Negative are pretty straightforward. If it helps establish or strengthen your market position, your value to clients, or your competitive advantage or it helps further your strategy, it is a Positive Force. Anything contrary is Negative. The relative strength of the Force must also be considered in evaluation. It should not be underestimated and should not be blown out of proportion. Quantify everything possible and if you cannot, consider performing a Gap Analysis for further enlightenment.

### Application

It should be obvious from the list of Forces and Factors that there is a list of questions to be asked for any element or aspect under scrutiny. Example: What Opportunities exist here? Are the Factors of this Opportunity Internal or External? What are the Positive and Negative Forces involved? The process repeats for Strengths Weaknesses and Threats.

The SWOT Analysis provides a structured method for evaluating important aspects and elements of nearly anything you can present. It creates the important information you need to make quality decisions about positions, situations, directions, and strategy. It is most beneficial and revealing when used in a collaborative environment engaging the entire organization, management, team, or department. The SWOT Analysis can and should be utilized to explore:

- New solutions to problems (Pain points)
- Barriers that limit goals or objectives (Road blocks)
- The Levels of the Pyramid of Purpose and Value
- Core Competencies

- Management Functions
- Market Competition
- Marketing Strategy
- Elements of the Value Chain
- Ten business Value Aspects
- Business Feasibility Dimensions
- Business Strategy
- Projects
- People and the People Process
- Ventures and Endeavors

## Matching and Converting Forces and Factors

In the evaluation of the results of the SWOT and the development of strategies, look for scenarios where Matching or Converting Forces and Factors help define or enhance a competitive advantage. Matching is simply identifying opportunities that can be matched with clear Strengths. You should also look out for compound Forces and Factors, such as Threats that Match with a Weakness to create a significant competitive disadvantage. Converting means looking for scenarios where a Weakness or Threat can be turned around into a Strength or Opportunity or at least negated. The possibilities for Matching and Converting are countless and only limited by your comprehension of all that is being analyzed and evaluated.

## Roadmap & Strategy

The ultimate goal of performing the SWOT Analysis is to feed this highly valuable information into your Roadmap & Strategy processes. Too many organizations do not perform real intrusive, in-depth studies of their organization until it is sick or failing and they are forced to by those brought on or in to save it. This tool should be treated as an annual health check if not quarterly to some extent. You should be using it when building your marketing strategy and when developing new products. If the use of this one tool even once could gain you a competitive advantage, why wouldn't you use it? In both Chapters 11 and 12—Business Strategy Meets Agile Execution and Case Study & Example—the SWOT Analysis is the tool of primary focus for getting the entire Roadmap & Strategy process rolling. Look to these chapters for specific examples of identifying and addressing SWOT results.

## Summary

The Gap Analysis in comparison to the SWOT Analysis is really a basic closed-loop process control tool. For any given aspect, it evaluates the current state compared to the specified desired values then proceeds to draw conclusions and prepare recommendations. The process is adjusted accordingly and then continues on. As mentioned before, the Gap Analysis is a standalone problem resolution tool. This is why the Gap Analysis is a great tool for focus on an issue once it is identified. Notice that something external to the Gap Analysis must have triggered the need for the Gap. We don't just go around pointing at things.

The SWOT Analysis is a true analysis tool in that it calls for data mining and inspection. It asks the questions and delves into the specifics but does not make any decisions, no matter how glaring the results of the analysis are. Its outputs are presented to the strategy system to do with as is necessary and desired. Even its inputs are unknown at the start. This tool is intended to be pointed at something like a flashlight is pointed into the dark—it reveals and inspects. In the next chapter we look at some extremely powerful Business Strategy tools to direct the output of your SWOT analysis toward.

If you find your problems are not completely revealed or addressed using either or both of these tools (Gap or SWOT), you should most certainly seek a more appropriate tool. And it's also my advice that if this is your scenario, you should most certainly seek outside help for your business. Failure to navigate complex issues could mean the difference between staying in business and losing everything. Don't ever let your failure to solve a complex problem due to the lack of proper resources be the reason for closing your business down.

Tool Tip: *Every Tool in the Box*

*If an organization is to meet the challenges of a changing world, it must be prepared to change everything about itself except [its basic] beliefs as it moves through corporate life...The only sacred cow in an organization should be its basic philosophy of doing business.*

– Thomas Watson, Jr.

# 5.0

## TOOLS & METHODS FOR REFINING YOUR BUSINESS

### Financial Statements

Financial Statements is the term used to describe the collection of various reports that an organization generates for the purpose of evaluating, sharing, and guiding their decisions related to the financial perspective of the business. Depending on the size of the organization, these reports can be anything from simple single-page printouts to complex and detailed multipage reports including detailed footnotes. Here again we come to point where the potential for discussion far exceeds the scope of this text, so I will cover the five most important reports mentioned when discussing the Financial Projections tool.

Every entrepreneur must understand at least these basic Financial Statements and what they reveal about your business and its financial health. If you are planning on borrowing money from the bank or seeking venture capital, these Financial Statements will not only be required but you may be expected to have them reviewed or even scrutinized by a Certified Public Accountant. Even if you never intend to borrow money from the bank or seek venture capital these reports are the source of the most important metrics for your business.

In business finance the rule is cash is king and it is the lifeblood of any business. The smaller the organization the more this rule holds true. You should always strive to have good liquidity—the ability to convert assets into cash (or cash equivalents) without significant loss. These reports show exactly where every dollar is and what is expected for expenses and income. In addition to the basic reports, I have also described two more analyses: the Break-Even Analysis and Cost Benefit Analysis. These give you an idea of the potential for actually making money on a new idea and some sense of how long before you will have recovered all the capital ventured on the idea.

## Balance Sheet

This report is a snapshot of an individual or business at a point in time and it details the assets, liabilities, and stockholders' equity as of the date indicated in the report. This is referred to as the business's position. It is called a balance sheet because it presents the debit information in a column on the left side and the assets in a column on the right side. The two sides must balance or there is something amiss in your finances.

This report is important to the bank or lender because it shows what the organization owns and what it owes. It can show your bank or lender if you are financially worthy to borrow or borrow more money. This report is important to you because it allows you to keep a vigilant eye on exactly where your money is tied up or held up. Remember that liquidity is important and this report is the primary key to keeping cash on hand and flowing as it should. Never tie up too much money; you will lose the ability to maneuver in your business by doing so. Cash and liquidity directly translate into operating options which means agility. Never forget this.

## Income Statement

This report shows the organization's revenue (income), expenses, gains, and losses for a specific period of time. It is often referred to as the Profit and Loss Statement (P&L) or Statement of Revenue and Expenses. An important difference from the Cash Flow Statement is that the Income Statement includes credit you have used and extended and the cash you fully expect to pay out and receive. It is typically run for the current month to date, quarter or year to date. The format for this report is not dictated but there are several common formats employed depending on the intended audience.

This report is important to the bank or lender because it discloses the revenue and expenses that are a direct result of the regular operation of the business. It is the breakdown of income and expenses that reveals how efficient your operation is. This report is important to you because it reveals the business's cash-generating ability. With this information, you can make day-to-day operating decisions that can affect the flow of your cash and therefore the agility of the business.

## Cash Flow Statements

The Cash Flow Statement should actually be called the Cash Flow Analysis because it is more of an analytical tool than just a report. This report shows how the operation is running by detailing where money is flowing from and flowing to. This report shows how changes in the Balance Sheet and Income Statement affect cash and the cash equivalents. It is an analysis of all operating, investing and financing activities. Most small companies do not have complex investing or financing activities but nonetheless, they exist and must be managed.

This report/analysis is important to the bank or lender because it is a picture over time of how money has ebbed and flowed in the business and it reveals anomalies in operations. If for example a large loan is suddenly paid off, it will be very noticeable on the balance sheet. Likewise a large cash distribution to a principal will also be very noticeable. This report is important to you largely for the same reasons. You need to manage cash for the long game as well as for short-term agility. This analysis does just that as the trends and anomalies indicated by this report help you to make plans for the medium and long-range future.

## Break-Even Analysis

This analysis intends to show you the point at which the revenue received for having done or created something matches the cost of doing or creating that thing. A Break-Even Analysis should include a margin of safety which takes into account the fluctuation of the market or volatility. This analysis is a requirement when considering anything that requires capital expenditure and should be considered even for changes to operation expenditures.

This analysis is important to the bank or lender because it will help them understand, validate, and calculate at what point they can reasonably expect to see returns on their investment in your organization or venture. It is important to you because it tells you at what point you can reasonably expect to begin seeing the return on your venture. Those returns are in the form of revenue and cash flow or an increase in production capability that will in turn generate the revenue or customer value.

## Cost Benefit Analysis

This analysis intends to help you evaluate and compare options you may be pursuing in any aspect of the business. When considering activities or avenues of remedy or even projects, you can weigh the strengths and weaknesses of each alternative presented and break them down into financial numbers, or dollars and cents. Because decisions are not (or should not always be) about the raw numbers and the money, you can interpolate the specifics of the options into client value and determine the weight given to that value.

This report is important to the bank or lender because it shows you have performed your due diligence. It can be used when presenting different options for funding your venture or making clear how you arrived at your decisions about how or why to approach a given market with a given offering at a given stage. This tool is important to you because it allows you to make informed decisions about the ventures and projects you choose to take on. By performing this analysis and saving the data and documentation, you can always recall on paper how or why you came to a decision and you can revisit to revalidate or rethink the decision.

**Summary**
Financial Reports can reveal the ability of a business to generate cash and where that cash is used. They will reveal whether a business actually has the capability to pay back a debt. They can also be analyzed over time to reveal valuable insight into the long-term performance of the business. I'll talk a little about these performance indicators in a later section. These Financial Reports often include supplemental notes of one form or another. These notes are the explanation of various activities of relevance, additional detail on accounts as necessary, and any other information mandated by the applicable accounting framework, such as GAAP or IFRS. Please see the Glossary for any terms used here that are not recognized or for further clarification.

# Leading Indicators

Technically, Leading Indicators are the measurable factors of any trending data that most reliably signal changes in the trending. To put it another way, they are the numbers to look to when evaluating a trend to get an early warning sign that the trend is changing or will soon change. In business terms when we refer to Leading Indicators, unless otherwise specified, we are usually speaking of the leading financial indicators. The Leading Indicators I present here in this section are all finance related because we need to plot and continuously evaluate the trends of the lifeblood of any business—money. There are of course leading indicators for every aspect, function, and dimension of your business and rest assured, I will cover many of these in a later chapter.

Although I will be pointing out several indicators that come straight out of the standard Financial Statements, there are countless other accounting numbers you could track if you so choose. My recommendation is to identify, understand and learn to track these as primary indicators first, then you can look deeper into the many other metrics and numbers as you find a reason to do so. And if you do identify an anomaly in some set of numbers on a report, by all means look into the numbers behind the numbers, but don't unnecessarily add clutter to your spreadsheets. Although your business can become complex, it does not mean that you must have complex methods for reading the signs of its health. Do not track trends for metrics that do not easily (if not instantly) give you the big picture you need.

By plotting and continuously evaluating the Leading Indicators of your business's finances you can gain valuable insight to the natural patterns and trends exhibited throughout the fiscal quarter and year. If you pay attention you will also learn to identify early warning trends and signs that indicate change must be implemented to preserve capital or avoid losses. Likewise you will also gain experience in recognizing when you need to hold your course—continue doing what you're doing and continue to capture great gains.

Everything about your business can be viewed as a machine and a process to be controlled. With your hands on the dials and your eyes on the gauges you really can tune everything for optimized performance. When I refer to the tool Leading Indicators I'm referring not only to the raw numbers from the Financial Reports but also the plotted values presented individually or grouped in some logical formation (see Figure 5-1).

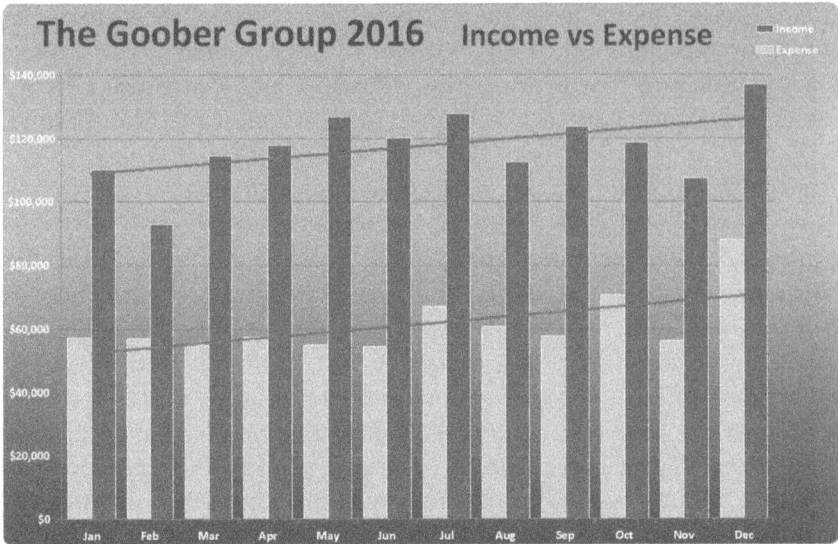

*Figure 5-1. Leading Indicator Trend Comparison - Twelve Month*

You must completely understand what each of these Leading Indicators represent in the big financial picture and you must also understand which forces can change these numbers. If Income is steadily increasing but Expenses are steadily dropping, you cannot just throw a party because profits are climbing too; you need to understand exactly why they are dropping. Hopefully it's a number you understand and have successfully caused to decline through your refinement of process, planning, strategy, or some other such positive action. But failure to understand this trend will eventually completely blindside you.

What if it's because you have switched vendors for some production materials but for some reason they are not billing you correctly. Three months from now you are going to receive the corrected billing statements and your numbers will be way off. In fact you could find you're not only nowhere near as profitable as you thought, but you have also paid out quarterly bonuses on profits that are inaccurate. Oh, and you are three or four months behind on the materials supplier invoices too.

To effectively use the Leading Indicators as a tool, you will need to track, isolate, and plot these metrics for a twelve-month rolling cycle. You can also plot them from fiscal year to fiscal year, as long as there is a cyclical method. I recommend using a spreadsheet and simply exporting the P&L information you need every month. Select the category totals you need and plot them on a graph. You can put each indicator on a graph of its own including a trend line, group them together as you see fit, or any combination that presents the data in a useful fashion (see Figure 5-2).

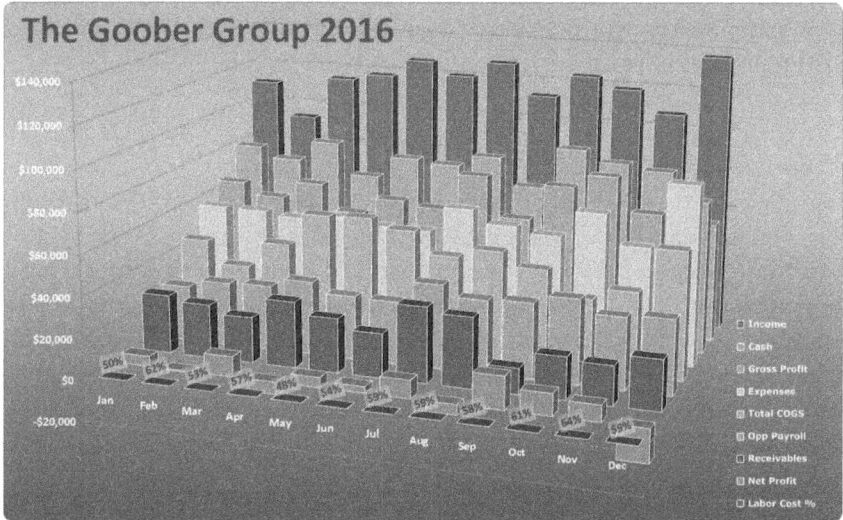

*Figure 5-2. Leading Indicators Graph - Twelve Month*

## Income

This is the total of all monies received by the organization through the general day-to-day operation of the business from sales of products and delivery of services. Income is calculated by multiplying the price received for products or services by the number of units (x) sold or delivered. You should be able to obtain this number directly from the Profit and Loss Statement, specifically the Total Income category. Income is often referred to as the Top Line or Revenue.

In the Chart of Accounts there is actually a category for other income the company may receive that is not related to the operations of the business. These other incomes would be line items such as interest income or rent received from other business properties. These two different Income categories can be referred to as Operating Income and Non-Operating Income. To be clear, this Leading Indicator is only about the Operating Income.

This number is important because it is the revenue or cash flow into the organization. If it's dropping you are in trouble. If it's steady and Expenses are increasing, you are in trouble unless you understand why

Expenses are on the rise, e.g. you are investing heavily in marketing or innovation, or you are ramping up for production. If it's rising this is usually good; again, as long as you understand why because you are, after all, looking for a consistent and steady profit. A healthy, stable, sustainable business does not move along in fits and starts; it paces along and makes steady gains. It may spike at times or drop, but never without the complete understanding of why.

## Expenses

This is the total of all monies spent by the organization through the general day-to-day operation of the business for everything not directly related to creating a product or delivering a service. In a typical business this would include rent, machinery, office equipment and supplies, insurance, marketing, advertising, officer payroll, travel and entertainment, and so on. You should be able to obtain this number directly from the Profit and Loss Statement, specifically the Total Expenses category.

Total Expenses does not include those costs for actually creating a product or delivering a service. Those are accounted for in the Cost of Goods Sold (COGS) section discussed next. The type of business you are running defines how each expense is accounted for and therefore where each expense line item will show up in the Chart of Accounts.

As with the Income category there is actually a category in the Chart of Accounts for other expenses the company may pay out. These would be expenses such as depreciation, amortization, and interest to name a few. These can be referred to as Operating Expenses and Non-Operating Expenses. To be clear, this Leading Indicator is only about the Operating Expenses.

This number is important because it is the necessary opposite of income which is required to run the business. Nonetheless, it must be controlled and you must always know why it changes, and you should strive to avoid upward spikes as these cut directly into profits if Income is holding steady. I would speculate that more than a fair number of organizations have gone under simply because they could not control this metric.

## Cost of Goods Sold (COGS)

This is the total cost of actually making a product or delivering a service. COGS includes materials, labor, and all the cost of running production machines. You should be able to obtain this number directly from the Profit and Loss Statement, specifically the Cost of Goods Sold (COGS) category. Again, the type of business you are running defines how each expense is accounted for and therefore where each expense line item will show up in the Chart of Accounts.

To help you keep Total Expenses and COGS clear think of them this way: Total Expenses is the cost of running the business itself (innovating a widget, marketing it, selling it, managing everything); Total COGS is the cost of making the new widget (parts to build the widget plus the labor to get it assembled).

This number is important because it indicates the true financial cost of creating your products or service. With this number you can know how efficient you are at producing your products and delivering your services. In any system efficiency is critical for optimal performance. If COGS is too high you do not have margin, and if you recall from the discussion of Porter's Value Chain, margin allows you to give greater value to your customers. In this book, customer value is a core competitive advantage that is extremely hard to push against and therefore COGS must be strategically managed for optimization.

### Operating Payroll

This is the total payroll not directly related to creating the products or delivering the service. This would include all officers, administrative, sales, and marketing staff but would not include machine operators or service delivery personnel. Remember that machine operators and service delivery personnel are considered labor which is part of the COGS. Operating Payroll is a subcategory of the Expenses category in the Profit and Loss Statement with its own total; as such you should be able to obtain this number directly from there.

This number is important because it can tell you if the cost of running and managing the business is out of tune with the cost of creating products and services. Many organizations, in an attempt to fix things or get the right people on board, find themselves with a bloated Operations Payroll. Examples include having an employee who is grandfathered in and happens to be making nearly as much as the principal of the organization, or when you hire a new sales force. Again, because this is a big number relative to the Income of the organization, it must be watched and managed.

## Gross Profit

This is the Income left over after having accounted for the Cost of Goods Sold. It is calculated with the simple formula: Income – COGS = Gross Profit. Gross Profit does not take into account the cost of running the business, i.e. Expenses. It also does not take into account the Non-Operating Income and Expenses categories mentioned earlier. You should be able to obtain this number directly from the Profit and Loss Statement, specifically the Gross Profit category.

This number is important because it indicates if you have a potential for making money. Notice I say potential since it is a Gross value not a Net value. This means you have additional math to perform but in general, if you can hold Operations Payroll and Expenses steady you can have a reasonable expectation of making a Net Profit, and that is money in the bank.

## Net Profit

This is the total Income for the organization after having taken into account COGS, Expenses, and both Non-Operating Income and Non-Operating Expense. It is calculated with the formula: (COGS – Expenses) + (Non-Operating Income – Non-Operating Expenses). Net Profit is often referred to as the Bottom Line. It indicates if a business is operating in the black or in the red, either making it or not. You should be able to obtain this number directly from the Profit and Loss Statement, specifically the Net Profit category.

This number is important because it tells you that you have in fact made money in the business. This is after all one of the most common benefits of taking on an endeavor—to make money. Of course you still have to pay taxes on that money and that alone could realistically put you in the red again if things are not managed correctly. I have seen companies state they would pay profit sharing based on the previous quarter's Net Profit only to find that although they made money the previous quarter, they would not be able to pay taxes if they pay out profit sharing.

## Receivables

This is the total of all outstanding debt accounts for all clients. Receivables or Accounts Receivable is the result of providing credit to customers for the products and services they consume in the normal course of business. Normally this benefit to the customer—of being allowed to purchase on account—also benefits the organization in that the client account incurs interest on the outstanding balance. There should also be reasonable limits to the extent of time the outstanding balance can remain, such as 60 to 90 days. This number will not be in the Profit and Loss Statement but in the Accounts Receivable Aging Report. You are looking for the total outstanding amount regardless of the number of days.

This number is important because it indicates how well you are managing your cash flow and to what extent you are playing the role of the bank. No small business should be the bank for another small business, at least not for anything but the shortest of reasonable terms if at all. I will once again speculate that this alone has caused the demise of too many small businesses simply because the math doesn't work. You cannot go into debt with your vendors because you extend credit to your clients. Most small businesses will incur fees and interest from their vendors while on the other side they will not be charging fees and interest to the clients. If you choose to extend credit to your clients there must be a reasonable extent to the amount, time, interest, and fees. Likewise there must be a rigorous process for managing all aspects of this client debt including contingencies for stopping services, holding up product shipments, and collections.

## Cash

This is simply the cash on hand at a given point. Although it may seem foreign to many businesses, this should always be a large positive number. It would not be unreasonable to have at least one month's payroll on hand at any time. Remember that cash is king and with it you have options and agility. In its early days Microsoft reportedly amassed no less than an entire year's payroll as insurance and protection. If you find this number is constantly dipping into the red you need to re-evaluate your business plan and model. Running your business in a cash poor state can easily become habitual, but this is not healthy nor sustainable.

## Labor Cost

This is the ratio of the cost of Labor to total Income or Revenue. This Leading Indicator can and will be calculated differently depending on the business you are operating. The cost of Labor includes not only the payroll of those who do the work but also the associated taxes, insurance and other benefits, incentives and so on. These numbers will come from the Profit and Loss Statement, specifically the COGS and Expenses categories and the total Income you already have.

If you run a small business this number can get tricky because quite often the owner is also part of the working crew. In these instances you will want to include that owner's Operating Payroll in your calculations. It's also not uncommon for a small operation to use the entire payroll because everyone is directly involved in creating or delivering the products or services.

This number is important because it indicates how well you are managing human resources and their compensation relative to Income or revenue. If you can tie the Labor Cost to the customer satisfaction you might see that as the Labor Cost percentage goes up, their customer satisfaction goes up, and likewise, if the Labor Cost percentage goes down their customer satisfaction goes down. This simply indicates over or under-staffing for optimal customer value and experience. You will need to recognize when an increase in Labor Cost yields no greater increase in customer satisfaction. At this point, you will need to improve some other aspect of your processes and understand that adding more people is not the complete answer.

**Summary**
Managing your business requires that you have a solid understanding of the financial Leading Indicators of the business. Failure to attend to these metrics simply means you will not see the train that runs you over coming through the tunnel. Getting a read on them and managing them means you are driving the success of the organization, not just watching its destiny unfold. Be in the driver seat and be strapped in.

Tool Tip: *Financial Statements*

# The Value Chain

This tool has already been introduced in Chapter 2 and some of that information is duplicated here although modified for the correct context and expanded. The concept of the Value Chain was introduced by the management professor Michael E. Porter in his book *Competitive Advantage: Creating and Sustaining Superior Performance*. The Value Chain is the concept that every organization can be broken down into the Primary and Supporting activities that are preformed when designing, producing, marketing, delivering, and maintaining a product or service. Once broken down, the Value Chain allows for systematic evaluation of the strategic and relevant activities of the organization and their interaction with each other. The goal is to fully understand the behavior of costs and the existing and potential sources of differentiation in the business.

Managing cost is a primary objective in any business and if done well can lead to a solid position of cost leadership in the market. Differentiation in any aspect of what you do to create or deliver your products leads to precious uniqueness. A focus on these two—Cost Leadership and Product Differentiation—coupled with a focus on your selected market (Market Focus), are the three generic business strategies that can result in a solid competitive advantage for any business. The key to differentiation is in clearly understanding the role of your organization's products and services in your customer's Value Chain.

The Value Chain displays total value of the organization which consists of value activities and Margin. Value activities are the distinct activities an organization performs in creating products and services. Margin is the difference between the total value created and the cost of performing these value activities. There are two broad types of value activates—Primary and Supporting. Each type of activity is broken down into several generic categories (see Figure 5-3).

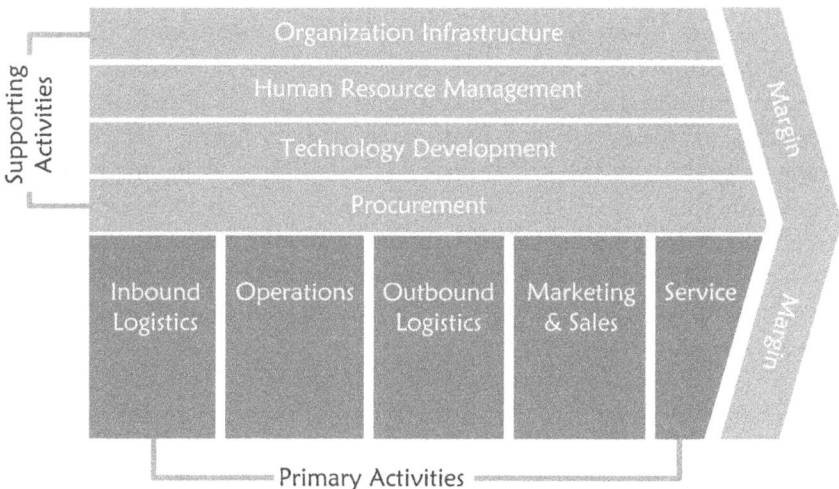

*Figure 5-3. The Value Chain*

## Primary Activities

These are the activities related directly to the creation of the product or delivery of the service including the after-sale assistance or after-service support. There are five generic categories for primary activities in the organization:

- Inbound Logistics – Activities associated with the scheduling, receipt, storage, allocation, and return of materials, as well as other inputs to the products and services being offered.
- Operations – Activities associated with the actual creation of the product or service being offered. This would include machines, operating systems, production, testing, and facility management.
- Outbound Logistics – Activities associated with processing, order processing, storage, scheduling, delivery, and returns of products and services.
- Marketing & Sales – Activities associated with presenting the Value Proposition of your offerings to the Target Market and facilitating their purchase or consumption of those offerings. This would include market analysis, product and service pricing, advertising, promotions, installation, repairs, and channel partnerships.
- Service – Activities associated with the support, maintenance, or enhancement of the products and services once delivered. This would include installation, training, repair, upgrades, and spare parts supply.

Each of these generic categories may play a significantly different role depending on the industry your organization operates in. For a restaurant, the Inbound Logistics are of critical importance. The freshness of meats and produce determine the quality of the food being delivered to the customer. A Competitive Advantage comes from your ability to source the best products with which to create your menu items. In a restaurant that does not handle takeout or delivery, the Outbound Logistics are largely non-existent as they mostly involve a trash compactor and a dumpster. There is not much of a Competitive Advantage to be leveraged here.

However if you are an Information Technology company, your Service activities are most critical as they are in fact your primary offering and foremost Value Proposition. In this type of service-based business, Service represents the single largest potential for Competitive Advantage. If the organization does not provide project-level services but only frontline service such as remote and onsite computer support, you would find that the Production Operations activities are minimal and therefore not a significant factor in Competitive Advantage.

## Supporting Activities

These are the activities that support the Primary Activities in that they provide the required resource management, technology, quality talent, and other organization-wide functions. There are five generic categories for primary activities in the organization:

- Procurement – Activities associated with purchasing of inputs (raw materials or even finished goods) used to create the products or deliver the services being offered.
- Technology Development – Activities associated with the research and development of new and existing products and services, innovations, and processes. This would include aspects of knowledge management, best practices, Core Competencies, and training.
- Human Resource Management – Activities associated with recruitment, pay, discharge, and replacement of personnel. This would include employee benefits and compliance with all applicable labor laws and regulations.
- Organization Infrastructure – Activities associated with general management, planning, finance, accounting, legal, regulation, and quality.

The concept Porter lays out states that competitive advantage cannot be understood by looking at the organization as a whole, but at the strategic and relevant activities of the organization and how they interact with each other. Products and service pass through the activities of your Value Chain in some semblance of order and at each activity, the product or service should gain value. Solid value should directly translate into Margin (profit). This Margin can then be used any way you wish within the organization. You could pour it into human resources, product development, marketing, customer incentives, and kickbacks or even pay it out in bonuses.

The Value Chain is only part of what Porter defines as the larger Value System. The value system shows how any business and their respective Value Chain has links to Upstream Value from suppliers and a link of Downstream Value to their customers. When your customer is also a business that creates products and services, they too become part of the Channel Value. This Channel Value Chain is created as each of these organizations link together, passing value through links. And finally there is of course the Channel Value created within the Strategic Partnerships that are formulated (see Figure 5-4).

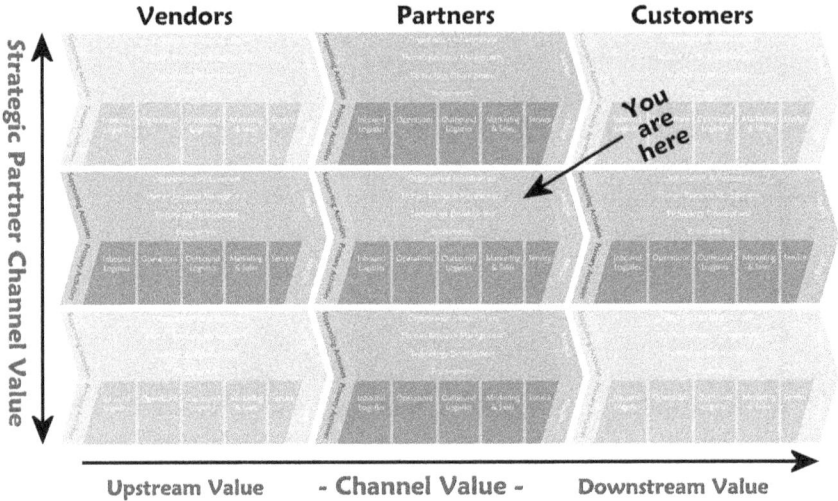

Figure 5-4. The Value System

## Summary

What I have presented here is but a scratch on the surface of Porter's Competitive Advantage and the Value Chain. I cannot emphasize enough how important these concepts and this tool are to your sustained success, success as a habit. If you can understand how the activities in your organization link together and are linked to activities and value in your strategic partners and vendors' Value Chains, that alone will give you a strategic advantage over your competition. The ability to constantly focus on product and service value as a prime motivation and goal versus only focusing on the margin (and hoping the value is there) puts you solidly out in front of the majority of your competitors.

# LEAN

I'm going to start with clarification of one extremely important point—Lean is not just for manufacturing and it is not just for big companies. This also happens to be true for Six Sigma. I won't spend much time discussing Lean, but I will provide a brief overview. Beyond trying to accurately convey what Lean is, delving any further into how to use Lean becomes a much bigger conversation that I do not believe could be covered in anything less than a chapter of its own. What you need to know is that Lean is in fact for you and it is easier than you think to get started.

The history of the term Lean goes back to the 1980s, the Toyota Corporation, and a book titled *Lean Thinking: Banish Waste and Create Wealth in Your Corporation* by authors James P. Womack and Daniel T. Jones. But the concept of time and waste management go back at least as far as Benjamin Franklin. This brings me to my main point about its implementation and use. You are likely already thinking and using Lean mindsets and methods, you just haven't learned the formal terminology and practices associated with today's prescribed best practices.

The authors Womack and Jones not only wrote the book on Lean, they are founders of the Lean Enterprise Institute and the Lean Enterprise Academy (UK), respectively. Interestingly enough each site presents a different definition of Lean.

From http://www.lean.org/WhatsLean/
The core idea is to maximize customer value while minimizing waste. Simply, lean means creating more value for customers with fewer resources.

From http://www.leanuk.org/what-is-lean
Rooted in Purpose, Process and respect for People, Lean is about creating the most value for the customer while minimizing resources, time, energy and effort.
So let's cut to the basics of Lean in a graphic that I believe will help you see that you are likely already Lean minded, you just need to realize it (see Figure 5-5).

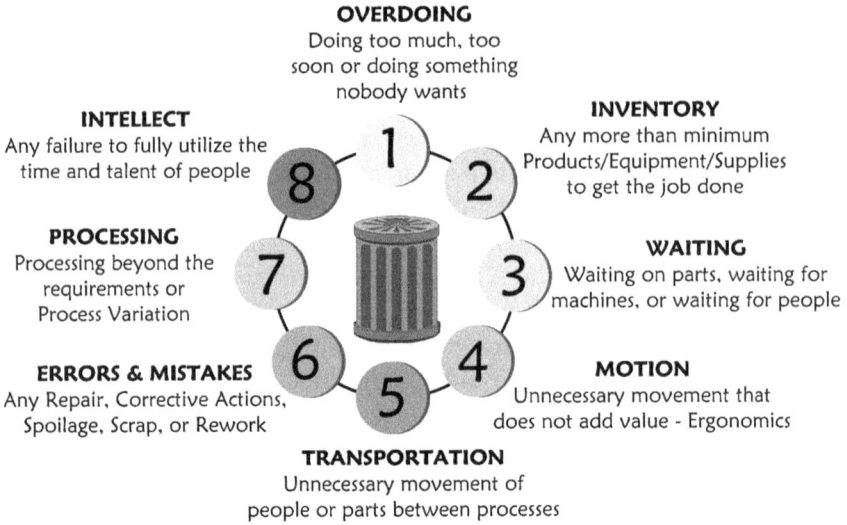

OVERDOING
Doing too much, too
soon or doing something
nobody wants

INTELLECT
Any failure to fully utilize the
time and talent of people

INVENTORY
Any more than minimum
Products/Equipment/Supplies
to get the job done

PROCESSING
Processing beyond the
requirements or
Process Variation

WAITING
Waiting on parts, waiting for
machines, or waiting for people

ERRORS & MISTAKES
Any Repair, Corrective Actions,
Spoilage, Scrap, or Rework

MOTION
Unnecessary movement that
does not add value - Ergonomics

TRANSPORTATION
Unnecessary movement of
people or parts between processes

*Figure 5-5. Lean Mindset*

Getting started with Lean as a core competency starts with something as simple as sharing the idea that through ownership of process, you and everyone in the organization can have a profound effect on the value of the end products and services. In all my years of experience, I have never worked in any business where there was a complete absence of people who cared about value. People who cared enough about the quality of the end product or service to speak up when they recognized waste. And they did this on their own based on their own interest in the organization they worked for or simply in the interest of pride in their workmanship. Just think what the people in your organization who think similarly could do if they were given a tool and a method to endear to.

## Six Sigma

The discussion of this tool will be one of the shortest in all three chapters mainly because, much like Lean, any discussion beyond an introduction to the tool would be neither simple nor short. But I will repeat the same opening statement from Lean as it applies to Six Sigma. Six Sigma is not just for manufacturing and it is not just for big companies. Unlike Lean, I cannot state that Six Sigma is easier than you think to get started, but it is for you.

To keep it simple, Six Sigma is about leveraging statistical process control, not just for the control function but also for driving the end value as a strategy. In the past, statistical process control was used to keep things running consistently while continuously introducing tighter tolerances, when possible, resulting in higher quality products being produced more efficiently. The higher quality trickled down to the customer as value and the efficiency trickled down to the bottom line of the organization as greater profit for the company.

But if you look at this same statistical process control from the viewpoint that the actual desired end value to the customer and process efficiency are driving the increased tolerances rather than the viewpoint of tighter tolerances driving greater value for the customer and better process efficiency for the company, statistical process control becomes the tool not the driver. Stated another way: It's not a push of higher tolerances that results in higher quality and efficiency, it's the requirement of higher quality and efficiency that drives the tighter tolerances. This is actually a paradigm shift in strategy, from using the tool to drive value to having the value drive the tool. This paradigm shift comes from the value-driven strategy for competitive advantage which has been a theme throughout this book.

Six Sigma was pioneered at Motorola Corporation and was subsequently trademarked by Motorola. Six Sigma got its name while at Motorola based on the set goal of six sigma for all of its manufacturing operations. A Sigma is the mathematical term for Standard Deviation. Targeting a quality level of Six Standard Deviations (Six Sigma) represents a process in which 99.99966% of all results are statistically expected to be free of defects. Six Sigma gave birth to the call for what has now become a highly sought after level of quality commonly known as Five Nines (99.999% defect free). Six Sigma quickly evolved from a strict process control methodology to a performance and management methodology. In the 1990s it was adopted by Jack Welch as a competitive strategy while at GM. Over the years it has been refined and redefined by large corporations all over the world for their own purposes and has become one of the most popular management methods in use to date.

The defining principal of Six Sigma is the DMAIC process (Define, Measure, Analyze, Improve and Control). It is this simple approach that allows anyone to implement Six Sigma, provided they can both accurately measure the important process metrics and affect them (see Figure 5-6).

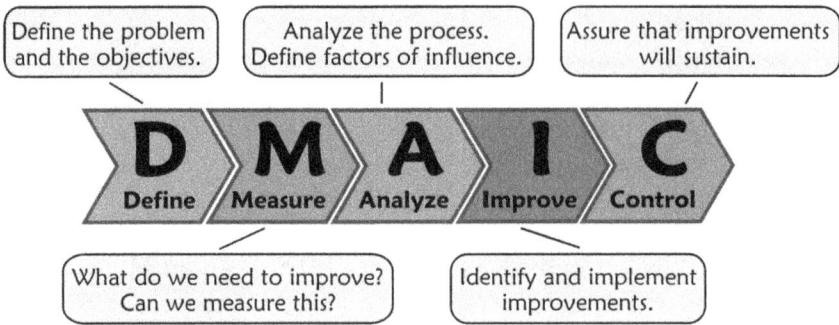

*Figure 5-6. Six Sigma DMAIC*

Unlike Lean, just mentioning the term Six Sigma and propping up a nice graphic will likely elicit at least one groan and have a negative effect on morale with the exception of the few who understand what it is and what it can truly do. As with Lean, start by tapping into the innate devotion of the people inside the organization to create great products and services for the customer. Introduce a tool and ask them if it will help; you might be surprised at how it takes hold. Six Sigma has a longer-term implementation timeframe but once it is instituted, it too can transform your organization. You can indeed attain your Five Nines.

Be open-minded to what can get you to the next level. And if it is not the right tool for your organization today, I guarantee it will be one day. There are excellent books being written every day on the subject of Lean and Six Sigma translated to small organizations including pure service delivery based organizations. Check out the Bibliography for a book titled *Lean Six Sigma for Service*.

## Balanced Scorecard

These next two tools are tied together in a specific way that precludes me from introducing them in the actual order you will use them. These two tools are complimentary and if used properly, can help you manage some of the most difficult tasks of creating success—translating, conveying, and gauging the progress of your business roadmap and strategy. Neither tool by itself nor both together represent a magic spell for creating success, but together they go a long way in effectively communicating to everyone exactly how you will convert your resources into value for the customer and for the business.

Developed first, the Balanced Scorecard was designed to be a comprehensive framework for executives to translate the business roadmap and strategy into a coherent set of performance objectives and measures. The Balanced Scorecard could be shared with everyone in the organization all the way down to the production floor, conveying the specifics of what initiatives would be undertaken and the targets for performance. It made perfect sense to the management but meant little more than noted performance expectations to the worker. What the Balanced Scorecard did not do was paint a picture of how the people in the organization were linked to anything but their performance objectives. It did not convey the cause and effect relationship that linked assets such as information capital, organization capital, and human capacity to the value proposition presented to the customer that creates revenue and profit.

The Strategy Map was developed later as a tool to help the organization translate the business roadmap and strategy into, for lack of a better term, human readable form. It was designed to provide a single-page view of the cause and effect relationship between the capital of the organization (including the human capacity) and the shared vision of the organization. Now everyone in the organization could see where they fit in the strategy and how they could best have a positive impact in the organization toward the shared vision, not just the performance measures they would be gauged by.

Today with both tools at hand, you would first build out your roadmap and strategy so you know where you are going. Next you would draw up your Strategy Map to translate the complex into the not so complex. And finally you would draw up your Balanced Scorecard to track and share your progress. Without the Strategy Map, the translation from roadmap and strategy directly to Balanced Scorecard would be much more art than skill. I will cover more on the Strategy Map later, but first let's discuss the Balanced Scorecard.

The Balanced Scorecard was developed in the early 1990s by Robert S. Kaplan and David P. Norton and detailed in their 1996 book *The Balanced Scorecard*. The Balanced Scorecard is a tool to help management focus on a coherent set of performance measures derived from the company's vision and strategy that, if accomplished, would help differentiate the organization from its competition while creating great customer value and stakeholder profit. Since its inception it has been refined into a powerful operating system for a strategic management process.

Norton and Kaplan revealed how the modern organization is moving away from building strategies around the creation of tangible assets and closer to strategies based on knowledge-based assets. Tangible assets such as inventory, property, plants, and equipment were historically measured using financial metrics to gauge performance and success. Knowledge-based assets such as customer relations, innovation, technology, employee competency, and motivation had to be measured using non-financial metrics to gauge progress and success. Thus the foundation for Norton and Kaplan's development of the Balanced Scorecard which allows the measurement of the overall strategy that supports the vision with respect to intangible assets.

The concept of the Balanced Scorecard centers on the team effort and how the team can support the strategy versus the outdated management model focused on measuring performance. The Balanced Scorecard does not simply do away with metrics and the concern of performance, but they are no longer the primary focus. The focus is now on a shared vision, the strategy for success and communicating it consistently and effectively. The Balanced Scorecard is for Strategy Focused organizations, not the Finance Focused.

The architecture of the Balanced Scorecard is quite different from the common graphical representation of the Balanced Scorecard. Let's look at the architecture first (see Figure 5-7). The architecture of the Balanced Scorecard is a cascading process that starts at the top with the shared vision and strategy of the organization. As there is no sustainable business without revenue and profit, the first perspective is the Financial Perspective. It addresses whether the organization's strategy, implementation, and execution are contributing to the bottom line. The next perspective is the Customer Perspective. It must address the value proposition which defines how the company differentiates itself from its competitors and endears the customer to the company's offerings.

## Vision and Strategy

### Financial Perspective

If we succeed,
how will we look
to our stakeholders?

### Customer Perspective

To achieve our Vision,
how must we look to
our customers?

### Internal Perspective

To satisfy our customers,
at which processes
must we excel?

### Learning and Growth
### Perspective

To achieve our vision, how
must the organization
learn and improve?

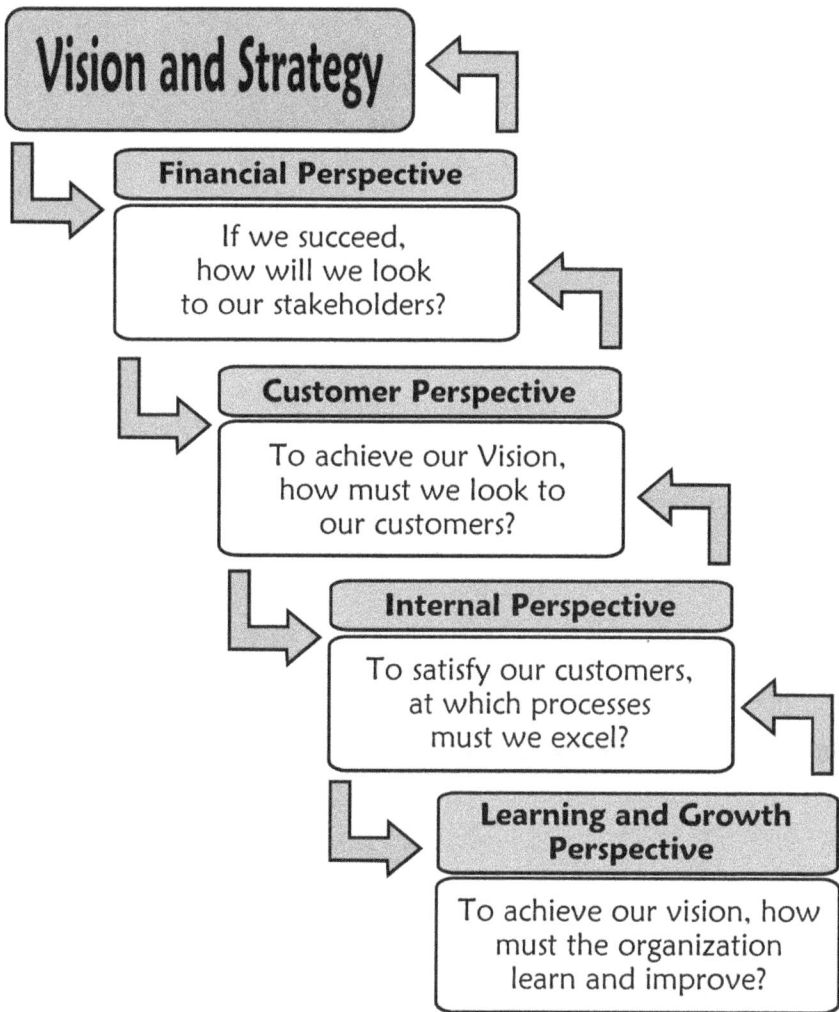

*Figure 5-7. Balanced Scorecard Architecture*

Next is the Internal Perspective which addresses the critical internal processes the organization must excel at to ensure the greatest positive impact on customer satisfaction and to support the financial objectives of the business. The final perspective, Learning and Growth, recognizes that the ability to execute on internal business processes relies on the organizational infrastructure, Core Competencies, Knowledge Management, and most important, the Human Element coupled with the Culture of the organization.

Each Balanced Scorecard perspective is a component of a strategic hypothesis that requires identifying the desired Outcome (lagging indicators) and the activities that are the Drivers (leading indicators). The primary question posed for each perspective is carefully constructed to illicit the response required to identify these Outcomes and Drivers (see Figure 5-8). Once created, the Balanced Scorecard is more suited to presentation as a clover leaf configuration if possible. After all, the clover leaf is actually a representation of balance versus the cascading depiction used when describing the architecture. The four perspectives allow for a balance between short and long-term objectives, desired Outcomes and their Drivers, and objective (hard) and subjective (soft) measures.

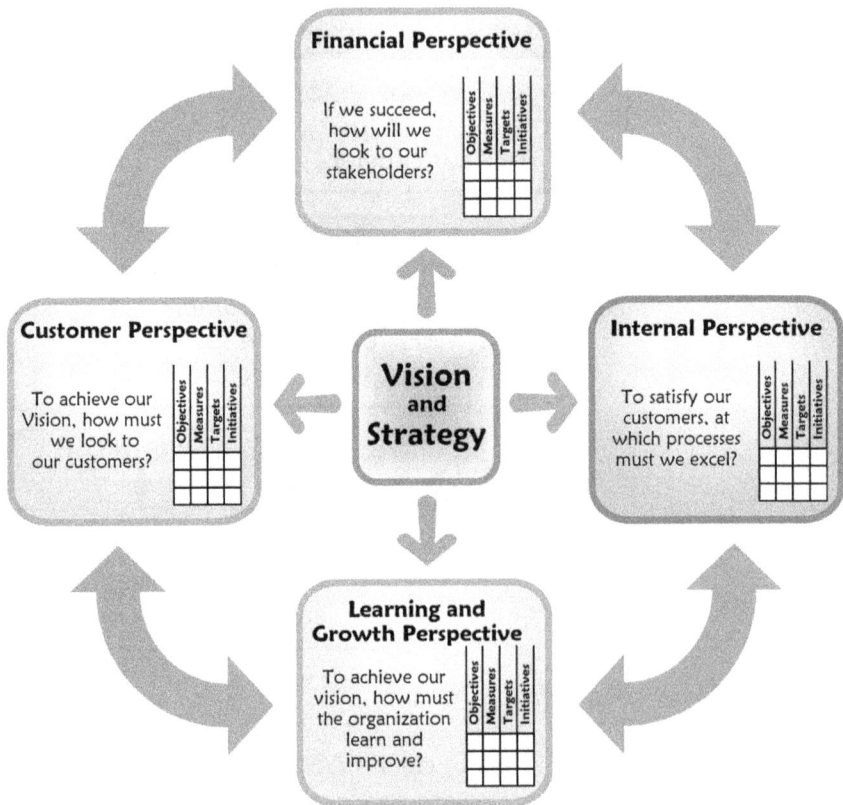

*Figure 5-8. The Balanced Scorecard*

Perspectives of the Balanced Scorecard
- Financial Perspective – Concerns are growth, profitability, and organizational risk.
  o Seeks to answer the question: If we succeed, how will we look to our stakeholders?
- Customer Perspective – Concerns are creating value and

differentiation from competition.
- o Seeks to answer the question: To achieve our Vision, how must we look to our customers?
- **Internal Perspective** – Concerns are priorities for business process directly related to creating customer and stakeholder satisfaction.
  - o Seeks to answer the question: To satisfy our customers, which processes must we excel at?
- **Learning and Growth Perspective** – Concerns are priorities for creating a climate that supports organizational change, innovation, and growth.
  - o Seeks to answer the question: To achieve our vision, how must the organization learn and improve?

Remember that the Balanced Scorecard cannot be stakeholder dominated KPIs and metrics, and it also cannot just present enough non-financial KPIs to balance the Customer and Financial Perspectives. Norton and Kaplan state that the best Scorecards are those that clearly reflect the strategy of the organization. The Balanced Scorecard will reappear in Chapter 8 (Pyramid of Purpose and Value – Blueprint for Success), Chapter 11 (Business Strategy Meets Agile Execution), and again in Chapter 12 (Case Study & Example). There I will show a completed scorecard and further the discussion on how it is conveyed to the organization, what objectives must be executed on, and how success will be measured.

Tool Tip: *Leading Indicators, The Value Chain, SWOT Analysis, Strategy Map, Pyramid of Purpose and Value*

## The Strategy Map

It certainly didn't take Norton and Kaplan very long to realize that although the Balanced Scorecard was a fantastic tool for conveying the most critical Outcomes and Drivers for the organization's roadmap and strategy, the actual translation of the roadmap and strategy was still more art than science. And the Balanced Scorecard by itself did not help significantly in that translation. Organizations were utilizing the Balanced Scorecard and executing on strategy but exactly how they were deriving the right objectives, measures, targets and initiatives was still largely unknown.

In their 2001 book *The Strategy-Focused Organization: How Balanced*

*Scorecard Companies Thrive in the New Business Environment*, Norton and Kaplan build upon their innovative development of the Balanced Scorecard with what could be considered the Rosetta Stone of strategy—the Strategy Map. The Strategy Map at its simplest is a graphical representation of the business Strategy showing the cause and effect logic connecting the desired Outcomes with the Drivers that will lead to those Outcomes.

Through their ongoing research and review of hundreds of Balanced Scorecards, Norton and Kaplan were able to identify clear patterns in how organizations were translating strategy into Balanced Scorecards. Using the information available, they mapped the patterns into a generic framework now known as the Strategy Map (see Figure 5-9). The Strategy Map presents a generic architecture for translating the organization's roadmap and strategy into a Balanced Scorecard. The example provided here can be used as a template when defining your business strategy. It shows the direct links and relationships of the intangible assets (Drivers) such as culture, leadership, knowledge, and teamwork to the desired value (Outcomes) for customers and stakeholders.

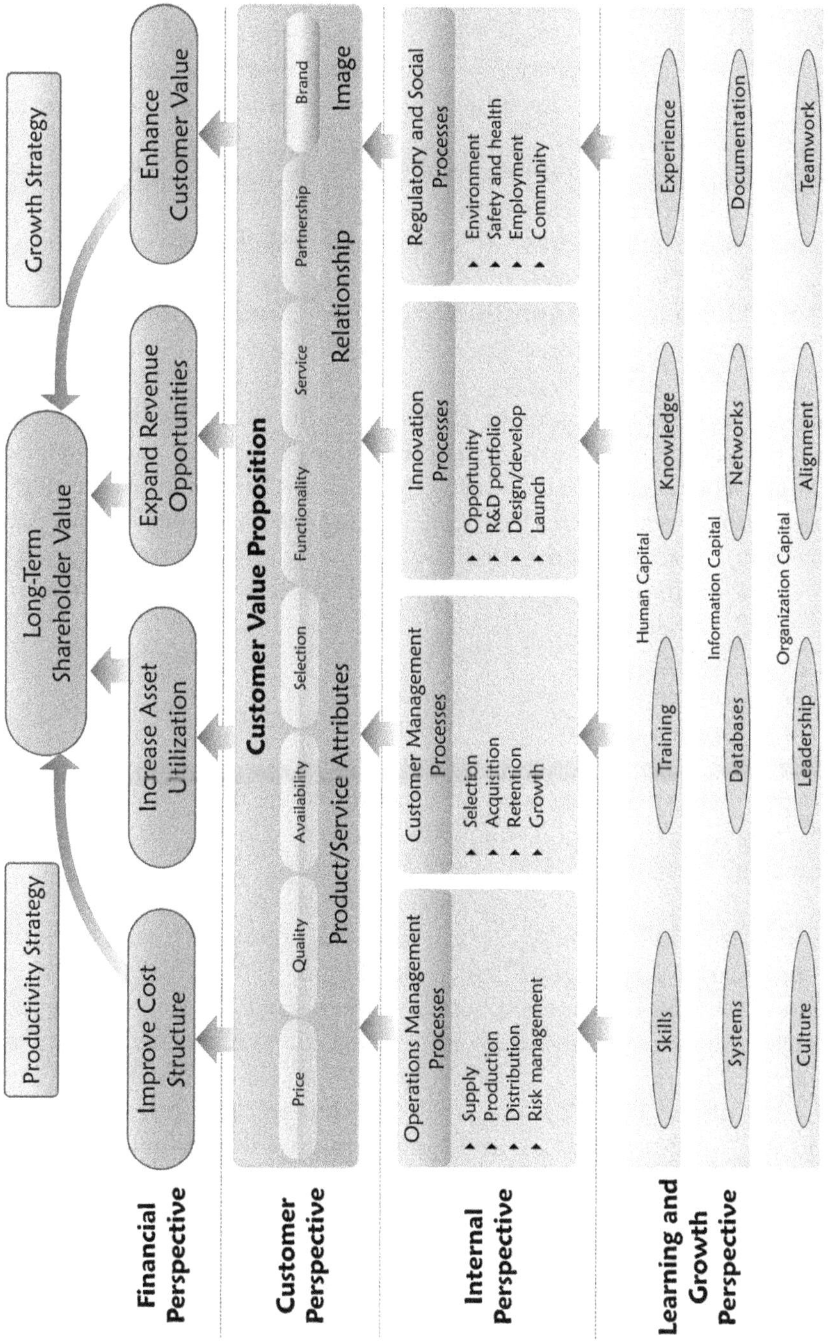

*Figure 5-9. Generic Strategy Map*

## Perspective and Strategy Breakdown for the Generic Strategy Map

- Financial Perspective – Strategy requires a balance between contradictory forces of long-term (Growth) and short-term (Productivity)
- Customer Perspective – Strategy is based on the differentiated Customer Value Proposition
- Internal Perspective – Value is created through the internal business processes
- Learning and Growth Perspective – Strategic alignment of intangible assets

Two additional dimensions of the Strategy Map must be discussed at least in brief: Generic Strategies for the Value Proposition, and Generic Strategy Themes. When translating the business Roadmap and Strategy into a human readable form and identifying the Customer Perspective objective, Measures, and Initiatives, it is common to refer to generic Value Proposition Strategies. Norton and Kaplan call out these four:

- Best Total Cost
- Product Leader
- Complete Customer Solution
- System Lock-In

My personal preference is to broaden the strategies you consider by referring back to Chapter 4 and both Porter's Generic Strategies and Bowman's Strategy Clock.

As for Strategy Themes, Norton and Kaplan specify four generic complementary Strategic Themes (see Figure 5-10). They found that most executives broke their overall business strategies out into several focused themes. Because they are defined individually, these singular Strategy Themes could progress, change, and succeed independent of each other. This allows the organization to deal with conflicting priorities of short-term growth, long-term growth, and profitability.

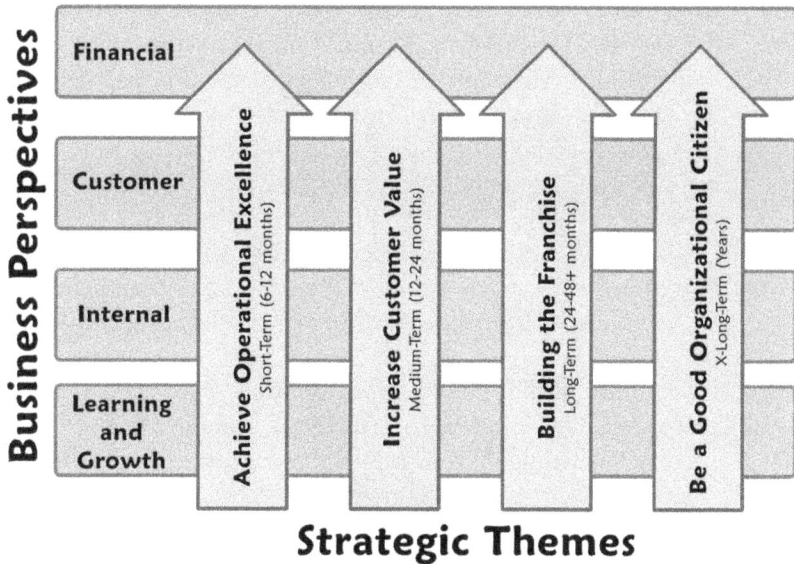

**Strategic Themes**

*Figure 5-10. Architecture of a Strategy Map*

It should be noted that each of the four generic Strategic Themes closely correlate to specific groupings of Internal Processes. The intention is that if your strategy focuses on a particular theme, Operational Excellence for example, you must therefore focus on specific Internal Processes to be successful.

- Achieving Operational Excellence will require primarily focusing on Operations Management Processes
- Increasing Customer Value will require primarily focusing on Customer Management Processes
- Building the Franchise will require primarily focusing on Innovation Processes
- Being a Good Organizational Citizen will require primarily focusing on Regulatory and Social Processes

You will see in the examples shown in later chapters that the use of Strategy Themes lends itself well to defining your business Roadmap relative to the overall business Strategy. It will allow you to leverage the Agile Methodology and the Business Agile Strategy Execution (BASE) process.

In retrospect, Norton and Kaplan also identified and clarified five important common principles of a strategy-focused organization. These principles are what must be supported and followed for the entire management system to work as planned.

- Principle 1 – Translate the Strategy to Operational Terms
  - o  Involves: Strategy Maps and Balanced Scorecards
- Principle 2 – Align the Organization to the Strategy
  - o  Involves: Roles, Collaboration, and Synergy
- Principle 3 – Make Strategy Everyone's Everyday Job
  - o  Involves: Strategic Awareness and Team Scorecards
- Principle 4 – Make Strategy a Continual Process
  - o  Involves: Budget, Analytics, and Learning
- Principle 5 – Mobilize Change Through Executive Leadership
  - o  Involves: Governance and Management Systems

Failure to support and follow these principles significantly reduces the ability for the organization to effectively execute on the strategy. Failure in even one principle represents a significant drop in the signal strength of the message and the conveyance of the strategy and shared value. Failure in two or more principles means the signal strength is weak at best. You must have everyone on board and tuned in.

I have mentioned many times and I will state again here—Building a solid business roadmap and strategy by itself represents a competitive advantage for any organization. Executing consistently and systematically on that strategy represents a significant competitive advantage. But what cannot be seen or understood cannot be effectively executed upon. The Balanced Scorecard and the Strategy Map are the most powerful tools for translating your strategy into a format that can easily be understood by the entire organization. Everyone will be able to understand the strategy and more importantly, find their place in the strategy. A place where they can contribute to the success by becoming aligned with the strategy which supports the shared vision they have already bought into.

I will provide a basic Strategy Map example in Chapter 8 (Pyramid of Purpose and Value—Blueprint for Success), Chapter 11 (Business Strategy Meets Agile Execution), and in Chapter 12 (Case Study & Example), but it is an understatement to say that delving even one level deeper into the Strategy Map is beyond the scope of this book. I do believe however that I have presented enough here that anyone can grasp the concept. For some it may even be enough to be able to construct a basic Strategy Map and Balanced Scorecard using the forthcoming example. Don't forget that this is not a magic wand; it does not plan your strategy for you. That remains the single greatest task before you. Taken as a collective work, you will find that most everything in this book is geared toward helping you figure out your roadmap and strategy and translate it into human readable form. Much of what has been presented in these last three chapters on tools is specifically intended to support the use of this one tool for a compelling reason. As your organization grows and the strategy of the business grows, you will need this tool ever more. No matter the size of the organization—even a micro operation—it will benefit from having a very clear picture of the roadmap and strategy to pin up on the wall and point at. Because of the potential represented by mastering these two tools, the Balanced Scorecard and the Strategy Map, I highly recommend that you research them in detail.

The Strategy Map represents that very clear and enticing picture I mentioned at the onset of this book. The Balanced Scorecard allows everyone to participate in the achievement of objectives that support the shared vision and track the progress toward success and to the next level. The cohesive energy that comes from having everyone on the team able to see their place on the ship and know their part in making history? Extremely powerful.

Tool Tip: *Leading Indicators, The Value Chain, SWOT Analysis, Pyramid of Purpose and Value*

## Business Maturity Index

The Business Maturity Index (BMI) is an innovation of my own resulting from the need to gauge an organization's overall subjective business maturity level. The subjective maturity of the organization is the side (viewpoint) that is not so easily gauged using solid KPIs and metrics such as the Balanced Scorecard or Leading Indicators. The subjective side of the organization must of course be evaluated using subjective criteria which are a little harder though not impossible to define. However once determined, an organization may, if they wish, compare its BMI to that of any other organization.

Because this tool is an innovation of my own that is not documented in any other text, it has an entire chapter dedicated to its definition and use. This section will only provide a basic overview of the BMI. I refer you to Chapter 9 (Business Maturity Index – Gauging Your Success) for the complete detailed narrative and example use of the BMI.

The BMI seeks to evaluate five Success Elements for each of ten Value Aspects of the organization according to a simple Capability Maturity

Model. Let's start with the Value Aspects which coincidentally were introduced in Chapter 1. They are:

- Communications & Collaboration – This aspect is not about the phone system, forums board on the website, or the white board in the conference room. It's more about the methods and culture around communications and collaboration.
- Finance & Accounting – Includes but is not limited to the invoicing, collections, payments, and day-to-day transactions of the operation, in addition to all the planning, budgeting, procurement, and effective utilization of the business capital.
- Human Resources – This aspect is concerned with the human side of the business and concerned with cultivation, acquisition, and assimilation of quality talent throughout the organization.
- Marketing – This aspect is concerned with defining the products and services that will be successful, differentiating them from your competitor's offerings, and letting the target market know you offer them.
- Organization Infrastructure – This aspect is concerned with management, legal, planning, information systems, leadership, government affairs, and quality management.
- Procurement & Logistics – This aspect is concerned with purchasing and all inbound and outbound logistics.
- Production Operations – This aspect is concerned with the transformation process that turns materials and people into finished goods and services.
- Research & Development – This aspect is concerned with the lifecycle of a product, from idea through viability testing to production.
- Sales – This aspect is concerned with activities in which the objective is to promote the customer purchase of your products or client engagement of your services.
- Service Delivery – This aspect is concerned with the coordination of the delivery of your products and services with client needs and desires.

Now I'll cover the five Success Elements each Value Aspect will be evaluated on. You should notice that the first three Success Elements are tied very closely to the three sections of the Pyramid of Purpose and Value introduced in Chapter 1 of this book. The additional two elements, Continuous Improvement and Continuous Refinement, are related directly to the continued quest for competitive and strategic advantage through the relentless pursuit of value. The five Success Elements are:

- Leadership and Staffing – This element addresses everything about the Human Element.
- Knowledge Management – This element addresses the creation, maintenance, and dissemination of Explicit and Tacit knowledge within the organization and when necessary, outside the organization.
- Roadmap and Strategy – This element addresses the future plans, goals, metrics, and cross-function alignment for a given business Value Aspect.
- Continuous Improvement – This element addresses the Continuous Improvement of every relevant process through statistical process control.
- Continuous Refinement – This element addresses Continuous Refinement, the relentless pursuit of creating the highest value products and services by focusing on the reduction or elimination of waste in all aspects of the business.

And finally, the five levels of maturity based on a standard Capability Maturity Model as applied to the organization.

Level 1 = Chaotic – Indicative of a Startup company that is Reactive in nature.

Level 2 = Aware – Indicative of the Pioneer company that is learning to be Proactive in nature.

Level 3 = Enabled – Indicative of a Success Oriented company that knows the value of process and wants to create value.

Level 4 = Managed – Indicative of an Organization Oriented business that has well-established process control with measurable metrics.

Level 5 = Optimized – Indicative of a Value Driven company that leverages all aspects of processes and systems to drive margin.

This tool is utilized in two stages: first for evaluating the individual Value Aspects, and second for the organization overall. For the first stage of utilizing this tool, you simply evaluate each Success Element of a given Value Aspect and assign the most appropriate Maturity Level 1-5, with 1 being the lowest level and 5 being the highest. Continue to evaluate each of the five Success Elements in each of the remaining ten Value Aspects. Find the average maturity level for all Success Elements in a given Value Aspect. This number represents the overall maturity level for that Value Aspect.

The individual Value Aspect maturity level can tell you a lot about the leading and lagging of processes and systems in the organization. You should not have critical aspects of your business with lower or significantly lower scores than other aspects. For example, if you are a service-based business and the Service Delivery Value Aspect is 1.1 but most of the other Value Aspects are 2.0 and above, you have a differential problem. You will need to figure out why your Service Delivery systems and processes are significantly lacking and therefore lagging. There is a point at which you simply cannot get to the next level if one or more aspects of your business are holding the others back.

For stage two, you simply average the maturity level of all the ten Value Aspects to determine the organization's overall maturity level or Business Maturity Index. Look to the BMI Graph below to see where your organization levels out (see Figure 5-11).

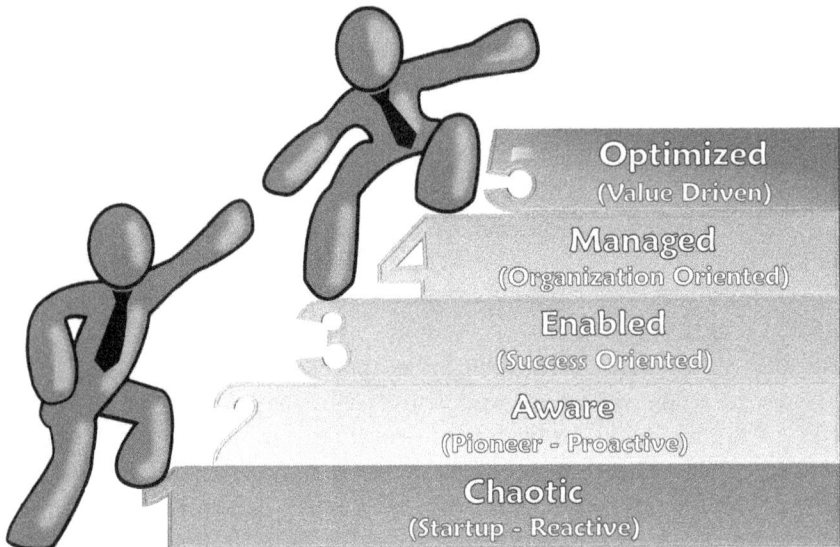

*Figure 5-11. Business Maturity Index Graph*

Don't get too excited or too depressed if you find your organization doesn't land where you think it should. There are tens of millions of businesses around the world and the overwhelming majority are in fact only at level 1 or 2. Think about it—If most businesses out there are sole proprietors or micro companies, how concerned with systems and processes are they? Your BMI is not a slight on you or your business, it is just a fair evaluat6.ion of your systems and processes. It takes a large, well-organized business with proper cash flow, revenue, and funding to build out level 5 systems and processes. However, it can be done by any size business if it is made the focus of the business roadmap and strategy. It can also be a great source of competitive advantage. Please look to Chapter 9 for a much more in-depth narrative on the BMI.

# BASE (Business Agile Strategy Execution)

This is the final tool to be presented and it has been saved until the end for specific reasons. This tool represents both the most powerful tool in its capabilities and the most complex tool in its application and use. Business Agile Strategy Execution is simply the synergetic melding of Business Strategy and Agile Execution into a formal process. Business Strategy refers to the business Roadmap & Strategy component of the Pyramid of Purpose and Value. Your Roadmap & Strategy is the plans and strategies for attaining objectives and goals with the intention of getting you and your business to the next level. Agile Execution refers to the Agile project management methodology which is the most modern process for developing applications and systems known. It allows for and encourages rapid execution on development.

What I propose is that after you break down your business Roadmap & Strategy into a logical order, there is no better way of executing on your plans than to implement Agile processes. In reality, your Roadmap & Strategy should already be logically organized into specific and time-bound goals, assuming you are utilizing the tools in your toolbox. And each of these goals should have largely been detailed with the measurable objectives required to attain those goals. The Agile methodology of execution intends to provide frequent iterations or versions of something, meaning continuous incremental improvement versus giant chunks or leaps of progress.

Why would you want little increments versus big steps? After all, you're trying to get to the next level, right? And those are big steps to climb. Remember the trick to eating an elephant? It's take one bite at a time. Agile lends itself well to small teams or even individuals with limited resources such as time. Most of the realistic plans for getting to the next level, although they can have big jumps, are more about the long play. Conversely, Agile also lends itself extremely well to large teams with ample resources.

As this is a concept of my own formulation that is not documented in any other text, I will refer you to Chapter 10 (Agile Execution) and Chapter 11 (Business Strategy Meets Agile Execution) for the complete detailed narrative of Agile and of the BASE process, but for the seeding of the concept and to help with comprehension, let's walk through a simple example of BASE.

Let's say your organization has identified three things that, if they can be accomplished this business year, will be the most relevant significant progress for the company, resulting in an increased competitive advantage over the closest competitor. For this example, let's say your business provides computer support and services. Your single greatest weakness and two biggest opportunities are:

1) Your service technicians are not tracking the time they spend fixing problems. You're losing money because you cannot bill the client for time that you cannot show you spent fixing things.

2) You need all of your technicians to be trained and certified on the new computer models being released next quarter. By having trained and certified technicians, you will receive exclusive referrals from the vendor for repairs on these new models.

3) The software you use to track customer requests for help has a new web-based version which allows for clients to use new chat and video help sessions. Your customers are already asking about these new technologies as options for getting technical support.

The strategy is simple: Get the technicians retrained and recommitted to logging all time, get them trained, and get the new application on line. But the actual breakdown of objectives, activities, and tasks turns out to be pretty long and detailed once written out. In fact it reads like a laundry list. From a time perspective, all of these goals overlap quite a bit too.

This is where Business Agile Strategy Execution comes in (see Figure 5-12). Agile allows you to break out the entire laundry list for each goal into bite-sized chunks that can be accomplished within a reasonable timeframe and within the constraints of your resources. Let's say the laundry list for each of the three goals is broken down into four chunks. Now you can assign the first chunk to an individual or group, and you can schedule it without overloading anyone or eating up too much time overall. One chunk at a time you, the members of the team, or the team together start to bite away at a chunk and incrementally make progress toward the goal.

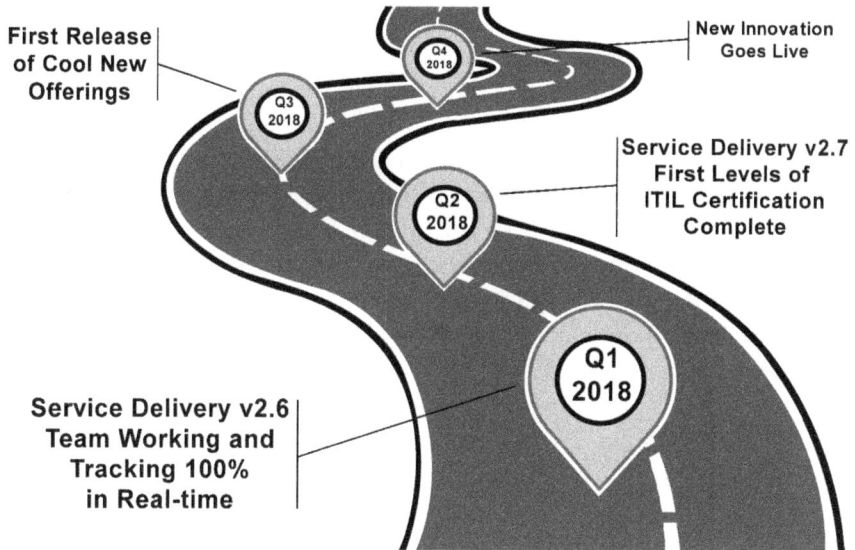

*Figure 5-12. Business Agile Strategy Execution*

Now to add one more important tie into some of the other tools discussed. If you look closely at the longer, more time-consuming and intricate of these strategies you're undertaking to get to the next level, it shouldn't be hard to see that these strategies must be clearly conveyed to everyone on the team and that they should be tied directly to creating value for the customer or value to the stakeholders. This is where a simple Strategy Map Theme and Balanced Scorecard tie in. You can get everyone on board and clearly define how their contribution is directly tied to the desired outcomes using the Strategy Map, and you can gauge your success as exhibited in the Balanced Scorecard.

This is just the low level introduction of the concept of Business Strategy combined with Agile Execution, intended to provide a very basic understanding. As with most of the material in this book, I intend to build on concepts as we move forward. To this end, as indicated previously, Chapter 10 (Agile Execution) and Chapter 11 (Business Strategy Meets Agile Execution) will provide a complete and much more detailed narrative of Agile and BASE. Before then, we will dive deep in the next chapter into the working of the Pyramid of Purpose and Value, including the Roadmap & Strategy. Beyond that is the chapter containing the Case Study and Example. By the time you reach the Case Study chapter, you should have a solid understanding of Business Agile Strategy Execution, with the example simply driving it home.

This closes out three consecutive chapters of tools for defining, analyzing, and refining your business. The discussion of many of these tools, while concise, will require an in-depth study before actually implementing them. My intention in introducing them was twofold. First, to present the most powerful tools I know of for defining, refining, and driving your business Roadmap & Strategy. Second, to show you that there are very specific tools to help you in ways you likely already know you need help, but perhaps did not realize that someone had already built the tool. Imagine what you could do if you systematically studied and implemented every tool in this tool box. I suspect it could very well help get you to the next level.

*Good business leaders create a vision, articulate the vision,*
*passionately own the vision, and relentlessly drive it to completion.*

– Jack Welch

# 6.0

# Pyramid of Purpose and Value – Culture

Everything written to this point has been in anticipation and support of the final two tools: The Pyramid of Purpose and Value; and the BASE of the pyramid, Business Agile Strategy Execution. These next three chapters will provide you with the specific details of how to design your pyramid from the top down. The three chapters following that—Business Maturity Index, Agile Execution, and Business Strategy Meets Agile Execution—will provide you with the tool for building your pyramid from the ground up. From there, you can begin driving the execution on strategy. Between design and build, you will have the opportunity to use every tool presented in the previous three chapters. This is in fact where we set our sails and get underway.

This tool has already been introduced in Chapter 1; some of that information is duplicated here although modified for the correct context and fully expanded. As I stated in Chapter 1, strategy planning and execution on the planned strategy are what will ultimately determine the success of any business. An essential component of execution is the ability to effectively convey the structure of the organization and the planned strategy. In these next three chapters I will fully detail the Pyramid of Purpose and Value and its use along with some closely related ancillary subjects.

I will show with detailed examples how to use the framework for defining each level of your pyramid from the top down and for presenting or sharing your Pyramid of Purpose and Value once completed. You will find that discussion for the top segment of the pyramid (Culture) is significantly longer than the other two (Compass, and Blueprint for Success). This is due to the fact that none of the tools previously laid out address creating your Vision, Mission, and Values or describing your Human Element; as such, the narrative required to guide you along in the right direction must be provided.

This tool, the Pyramid of Purpose and Value, is a simple framework for laying out and graphically depicting an organization's structure, strategy, and business identity. It is the representation of your organization's Micro Environment and everything within it. It is of great importance because it is the mechanism you will use to collect and convey everything about your organization's structure. Throughout this chapter I will tap into the example content from the case study subject company to help bring the pyramid to life. You can find the complete Case Study & Example in Chapter 12.

The choice to use the pyramid for business-related subjects in general is deep-seated in the mysteries of the seven wonders of the ancient world. The structure of the pyramid is used so often for the graphical depiction of an organization because it is considered the most resilient known to mankind and is in fact time proven. For my purposes, the shape and layers of the pyramid lend themselves to my belief that the most important components of a feasible, healthy, and well-balanced organization stack and interlock in a significant way. Each level of the pyramid from the top down must be designed and built solid enough to support all the levels above it.

The Pyramid of Purpose and Value includes elements of your business that are high level and esoteric such as the business Vison and Mission. These higher level elements are easily conveyed but not always easily translated into actions. The pyramid also includes elements that are as specific and detailed as the strategies and tactics you focus on every single day. These low level elements are hard to convey in simple terms but if properly laid out are easier to translate into actions. See Figure 6-1 as I provide an overview of each segment and section.

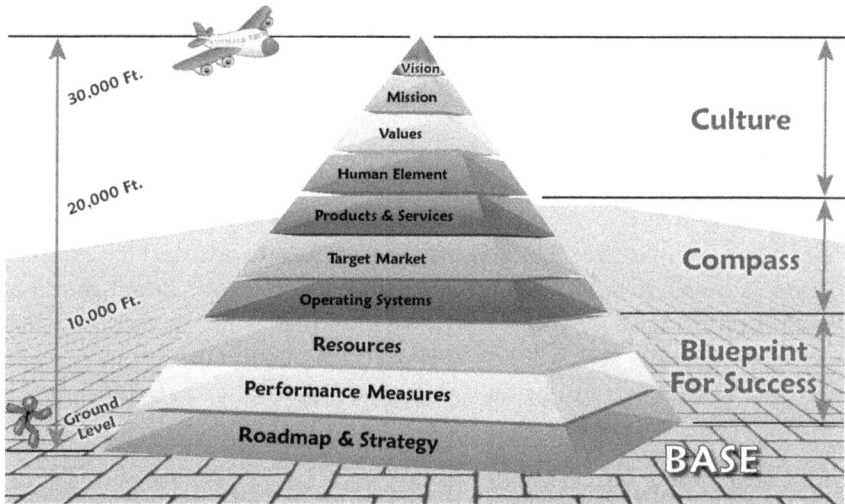

*Figure 6-1. The Pyramid of Purpose and Value*

At the lower levels are the things that are most tangible and interactive with the day-to-day operations of the organization when creating value for your clients. These are the things that can most quickly affect the long-term stability of the organization and its ability to support everything above it. As you move up the pyramid to higher levels, you move to things that are less tangible and more conceptual. These are the things that must be embedded and infused into everything you do so as to ensure and maintain unity of purpose.

Specific levels of the pyramid are grouped together into three segments that represent the outward facing definition of your business. These segments are your organization's Culture, Compass, and Blueprint for Success. First I will describe each of the three segments; then I will detail each segment one level at a time including examples.

The top segment of the pyramid defines your organization's Culture. It is the essence of what your organization is at its heart. It is the answer to the question of "Who are we?" You will notice it includes a special level called Human Element. The Human Element is not the same as the Human Resources aspect of your organization; it is much more. It is an expression of how you feel about the human element of your organization, and it is the clear parameters of what you want to cultivate for talent in the organization. It is strategically placed here because you must have the right people caring for and conveying the Vision, Mission, and Values of the organization. The Human Element is the single most valuable intangible asset the organization has and it is what couples your Culture with your Compass. The Human Element is also the single most powerful determinant of your success.

The middle segment of the pyramid defines the organization's Compass. It is the clear and well-defined direction the organization and business is headed. It is the needle that points you toward the horizon and it is the course you steer your ship along. It calls out not only what you will and will not offer for products and services, it also very specifically details who are and who are not your target markets in addition to defining your ideal customer. And finally, it specifies the tools and systems you will rely on to accomplish your ultimate goals, execute on strategy, and bring to life your vision; the shared vision.

The lower segment of the pyramid defines your Blueprint for Success. Each successive lower layer of the pyramid is more detailed than the one above it but none so specifically as the layers in this segment. This segment begins with the details of time, energy, money, and equipment required to create success. This segment is where the strategically directed actions of the organization are translated into measurable results. Here is where the Roadmap & Strategy are laid out and translated into Strategy Maps for clarification and Balanced Scorecards for success measurement. Every level of your pyramid must be carefully thought out and detailed, but these levels more directly determine your success than any others if properly focused and executed upon.

The Pyramid sits on a solid foundation or BASE. For our purposes, this BASE is the Business Agile Strategy Execution methodology used to execute every day on the most important elements of every aspect of your business in order to get it the next level. BASE is the wind in your sails. If your execution (BASE) is weak, you will not get anywhere. If there is no commitment to the purpose (Culture), you will not get anywhere. And worse, if you have committed to and are executing on as planned but you are off course (Compass), you will get nowhere fast. I will detail the Business Agile Strategy Execution methodology in Chapters 10 and 11.

Next I'm going to break down each level of the pyramid and provide some direction and instructions for how best to present the information each level is intended to convey. Remember that the pyramid is a simple framework for laying out and graphically representing the organization's overall business identity, structure, and strategy. I will present the examples of completed layers and segments just as I would if presenting this information to the team or to the stakeholders as a slide deck. You may choose to create an interactive website or even a flipbook style pamphlet. The level of detail for certain sections will of course need to be restricted depending on the audience. For example, you will not want to have specifics such as the Strategy Map available to those outside the organization. And likewise, you will not want to divulge finite details of your target market demographics to partners if it is not necessary.

## Your Organization's Culture

To build your Pyramid of Purpose and Value, you begin by designing it from the top down. As you will come to see, you cannot do it any other way. First you formulate or clarify the Vision of your endeavor. Then you cultivate the mission statement for how the Vision will come to be. Next you express your Values and the Values of the organization. Then you define what leadership and talent will be required to accomplish this Mission. This includes setting the landscape for the organizational culture (see Figure 6-2).

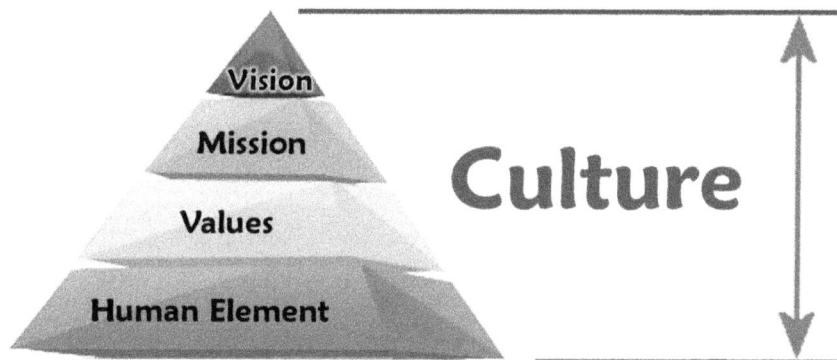

*Figure 6-2. Top Segment of The Pyramid*

## Vision

The Vision statement of the organization usually begins with the person or people who start the endeavor. They had some idea, some beautiful future vision for what the world could look like if they succeeded at creating their vision come true. They painted this very clear and enticing picture and told a compelling story. This is ideally where it all starts but as I've mentioned, it is most common in small and medium-sized businesses that although the entrepreneur had a vision or even a glimpse of a vision, they quickly moved forward with formulating a mission and strategy and never looked back. Those companies may very well have been around for years and they may very well have succeeded somewhat, but they will never get to the next level without a solid vision.

The vision of the organization should transcend time in that there should be no restriction from or bindings to timeframes. A good vision statement will outlive the founders, principals, and stakeholders. The vision statement should be embedded in everything the organization does so it can be seen by everyone who looks at the business. The vision statement should in fact help the person hearing the vision statement see the mental picture that is the business's shared vision. And last but of most importance, the Vision statement should inspire or at the very least make people imagine.

The statement should use clear and concise language that does not need dictionaries and definitions to understand. The best vision statements are very short and make big, bold statements. I encourage you to use organizational Values in expressing the shared vision if you already have honed in on them. After all, this is the intention, to get people excited about what you care about and what you would like to see come to fruition.

Examples of shared Vision statements:

**IKEA Corporation** – To create a better everyday life for the many people.

**The Goober Group (our example company)** – To empower business through Information Technology.

See Figure 6-3 and Figure 6-4 for the narrative version and graphic version of the Vision statement, respectively.

Figure 6-3. *Vision Statement*

Figure 6-4. *Vision Statement Graphic*

Don't get me wrong when I say that failure to have some form of vision is failure in itself. You must have struck out on your own or put together this endeavor for some reason. There must be some picture you formulated in your mind of how you doing what you do better than anyone else would look. It's understandable to say you don't know how to translate it into words or how to express it. And if that is the case then get with a mastermind group or your team and start brainstorming. Come up with something and refine it as time goes on, but don't keep going without one.

If you really don't have a vision and you really cannot come up with one, we already know you certainly can proceed (or continue) to do business and grow some big, beautiful thing. But I promise you, you will not go as far or as fast as you will with a clear and concise vision. There is an old saying that if you want to go fast, go alone but if you want to go far, go together. Vision is what binds people together. Without it you will keep finding yourself going alone.

## Mission

The Mission statement is a short to medium-term statement of intention. The power of intention is that which makes things happen. The Mission statement explains what the business intends to do to realize the Vision of the organization. Unlike the Vision statement, the Mission statement is often something that can be measured in some fashion, something tangibly attainable. Because the Mission statement can actually be attained, it can and often should change depending on the strategy and goals of the organization.

It is very common for organizations to interchangeably use the term vision and mission and to only have one statement. In the corporations of old, there is usually a Vision statement that sits on a plaque in the halls and is on letterhead, and it has been there for a hundred years. Meanwhile, the Mission statement is embedded into the strategy and corporate reports and is revised whenever the business model is revised or new management comes in.

Many organizations create only a single (usually more Visionary) statement to share with the world. I'm going to say it's okay to have only one statement and to refer to it as your Mission or as your Vision as long as it exists and it gets people excited and onboard, but they are not the same and you should have both. I will also say I do not believe it is that hard to formulate both for the best clarity of this most important endeavor—your business. As with the Vision statement, if you need to borrow someone's imagination to get it formulated, then do so.

On the supporting side of having both a Vision and Mission, let's take a closer look at IKEA's shared Vision and their supporting business ideas (Mission statements). As shown previously, their Vision is "To create a better everyday life for the many people." If you look at their website, you will also see their two supporting ideas:

The Business Idea – We shall offer a wide range of well-designed, functional home furnishing products at prices so low that as many people as possible will be able to afford them.

The Human Resource Idea – To give down-to-earth, straight-forward people the possibility to grow, both as individuals and in their professional roles, so that together we are strongly committed to creating a better everyday life for ourselves and our customers.

These are followed by two additional clarifying statements:
- It takes a dream to create a successful business idea.
- It takes people to make dreams a reality.

I will say I love how they have put their shared Vision together and how they have tied it into their business's Values and Mission. I wonder if this has anything to do with their global success.

Example Mission statements:

**IKEA Corporation** – We shall offer a wide range of well-designed, functional home furnishing products at prices so low that as many people as possible will be able to afford them.

**The Goober Group (our example company)** – Our mission is to enable your company to focus on its core business and operate smoothly because we focus on the technology as our core business.

See Figure 6-5 and Figure 6-6 for the narrative version and graphic version of the Mission statement, respectively.

When you are creating your Mission statement, be certain that what you set out as your stated mission actually supports your Vision. This might sound a bit unnecessary to state but trust me, if the stated mission doesn't actually support the Vision, you are already off course.

**Mission**

{ Our mission is to enable your company to focus on its core business and operate smoothly because we focus on the technology as our core business }

*Figure 6-5. Mission Statement*

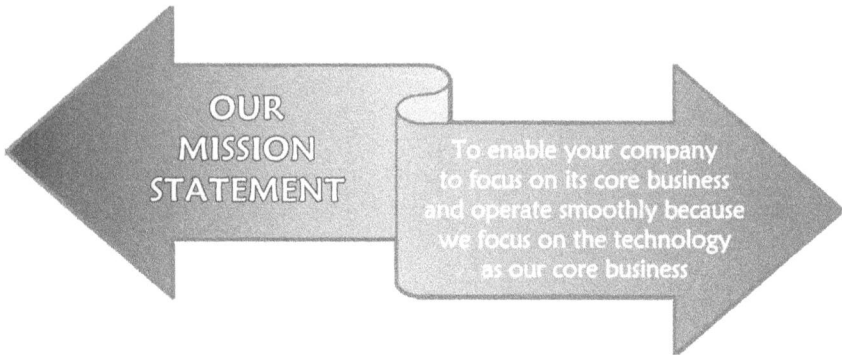

OUR MISSION STATEMENT

To enable your company to focus on its core business and operate smoothly because we focus on the technology as our core business

*Figure 6-6. Mission Statement Banner*

## Values

Nothing becomes more transparent than your stated shared Values as an organization. You may firmly believe that you are living up to them, but if the perception from the outside world is that you are in fact not, it's very hard to defend. After all, we are who we are every day, as an individual and as an organization. If you demonstrate significantly different values than what you publicize, people will call you on it. Ask Walmart—They have been running for years from the persona that they are just a big boxmart trying to make huge profits while exploiting their employees, a reality that is in stark contrast to the founder's stated vision and values. And they have embarked on multi-million dollar campaigns to fix this persona. I have a bit more to say on this subject, but I will save it for the closing of this segment.

You may recall from Chapter 3 the tool known as the McKinsey 7S Framework, developed by Tom Peters and Robert Waterman and discussed in their book *In Search of Excellence*. One of the key conclusions they came to in their search for excellence and discussed in the book was that "Every excellent company we studied is clear on what it stands for, and takes the process of value shaping seriously. In fact we wonder whether it is possible to be an excellent company without clarity on values and without having the right sort of values." Peters and Robert Waterman's conclusion is engrained in their 7S model. At the center of that model is the Shared Value of the organization which everything else around it must be in balance with. I believe they drive it home best with their qualifying statement that how strongly the people in the organization believe in and faithfully carry out the basic precepts transcends the success realized through effective leverage of technology, economic resources, organization structure, innovation, or even timing.

Defining your values is not easy and in my opinion, it's actually harder than coming up with a Vision statement. To get started, you should look closely at your Vision and Mission statements and consider what passion they elicit in you. What values do you hold at your personal core? What values would you like to ensure are built into the organization? Get help from your mastermind group or your circle of council. And don't be afraid to try some values on and see how they fit. Remember, you are free to change your Vision, Mission, and Values as you see appropriate as a fledgling company. You do want to settle in to fixed ideals at some point, but no one expects you to nail it on the first try. In fact, some organizations sit down with the kick-off team and formulate the values based on those core people and the intended vision.

Whatever values you pick, they must be sustainable in that the people in the organization can actually affect them directly with their day-to-day actions and work product. I would highly recommend not using short, one-word values that somehow put people directly on the spot for the organization. Putting values like honesty and ethics up front can really be hard for the average worker to feel they have any control over considering the behemoth organization they stand behind. It's not that these are not valid or admirable values, but the average worker is going to feel heavily pressured if they are expected to be the custodians of the organization's honesty and ethics. It's quite another, more realistic thing to ask them to be custodians of quality work or care for the environment. Let's look at IKEA first and then look at the Values statement for our example company, The Goober Group.

Example of IKEA's Shared Values from their website:

## IKEA Corporation

- Humbleness and willpower – Our managers try to set a good example, and expect the same of IKEA co-workers.
- Leadership by example – Our managers try to set a good example, and expect the same of IKEA co-workers.
- Daring to be different – We question old solutions and, if we have a better idea, we are willing to change.
- Togetherness and enthusiasm – Together, we have the power to solve seemingly unsolvable problems. We do it all the time.
- Cost-consciousness – Low prices are impossible without low costs, so we proudly achieve good results with small resources.
- Constant desire for renewal – Change is good. We know that adapting to customer demands with innovative solutions saves money and contributes to a better everyday life at home.
- Accept and delegate responsibility – We promote co-workers with potential and stimulate them to surpass their expectations. Sure, people make mistakes. But they learn from them!

## The Goober Group (our example company)

See Figure 6-7 and Figure 6-8 for the narrative version and the starburst version of the Values statement, respectively.

**Values**

**Integrity** – We are who our clients think we are and we strive to be worthy of their partnership.
**Passion** – We look to the inner driver of individuals to do what they love to do the best they possibly can.
**Knowledge** – We leverage information by encouraging people's innate desire to know more.
**Experience** – We cultivate our core competencies through crowdsourcing of skills, each of which relies on the mastery of the individual.
**Collaboration** – We love to share and grow ideas any way we can for the continued development of our ability to better service our customers every day.
**Stewardship** – We care about things beyond our arm's reach - the community, the environment, the world.

*Figure 6-7. Values Statement*

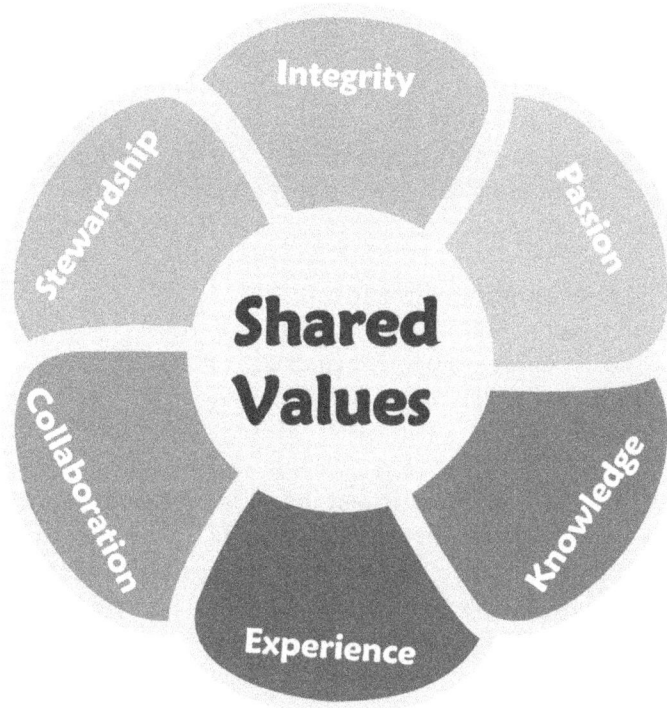

*Figure 6-8. Values Statement Starburst*

I would like to point out how easy it was for me to find IKEA's Vision, Mission, and Values. In my research for this book, I thought of many of the great statements I have heard over the years from companies like Microsoft, Apple, Nike, and so on. But actually finding the complete and concise Vision, Mission, and Values statements for any of them is not as easy as it was for IKEA. I believe IKEA holds these elements of their business identity to be extremely important, not only to the company itself but to anyone who looks at them, because they made certain it was easy to find these statements in the most prominent place they could. When you go to look for any organization's Vision, Mission, and Values statements, how easy are they to find? How important is it to that organization to share them with you?

I would also like to highlight one of the Values called out by our example company, The Goober Group:

Stewardship – We care about things beyond our arms' reach—the community, the environment, the world.

This represents a common thread in many organizations to realize that there are cultural requirements for us all to be concerned about, more than just ourselves. This example Value is drawn directly from the book *Focus: The Hidden Driver of Excellence*. In the book, author and psychologist Daniel Goleman talks about how leaders should have three important focuses that, when woven together, properly become a hidden driver of excellence.

Goleman points out these three focuses:
- Inner focus: The Culture and Climate in the company.
- Other Focus: Competitive landscape we are in.
- Outer Focus: The larger realities that shape the environment the outfit operates in.

Just as with the Mission statement formulation, be certain that the Values you call out here can actually be aligned with the Mission and Vision statements. If they cannot, you are not only off course, but you will also find coupling the Culture of the organization with the Compass to be exceptionally hard. If the people you bring on cannot make the connection, you lose significant power of clarity.

## Human Element

What is the Human Element? It is the most valuable intangible asset of any organization. The Human Element is the actuator, custodian, and perpetuator of the organization's culture. It is the single most powerful determinant of success for a healthy and viable business. Only with a healthy company culture can an organization truly focus on next level innovation.

Let me explain and clarify the Human Element. In business, people are considered resources because they are in fact the brains and the brawn of the operation. In today's global industries, brawn means everything from the individuals assembling the robots to the individuals programming and oiling them. We have a ways to go before there is no more heavy lifting whatsoever required in making a business run. The business function that deals with managing the recruitment, pay and discharging, etc. of people is formally called Human Resources. The Human Element is the innate skills, talent, emotion, drive, and culture that only come from humans. The Human Element is what gives the organization's Values meaning and it is the driving force that makes the Mission valid.

A corporation is equipment, inputs, specifications, criteria, requirements, and strategy. The human element is the driver. It is only through the application of the Human Element that all of this comes alive. A corporation is not a person, it's a machine filled with people, and it only appears to be alive for the sake of the Human Element. Considering a corporation to be a person is tantamount to offering a certificate of live birth to a robot running artificial intelligence software. Even here, it is only the Human Element that gives this creation the possibility of being considered truly alive. The corporation is the machine and the Human Element is the life force within.

When discussing the direct links and relationships of the intangible assets (Drivers) such as culture, leadership, knowledge, and teamwork to the desired value (Outcomes) for customer and stakeholders, it is only through the presence of the Human Element that these can happen. It involves the entire spectrum of human activities performed by the many and various teams, departments, and units of the organization. It encompasses and embraces anything that positively influences the effective interaction between a human and any other human, system, or machine. It is also what melds the Culture segment of the pyramid and organization to the Compass Segment.

This may be one of the hardest components of your pyramid, of your business identity, to put into words. As with the other elements, it is not impossible and you should carefully consider what you do put down. Luckily I have some great examples to help guide you. In fact, there is nothing in the world to keep you from taking the inspirational ideas and statements you find here (or anywhere for that matter) and incorporating them as your own if they truly resonate with you. After all, it's highly likely that any time the Human Element is discussed, the terms used will be very common and easily transferable to any organization that finds these traits important to their own success.

The Human Element is the intangible asset that couples the Culture with the Compass and drives the business Blueprint for Success. So how exactly are you supposed to define the Human Element for your organization? It all sounds so esoteric and imaginary. The answer is actually fairly simple. Consider who you want in the organization to run and operate this business—what type of people. I would encourage you to always and only select the best people you can find and people you actually like. They travel long distances together better than those who do not carry their own weight and do not get along with others.

Two slices of inspiration before I move on to the examples. First, one of my favorite executives and management masters Lawrence (Larry) Bossidy, former CEO of Allied Signal, made this qualifying statement more than twenty years ago: "I am convinced that nothing we do is more important than hiring and developing people. At the end of the day, you bet on people, not on strategies. Strategies are intellectually simple; their execution is not." And second, the professor and management consultant W. Edwards Deming said, "Research shows that the climate of an organization influences an individual's contribution far more than the individual himself."

How better to cultivate the best environment for people to succeed in than to endear to the Human Element and seed it with the right ideas and mindset? Culture and Compass come from the top of an organization and if left unseeded and uncultivated, your organization will get what grows from the bottom up, and you may not like what you get.

So let's look at some seeds for your Culture and inspiration for your Human Element, starting with the company Zappos. Among the Family Core Values that Zappos has posted on the website is the following: Create Fun and A Little Weirdness. I have no problem listing this as a core value, but tell me this is not a call to the Human Element they wish to draw to their teams and to bring into their family. I absolutely love it, and I have no doubt it is one of the elements of success for Zappos simply because it draws a certain kind of person to not just apply to work there but actually really want to work there.

Now let's take a peek at Google's How We Hire web page. It simply states, "There's no one kind of Googler, so we're always looking for people who can bring new perspectives and life experiences to our teams. If you're looking for a place that values your curiosity, passion, and desire to learn, if you're seeking colleagues who are big thinkers eager to take on fresh challenges as a team, then you're a future Googler." This is the Human Element statement for Google. Yes, it directly incorporates many of their values, but it is undoubtedly put together to illicit something more than a strict "We only hire the best so if you're the best" mantra of days gone by.

Let's look at IKEA one more time and then look at the Human Element statement for our example company, The Goober Group.

IKEA calls out two components on two separate pages of their website:

### IKEA's Working Here Page - A positive team spirit
- We're a diverse group of down-to-earth, straightforward people with a passion for home furnishing. We come from all over the world but we share an inspiring vision: "to create a better everyday life for the many people". How we realize this vision is based on our shared humanistic values. These values are the foundation of our work and our inclusive, empathizing, open and honest culture.
- Working with us is like working with your friends. Our culture is based on the spirit of togetherness, enthusiasm and fun. And we're always looking for people who share our positive attitude and values

### IKEA's Culture Page - Work hard, be yourself
- An ability to do the job is obviously the starting point. But beyond that we look for many other personal qualities such as a strong desire to learn, the motivation to continually do things better, simplicity and common sense, the ability to lead by example, efficiency and cost-consciousness. These values are important to us because our way of working is less structured than that of many other organizations.

### The Goober Group (our example company) Human Element
See Figure 6-9 and Figure 6-10 for the narrative version and word cloud version of the Human Element statement, respectively.

One last reminder—Your Human Element statement is the last piece of the top segment of the pyramid, and what you call out for to seed the organization's culture had better align directly to the Values stated previously. It should be easy for anyone in the organization to draw a direct line from any of the Human Element statements up through the Values, up through the Mission, and truthfully say that they can see the direct connection. Each level of the pyramid supports the levels above it.

## Human Element

**We** strive to seed our company with what we believe are core principles of Unity because we know that harmony enables excellence and excellence coupled with our Values, Mission, and Vision will allow us to become the best we can be.

**We** demand emotional fortitude to accept points of view that are not our own because it allows us to deal with conflict and it gives us the confidence to encourage and accept challenges.

**We** rely on truth over harmony as the candor helps discourage the silent vetoes that stall initiatives and cause rework.

**We** encourage Authenticity (Keeping it real), Self-Awareness (Know ourselves), Self-Mastery (Expanding ourselves), and Humility (Containing our ego).

**We** look for people who believe in the potential of our Vision because if they believe then it will be realized.

*Figure 6-9. Human Element Statement*

*Figure 6-10. Human Element Statement Word Cloud*

I have spent a significant amount of time just on the top of the pyramid—the Culture—but I maintain that this is required for your organization to get off to the right start and to have a chance at true sustainability and longevity. If you are revamping your organization, it's no different. You must get this part right or you will suffer deeply for it. Yes, it will be a work in progress for a while and you may start out with minimal design, but you can never let up until it is done and done right.

I also know that I have placed more quotes and external references in this single section of the book than in any single chapter if not the remainder of the book. This is because I need to drive this theory of Culture and all of its components, especially the Human Element, solidly home for the sake of your business. I have included these specific quotes so you can see this is not all just fodder of my imagination. Every one of the top management professionals and masters I know of also hold this to be true.

In the book *In Search of Excellence*, Peters and Waterman developed a thesis based on their research that includes this simple statement: "I believe if an organization is to meet the challenge of a changing world, it must be prepared to change everything about itself except those beliefs as it moves through corporate life." In his book *Good To Great*, Jim Collins stated that one of the most revealing results of his research into companies that did in fact make the jump from good to great indicated the leaders were hyper-focused on "getting the right people on the bus … in the right seats." Only then would they begin to decide the direction of the business. They prioritized the Human Element well above and in front of the strategic planning.

## Culture Crosscheck

Getting your culture right is just the beginning. Once you have built this crucial and pivotal piece of the pyramid, you have to diligently protect it, and that may mean making very hard choices as the organization grows. There are forces which are very strong that will work against your culture in ways you may not have realized they could. One specifically is the greed for money by those forcing the profit motive in front of the purpose motive. This can only happen if the culture of the organization is compromised or wholesale abandoned.

As your business grows and other stakeholders and principals are allowed in at the top level, their desire for money may influence decisions; this can compromise or undermine the culture of the organization. If your business ever goes public (becomes a publicly traded entity), it will subsequently have shareholders to which the organization would have a legal obligation to above and in front of everything else in the organization, including the culture. The board of directors' decisions can in fact compromise or undermine the culture of the organization.

If your business never goes public and you never share the stakeholder role, you will never have to allow the profit motive to get in front of the purpose motive if you choose not to. Of course just because you do take on shared stakeholders or the organization goes public, it still does not mean that the profit motive will get placed in front of the purpose motive, provided it is protected and cared for. Your culture has a chance to be championed and prevail if you have in fact woven your values and beliefs into the Vision, Mission, Values, and Human Element of the organization. With this in place, it can hold up against these forces even after you are gone or no longer the only one steering the company. Walmart here is the antithesis.

The founder of Walmart, Sam Walton, began writing a book *Sam Walton: Made in America* which would unfortunately not be released until after he passed away. In the book, Walton clearly describes his belief in why Walmart was still around while 76 of the 100 other discounters were all gone. He calls out specifically caring for his customers first by caring for his employees:

> "They were bright stars for a moment, and then they faded. I started thinking about what really brought them down, and why we kept going. It all boils down to not taking care of their customers, not minding their stores, not having folks in their stores with good attitudes, and that was because they never really even tried to take care of their own people. If you want the people in the stores to take care of the customers, you have to make sure you're taking care of the people in the stores. That's the most important single ingredient of Wal-Mart's success."

Today, Walmart boasts "Our Story." Not their Vision, Mission, Values, or Human Element, but rather their Story as "Innovative thinking. Leadership through service. And above all, an unwavering commitment to saving people money. It's what makes us the business we are today, and shapes the company we will be tomorrow."

The "take care of the customer" components of Mr. Walton's beliefs are certainly in the statement, but it says nothing about the "most important single ingredient," taking care of the people in the stores. If we look at the exhibited behavior of the organization, it's easy to clearly see a long and sullied history of issues involving low wages, grim working conditions, inadequate healthcare options, anti-union stands, and even misogyny. Those who have inherited and carried forward the organization since Walton's passing certainly have created the business they want—low costs above all.

If Sam Walton wanted his "most important single ingredient" to be endeared to, to permeate all the way to the bottom levels of the organization and to resonate throughout, he probably should have embedded these specific beliefs into the culture. But because these core beliefs are nowhere in sight, they had no chance of survival, even if there were people in the organization after Walton passed on who wanted to protect and care for them. Price point is after all a competitive strategy, and if you are the definitive price leaders, you have a competitive advantage and a powerful one at that. But in Walmart's case, does it come at the wholesale cost of Sam Walton's core belief? Are you building a Walmart or an IKEA, Google, or Zappos? You get to decide. The top segment is the most visible piece of your pyramid and it will be seen by more people than you can imagine or may realize. It must not only look right, it must be designed and built to withstand the test of time. Each level of the pyramid must be solid enough in its design and structure to support all the levels above it. Protect the Human Element because it supports the Values. The Values support the Mission, and the Mission supports the Vision. Problems at the Human Element level will cause problems all the way up to and including the Vision.

I don't have a problem with you choosing to embed or weave your Human Element into your Vision, Mission, and Strategy versus having it be a level all its own. Just don't forget that the Human Element is in fact what couples the Culture with the Compass. And without a Compass, you will certainly get off course.

Required Reading:

Simon Sinek – *Start with Why: How Great Leaders Inspire Everyone to Take Action*

Daniel H. Pink – *Drive: The Surprising Truth about What Motivates Us*

Jim Collins – *Good to Great: Why Some Companies Make the Leap… And Others Don't*

Larry Bossidy and Ram Charan – *Execution: The Discipline of Getting Things Done*

Thomas Peters and Robert Waterman – *In Search of Excellence: Lessons from America's Best-run Companies*

Peter F. Drucker – *The Essential Drucker: The Best of Sixty Years of Peter Drucker's Essential Writings on Management*

*The man who will use his skill and constructive imagination to
see how much he can give for a dollar, instead of how little he can
give for a dollar, is bound to succeed.*

– Henry Ford

# 7.0

## PYRAMID OF PURPOSE AND VALUE – COMPASS

### Your Organization's Compass

Once you have completed the top levels of the pyramid (Culture segment), then can you begin imagining and innovating the Products & Services you wish to offer for your value proposition. With your proposed Products and Service line card filled out, you now can begin to identify your ideal Target Market and determine the Operating Systems that you will need to present these Products and Services to that Target Market (see Figure 7-1).

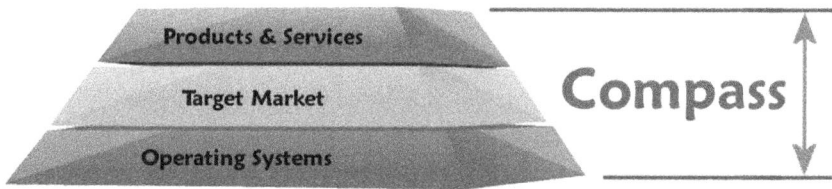

*Figure 7-1. Middle Segment of The Pyramid*

### Products & Services

Now we come to the first tangible elements of the business—the products and services that will make up the value proposition offered to potential customers. The only thing that might make this difficult is properly categorizing your products and services in a logical fashion that can be presented clearly and easily. If you are running a bead shop or supermarket, you probably have thousands of products to list. If you provide plumbing services, it may be a significantly shorter list.

A Product or Service Line Card (digital or print) is a brochure for sales and marketing purposes which lists every product and service you offer and may include some pricing information. Although you will need to create and maintain a Product or Service Line Card, this is not the place for the entire brochure.

For this level of the pyramid, you should present the most prominent offerings that represent the focus of your core business. You would present your flagship products or services and may mention the supporting or related offerings only to the extent they represent a significant piece of the value proposition. You would not list or represent lesser products or services that are not a relevant revenue center or do not somehow link to a significant customer stickiness (attraction) factor. You would also emphasize any specific products or services that you would like to be known for.

If you have strategic partnerships with vendors, you would want to exhibit the logo for these companies and possibly include a partnership statement if appropriate. A strategic partnership is one in which the association with the other organization creates a solid connection to some component of value and usually with the intention of gaining a competitive advantage. The partnership could be exclusive or non-exclusive. Most often you choose to partner with a vendor to access upstream value and infuse components they offer into your products and services in order to create a greater value for your customers. The vendor partner may gain exposure for their brand (if you show it off), or they may simply gain access to your target market as an opportunity to sell more products through your use or resale of them. It is also common for the customer organization to gain access to the target market of the vendor if the vendor shows those companies that use their products or services. The possibilities and combinations are vast. Refer back to the Value Chain and the discussion of the larger Value System.

When considering strategic supplier partnerships to showcase, do not list here the solution provider of the equipment or products you use to actually create your products or deliver your services. For example, if you ran a restaurant, you would list your exclusive local Farm-to-Table produce supplier because it represents a strategic partnership with a food producer. That producer may also likely boast that they are the exclusive provider of your restaurant's produce. This adds to the value proposition because those who find value in eating at wholesome restaurants would recognize both local establishments and their partnership as favorable.

However, you would not likely list the computer program you use to track table seating, reservations, and wait lists. The computer program you use to track these things, however critical to your operation, does not necessarily add to the value proposition unless somehow you can show it magically reduces wait time for the customer. Perhaps if it allowed for online reservations, changes, and wait time updates like an airline flight status, you might then just boast the use of this application. Regardless, those things that support the delivery of your products and services but are not the actual product or services being sold or delivered would be listed below in the Operating Systems level of the pyramid, if appropriate.

I'm going to provide a few more examples for clarification before I move on. If you are running a Dry Cleaning service, you might exhibit the brand of the environmentally safe chemical you use, but you would not likely note the vendor for your hangers unless there is some specific feature that adds value as perceived by the customer, such as reusable plastic versus the thin metal ones everyone recycles or throws away. For our IT Services Provider example company, they may choose to exhibit the Antivirus solution they use to protect computers from malicious attacks. They would do this only because the Antivirus vendor is a well-known brand name company and pointing out their association with such a vendor would be a valuable market attractant due to the vendor being readily recognized and trusted. Potential customers who favor this Antivirus solution may look favorably on IT Service Providers who employ this solution and they may even prefer to only work with providers who employ this solution. On the other hand, if the IT Service Provider would like to reserve the ability to change Antivirus solutions without affecting their market attraction based on the Brand name of the solution they use, they would not list it here.

Now for a look at our example company, The Goober Group. The Goober Group is a technology company that provides products and services to businesses to support their information technology (IT) infrastructure. The correct term for their primary offerings is Information Technology Service Management ITSM. They are what is known as an IT Solution Provider because they build solutions to meet ITSM needs. We're going to look closely at the specific Products and Service they choose to offer (see Figure 7-2). They start with the short, concise, but big and bold Value Proposition statement. Every organization should be able to stand up and state what their value proposition is in a way that garners attention. If you cannot or are not willing to, you are never going to be number one or even close to it. Think of those taglines and slogans you see that get your attention; they are that business's big, bold statement.

Next let's look at their flagship Managed Service Offering, The Goober Group Goober Care™ Service Offerings (see Figure 7-3). And finally, let's look at The Goober Group Product Offerings (see Figure 7-4).

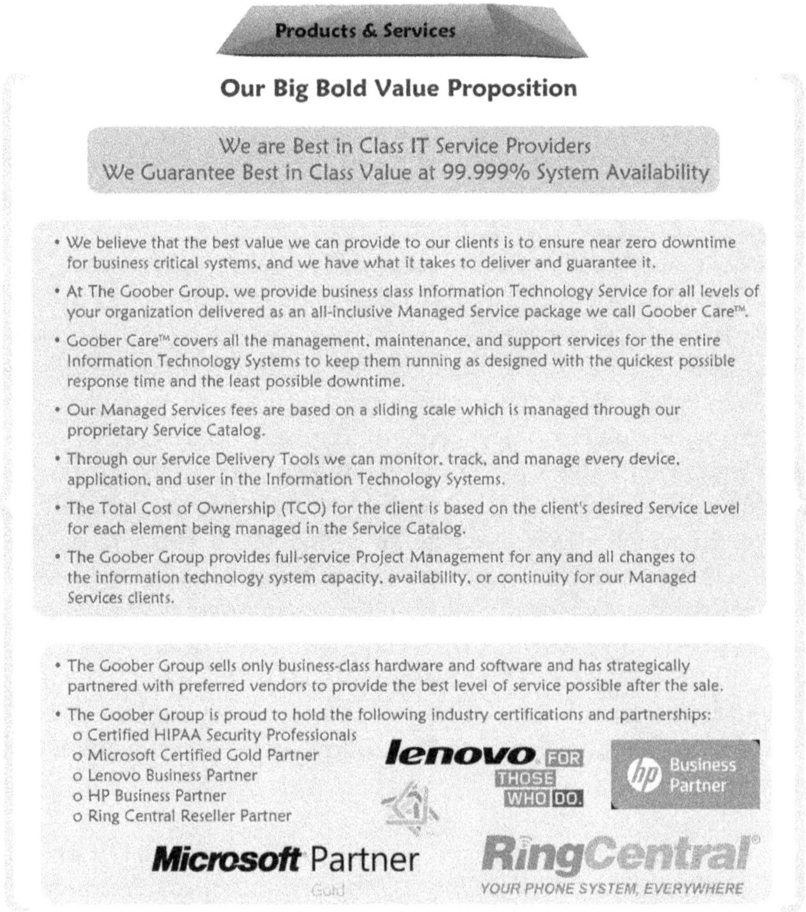

**Products & Services**

**Our Big Bold Value Proposition**

We are Best in Class IT Service Providers
We Guarantee Best in Class Value at 99.999% System Availability

- We believe that the best value we can provide to our clients is to ensure near zero downtime for business critical systems, and we have what it takes to deliver and guarantee it.
- At The Goober Group, we provide business class Information Technology Service for all levels of your organization delivered as an all-inclusive Managed Service package we call Goober Care™.
- Goober Care™ covers all the management, maintenance, and support services for the entire Information Technology Systems to keep them running as designed with the quickest possible response time and the least possible downtime.
- Our Managed Services fees are based on a sliding scale which is managed through our proprietary Service Catalog.
- Through our Service Delivery Tools we can monitor, track, and manage every device, application, and user in the Information Technology Systems.
- The Total Cost of Ownership (TCO) for the client is based on the client's desired Service Level for each element being managed in the Service Catalog.
- The Goober Group provides full-service Project Management for any and all changes to the information technology system capacity, availability, or continuity for our Managed Services clients.

- The Goober Group sells only business-class hardware and software and has strategically partnered with preferred vendors to provide the best level of service possible after the sale.
- The Goober Group is proud to hold the following industry certifications and partnerships:
  o Certified HIPAA Security Professionals
  o Microsoft Certified Gold Partner
  o Lenovo Business Partner
  o HP Business Partner
  o Ring Central Reseller Partner

**lenovo** FOR THOSE WHO DO.          **hp** Business Partner

**Microsoft** Partner
Gold

**RingCentral**
YOUR PHONE SYSTEM, EVERYWHERE

*Figure 7-2. The Goober Group Value Proposition*

**Products & Services**

## The Goober Group Goober Care™ Service Offerings

- **Managed Services**
  - o Service Level Management
  - o ITSM Finance Management

- **Business Continuity**
  - o Policy Compliance
  - o Security & Risk Management
  - o Backup Management
  - o Disaster Recovery
  - o Continuity Planning

- **Project Management**
  - o Capacity Management
  - o Availability Management
  - o Continuity Management

- **Help Desk**
  - o Incident Management
  - o Self Help
  - o Customer Chat (Text, Audio, Video)
  - o Best Practices

- **Field Service**
  - o Problem Management
  - o Solutions Training
  - o Onsite Remediation

- **Network Administration**
  - o Asset Lifecycle Management
  - o Change Management
  - o Configuration Management
  - o Release Management

- **Network Operations**
  - o Remote Monitoring
  - o Event Management
  - o Patch Management
  - o Automated Remediation

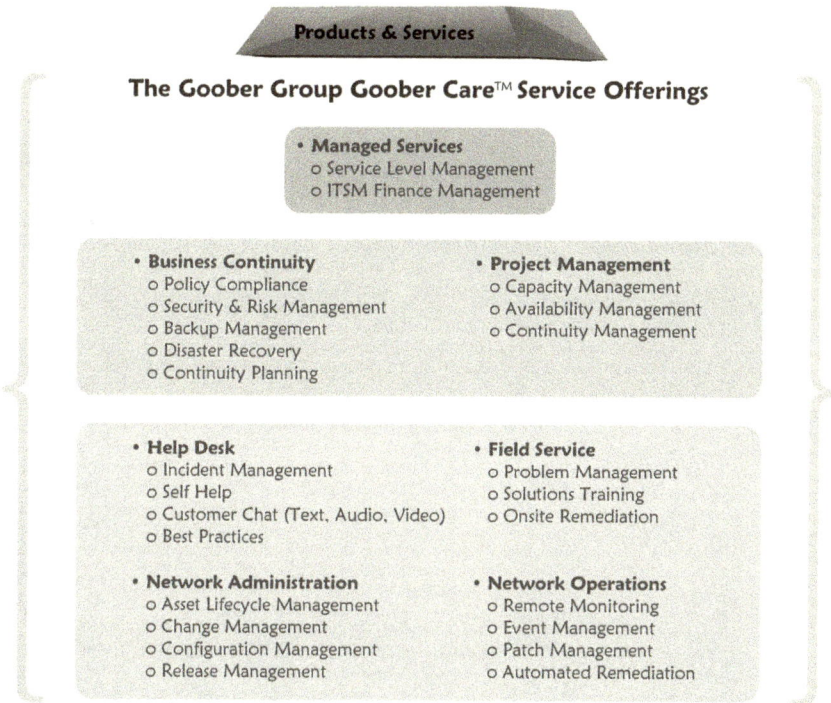

*Figure 7-3. Goober Care™ Service Offerings*

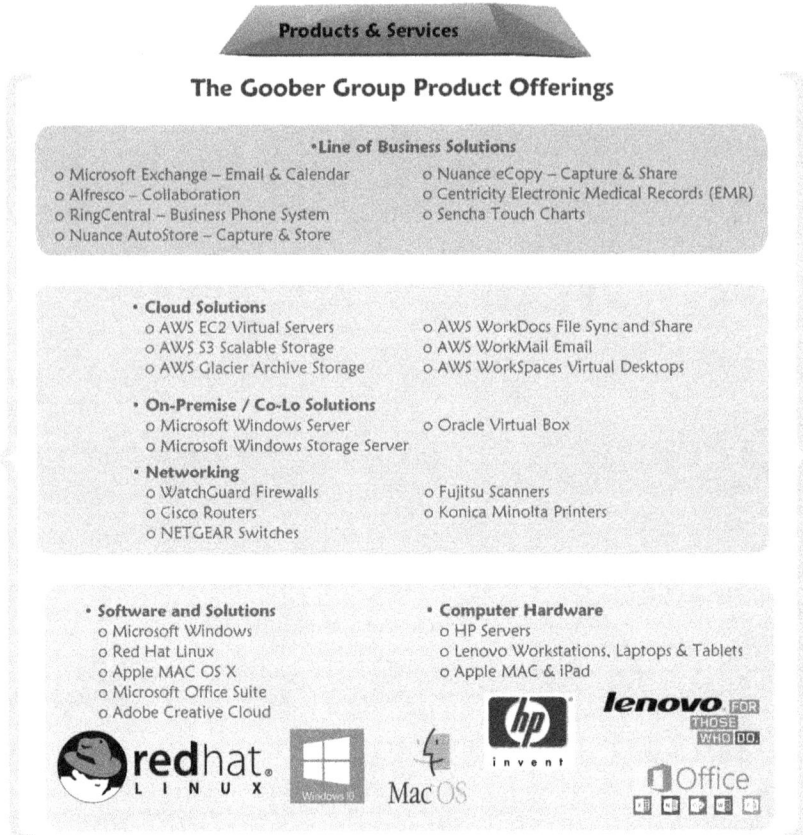

*Figure 7-4. Goober Group Product Offerings*

Services are listed first because Information Technology Service Management is The Goober Group's primary offering. Products are listed second because as a Solutions Provider, all the products they sell or resell are just the building blocks for the solution they present to the customer to meet their IT needs. Every product and service listed here can be directly linked to the targeted primary needs or desires of the customer, in this case their IT needs and desires, and therefore represent (individually or combined) a value proposition.

Every product listed is specifically called out by brand and name because there is some benefit to associating The Goober Group with these specific products. Many of these vendors are strategic partners and others are recognized brands. Some of the products listed represent a strategic advantage in that they are particular to the Target Market and Ideal Customer. This product focus creates a vertical market targeted by the organization in order to create a competitive advantage. I will cover more about these benefits of association, strategic partnerships, and strategic and competitive advantages in the Target Market, Operating Systems, and the Roadmap & Strategy levels.

Because the example used here is so technical, I would like to add one simple example for clarification. If the example company were a restaurant, this list would be constructed essentially the same but it would be broken down into menu fare—Seafood, Grill, Salads, etc.—and it would list signature dishes and their main attraction points such as the unique ingredients which make it different from other restaurants. Services would also be quite similar but would list Online Seating Selection, Outdoor Roof Top Dining, Dance Floor, Valet Parking, and so on.

Notice that there is no pricing on the products and services in this list. This is not the line card and it is not for advertising or marketing purposes. All of the concerns over pricing are addressed in the feasibility study, business plan, product lifecycle planning, target market analysis, and so on. Pricing is discussed extensively in the lower levels of the pyramid where you must be concerned with the costs of resources and margins on revenue, but it normally has no purpose here.

## Target Market

There are two components being defined in this section: the Target Market, and the Ideal Customer. The two are not the same and only one of these two sets of criteria can be researched—the Target Market. You have been introduced to all of the tools you need to determine where your products and services should best be received and valued. There are no guarantees, of course, but once you start doing business and moving into the selected market, you will find out relatively quickly if you are paying attention to the market's response to these offerings. Hopefully you already have estimated numbers for expected penetration over the first quarter, second, and throughout the coming year so that you will be able to adjust accordingly. Let's start with the already pretty well understood Target Market and then move on to the Ideal Customer (The Box).

If you recall, the Target Market is carved out of the Serviceable Available Market (SAM) and represents very specifically who you believe would find value in your offerings. Your Target Market should be defined as specifically as possible and it should identify the Primary and Secondary segments. The primary market is where the bulk of your marketing and advertisement is aimed. The secondary market is where you may aim marketing and advertising but should not expect deep penetration.

A good example of a secondary market: If you were a restaurant, you may market to businesses in the area with weekday lunch specials. The dinner menu is where the big revenue is but by advertising the lunch menu to the nearby businesses, you build brand recognition. And even better, those business people may very well decide your menu is so tasty looking and they hear such good things about your food, they may very well come in for dinner one evening. I don't want to oversimplify the secondary market because it can in fact become extremely complicated depending on your business offering and your industry. Suffice it to say you should have a net you cast for your primary market and a net you cast for your secondary market.

If you have defined your Target Market so specifically and restrained it to only a small segment of the SAM, you are said to have defined a Vertical Market. This sliver of the SAM will be referred to as A Vertical or Your Vertical. Most restaurants typically do not want a vertical, but if you are a five star restaurant at the top of a glacier in an ice hotel, you have one. Your market is confined to those who can afford to get there, those who like to be in that climate, and those who have a discerning taste for your fare. Take note by the way that the selected location for the restaurant (in an ice hotel) imposes external forces that dictate some of the demographics that define the target market and the thinner slice vertical market.

You select a vertical because you want to restrict your offerings to a narrow group of potential customers as a strategic competitive decision. There are countless factors that determine what the end result target market for a product or service will or can be. It is of course beyond the scope of this book to condense the entire subject of a Vertical Market into usable form here, so let's move on to our example company. I will, however, add to the clarification of a Vertical Market when I briefly discuss The Goober Group's specific selection of a Vertical Target Market in several of the remaining levels of the pyramid, as well as in the chapters on Business Strategy Meets Agile Execution and Case Study & Example.

Our example company has decided their strategy will be to move into a Vertical Target Market by providing IT services to healthcare providers that work with cardiology equipment, specifically cardiology offices. One of the major deciding factors being that The Goober Group completely understands and has extensive experience with the most commonly used cardiology management applications used in the healthcare industry. Refer back to the list of Line of Business Solutions in the Products & Services section; you will notice the entries for the Nuance capture & store application, Centricity Electronic Medical Records (EMR), and Sencha Touch Charts. Each of these applications requires special knowledge which then presents an opportunity for those service providers who know and can manage them; this can be a competitive advantage.

Another important competency The Goober Group possesses is HIPAA certification for all of its engineers. The Health Insurance Portability and Accountability Act (HIPAA) is a piece of U.S. legislation (law) that imposes certain requirements on the medical industry and extends to those who intend to service their IT systems. Translation: This core competency makes The Goober Group one of the few IT Service Providers who can fully manage the IT systems for most medical offices within federal legislation. Think of it like being a BMW certified mechanic. Without the proper certification, you cannot work on a BMW without voiding the warranty. Except that HIPAA is a law, not a manufacturer's ploy to tie you exclusively to their service centers.

Now we are ready to cover the Target Market (primary and secondary) for The Goober Group. It starts with a brief narrative describing their target market and how the target market is divvied up into primary and secondary (see Figure 7-5).

**Target Market**

## The Goober Group Target Market

The Goober Group has identified a vertical market where we believe we can be most successful if we can effectively assert our strategic competitive advantages.
We believe that engaging with medical offices and clinics that specialize in Cardiology will allow us to leverage our core competencies and retained knowledge related to the unique IT needs of these types of businesses.

**Our primary Target Market focus will be Cardiologist medical offices**
- We know that offices of sufficient size require teams of doctors and supporting staff.
- We believe that we will be able to build solid, long-term relationships with these teams by effectively translating their IT needs into understandable technology roadmaps.
- Due to the nature of these offices, there will be greater need for project work; therefore the average revenue per user seat will be higher.
- We believe these offices will see high value in our service offerings and service levels in addition to their return on investment.

**Our secondary focus will be clinics that provide Cardiology scanning services**
- These clinics typically have less cohesive teams and are often more corporate driven.
- We therefore believe that although we will be able to service their IT needs, we will not be able to build as solid of a working relationship as with staffed offices.
- Due to the nature of these clinics there will be less need for project work than Cardiology offices; therefore the average revenue per user seat will be lower.
- Our skills, certifications, and retained knowledge will be of great value to these clinics.
- Our relationship with these clinics may provide inroads to other Cardiology offices.

**Primary Target Market Demographics**
- Cardiology offices with gross revenue between $5 million and $35 million.
- 15+ Users and complete EMR and Cardio Scan systems.

**Secondary Target Market Demographics**
- Cardiology Clinics with gross revenue between $15 million and $50 million.
- 10+ Users and complete EMR and Cardio Scan systems.

**Geography**
- Medical Offices within 50 U.S. miles of The Goober Group's home office.

**Psychographic**
- Organizations that do not have an in-house IT department.
- Organizations that are highly competitive and who see IT as potential for strategic competitive advantage.

**Behavior**
- Businesses that have an IT budget of at least 3% of gross revenue.
- Businesses that have strict guidelines for systems and equipment replacement and refreshment as technology moves forward.
- Businesses that have strict guidelines for systems and equipment warranty and licensing.
- Organizations in which security and compliance are held at high priority.

*Figure 7-5. Target Market*

Independent of the Target Market definition you have the criteria for an Ideal Customer. The criteria for the Ideal Customer and the Target Market are independent of each other because you could develop either in the absence of the other and neither ties to or relies on the other. Furthermore, the set of criteria for the Ideal Customer is not something you can pass off to a marketing or advertising agency and expect them to act on it. This is because the Ideal Customer is a set of criteria that, for the most part, cannot be evaluated until after you have started the relationship, unless of course you have some very reliable if not tangible supporting data. You will see this more clearly once the example criteria are presented from our IT Service Provider example company.

### The Goober Group's Ideal Customer (The Box)
- Is highly IT Dependent
- Is at Level 2 or 3 on the Business Maturity Index
- Actively participates in the well-being of the company's IT
- Values the service we provide
- Respects us and trusts our advice
- Likes us as an organization and our people in general
- Does not mistreat our employees
- Pays us on time and as agreed

First, notice how none of these criteria can be validated or verified by selecting demographic information checkboxes for a Market Analysis. These criteria are about the ideal customer's dependence on what you provide for services, their business maturity, how well they participate in the well-being of their own success, and how they interact with you as their service provider. I highlight the criteria for The Goober Group for a very particular purpose. We do business with people we know, like, and trust, and the world is too small of a place for anyone to be forced to do business with people who don't fit their model for an ideal customer. And it's okay to have requirements such as those I have laid out here. Whenever I talk about the Ideal Customer, I use the question "Do they fit in The Box?"

Before I continue, I will state that identifying the right criteria can be a little elusive depending on your business type and model, but "The Box" can be defined and employed by any business. It does lend itself best to those organizations that have a finite client list such as our example company, but it is extremely hard to apply to a fast food drive-up restaurant. What I present in the next few paragraphs is tailored for the example company and those like it, but what I lay out for using The Box as a method for culling less desirable clients can be applied to any business model.

Every person and organization has choices of who they partner with, vend to, or service. Many small businesses find themselves tied to customers who mistreat their employees, don't pay on time, or in the case of our example company, just don't understand how much their business relies on the technology they use. Yet they cling to them for fear of the loss of revenue. However, as discussed previously regarding Values and the Human Element, you can only be the best organization you can be if you do business with people who are also trying to get the next level and who have similar values.

The Ideal Customer criteria could be considered an alignment check for the customer, even a scorecard if you like for the relationship with the client. To the extent possible, you identify the likelihood that these criteria will be met while you are courting the potential client. If they seem to be in alignment, you take them on as a client and go to work. As the relationship progresses, you learn more about how closely you are aligned. If the customer becomes too far misaligned, you must take corrective actions. Understand that it's not unreasonable for the customer to have a similar Ideal Vendor criteria list, or for the potential customer to check you for alignment with their core business Values and Human Element.

Every size organization is faced at one time or another with the problem of reaching capacity and having to decide how they will handle the new demand or the expansion of the production. The smaller your organization, the more you feel the pain. The cost of bringing new talent on board and training them is weighed against the potential revenue from adding a new client. It's a never-ending cycle, and I certainly hope it's always one of your biggest problems. But to get to the next level, you must also have a method for shifting the focus of your organization as it matures to higher levels.

Consider the option of being able to look at your client base on your radar and having the option to manage the relationship with these clients based on how well they fit in The Box (see Figure 7-6). The intention is to track the top 20% of the clients that bring you 80% of your revenue and put them on a radar graph. Not only can you use the plotting to manage the client base, but you can also use it to decide who is going to continue to be your client as you move to the next level.

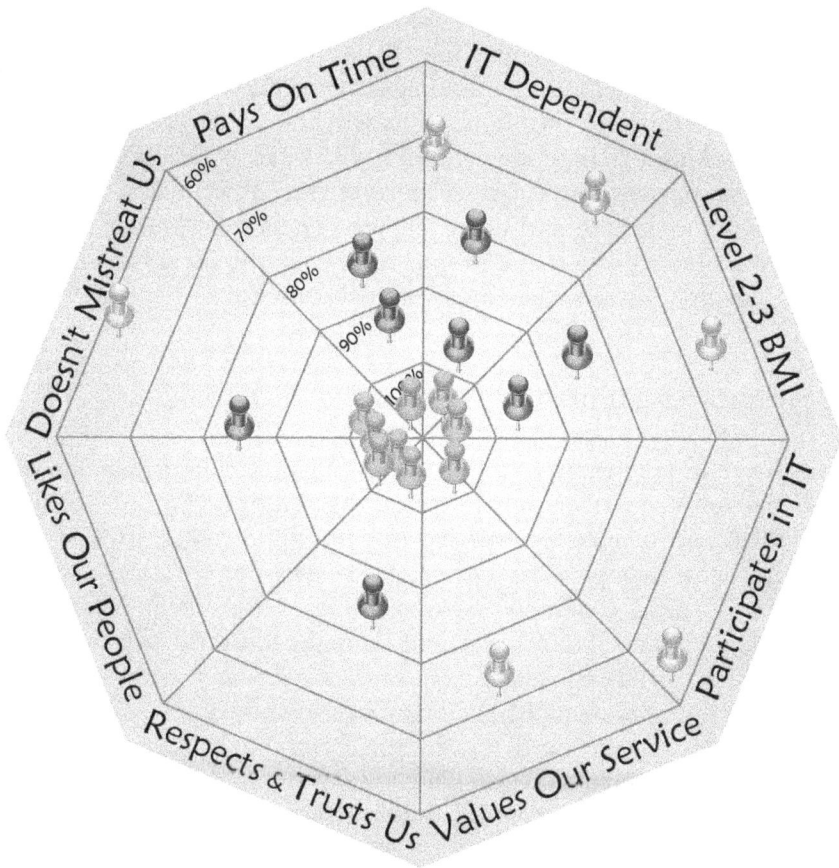

*Figure 7-6. Ideal Customer Radar Graph - The Box*

When faced with the dilemma of expanding operations or staying the same size but turning customers away, there are other options. It's not uncommon for a business to drop a client who just does not align with their business model, Culture, and Compass. You would simply review the customer relationship history, and if a client just doesn't fit in The Box and, given guidance and choices, has no intention of doing so, you must drop them from your list.

You actually have a duty to do so if you wish to uphold the values, mission, and vision of your organization. If the client isn't moving in the same direction as you are, you must part ways. Failure to do so will hold you back and you will not get to the next level. But if all your clients are moving along with you because they too are trying to get to the next level, then you should hold off on taking on a new client or expanding. I certainly hope that becomes your biggest problem.

As for where to place your Ideal Customer in the Pyramid of Purpose and Value, I would present it immediately after the Target Market as a second page, or as an additional slide similar to how the Values Statement Starburst or the Human Element Statement Word Cloud are presented. Although both are definitions of who specifically you would want to do business with, one is more internal (the Ideal Customer) and one is more external (Target Market). The Target Market is most directly related to your value proposition while the Ideal Customer is more directly related to the organizational culture.

## Operating Systems

The Operating Systems (OS) of an organization refers to the organization-wide collection of systems (hardware, firmware, software, cognitive) and their accompanying principals, processes, procedures, and practices. In large corporations, these are often formally referred to as a Business Operating System (BOS) which is in fact much more defined, specific, and integral than those of the typical small and medium-sized organization. Regardless of which name you use, these Operating Systems of the organization should not be confused with the simple software that is run by a computer to enable human interaction and perform work. Those software operating systems are just a fragment of the Operating Systems I am referring to here.

For my purposes I choose to use the simpler term Operating Systems (OS) for small and medium-sized organizations and the more formal term Business Operating System (BOS) for large organizations. I parallel the distinction between OS and BOS to the difference between the requirements and implementation of Operating Systems of small or medium-sized organizations and the implementation of a Business Operating System of large organizations. Large organizations absolutely must have a high degree of uniformity and integration in their BOS which is intricate and complex. Small and medium-sized organizations certainly should have a high degree of uniformity and integration, but the benefits typically do not outweigh the cost until the operation itself becomes significantly larger. These small business OS are nowhere near as formal, intricate, or complex.

I will clarify these two terms further but the gist of their differences is that for the typical small and medium-sized business, the organization-wide collection of systems is usually a long list of subsystems (plural) that have been patched together, whereas in the large organization, it is one big integrated system (singular) that has been built. Think of the small and medium-sized business OS as the less mature, light versions of a fully mature large corporation BOS.

In large organizations, a BOS is an integral part of the organization and incorporates the enterprise-wide standards, processes, structure, principles, and practices necessary to drive the organization. They have created these systems over time by mashing together their finance and accounting package to integrate with the shipping and receiving system and then coupled these with the quality control systems and more. They did this because it is strategically and logistically the best way to have uniformity of systems across the entire organization. These organizations typically have extremely large operations spanning the globe. There must be a high degree of uniformity in systems for there to be any chance of managing these systems effectively.

Often this BOS has a fancy name that is tied to the process or system it is built for. One example is the aerospace manufacturer Boeing who has the Boeing Production System. The automobile manufacturer Toyota has the Toyota Production System or TPS. What is important to note is that many of these large, formal BOSs do in fact share common features. This is because these systems are in fact derived from other well-known and time-proven methods, best practices, and systems. One example of the incorporation of well-known and time-proven methods is the use of Agile, Lean, and Six Sigma in production and other operations. It should be noted that these three methods are used all over the world today but a mere fifty years ago, they were either non-existent or the voodoo of only big corporations.

In small and medium-sized organizations, the OS are critical and may be integral but most often, components or even the entire system can be revamped or replaced with relative ease. This is in stark contrast to the BOS of large organizations where even saying the word BOS revamp could cause a high-level executive somewhere in the company to start drinking heavily. Smaller organizations typically are patching systems together to get them to work as best as they can until they can afford better wares. They may have custom built a single-purpose solution but it's not likely integrated to the level they would like it. As the organization grows and can afford better solutions, they move to them and things slowly become more and more integral and embedded. As smaller organizations grow more mature, they plan for these changes as part of their strategy to get to the next level. Regardless of how integral or embedded the Operating Systems of the small and medium-sized organization are, they must be defined for the purpose of understanding where value is created and lost.

The Operating Systems of the organization are the specific tools, processes, and secret recipes used to create and deliver the value proposition. Your OS are comprised of every relevant system you utilize in any of the ten business Value Aspects: Communications & Collaboration, Finance & Accounting, Human Resources, Marketing, Organization Infrastructure, and so on. I will specifically cover Resources in the next chapter but for clarification of Operating Systems, let's get a head start now. Resources are the human, financial, physical, and knowledge factors that provide an organization the actual means to perform the processes of the business. Think of it like this—Resources are the money to buy the parts and pieces, rent a place to assemble them, hire the people to do the assembly, and even the knowledge of how to assemble them. Operating Systems are the machines, software, methods, and processes the people use to do the assembly and track production, sales, resource usage, and so on.

If you are an auto mechanic shop, your OS are the software you use to manage finances, the repair and restoration estimating software you use to create quotes for work, and the time tracking software you use for tracking labor, and possibly even the hydraulic lift you use to get vehicles off the ground. They are the teardown and repair reference material you use, and they are the point of sales machines you use to collect money from customers for parts and service. If you are a restaurant, they are the guest wait list management application you use, the point of sales system, the order entry system, the payroll system, and the employee scheduling system. They are the refrigeration and storage methods for meats, produce, and dried goods and they may even include the ovens you use, depending on how you use those ovens.

You may have already deduced that there is or can be a crossover of tools and machines between the Resources level of the pyramid and the Operating Systems level. Any tool or machine you purchase for your organization is obviously a resource and is accounted for as such. These same tools or machines may also be considered part of your Operating Systems if they are key to the value creation process in some discernable way. One example would be the hydraulic lift I mentioned when listing Operating Systems for the auto mechanic. To put it simply, if it's just another machine you need for the normal day-to-day function of a shop, it is a resource and not necessarily part of your OS. If however your lift has an integrated tire balance machine and comes with the control terminal, you have a component of your OS. You leverage what this machine can do as part of your value proposition and it is integral to your operation.

This opens up the discussion of channel value and vendor value. If you recall the discussion on the Value Chain and the Value System, I indicated how your vendors and partners can have a great effect on the value you pass to your clients. Consider the vendor who has put together a well-thought-out line of solutions specifically for the type of business you run. Now I will also revisit the discussion from the previous section on the computer program you use to track table seating reservations. What if that vendor does in fact have modules that you can purchase to allow for online reservation, changes, and wait time updates just like an airline flight status? And what if they also have a module that integrates communications to the valet? Letting the valet know that the guests at table twelve are now done with their dining and are in fact headed to the front of the restaurant, the valet could then round out the guests' wonderful evening by having their car waiting.

When presented with this type of clean solution for more than one need in your business, it only makes sense to buy into the whole package and leverage every element to the greatest value for your customers. If you do it right, you can certainly create a competitive advantage for your business. And you must know that this is exactly what the vendor wants you to do. They have planned out the solution package carefully and specifically, and they will most likely have detailed how to link these modules together and use them to greatest advantage. They want to be your strategic partner and help you create success. And why would they do this? Because their business is building superior solutions for your business. Not so coincidentally, the purpose of their business is exactly the same as yours—to attract customers with their offerings and to endear them to their organization as the preferred provider of the things they want, need, and find valuable. This is a strategic partnership that makes sense and can work.

Not every business that sets out to build a complete solution line or package gets it right. Sometimes they are in touch with one part of their target market and out of touch with another. You will see offerings that fit most of your needs but not all, and you may find that the vendor doesn't seem to care. You will also find solutions that fit the majority of your needs and are backed by vendors who are receptive to modifications. With these solutions, you may elect to engage the vendor to do the modifications to get the final pieces to link up, or you may turn to a third party solutions. And sometimes this can be achieved with little time, energy, or effort. The point is that when you find a solution that you can plug into your Operating Systems which has value creation or retention capabilities, you have a strong potential for competitive advantage. Then it is up to your strategy to actually drive this potential. This is why you need to clearly define your Operating Systems, so that the strategy planning can see clearly what you have at hand to create your value proposition.

Now I turn to the OS for our example company. This may seem overly detailed but for an IT company that already sees the value of strategic partnering and has identified the solutions packages that are right for them, but it is not. In fact, having this level of detail allows the planning and execution of strategy to be very precise. The Goober Group didn't just pick a handful of solutions that sounded good or seemed to be able meet their needs. Each one is hand-picked and battle-tested over time. Where you see solutions that are multiple modules from the same vendor, this is because The Goober Group believes there is value and competitive advantage potential in using this solution package. If this is your OS for your organization, you should be able to defend every item on the list with a simple statement of how you believe this will either create or preserve value in some relevant way. You can see much of the reasoning behind the selected list our example company uses in the chapters for Business Strategy Meets Agile Execution, and Case Study and Example (see Figure 7-7).

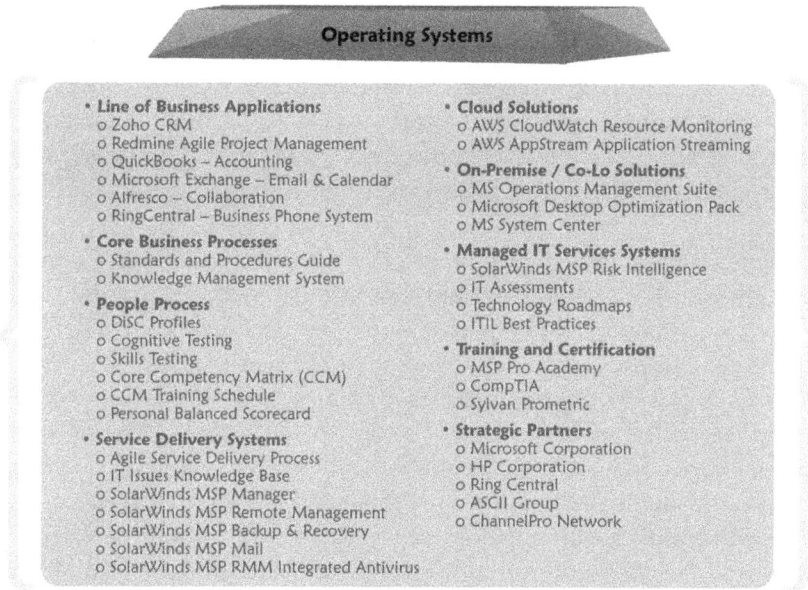

**Operating Systems**

- **Line of Business Applications**
  o Zoho CRM
  o Redmine Agile Project Management
  o QuickBooks – Accounting
  o Microsoft Exchange – Email & Calendar
  o Alfresco – Collaboration
  o RingCentral – Business Phone System
- **Core Business Processes**
  o Standards and Procedures Guide
  o Knowledge Management System
- **People Process**
  o DISC Profiles
  o Cognitive Testing
  o Skills Testing
  o Core Competency Matrix (CCM)
  o CCM Training Schedule
  o Personal Balanced Scorecard
- **Service Delivery Systems**
  o Agile Service Delivery Process
  o IT Issues Knowledge Base
  o SolarWinds MSP Manager
  o SolarWinds MSP Remote Management
  o SolarWinds MSP Backup & Recovery
  o SolarWinds MSP Mail
  o SolarWinds MSP RMM Integrated Antivirus

- **Cloud Solutions**
  o AWS CloudWatch Resource Monitoring
  o AWS AppStream Application Streaming
- **On-Premise / Co-Lo Solutions**
  o MS Operations Management Suite
  o Microsoft Desktop Optimization Pack
  o MS System Center
- **Managed IT Services Systems**
  o SolarWinds MSP Risk Intelligence
  o IT Assessments
  o Technology Roadmaps
  o ITIL Best Practices
- **Training and Certification**
  o MSP Pro Academy
  o CompTIA
  o Sylvan Prometric
- **Strategic Partners**
  o Microsoft Corporation
  o HP Corporation
  o Ring Central
  o ASCII Group
  o ChannelPro Network

*Figure 7-7. Operating Systems*

## Compass Crosscheck

I have covered a lot of ground in this segment of the pyramid and I hope it is clear how the three levels—Products & Services, Target Market, and Operating Systems—combine to determine the direction the organization is going in. They are the compass and they point to where you are going as an organization and they determine who you will partner with and who you will build your relationships with.

Everything about the levels in this segment has been carefully designed to support every level above it. The Operating Systems are specifically selected to effectively create and deliver your products and services to the Target Market, which is carefully selected based on the Products & Services you intend to offer. These are in line with and therefore support the Human Element and so on up the levels all the way to the top. As a whole segment of the pyramid, the organization's Compass must support the entire segment above it—the organization's Culture. If anything in this segment falters or fails, it will shake the Culture segment above it which could have a lasting effect on every level in that segment. I'll provide an example of how this happens shortly.

As the design of your pyramid progresses, you will see in the discussion on the bottom segment that the levels in that segment—

Resources, Performance Measures, and Roadmap & Strategy—must also be aligned properly or you will get off course. If the Blueprint for Success segment is not properly designed and you are not effectively supporting the organization's Compass, you can certainly do business but at nowhere near the level you intend to and with nowhere near the competitive advantage you intend to create and leverage.

To demonstrate how the failure in the lower levels of the Compass segment can shake if not topple an entire organization, I present the IT infrastructure failure that occurred at Southwest Airlines in July 2016. Southwest Airlines posted on their blog, "Southwest Airlines began experiencing intermittent performance issues earlier this afternoon with multiple technology systems as a result of an outage." Starting at the failure date of July 20, 2016, Southwest reportedly ended up cancelling some 2,300 flights over the next 4 days with more than 8,000 delays. The end result was arguably one of the worst infrastructure failures of any airline to date and certainly the worst for Southwest. The blame was put squarely on a critical piece of information technology called a router.

In the 2003 book *The Southwest Airlines Way*, author Jody Hoffer Gittel begins her book with a short list of accolades about Southwest including the airline's track record of being profitable for 31 years consecutively while their competition struggled to stack more than four or five years in a row. She mentions how *Fortune* magazine listed Southwest as one of the "100 best companies to work for in America" and how *Fortune* also names them as "the most successful airline in history." Gittel's book is all about unlocking the secret sauce of Southwest Airlines, and it does a fine job of doing so with highlights on their LUV culture and their unique communications coupled with what she refers to as "High Performance Relationships."

The LUV culture refers to a place and time back when Southwest was a small central carrier based in Love Field Texas (Airport code LUV) and their early culture. Their stated Vision is: To become the world's most loved, most flown, and most profitable airline. There are more than a dozen books on the subject of Southwest Airlines and what made them special and how they got to the top. Some focus on Chairman Herb Kelleher but all delve deeply into the most powerful driver—the company culture. Southwest went stratospheric and it is largely attributed to their culture and how they bound the organization together cohesively to execute on a brilliant strategy over time to become number one.

Southwest's strategy is not always the focus of their story because somehow it is always outshined by the reality that great strategy is powerful, however, without having the vision, mission, values, and everything on down the pyramid in place, you won't actually get anywhere. Strategy can also become a complex discussion and people tend to look for the one golden nugget to take away. And let's face it, a great company culture is more fun to talk about. But their strategy is central to this discussion as we look at Southwest's chosen direction for their services, target market and operating systems.

I will highlight one of the primary focuses that Southwest identified would lead to a significant competitive advantage, namely to develop a solution to shorten the turn times for their airplanes. They knew if the plane was sitting on the ground, i.e. not flying, they were losing money. If they could slice five minutes off the turn time (time to deplane passengers and load up again), they could multiply this by the number of flights in a given day and thus shave several hours a day per airplane, which is a measurable increase in efficiency. But what does a strategic objective like this require to be successful? Operating systems.

In the 1990s when Southwest was building their information technology infrastructure and cultivating what would be the operating systems they use to deliver their services and support their customers, there was a simultaneous surge in high technology which made it all conveniently possible. The internet as we know it today was very new, but Southwest learned to leverage it as did every other airline. As time moved on, Southwest's operating systems and infrastructure grew to meet the increasing demand as it grew. And today, their systems are a conglomeration of new and legacy systems. Legacy systems are those that may be less than modern but are relied upon heavily and are not easily replaced or revamped.

On July 20, 2016, the day of the Southwest meltdown, I was talking with a close friend who spent nearly a dozen hours stranded at his home airport waiting for a flight out to an event we were both attending. When he finally arrived, he arrived without his luggage, and for the next few days it seemed he was constantly on the phone trying to book his return flight and find his missing luggage. He shared several firsthand anecdotes of interactions between livid Southwest customers and extremely stressed and pressured Southwest agents and employees. He told of irrational passengers blowing up in anger and expecting miracles, customers who really just didn't quite understand how complex these systems can be and how little control anyone standing at a keyboard really has.

Of all of this, what made me feel most sad was not the story of the customer in line who really didn't understand these complex systems, but rather the story of a Southwest agent who completely lost their composure. Granted it was after more than fifteen hours of downed systems and probably hundreds of irate passengers and untold issues related to the cascading problems which started with the downed system. But to be crystal clear, it's not about just any airline agent losing it, it's about a Southwest agent losing it. I felt that if the Southwest agents are stressed to this level, you have in fact pushed them to serious extremes. I do not have the same respect or expectations for customer service from any other airline as I do Southwest. After hundreds of flights and thousands of miles of service, you feel like you are part of their family. Of course it's not unheard of to rattle a Southwest agent, but when put to the test, they will typically far outshine those of other airlines by far. Why do I say this, why do I believe this? Because they have proven it over time and their reputation shows it. Southwest's infrastructure failed and their employees banded together, tapped into the reserves of their powerful culture, and held together. But there were casualties on the inside and the outside.

I have no real concern for exactly why the Southwest system went down, what I am concerned with is how their operating systems could have become so stressed as to fail to this extent when their entire Purpose is, as prominently stated on their website, to "Connect People to what's important in their lives through friendly, reliable, and low-cost air travel." Southwest places their Purpose above their Vision, Values, and Mission on their website. If your primary offering is air travel and your aim is to be the best in the industry at delivering, it requires the highest efficiency and reliability, and your operating system had better be in line with this goal.

In a *Dallas News* interview with Southwest CEO Gary Kelly on July 30, 2016, he was quoted as saying, "We were at a dead start when I got here in the 1980s. There was virtually no technology and then the technology we added in the 1990s was very immature." My personal opinion is that somewhere along the way as Southwest grew and moved forward, they relied too heavily on the technology without recognizing its significance in their business. The technology they employ as a central component of their operating systems was not given proper consideration relative to their stated purpose. Kelly did in fact clearly recognize the hit that Southwest's image took, stating, "There's no lingering effect of that event other than the way people feel," and, "We're mainly focused on winning back our customers that we didn't serve well, we care about that."

In the end, there is only the failure of the inadequate operating systems of Southwest that should have been supporting the delivery of the value proposition to their target market. It will in fact change the course of Southwest, their Compass direction. Kelly also stated in the *Dallas News* interview, "This happened. We have to do everything we can to understand it and prevent it from ever happening again." And he's right, but my question is still this—How do you grow the second largest airline in the world and overlook the operating systems that support it?

Southwest's failure of a critical component in their operating systems shook the Compass of that organization, and they must reset their heading and press on. The shudder of their Compass shook the Culture of the organization and tested it. What is the price they will pay, what is the toll? For their organization, the shudder of this event was felt all the way to the top. They took a hit on their profits, they lost some trust which will lose them some customers, and they lost some LUV. A lesser airline could lose a significant market share with an event like this. If we were in the middle of an economic downturn, it could have cost them their entire business.

In the long run I believe that Southwest will recover and be just fine. Why? Because they have an extraordinary vision and mission that are worth pursuing. These coupled with their values and stated purpose have seen them through a few rough times including the terrorist attacks in the U.S. in 2001 and the economic downturns of 2000 and 2008. Resiliency comes from a solid Culture built out of a compelling Vision, Mission, and Values. In the end, the Compass segment of the pyramid must be designed to support the Culture segment, but if the Culture is solid, it won't crumble so easily when the Compass is threatened.

*Performance of management should be measured by potential to stay in business, to protect investment, to ensure future dividends and jobs through improvement of product and service for the future, not by the quarterly dividend.*

– W. Edwards Deming

# 8.0

## Pyramid of Purpose and Value – Blueprint for Success

### Your Organization's Blueprint for Success

Once you have completed the middle levels of the Pyramid of Purpose and Value (Compass segment), you can begin to identify the Resources required to utilize the Operating Systems you have just defined. Only then can you begin to set Performance Measures and targets for the utilization of Resources to ensure quality, value, repeatability, reproducibility, efficiency, and profitability. And finally, once all these are completed, you can begin to plan the specific Roadmap and Strategy you will execute over the coming years to get to the next level (see Figure 8-1).

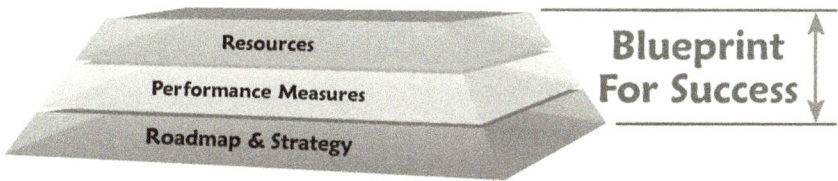

Resources

Performance Measures

Roadmap & Strategy

Blueprint For Success

*Figure 8-1. Lower Segment of The Pyramid*

### Resources

Resources are simply a source of supply (Natural and Capital) or support (Human) used in the generation of products and services. They are the means or inputs to the business processes that create the value proposition. Natural resources include elements or things found in the environment such as land, minerals, water, etc. Capital resources include things man-made, knowledge, money, assets, tools, and equipment. Human resources include people as well as the capability and capacity to create knowledge. Note that knowledge is a Capital resource because it can be bought, sold, and transferred. The ability to actually create knowledge is a Human resource.

The resources of an organization and the resource needs of the organization must be well understood and managed. The proper configuration of resources within the challenging environment of the market that the organization operates in makes it possible for the business strategy to establish a competitive advantage. Failure to acquire and configure the right resources means that the strategy, no matter how well planned or executed, will fail.

A perfect example: If you are planning to sail across the ocean, you should build your ship from good, solid wood or steel rather than salt blocks. Even then, you must treat each piece of wood the correct way in preparation for their extended life soaking in salt water. You must also have a sufficient amount of the right materials to build a ship large enough to hold your required provisions for the long journey. This may seem an overly simplified example but it is nonetheless an appropriate one to show how quickly the considerations for any endeavor are distilled down to the resources required for success.

Recall the details of the Feasibility Study and Business Plan; they were largely a description of what resources would be required and how they would be used to create success. Certainly money represents most of the resources being requested, but where would that money go? To buy buildings, machinery, and tools; hire people; order supplies to build the widget; and even purchase materials to package them for delivery. Financial resources are the single most significant determinant of the ability of the business to execute on a strategy. The overall resources of the organization directly determine its ability to produce and the capacity at which it can produce. This is why they must always be counted, measured, horded when necessary, and certainly protected from internal and external forces who may seek to misappropriate them.

All resources have an associated abundance and scarcity relative to time and space. That is to say, whatever resource you have a need for will at any given time, depending on where in the world you are, be either abundant or scarce. But in the modern world, of all the resources that have the power to tip the balance of any other resource from scarce to abundant, cash pretty much tops them all. There is an old saying that cash is king, and there is a reason for that. Cash directly translates into agility and options. With cash you can buy anything from precious materials to people, sad but true. The point is this—In the operation of your business and in the accounting of your resources, cash reserves should be the most coveted and protected. We see this whenever we look at large organizations. The first question is always, "What are they worth?" and the second is, "What is their liquidity?" or, "How much cash do they have on hand?" For this reason you should always post your financial resource strength at the top of the list.

The Resource level of the pyramid is not just about listing the resources to show what you have stockpiled and in reserve. It is also not intended to be any kind of Balance Sheet report or Statement of Assets. For the purposes of the Pyramid, what you really want to showcase are the resources that are most important and relevant to the production and delivery of your products and services, and you will want to show how this directly translates into production capability and capacity for the organization. Capability and capacity are the key words here as they represent the organization's potential to produce. To be able to share the capability and capacity of the organization in a meaningful way, you must either do the math or come to some reasonable assumptions of what your capability and capacity are.

Here is a simple example. If your business is a restaurant, you would list out the major factors in capability and capacity such as:
- Number and capacity of food holding ovens and refrigerators
- Number of kitchen staff (Chefs, Leads, Preps, etc.)
- Number of wait and support staff
- Number of tables in the restaurant
- Number of seats at each table
- Average table turnover time
- Average number of guests
- Average table total bill
- Average product consumed per table

With this information you could calculate how many customers your restaurant is capable of serving per shift, day, week, month, and year. Note that the widget of a restaurant is the complete meal, i.e. We count our day's success by how many meals we served. It should also be noted that you should calculate the amount of food product consumed per day so you know if your capacity to serve customers is limited by your ability to store enough food with which to feed them all. On the other hand, if your capacity for food storage exceeds your capability to move that many people through the restaurant in a day, then your production is limited by your number of seats, staff, etc. The desired end result being that you can now in fact state that your restaurant has the capability and capacity of serving X number of clients annually and at an estimated revenue of $Y.

Before we get too far along, I must address the concerns that will be presented most commonly by small organizations about what information is being shared with the staff. It is common that the sole proprietor initially sees no reason to list this information let alone share it with anyone, but when the sole proprietor organization becomes a two, then three, then four-person operation, there is a genuine fear of sharing this information. The primary fear is that the owner does not want the staff to know what the business is making and potentially what the owner is taking home. They also do not want anyone thinking there is money just lying around that should be spent on better things like higher wages or better tools. Oddly enough, I have heard these concerns expressed by companies with as many as one hundred employees.

I do not think that the entire company budget or financials should be freely posted or shared, but I certainly believe that the single most important representation of the growth or strength of the organization (in some form or another) should be. When these same entrepreneurs are at conventions and other such events, they freely answer the question "How big is your business?" with a solid number (and often with embellishment), such as, "We're at $800 thousand and growing." But heaven forbid you should go to your employees once a quarter and tell them this. The employees might start breaking up the furniture, build a bonfire, and go on strike because after all, we're a very small company and that's a lot of money for one person to be making.

What you must do, even if you are a small business, is share the numbers that can express your progress as a business in the best way that makes the most sense. There are numbers that can express the growth and potential strength of the business without revealing the total revenue, such as Earnings Before Interest, Taxes, and Amortization (EBITA). And there are numbers for expressing cash relative to revenue and so on. The point is even if you are a sole proprietor, you must have these important numbers posted and ready to share, even if it's only with your spouse and your cat at the dinner table. Regardless, if you are listing them here as Resources that represent potential or listing them in the next level down on the Pyramid (Performance Measure) for the purpose of driving them higher, they are a critical element of what defines the business, what the business is capable of, and where it is going.

Here are my final words regarding the sharing of most any financial numbers of the organization with the staff. Some number that represents the financial strength of the organization and its cash reserves or retained earnings, in addition to the Leading Indicators of the business, should be shared with the entire company. If you are actually running your business as if you want it to be around in five or ten years and you are not using it to siphon money into a getaway fund, you need everyone to see where you are and where you're trying to get to. After all, these are all parts of the big picture and the compelling story they (the staff) are a part of. If there are concerns of being held up by an employee for more pay as the revenue grows, you either have the wrong people on board or you're not actually paying them what they are worth.

Think of the Resources level of the pyramid as the big, bold statement of "This is what we have to work with and this is what we're capable of." To present the resources of the organization you simply need to list them out in some logical order. Depending on the size and nature of the organization, the presented list could be quite different although certain information would always be common among them, such as annual revenue, cash holdings, etc. If the resource does not significantly contribute to the capability or the capacity of production, do not list it.

Looking to our example company, The Goober Group, some examples of resources that do not significantly contribute to production capability or capacity would be the Knowledge Management System and the entire People Process listed in the Operating Systems level. Both certainly are knowledge resources. As for the Knowledge Management System specifically, while it may contribute to production capability it will not likely contribute to capacity. Since it can contribute to capability the only question then would be "Does it do so significantly?" For this organization at its current maturity the answer is no, as such it would not be mentioned.

As for the People Process, it too certainly contributes to the capability of production if it is properly applied. It is a vehicle for increasing capacity in that you employ the process to select the next person who will represent an increase in capacity, but that person, no matter how good your People Process is, will not be able to put in more hours than another person. There are still only 24 hours available to any human being. Here again the capability of the production system may be positively affected but not so significantly as to be noted. If a direct correlation can be drawn between any resource and a measurable increase in production capability or capacity, then list it.

Here are the important and relevant Resources numbers for our example company. Note that the widget for this business is time. Everything they do can be boiled down to time: how long it takes to perform certain common tasks, installing software, hardware, completing projects, maintaining systems, everything. As you will see in the next section, management and efficient use of time are the most important metrics to be managed. Some calculations are required to obtain the capacity total for The Goober Group; the formula is shown below to support the example.

Here is how the end result Resources for The Goober Group would be presented (see Figure 8-2). For the last number (Revenue or Value Potential), we need to assume a standard service rate for The Goober Group. I've selected a common rate of $150 per hour.

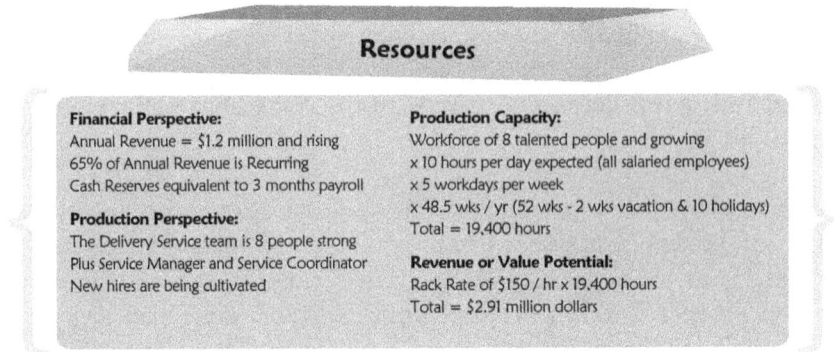

### Resources

**Financial Perspective:**
Annual Revenue = $1.2 million and rising
65% of Annual Revenue is Recurring
Cash Reserves equivalent to 3 months payroll

**Production Perspective:**
The Delivery Service team is 8 people strong
Plus Service Manager and Service Coordinator
New hires are being cultivated

**Production Capacity:**
Workforce of 8 talented people and growing
x 10 hours per day expected (all salaried employees)
x 5 workdays per week
x 48.5 wks / yr (52 wks - 2 wks vacation & 10 holidays)
Total = 19,400 hours

**Revenue or Value Potential:**
Rack Rate of $150 / hr x 19,400 hours
Total = $2.91 million dollars

*Figure 8-2. Resources*

You may be asking yourself, "How is it that The Goober Group has the capacity to do 19,400 hours of work per year representing a potential to earn $2.91 million dollars, yet their entire revenue for the year was only $1.2 million dollars?" Well the answer is quite simple—operational efficiency. Everything about the capability of the resources in the organization, including and especially the internal processes of the organization, must be finely tuned in order to realize anywhere near the potential of the organization. This is precisely why these numbers are presented, so that everyone can see what the potential of the business truly is.

Even if we look at the numbers related to the restaurant example from earlier, the potential of the business would far exceed the actual or realized yield. Ask any restaurant owner how may seats they have, how fast they can cook a meal, and how fast they can turn a table, i.e. what their potential is. Then ask them how many seats and tables they actually turn. You will find that even the restaurants that are packed from open until close are nowhere near their potential. But they are all trying to continuously and incrementally improve their process and their yield in any way they can.

This fact about potential and actual yield is true with any business, and it is the exact reason you must understand resources and how to manage them. It is also true that for any business there must be an understanding of what the realistic efficiency of that type of business is. If it is not known then the organization must do as The Goober Group is doing—track the numbers, do the calculations, and then set Performance Measures to drive the efficiency and therefore the revenue up, while ensuring the highest possible value to clients. This brings us to the next level of the pyramid.

## Performance Measures

At the core of any enterprise are the internal processes that create and deliver the products and services (the Value Proposition). If properly designed, the internal processes (when followed) will ensure quality, repeatability, reproducibility, efficiency, and hopefully represent value for the customer and profit for the business. This is true at any level of business maturity and in every valid business. In fact once the business is defined and running, the internal processes by which products are created and services are delivered usually become the single greatest determinant of efficiency, profitability, and growth potential. If your internal processes are optimal, it means you are making the most of the resources possible and perhaps even operating at maximum potential. Performance Measures are the gauge you will monitor when managing all processes and activities of the organization that determine if progress is being made, goals are being met, and if adjustments must be made.

With a highly efficient internal process you have repeatability, reproducibility, efficiency, and profitability, meaning you have the ability to scale or clone the operation. Think of any franchise you can name. Only when the business model and internal processes are so systematic and efficient can they put the whole business into a box and sell the concept to anyone with the right amount of cash for buy-in. The franchisee opens the box, follows the instructions to get set up, and then begins learning and practicing the exact prescribed processes to create the franchise products or services. If they follow the processes exactly, they have the highest statistical probability that their results for production efficiency and profit will be as promised. You should strive for no less efficiency in your operation regardless of size or future plans.

But how will the business owner know if they are doing it right? How will they know if the internal process is working like it is supposed to and how will they know if it is producing the results promised? How will they know they are creating true value for the customer and profit for the organization by design and not by happenstance? The key to all success in production is the Performance Measures coupled with Process Control. The subject of Process Control was briefly covered early in the first tools chapter.

In looking to identify Performance Measures for the organization and its internal processes, the conversation circles back to Process Control. If you recall from that brief discussion, the basics of Process Control can be boiled down to Plan, Do, Check, and Act. You Plan your internal process for production or delivery, you Do that process, you Check the outputs or results, and you Act on the results to adjust or correct the process accordingly. Performance Measures are what you Check when you Do the process, and the Plan and Act are the controls of the process.

To this point I have only focused on the internal process of the organization because this is where nearly all value is actually created. There are of course three other perspectives of the business that must be included in the discussion of Performance Measures: Financial, Customer, and Learning and Growth. The Financial perspective is addressed when you consider superficially how you will attain the desired progress, performance, or results for the business stakeholders. The value you are creating, of course, needs to be focused on the Customer perspective if you intend to keep or expand your market share. And it is only through Learning and Growth that all these internal processes can be performed with any competency let alone optimized well enough to attain maximum production potential.

## Measures, Metrics, and KPIs

There are several names used for Performance Measure (PM) including Performance Metric and Key Performance Indicator (KPI)—the common word being Performance. When you remove the word Performance you end up with the more generic terms Measure, Metric, and Indicator. It may seem elementary but the terminology must be clear before we continue. Measure, Metric, and Indicator are everywhere but they may not necessarily indicate Performance and even if they do, they may not have been identified as Key.

Measures, Metrics, and Indicators by themselves are generic terms for a set point for monitoring or controlling a process, including the digital state (On/Off, Yes/No). When the word Performance is added to the generic term, it's because the Measure, Metric, or Indicator is no longer just a set point for monitoring a process. It has been identified as an indicator to show that the specific desired performance is in fact being attained or specific desired results are in fact being obtained. Regardless of the term used, if it is measuring specific desired progress, performance, or results, it is a Performance Measure.

Some examples of Performance Measures are:
- Revenue
- Cash Flow
- Expenses
- Build Strategic Partnerships
- Build Brand Awareness
- Average Table Wait Time
- Average Table Turn Time
- Project Payment Lag Time
- Define the Ideal Client
- Solidify Office Manager Competency
- Identify Core Competencies
- Establish Marketing Competency

Any of these Metrics can be declared Performance Measures if and only if it is identified as the prime indicator of specific desired progress, performance, or results in one of the four perspectives: Finance, Customer, Internal, and Learning and Growth. For each of these metrics a selected gauge scale must be used. For many it is simply an analog scale; for example, Revenue is simply gauged by the month's end revenue in dollars. Others such as Build Brand Awareness or Build Strategic Partnerships are a little trickier and must be gauged by polling of an audience or level of engagement respectively. And others are very digital in nature and can be either completed (Yes) or Not yet Completed (No), such as Solidify Office Manager Competency.

### Getting it Right

What really matters is that the right measures for progress, performance, or results be selected. You cannot just pull a number from the financial statement and declare it to be a Performance Measure. Leading Indicators for finances can be used for Performance Measures but they are not automatically considered Performance Measures, nor can you just grab a handful of numbers from the report that your Operating Systems generate and claim these to be the measures you will use to gauge performance.

The most common mistake in trying to measure progress, performance, and results is selecting the wrong Performance Measure or KPI to monitor. Unfortunately, many of the vendors of the software and applications a business may employ to manage and run their business feel it necessary to call out what they consider to be useful performance indicators. It may be that their intention is to boast a feature of the application while intending to help the business owner manage their process better. But these indicators may not actually be tied to any relevant business perspective or they may be gauging metrics you should not be wasting time staring at.

One example would be the software application the restaurant uses to manage table wait times in our example for Chapter 7. The vendor of the program may call out that the cycle time (time it takes to get a table cleared and new customers seated) would be a useful KPI to monitor. But what if part of the restaurant's Value Proposition is to never push a client out the door, but rather encourage them to sit and enjoy their time, maybe even long enough to feel the need for a tasty desert and beverage? After all, this is fine dining, not fast food. The business owner is then prompted to use the cycle time for a performance indicator when in fact it is contradictory to the desired customer experience.

It is also true that the vendors of these applications have a very good understanding of the businesses that actually use their applications as well as the processes of those businesses. In this case, their selection of preferred metrics to track and understand may very well be of great value in managing certain processes. But this brings us to the biggest pitfall for small and medium-sized businesses when selecting Performance Measures. Look back at the list of Operating Systems laid out by The Goober Group. There are more than a dozen different applications or systems managing and manipulating countless processes and their associated metrics. Identifying the Performance Indicators that can actually indicate progress, performance, or results that create value from the potentially hundreds of metrics is nearly impossible. This by the way is one reason why, as organizations grow, they choose to build a single all-encompassing Business Operating System to suit their needs.

If there could in fact be hundreds or even thousands of metrics to monitor and select as KPIs for the many Value Aspects of a given business, where do you start? The ultimate goal is to differentiate the organization from its competition while creating great customer value and stakeholder profit. This means the Performance Measures must be derived directly from the vision of the organization and the strategy for success. The answer lies with the Balanced Scorecard.

If you recall, the Balanced Scorecard looks at the four most important perspectives of the business: Financial, Customer, Internal, and Learning and Growth. It forces you to ask important questions such as: If we succeed, how will we look to our stakeholders? To achieve our vision, how must we look to our customers? To satisfy our customers, which processes must we excel at? To achieve our vision, how must the organization learn and improve? The Balanced Scorecard focuses on a coherent set of Performance Measures derived from the company's vision and strategy. By looking to the actual strategy of the organization and allowing it to dictate the Performance Measures, the likelihood of success is significantly higher.

### The Secret of The Pyramid

Since the beginning of this book I've described the process of designing your pyramid as a top- down process. This is correct but there is one small variation required for the Performance Measures and Roadmap & Strategy levels. We are currently at the Performance Measures level of the pyramid; the next level below is where the strategy is actually developed. You may be able to identify certain useful Performance Measures given what you have defined so far about the business, but they will not be correctly derived from the actual business strategy and will not likely represent the four perspectives you care the most about. The next step then is to move to the Roadmap & Strategy level and begin defining the strategy which in turn will allow you to identify and extract the most beneficial Performance Measures. To state it another way—These two lowest levels of the pyramid are actually formulated simultaneously but presented separately.

To this point, I have covered a bit on what Performance Measures are, why they matter, and how to identify them. The bulk of the actual extraction of Performance Measures will be covered in the next section as the Roadmap & Strategy is developed. Here at this level is where you present the Performance Measures in the appropriate order in the pyramid using the Balanced Scorecard (see Figure 8-3). I will cover more on how these measures came about and how they were selected, both in the next section as well as in the chapters for Business Strategy Meets Agile Execution and Case Study & Example.

For the remainder of this chapter and specifically the Performance Measures and Roadmap & Strategy graphical examples, I will use the Balanced Scorecard, Strategy Map, and the data from the example company. The focus will be on the long-term strategy defined by The Goober Group targeted for execution in 2017. I recommend reviewing the sections on the Balanced Scorecard and Strategy Map (near the end of Chapter 5). I also recommend reviewing the Case Study and Example on The Goober Group, specifically the SWOT analysis and the resulting Strategy Maps and Balanced Scorecards.

**Performance Measures**

| | Theme: Build The Franchise | | | |
|---|---|---|---|---|
| | Balanced Scorecard | | | |
| Perspective | Objective | Measure | Target | Initiative |
| FINANCIAL | • Increase Recurring Revenue<br>• Increase Per Client Revenue | • % of Total Revenue<br>• Ave. Revenue Per Seat | • 80%<br>• $4,500 | • See Client Refocus Below<br>• See Client Roadmap Below |
| CUSTOMER | • Be the Complete IT Solution<br>• Refocus Existing Clients to the MSP Offering<br>• Attract New Clients in Vertical<br>• Reduce Average Ticket Age<br>• Reduce Average Time on Ticket<br>• % Unscheduled Downtime | • % Project Ownership<br>• % Converted<br>• # Assessment Requests<br>• # of Days Old<br>• # Minutes Per Issue<br>• Average % Downtime | • 100%<br>• 100%<br>• 3/Mo.<br>• < 45<br>• < 50<br>• < 0.10% | • Client Roadmaps Phase III<br>• Operation Client Focus<br>• Marketing 2.0 WIIFM<br>• Ticket Targeting<br>• Escalation Process<br>• Op. Goober Care Phase II |
| INTERNAL | • Partner with Vendors for MDF<br>• Increase Project Efficiency<br>• Fine-tune PSA and RMM for MSP<br>• Lower Ave. # Outstanding Issues<br>• Manage Service Delivery Backlog Hours | • % Marketing Budget<br>• % Budgeted Time<br>• Valid MSP Reports<br>• Ticket Count<br>• # Days Backlogged Projects & Service | • 5%<br>• < 100%<br>• 100%<br>• < 250<br>• < 5 | • Lunch & Learns<br>• Op. Agile Project Phase III<br>• Op. Goober Care Phase II<br>• Agile Service Delivery Phase II<br>• Agile Service Delivery Phase II |
| LEARNING AND GROWTH | • Establish ITIL Certification<br>• Establish HIPAA Compliance<br>• Establish EMR and Scan Systems as a Core Competency<br>• Get Everyone On Board<br>• Team Informed and Aligned | • % Team Trained<br>• % Team Trained<br>• % Team Trained<br>• % Employees Aware<br>• % Employees @ % Standups | • 100%<br>• 100%<br>• 100%<br>• 100%<br>• 100% | • ITIL Certification Phase 1<br>• HIPAA Compliance Phase 1<br>• Final Friday Training<br>• Q4 2016 Company Retreat<br>• Weekly Standups |

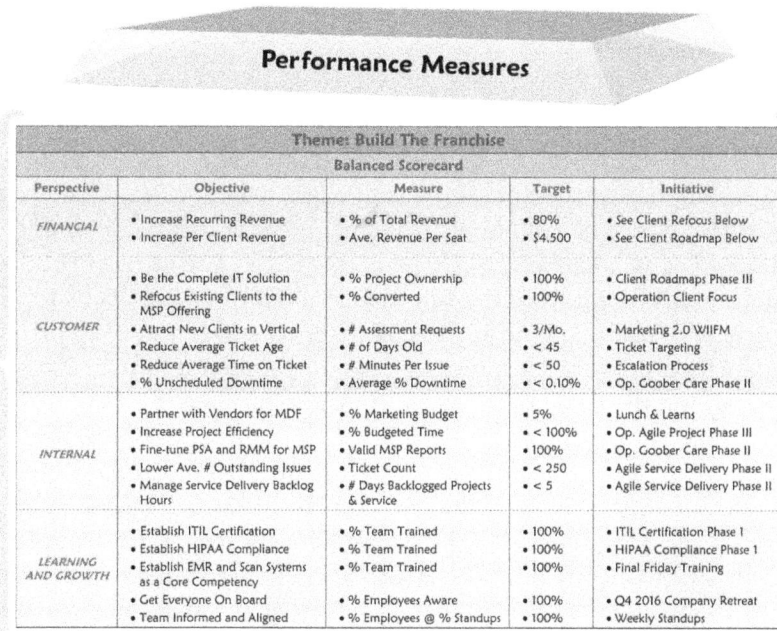

*Figure 8-3. Performance Measures*

## Summary

While you are free to select any performance measures you like to manage your processes and gauge your business's success, you have a responsibility to select measures that support the vision and mission of the organization and that create the greatest value for the customer and the business. Failure to do so typically results in stagnation and aimless wandering. But get it right and you will see continuous improvement, measured progress, and desired results.

Developing a strategy and selecting Performance Measures is unfortunately not a cut and dry process. Early on you will likely select some performance measures that really don't tell you anything or don't tell you what you need to know. You must tune in to your business and you must rely on your managers and leads to help you. Together you can better identify and calibrate the right metrics based on the business vision and strategy relative to the finances, customers, internal, and the learning and growth perspectives of the organization. The maturity of the performance measures of the organization will be commensurate with the maturity of the organization itself and the strategies employed. As I stated before it is a skill, but a learnable skill nonetheless.

# Roadmap & Strategy

The roadmap of an organization is the chronologically ordered and prioritized list of prime objectives based on the long-term business strategy. The roadmap can be seen as a tracker for the organization's progress and advancement. Major landmarks (significant initiatives or their phases) may be called out or highlighted. It can be as simple or as detailed as you like and it can be presented in any fashion you like. Some organizations actually post their roadmap on their websites for customers to see. They want the customer to know how they plan to advance their internal learning and growth and their internal processes to strengthen the value proposition for the customer.

Nearly every organization that has well-formulated roadmaps creates slide decks and presents them at company meetings and internal quarterly and annual events. The top organizations publish pamphlets for everyone in the organization and they post the roadmap everywhere for everyone to see all the time. To get it right you must also properly couple the roadmap and strategy of the organization together so that everyone knows not just where the business is, or where it's going, but also what part they play in the strategy.

The strategy of the organization is the specific plan of how the prime objectives for each of the four perspectives of the business will be attained in order to differentiate the organization from its competition while creating the greatest customer value and stakeholder profit. The strategy is what must be effectively executed as a discipline of the day-to-day operations of the business. In this example of the Pyramid of Purpose and Value, the business strategy can and will be presented using the Strategy Map. Recall that the Strategy Map helps the organization translate the business strategy into readable form which can easily be conveyed and requires only minimal narrative to describe.

### The Magic of The Pyramid

If there were any magic in the Pyramid it would exist here at this level where everything somehow miraculously culminates into the strategy for success. Fortunately you do not need to rely on magic, but the transformation will nonetheless be miraculous. Every concept, construct, and tool I have presented in this book is intended to help you define your business from the top down and build it from the bottom up, but none have the power to actually create strategy or make the decisions required to formulate strategy—not one.

My intention is to make the actual formulation of strategy significantly easier through the use of the concepts, constructs, and tools outlined in this book. Nothing less than the power of human intellect is the required key ingredient. To take the next critical step you need only examine closely the Case Study & Example of The Goober Group and follow suit. It will give an overview of the process and identify the key elements as we move along. The chapter on Business Strategy Meets Agile Execution also provides valuable insight into the process.

The Goober Group is ready to begin formulating their Roadmap & Strategy and identify their Performance Measures. At this point in the design of their pyramid, they have defined almost everything about the organization from the top down and they have all of the studies, plans, and analyses of and for the business. As The Goober Group endeavor is a revamp and rebuild of the business, they also have a complete business analysis including a SWOT analysis and resulting solutions recommendation. With this data they can begin to identify the objectives of the strategy, such as: attract new clients in the vertical market selected, increase recurring revenue, increase project efficiency, and so on.

When The Goober Group performed a complete business analysis, they discovered where their pain points were, what issues they had internally, what opportunities and threats existed on the outside of the organization, and where their strengths lie. The results of the analysis were in essence a laundry list of issues to be addressed, organized according to the ten business Value Aspects for easy reference. To supplement this laundry list and help define the strategy, the intentions and desires of the organizations principals are added along with their desired direction for the business.

These additional supplements represent the requirements that must be met and constraints that must be navigated. Requirements include things such as the overall business strategy of Customer Intimacy selected by Fiona, the owner of the organization, or the requirement that her husband, Esteban, be replaced as soon as possible so he can get back to his chosen career. Constraints include things like the chosen value proposition and vertical market, both chosen based on the market studies and the desired focus of the owner.

Not everything on the laundry list can or will be addressed by the business strategy. Some items represent dependencies that must be resolved before the strategy can be finalized or execution can begin. A perfect example is the sales person on staff for The Goober Group. It was decided this was the wrong person to be in that role and that laying him off is not part of a short-term strategy. Rather, laying off a non-performing employee is a part of the day-to-day operations of a business and is simply a correction to be made immediately. Other items are just not going to add to the customer value or business value in a relevant or measurable way and therefore should not be allowed to consume the organization's energy.

## Identifying, Sorting, and Prioritizing

The first step of strategy formulation is identifying and sorting the actual Strategy Objectives that will help take the business to the next level. The task at hand is to evaluate issues from the laundry list, group them with closely related items, consider the requirements and constraints, and identify specifically what the objective should be. Each objective identified must address one or more issues or recommendations from the laundry list and it must represent either a Driver or an Outcome relative to the four perspectives of the Balanced Scorecard. For example, the objective to Acquire Sales competency resolves several issues related to the Sales business Value Aspect. It would be identified as a Driver and would therefore land squarely in the Learning and Growth perspective. The Increase Recurring Revenue objective would address several business growth requirements, is an Outcome, and certainly belongs in the Financial perspective.

Once the Strategy Objectives are all identified and sorted into the appropriate Balanced Scorecard Perspective, they must be prioritized. The prioritization is relative to time, energy, and resources. Not every objective can be met just because it has been identified. Some items must be budgeted for and funded over several months or even years. Other objectives may have a prerequisite component in that they can only be met once certain other objectives have been successfully completed. The organization must fully understand what it has the capability to accomplish in a given business quarter and year. As the objectives are prioritized, the initial formation of strategies should begin naturally and progress homogenously.

## Strategy Formulation

As objective timelines, deadlines, budgets, requirements, and constraints are evaluated, there should appear a need to have a short-term strategy, medium-term strategy, and long-term strategy to address things in the appropriate time frames. Notice how The Goober Group defined four specific strategies each with its own theme. They knew that they needed to have a short-term strategy to get the organization realigned; this would address certain highly important issues that other strategies would build upon. Each strategy had a specific theme and was intended to address issues that were closely related with respect to the Balanced Scorecard Perspectives.

Developing a business strategy is part science and part art. The science side is represented by the logical ordering and organizing of information and the adherence to constraints and requirements. The art side is represented by the human intellect and its ability to perform critical thinking on complex subjects. After applying the science of strategy formulation, the art of strategy formulation will then begin to emerge. You are, in effect, building a collage that represents the picture you see of the future for this organization. And although there were requirements of what the design should represent and constraints on the materials and tools you could employ, it is now up to you to make it look enticing and like an endeavor your team will buy into and get on board with.

With the optimal number of strategies formulated for the coming year or years, each with the most logical and efficient focus over the appropriate time frame, the objectives can now begin to be evaluated to identify which specific Performance Measures will indicate if progress is being made and goals are being met. This last item is most critical as it relates to the Balanced Scorecard. Provided a given Strategy Objective is valid, relative to the organization's Financial Perspective, the indicator selected must either show how you are selling more or spending less. Everything else is background noise. Provided a given Strategy Objective is valid relative to the Customer Perspective, the indicator selected must show how you are increasing the value in the Value Proposition. Again, everything else is background noise. Similarly, provided a given Strategy Objective is valid relative to the organization's Internal Perspective, the indicator selected must either show how you are improving or leaning down your processes. And provided a given Strategy Objective is valid relative to the organization's Learning and Growth Perspective, the indicator selected must either show how you are growing your intangible assets or increasing the effectiveness of them.

For each Strategy Objective there must be an Initiative(s) which represents the actual effort and work required to obtain the objective.

Each Initiative can be seen as an organized effort, from a simple one-off task to be performed all the way up to a full-sized project. As with any kind of goal, both the Strategy Objectives and the supporting Initiatives must be time bound. When properly laid out, the Strategy Objectives and Initiatives chronologically represent the Roadmap for the organization relative to its Strategy. By selecting the most significant Strategy Objectives and presenting them in chronological order you have the major landmarks of progress for the Strategy. The specifics of how these Strategy Objectives, supporting Initiatives, and the work efforts required to attain them is outlined in the next section (The BASE). The subject is also expanded upon in the chapter on Business Agile Strategy Execution.

At this point, the entire Balanced Scorecard is well-defined as seen in the previous section. You have created a Roadmap that reflects landmark progress in the strategy based on the significant Strategy Objectives and supporting Initiatives. The Roadmap may be a text list or it can be graphical; for The Goober Group it is graphical. The 2017 long-term Roadmap and Strategy Map for The Goober Group is presented in Figure 8-4 followed by a short narrative of that organizational strategy.

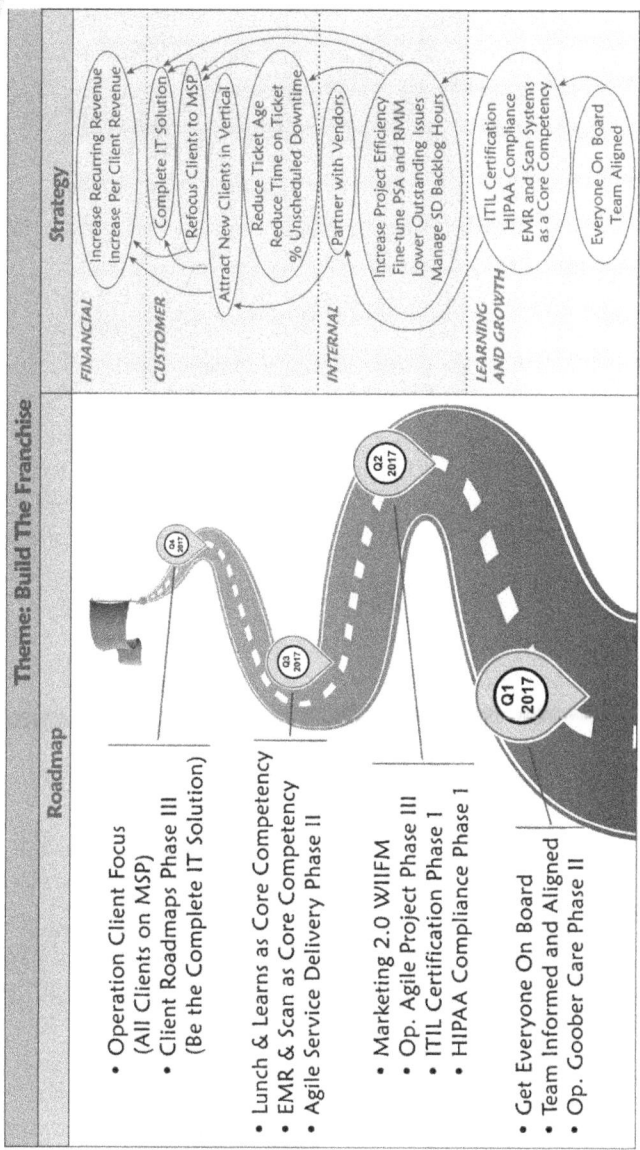

*Figure 8-4. Roadmap & Strategy for The Goober Group*

## The Strategy Narrative

Financial Perspective

- The Goober Group is pursuing an overall Customer Intimacy Strategy with this coming year's focus on Build the Franchise.
- Our goals are to Increase Recurring Revenue by presenting a higher value proposition to existing and new customers through our newly completed MSP Offering.
- We also intend to Increase Per Client Revenue by showing that we can be the Complete IT Solution for the customer.

Customer Perspective

- We intend to build stronger client relationships by establishing ourselves as the Complete IT Solution. As new and existing clients are focused on the new MSP offering, we intend to leverage specific relevant internal processes and to help clients build out their long-term IT roadmap. This will also show our brand and shared values.
- By refocusing existing customers to the newly completed MSP Offering we believe we will increase their return on investment through higher availability and reliability (% Unscheduled Downtime) with quicker time to resolution (Reduce Average Ticket Time and Average Time on Ticket).
- We believe we can attract new clients in the vertical market we have selected by offering free assessments and presenting the new MSP offering. The new MSP offering represents a value proposition we do not believe they currently have access to.

Internal Perspective

- In order to build relationships with potential and existing customers we must provide them with needed education and training about their systems. By tapping into our vendor Marketing Development Funds we will not only establish strategic partnerships with certain vendors but also tap into sources of valuable information and training for our customers that we may not currently possess.
- To show the customer we can in fact be the complete IT solution we must Increase Project Efficiency measurably.
- To provide higher availability to the customer and reduce time to resolution we must continue to Fine-Tune our front line tools. This tuning will allow us to actually show the customer the results in usable reports.
- To ensure quicker time to resolution we must effectively manage the Service Delivery Backlog and we must focus on Lowering the Average Number of Outstanding Issues.

Learning and Growth Perspective

- To attract new clients in our selected Vertical Market and Be the Complete IT Solution we must establish certifications in ITIL and compliance with HIPAA.
- To support many of the objectives for this year we must continue to strengthen the Core Competencies related to key client systems including EMR and Scan Systems.
- To succeed we must constantly be endearing Team members to the strategy and keep them Aligned with the objectives. Everyone has a place in this organization and a destiny in the success of our endeavor.

**Summary**

Defining an effective strategy for your business may be one of the most difficult tasks you ever take on. I believe that by using the tools and methods I have outlined in conjunction with the Case Study and Example, you can in fact learn to formulate effective strategy as a core competency. I promise that if you do, this competency itself represents a competitive advantage over the vast majority of your competitors.

# The BASE

The BASE that the pyramid sits upon is where all the actual effort to build the pyramid is performed. It is where the efforts of the organization are applied to the objectives and initiatives of the strategy. This work must be ordered and organized and executed on with prudence in line with the strategy for success that the organization has defined. As with anything we choose to construct with the intention of standing the test of time, we must build on solid ground. The BASE I refer to here is the most solid foundation any organization could choose to build on. BASE refers to the concept of Business Agile Strategy Execution, my own innovation in bringing Agile Methodology to Business Strategy. It represents the single most powerful tool I have presented in this book and if you tap into this power, I believe it can provide you with a core competency and significant competitive advantage over your competition that is unparalleled.

These last three chapters have been focused on the Pyramid of Purpose and Value itself and should be seen as a trilogy for designing your organization's Culture, Compass, and Blueprint for Success. The entire subject matter of executing on strategy is best presented in its own trilogy. Therefore, the complete and detailed discussion of

Business Agile Strategy Execution will be covered in Chapter 10 (Agile Execution) and Chapter 11 (Business Strategy Meets Agile Execution) with application to Chapter 12 (Case Study and Example).

## Blueprint for Success Crosscheck

Getting your Blueprint for Success right can mean stratospheric success or at the very least dominant competitive advantage. Getting it wrong can also mean being the one that is still standing on the ground, being totally dominated, or even being run out of the game. In my experience, the most common mistake made in strategy formulation is rooted in the concept of build it first then make it good. The best example of the mindset is the American term "fake it until you make it".

There are entrepreneurs who set up shop and start creating products or delivering services without any concept that they are building their brand every day and in every way that they do business. They are externally driven by that all-important need to make money to pay the rent and keep the doors open. Most are internally driven to actually take time to build the product right or refine the service process so that they are delivering what they intend or promise to. But most often, the time to do so is never available, so instead they churn faster in hopes the slack time will one day appear.

The end result is an organization that is wanting, intending, and trying to provide top level products or services but is in such a hurry to sell more to grow faster or find slack time that they become just another vendor of the same old stuff. They have created a brand that no one really knows or would likely recognize if quizzed or is just tarnished from improper care.

The root of the problem is in the strategy and the execution, or lack thereof. Of course there is a lot to be said for those small businesses that face the everyday requirements of paying rent just to stay in business, but there is no excuse for any business that has matured enough to have a handful of employees, a real business budget, and who is making payroll regularly. And for those organizations that mature into multi-million dollar businesses, there is even less of an excuse for not taking the time to build the products right or designing the services properly.

Even if the ultimate business strategy is to be a cost leader, there is still a strategy to doing it right. We have seen this with Wal-Mart and many others. So why would an organization intent on being the best of the best follow a strategy that is "fake it until you make it"? It is only one of two reasons—fear of losing ground in hard-won progress, or the neglect of long-term strategy for short-term gains. But what would it look like if an organization became the far and away leader at delivering a service before presenting the value proposition to the customer? What if they were to build the extremely high value proposition first and then offer it to the customer for a premium price, instead of the other way around?

In 2010, I was backpacking in Europe and just before the trip home, I realized if I had a few big duffle bags we could simply drop our entire backpacks into the duffle bags and check them as luggage for the trip home. We'd carry a shoulder bag and be free of the weight and the hassle. I went online and checked Amazon.co.uk for what I needed, and the bags showed up at my doorstep in Italy three days later. Nice, considering I didn't pay extra for expedited shipping. I also recall ordering something from Amazon in 2012 where my order showed up in only two days. Again, nice considering I did not pay for two-day shipping.

Fast forward to late 2014 when I ordered something from Amazon and it showed up the same day. I wasn't even willing to select two or three-day shipping, and yet it showed up the same day. Just when I thought it couldn't get any better, an item I ordered from Amazon in early 2015 appeared on my doorstep in short order and on a Sunday at that. I can't ship a box across town and get it delivered on a Sunday for anything under $25 US, regardless of the lead time. Amazon had been slowly refining their process without asking for a single dime more for the value. I recall sharing my experience with others and advising them not to be suckers, don't click two or three-day shipping because it's likely going to show up in twenty-four to forty-eight hours anyway.

And then the day came, when no matter what I ordered it came as promised in five to seven business days. No more speedy delivery, unless you paid extra for expedited shipping or you subscribed to the Prime membership. Prime was a program Amazon started back in 2005 and in their own words is an "all-you-can-eat express shipping membership program". I also noticed that more and more Amazon items started to only be available to Prime members. I felt confused, let down, and excluded all at the same time. I had the overwhelming feeling that I was somehow receiving worse service from Amazon now. But I wasn't, I was in fact getting exactly what I was promised—five to seven business days unless I select expedited shipping or become a Prime member.

I was confused why Amazon would just stop delivering things as fast considering they were obviously capable of doing so. Why wouldn't you, for the sake of moving product and customer satisfaction? The answer was simple—they had improved their internal processes for shipping and logistics to the point that they knew they could deliver faster than anyone else in the business. They proved they had created a core competency to deliver in under twenty-four hours to any densely populated area in the world. They also created a craving for this fast shipping because it meant customers could order and receive their impulse purchases possibly as early as same day, and that has value. This is how Amazon built the value proposition for their Prime membership and how they established their significant competitive advantage.

What this represented for Amazon was that their long-term strategy to create customer value could now begin to pay off in value for the organization. According to Amazon themselves, in 2014 alone their membership to their Prime program increased 50% with tens of millions of subscribers. That's a billion dollars for every ten million subscribers per year. Amazon first proved they could deliver on the value and then they began to charge accordingly for it, and rightfully so.

What if your organization could have the patience and the resolve to build a value proposition like no one else in the market you do business in? What if you could work a long-term strategy that ensured your strategic competitive advantage and created a value proposition the client could not do without? The answer is simple—you would get to the next level and you would find there are few if any competitors there. My recommendation is that you develop balanced short and long-term strategies that build value into the products and services and that you never set aside the long-term strategies for short-term gains.

*It doesn't matter where you are coming from. All that matters is where you are going.*

– Brain Tracy

# 9.0

## BUSINESS MATURITY INDEX – GAUGING YOUR SUCCESS

I believe that any business needs a way to benchmark its overall maturity but I do not necessarily believe it must always be relative to any other business. Of course if the measuring system you select can in fact help gauge your maturity relative to other businesses, especially if they are similar yours, then of course this can be a nice additional feature. Either way it all starts with the empirical question: Are we actually maturing as an organization? It's fair enough to say that if we can actually answer this question in any substantial way, the very next question will in fact be: How mature are we compared to other companies that do what we do? This then is where that previously mentioned "nice additional feature" comes in.

While developing my Getting To The Next Level methodology I recognized the need for a subjective business maturity measurement tool, but I have not found anything that suited my purpose. Most of what I came across touched on some aspects or elements of the business, but there was nothing to take in the subjective elements and see the big picture across the many aspects of a business. It is fairly common to find tools for *measuring the financial health of your business and even your standings relative to other businesses with similar operations. But if you measure the maturity of any business solely on their financial strength and position, you are missing a significantly large portion of that business's true maturity indicators. In fact, I propose that the financial strength is not even a factor in a business's maturity. How they manage money and how their systems deal with finances, however, is. Remember that you are out to build something that can withstand the tests of time, not just produce a decent profit and disappear.

In this chapter, I will detail my Business Maturity Index (BMI) that was briefly covered in Chapter 5. Some of that information is duplicated here although modified for the correct context and expanded. The Business Maturity Index is a grading or scoring tool for identifying your overall business maturity. The BMI is based on ten specific Value Aspects of your business which are then broken down into five specific Success Elements. Your BMI is expressed as a number between 1.00 and 5.00. The BMI is the actual business maturity level score for your organization. This score can be represented on the Business Maturity Index graph I introduced in Chapter 1. The BMI Graph is the measuring stick you refer to with your overall BMI score to see where you fall on the universal maturity scale of organizations.

## The BMI Framework

I'm going to describe the two components of the Business Maturity Index (BMI), first on a basic level with an example, and then later in detail. These two components are the business Value Aspects and the Success Elements. I will give an example of how the components combine to give you the overall Business Maturity Index, and I will show you how to apply them to the BMI graph so you understand how to use this tool to gauge and share your organization's own overall business maturity.

Any business can be defined by, broken down into, and evaluated on a finite number of functions and activities. I choose to use the term Value Aspects as opposed to Functions or Activities as it is a more accurate term to describe the fluid and symbiotic workings of a business and the value they create versus the strict segmentation of processes that are performed. I'll expand more on this later.

The list of ten Value Aspects, which I first introduced in Chapter 2, were derived from a careful culmination and evaluation of the business functions and activities consistently used by leading business management professors, authors, and masters over the last fifty plus years. These references include management authors such as Norton, Kaplan, Peters, Waterman, Porter, Drucker, Pink, Deming, Bossidy, Charan, Collins, and many others. See the Bibliography and the Glossary for a complete list of references on these sources.

In my evaluation, I found the standard list of commonly used business Value Aspects, while adequate, was missing something important. There is a specific Value Aspect of any operation that I find is significantly overlooked in modern business today. We do business very differently than ever before in today's interconnected world. We do business and collaborate with suppliers, partners, and clients all over the world as if they were right next door, twenty-four hours a day. But we are horrible at communications and collaboration. For this reason, I have called out an additional and specific Value Aspect: Communications and Collaboration.

The complete list of ten business Value Aspects is:
- Communications & Collaboration
- Finance & Accounting
- Human Resources
- Marketing
- Organization Infrastructure
- Procurement & Logistics
- Production Operations
- Research & Development
- Sales
- Service Delivery

To this point, I have defined the most common and prominent Value Aspects applicable to most any organization. I can now call out the critical Success Elements that will be evaluated for each of these Value Aspects. As with the Value Aspects, I will first give the basic layout of the Success Elements, and then provide the detailed explanation later in this chapter.

You should notice that the first three Success Elements are tied very closely to the three sections of the Pyramid of Purpose and Value introduced in Chapter 1 and detailed in Chapters 6-8. The additional two elements are related directly to the continued quest for competitive and strategic advantage through the relentless pursuit of value. They are Continuous Improvement and Continuous Refinement. You should also notice close ties of all the Success Elements to many of the concepts, tools, and subjects discussed throughout this book. The five Success Elements I chose to use are:
- Leadership and Staffing
- Knowledge Management
- Roadmap and Strategy
- Continuous Improvement
- Continuous Refinement

Now that I have described each of the five specific Success Elements that the ten Value Aspects will be evaluated on, let me explain the scale used for scoring the five Success Elements. In Chapter 1, I introduced the BMI graph with some narrative but not the full detail of how it came about. The BMI graph is a simplified representation of what is known as a Capability Maturity Model.

What is a Capability Maturity Model? The concept was conceived as early as the 1970s for benchmarking the maturity of processes and how well they are being actively adopted and accepted as culture with respects to the quality of products and services. As time moved forward, large strides were made in the advancement of the Capability Maturity Model by Carnegie Mellon University while working with the U.S. Department of Defense. The end result is that there is now a universally accepted Capability Maturity Model (CMM) that can be effectively adapted not only to processes and systems, but also to an organization as a whole. For our purposes, I choose to apply the Capability Model to the organization and refer to it as simply the Business Maturity Index.

The BMI graph is a structured set of five levels which can express how well the processes, procedures, and best practices of an organization are becoming the "embedded as culture" behaviors that can reliably and sustainably produce the desired and optimum outcome. This tool fits your needs well as it can be used as an aid in understanding the continued growth and maturity throughout your organization over time. Further, it can be the benchmark for comparison to other organizations, assuming they can properly score themselves using the same method outlined here.

The five maturity levels of the Business Maturity Index graph are as follows:

Level 1 = Chaotic – Indicative of a Startup company that is Reactive in nature. No uniform processes or no processes at all, and what does exist is usually disorganized. Success is almost always due to the heroic efforts of individuals. Repeatability and Reproducibility are not words used to describe the work product, and Rework and Duplicate Work are common.

Level 2 = Aware – Indicative of the Pioneer company that is learning to be Proactive in nature. They recognize the need for process control and they are establishing it at the best rate they can. They realize that if they can get the processes documented, they can be Repeatable and Reproducible and begin to drive Rework and Duplicate Work out of the system.

Level 3 = Enabled – Indicative of a Success Oriented company that knows the value of process and wants to create value. They have the most important processes defined and documented; they have established internal standards and procedures. Projects and most general work are Repeatable and Reproducible. Rework and Duplicate Work are uncommon.

Level 4 = Managed – Indicative of an Organization Oriented business that has well-established process control with measurable metrics. They have established systems and are a learning company. They focus on the innovations that can bring the most value to their customers. They rely on Repeatability and Reproducibility. Rework and Duplicate Work are low percentage metrics.

Level 5 = Optimized – Indicative of a Value Driven company that leverages all aspects of processes and systems to drive margin. They are truly innovative and they know that Margin can be directly converted into Value for the client. They focus on the core functions of the business and outsource everything else. Repeatability and Reproducibility are long embedded watchwords.

As you will see shortly, the BMI criteria applied to a given Success Element of a Value Aspect has been customized specifically for that Success Element. This is because you cannot gauge the maturity of your Leadership and Staffing the same as you gauge the maturity of your Knowledge Management. The criteria and terminology are much different for each Success Element. But notice that once the Maturity Level criteria is defined for a given Success Element, it does not change regardless of what Value Aspect it is applied to. The desired result is that the maturity of any Success Element is evaluated exactly the same across all Value Aspects.

## The Index and Graph in Action

Now that all the pieces have been laid out, let's put them together to calculate the Business Maturity Index and see where we are on the BMI graph. There are ten Value Aspects broken down into five Success Elements. Each Success Element has a simple five level scale to represent the maturity of that element, from 1 to 5. (Note: The Scale for each Success Element has a deeper meaning and is explained in greater detail below.) Now let's assume an honest and deeply introspective evaluation is performed of each and every Success Element for each of all ten Value Aspects. What we end up with is individual maturity scores for each Value Aspect, and when all ten are averaged out, we will also have the overall Business Maturity Index.

Now let's turn to the example below where I highlight the Communications and Collaboration Value Aspect (see Figure 9-1). First a deep, introspective evaluation would be performed for each element to come up with a score. What we're looking for is the average; as such, we would add together the Success Element score totals for this particular Value Aspect and then divide the total by 5. The result is a single number between 1 and 5 which represents the BMI for this Value Aspect.

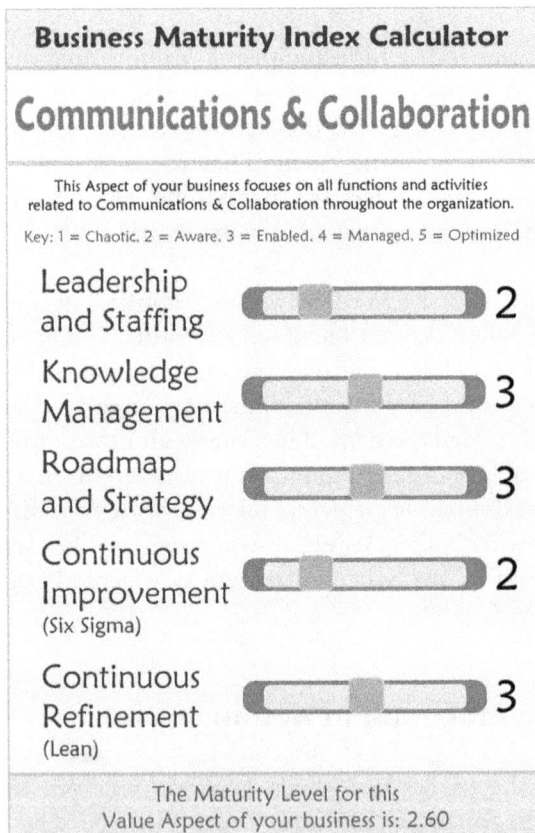

**Business Maturity Index Calculator**

# Communications & Collaboration

This Aspect of your business focuses on all functions and activities related to Communications & Collaboration throughout the organization.

Key: 1 = Chaotic, 2 = Aware, 3 = Enabled, 4 = Managed, 5 = Optimized

Leadership and Staffing — 2

Knowledge Management — 3

Roadmap and Strategy — 3

Continuous Improvement (Six Sigma) — 2

Continuous Refinement (Lean) — 3

The Maturity Level for this Value Aspect of your business is: 2.60

*Figure 9-1. Business Maturity Index Calculator*

Based on the example, we can now actually state that we have a business Maturity Level of 2.6 for the Communications and Collaboration Value Aspect. Next, we need to perform the same deep, introspective evaluation of the remaining nine Value Aspects. Once again, we are looking for the average of all of the ten Value Aspects. This will be the overall cumulative Business Maturity Index of all Value Aspects (see Figure 9-2). We see that each Value Aspect has been scored, and if we average them as indicated, we can confidently state that you have an overall Business Maturity Index of 2.35.

| Your Overall Business Maturity Index Is: 2.35 | |
|---|---|
| Communications & Collaboration 2.6 ◀ | Procurement & Logistics 2.0 ◀ |
| Finance & Accounting 1.5 ◀ | Production Operations 2.5 ◀ |
| Human Resources 2.5 ◀ | Research & Development 2.0 ◀ |
| Marketing 2.9 ◀ | Sales 2.0 ◀ |
| Organization Infrastructure 3.0 ◀ | Service Delivery 2.5 ◀ |
| Note: Maximum Possible Score is 5.0 | Please note: Numbers may appear larger than actual. This is a self-evaluation so please understand that your Business Maturity Index may not be completely accurate. |

*Figure 9-2. Value Aspect Scoring*

Next we find our benchmark spot on the Business Maturity Index graph at about the midpoint of level two (see Figure 9-3). By definition, the organization is right at the midpoint of maturity as a Pioneering Proactive organization. We can stick a pin in the graph and put it up on the wall for everyone in the organization to see. We can even compare it to other companies regardless of their industry, products, or services, assuming of course that they have used the same criteria for scoring their organization.

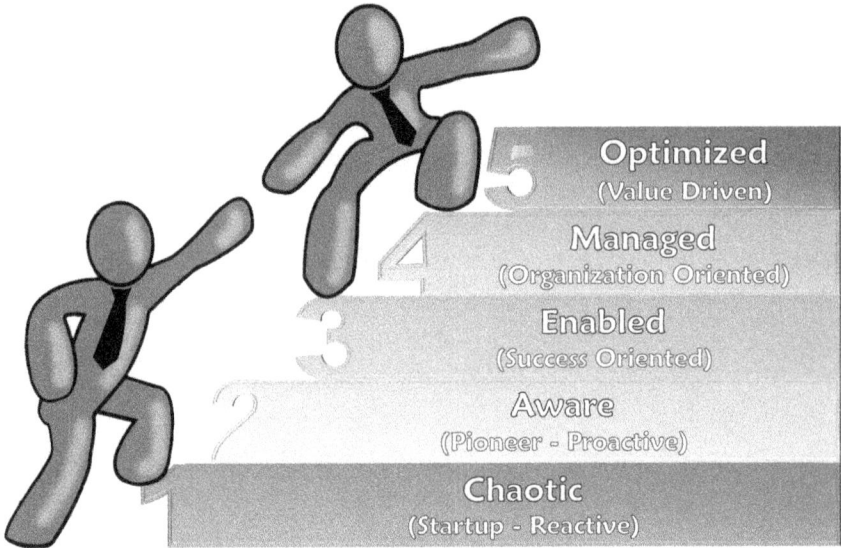

*Figure 9-3. Business Maturity Index Graph*

## BMI Summary

What I have proposed here is a straightforward method using a framework built from generally accepted business and industry standards for gauging an organization's overall business maturity. For my purposes, this tool is a critical step in evaluating any business and discerning where an organization is at and what the next level looks like.

Be sure to review the original introduction and discussion on Your Business Success and Maturity in Chapters 1 and 5. The concepts and details laid out in this chapter help explain and support those and vice versa. A reminder now of one important message: The Business Maturity Index for an organization is typically not a fast moving thing. Companies may trudge along for a dozen years or more and never break out of level one. Conversely, an organization which comes to the realization that building out their processes and pushing from Level one (Reactive) to Level two (Proactive) will transform their business and their market position significantly, can make it happen in a matter of months given the resources and drive.

The BMI is a versatile tool in that it allows you to look specifically at and evaluate each Value Aspect of the business independently of the others, and when desired, compared to each other. As shown in the example, Communications and Collaboration were scored 2.6 while

Procurement and Logistics were scored 2.0. If this was a large company with resources, we could define the very unique but specific roadmap for each of these Value Aspects in order to get each of them to the next level independently of each other. And of course, if this was a smaller business where each individual Value Aspect is not going to make significant progress relative to the entire organization, we could simply and safely focus on the overall Business Maturity Index for our progress metric and landmark.

In the next two chapters, I will define the agile project methodology and I will discuss the agile project management system I use to drive your business roadmap and strategy. I call it Business Agile Strategy Execution, and the BMI fits very well within this agile tool. I will show you how to systematically execute on your defined business roadmap and strategy. I will also show you how to precisely measure the progress of the individual Value Aspects and the organization overall using the BMI.

Let's now wrap up this chapter with the breakdown of the ten Value Aspects and the five Success Elements.

## The Ten Business Value Aspects

As I mentioned previously, I prefer to use the term Value Aspect versus either Function or Activity, first and foremost because the word aspect more accurately describes the symbiotic relationship of the processes, procedures, and operations that are routinely performed throughout an organization to attain the ultimate mission. Mostly when planning, and certainly when managing, the strict boundaries associated with the word's function and activity cause segmentation that restricts one's ability to craft robust strategy. Also, the ten business Value Aspects I have selected are largely derived from Michael Porter's Value Chain and I certainly subscribe to his concept that a mature business is Value driven. Thus, business Value Aspect versus business Function or Activity.

The business Value Aspects listed here are mostly self-explanatory with a few important clarifications, starting with the differences between Production Operations and Service Delivery. These two Value Aspects are significantly different depending on whether your business is Product-centric or Service-centric. Although the difference between them may, for some businesses, be hard to discern or seem irrelevant, it is in fact neither. You only need to look at them relative to how a Product-centric or Service-centric business defines their core processes and more importantly, defines their roadmaps and strategy for getting to the next level. Before getting into the examples, let me ask a clarifying question: Is the primary value proposition of your business creating products that require service (Product-centric) or delivering service of products (Service-centric)?

Product-centric – If your business is a Bakery or a Plywood Manufacturer, these two business models are distinct and simple Product-centric entities. As a Baker, your Production Operations is everything about making bread products. If your business is a Plywood Manufacturer, Production Operations is about making plywood. For both of these businesses, the Service Delivery is everything about servicing the items you have sold, including: sales counter, parts, repairs, replacements or returns, service scheduling, etc.

If however you are in a Service-centric business, such as Heating Ventilation and Air Conditioning (HVAC) or IT Computer Services, it can get a little confusing. In these two examples, there is a huge component of the business that is about selling these new devices and systems to your clients, but there is also a significant, if not larger portion of the revenue that comes from servicing these devices and systems.

In this example of Service-centric, your Production Operations is the build-out of a unit (Heater or Server) and usually includes the delivery, installation, and setup of the unit. And if you're doing it right, you're running the build, delivery, and installation as a project. Service Delivery is provided as a support function for existing devices and systems, usually regardless of who the client purchased the devices or systems from. It includes the administration of service such as the Service Management, Service Coordination, plus the majority of your service delivery staff.

This implies that your higher level engineer team and the design function of their job is part of Production Operations while the Tier Three support function they provide to help your service team is Service Delivery. You could also think of it this way—In the service industry, time is your widget. If you are creating a need for the widget or creating something that gets widgets sold out the door (a project), it's Production Operations. If it's just delivering the widgets, maintaining the things you've sold, it's Service Delivery.

Although the business Value Aspects listed here are in what I believe to be a specific priority order, there should be no misunderstanding that not one aspect can be ignored, dispensed, or otherwise neglected. You must have balance and symmetry in the operation of your business or you will be running lopsided and you will not get to the next level. The failure of even one business Value Aspect to properly mature will keep your entire organization from getting to the next level. It is a physical impasse and it is always revealed upon scrutiny.

## Communications & Collaboration

This aspect of your business focuses primarily on all functions and activities related to Communications & Collaboration throughout the organization. This aspect is not about the phone system, forums board on your website, or the white board in the conference room. It's more about the methods and culture around communications and collaboration. It deals more with the advancement of your team skills, practices, and utilization of the tools available to use such as the phone system, forums board on your website, or the white board in the conference room. While this is the most esoteric (least tangible) of all the business Value Aspects, it is also the most crucial aspect for building great teams and organizations.

## Finance & Accounting

This aspect of your business focuses primarily on all functions and activities related to Finance & Accounting throughout the organization. Finance & Accounting is at the heart of the organization as it deals directly with the lifeblood of the business. It includes (but is not limited to) the invoicing, collections, payments, and day-to-day transactions of the operation, in addition to all the planning, budgeting, procurement, and effective utilization of the business capital.

## Human Resources

This aspect of your business focuses primarily on all functions and activities related to Human Resources throughout the organization. This aspect is concerned with the human side of the business and concerned with the cultivation, acquisition, and assimilation of quality talent throughout the organization. It includes (but is not limited to) training, advancement, wages, hours, and related policies and regulations.

## Marketing

This aspect of your business focuses primarily on all functions and activities related to Marketing throughout the organization. This aspect is concerned with defining the products and services that will be successful, differentiating them from your competitors' offerings, and letting the target market know you offer them. It includes (but is not limited to) defining the target market, market research, execution of advertising, and promotions.

## Organization Infrastructure

This aspect of your business focuses primarily on all functions and activities related to Organization Infrastructure. This aspect is concerned with management, legal, planning, information systems, leadership, government affairs, and quality management. It includes (but is not limited to) the cultivation of the business roadmap and strategy in addition to the entire IT infrastructure and operating systems the business runs on.

## Procurement & Logistics

This aspect of your business focuses primarily on all functions and activities related to Procurement & Logistics throughout the organization. It is concerned with purchasing and all inbound and outbound logistics. It includes (but is not limited to) order processing, shipping, receiving, material handling, inventory control, warehousing, returns, exchanges, and supplies.

## Production Operations

This aspect of your business focuses primarily on all functions and activities related to Production Operations throughout the organization. This aspect is concerned with the transformation process that turns materials and people into finished goods and services. It includes (but is not limited to) organizing effective method of production and controlling of machining, assembly, packaging, maintenance, and facility operations.

## Research & Development

This aspect of your business focuses primarily on all functions and activities related to Research & Development throughout the organization. This aspect is concerned with the life cycle of a product, from idea through viability testing to production. It includes (but is not limited to) innovation, research and development, design, revision, refinement, processes, procedures, and documentation.

### Sales

This aspect of your business focuses primarily on all functions and activities related to Sales throughout the organization. This aspect is concerned with activities whose objective is to promote and facilitate the customer purchase of your products or client engagement of your services. It includes (but is not limited to) customer relationship management, planning of  advertising and promotions, market awareness, public relations, fulfillment, refunds, returns, and exchanges.

### Service Delivery

This aspect of your business focuses primarily on all functions and activities related to Service Delivery throughout the organization. This aspect is concerned with the coordination of the delivery of your products and services with client needs and desires. It includes (but is not limited to) client management, scheduling, installation, maintenance, repair, training, parts supply, third party interaction, and customer satisfaction.

## The Five Success Elements

Listed below are the five most critical Success Elements of any business Value Aspect, again in priority order. The Success Elements are those core competencies that are critical to the success of the organization as a whole that failure to cultivate and progress in any one area will actually block an organization from getting to the next level. Failure to keep these elements in balance will hold the organization back from becoming the truly excellent business they wish to be. Imagine never getting Gold, never getting the #1 spot no matter how hard you try. There must be some element of your game that isn't mature enough. But if you identify it and remedy it, you certainly can get to where you are going.

I will start with a special note about the last two elements and address any idea you may have of either eliminating or replacing them. The last two elements are: Continuous Improvement and Continuous Refinement. The primary gauge for Continuous Improvement is Six

Sigma, while the primary gauge for Continuous Refinement is Lean. I discussed Lean and Six Sigma in Chapter 5 to a necessary level as an intentional prerequisite to the upcoming discussion. These two Success Elements have a greater significance than most will readily recognize.

The gauges used for these two particular Success Elements—Six Sigma and Lean—represent the Yin and Yang of your organization's process and systems improvement efforts. This Yin and Yang are present and manifested in every organization whether you believe it or know it. It may be the clarification of a structured protocol and the formality that gives one the impression that they are only for big companies or that they do not exist in every corner of every entrepreneurial endeavor around the world. As you will read shortly, these two (Six Sigma and Lean) address a single end result from two opposite sides.

Yin is the quiet mind and active body while Yang is the quiet body and active mind. Both are ever present, and the decision to develop them is left to the free will of the individual. I believe the best and most accurate correlation is to consider Six Sigma and Lean as the two most prominent options for creating anything, such as a piece of art. Six Sigma is the building up of something from nothing but only ever selecting actions and materials that will give value, e.g. a painting. Lean is starting with something, then removing only materials or substances that do not give value, while also having the discipline to refrain from additional actions that would not give value, e.g. a sculpture. You could actually reread the previous sentences with the words Continuous Improvement and Continuous Refinement in place of Six Sigma and Lean, respectively. Final word: Six Sigma is Continuous Improvement while Lean is Continuous Refinement. Now to move on to the list of Success Elements.

## Leadership and Staffing

This Success Element addresses everything about the Human Element. This Success Element strongly determines how well the organization's mission, vision, culture, and compass are adopted from the top down. The maturity of your leadership and staff also strongly affects your ability to successfully cultivate talent from within.

If you do not have a mature team (leaders and followers), you will not achieve the desired results of your grand plans, i.e. selling the organization roadmap and strategy to your own people, let alone being able to execute on them. You strive for Leadership and Staff that possess emotional intelligence and are mature in their understanding and mastery of each business Value Aspect as these are the true determinants of your ability to leverage knowledge and actualize operational philosophies.

This is not in conflict with the business Value Aspect of Human Resources as HR is about the function of finding, hiring, and maintaining quality talent across the entire business. The Leadership and Staffing Success Element is about the maturity of a given business Value Aspect. For example: We do not have seasoned and mature Sales people, i.e. we have an immature Sales department. However, we do have a great HR team, and they are more than capable of finding the people we need provided we properly fund the endeavor.

Level 1 = Chaotic – Yeah, we're very mature. We're all adults here! – Relative to this business Value Aspect, our people have low competence but high commitment, and our leadership is mostly oriented toward instructions for the task versus development of the person. We demonstrate an overall low autonomy, mastery, and sense of purpose.

Level 2 = Aware – We recognize the importance of having the right people – Relative to this business Value Aspect, our people have growing competence but low commitment, and our leadership is mostly oriented toward coaching staff and selling the company culture. We demonstrate an overall low autonomy, medium mastery, and a developing sense of purpose.

Level 3 = Enabled – We recognize the significance of Autonomy, Mastery, and Purpose – Relative to this business Value Aspect, our people have high competence but a varying commitment, and our leadership is mostly oriented toward supporting and sometimes still participating in work. We demonstrate an overall developing autonomy, high mastery, and a developing sense of purpose.

Level 4 = Managed – We actively invest in the cultivation of our leadership and talent – Relative to this business Value Aspect, our people have high competence and high commitment, and our leadership is mostly oriented toward delegating and organizing work. We demonstrate an overall strong autonomy, high mastery, and strong sense of purpose.

Level 5 = Optimized – We have a robust people process and we create our own success – Relative to this business Value Aspect, our leaders possess emotional intelligence and they develop staff effectively through coaching, mentoring, development programs, and learning projects. Our staff largely possesses both the internal and external core competencies required to demonstrate their ability to develop, grow, and self-nurture for sustainable success. We demonstrate an overall high autonomy, mastery, and sense of purpose.

## Knowledge Management

This Success Element addresses the creation, maintenance, and dissemination of Explicit and Tacit knowledge within the organization and when necessary, outside the organization. Although Knowledge Management (KM) should be a core competency of any organization, it is often significantly segmented. What you end up with is each business Value Aspect having a KM maturity that is usually relative to the maturity of the other elements of that business Value Aspect.

This Success Element includes (but is not restricted to): Processes (Internal & External), Policies, Standards, Procedures, Best Practices, Documentation, Training, and Learning.

Level 1 = Knowledge Chaotic – Yeah, we have some notes on this somewhere! – We have documented a few critical things relative to this business Value Aspect, but the documentation process and quality depends greatly on the heroics and effort of a few key people.

Level 2 = Knowledge Aware – We have a place to put everything and everybody is on board – We recognize the importance of Knowledge Management relative to Business Maturity and we have our own fledgling system in place that endears to this business Value Aspect.

Level 3 = Knowledge Defined – Documentation is what we do! – We largely utilize the resources provided by management to drive our maturing Knowledge Management system relative to this business Value Aspect. We are looking for ways to expand our Knowledge Management system.

Level 4 = Knowledge Managed – Knowledge is power and we're getting stronger every day – Leadership lives up to the accountability assigned by management. We do our part to have a significant, positive impact on the resulting Knowledge Management system relative to this business Value Aspect.

Level 5 = Knowledge Optimized – We leverage our retained knowledge for competitive advantage – We fully participate in the organization's mature and robust Knowledge Management system by being custodians of these systems relative to this business Value Aspect.

## Roadmap and Strategy

This Maturity Element addresses the future plans, goals, metrics, and cross-function alignment for a given business Value Aspect. Although there should always be a top level master business Roadmap and Strategy, you must ask: Are the components relative to this business Value Aspect mature and future looking (to the extent possible) for 6 months out? 1 year out? 3 years out? 5 years out? Are the goals and metrics set out for this business Value Aspect (think Balanced Scorecard) in realistic alignment with each of the other business Value Aspects to create success, growth, and value?

Level 1 = Roadmap and Strategy Chaotic – Who needs a map? – Hey, we just do whatever it takes to get though the day to help pay the rent and keep the lights on. We're not really clear on how this business Value Aspect would be addressed in a business Roadmap and Strategy.

Level 2 = Roadmap and Strategy Aware – We see the forest for the trees – We recognize the importance of having plans for the development of this business Value Aspect specifically called out in the overall business Roadmap and Strategy.

Level 3 = Roadmap and Strategy Defined – We know where we are – We have general language in the overall business Roadmap and Strategy that addresses the most critical goals and metrics relative to this business Value Aspect and we are committed to keeping our progress in line with all the other business Value Aspects.

Level 4 = Roadmap and Strategy Managed – We know where we're going – We have specifics called out in the overall business Roadmap and Strategy that address every important goal and metric relative to this business Value Aspect and we are driving our success in near lockstep with all the other business Value Aspects.

Level 5 = Roadmap and Strategy Optimized – We know how we'll get there – We have specifics called out in the overall business Roadmap and Strategy that address every important goal and metric relative to this business Value Aspect and we are driving value in lockstep with the other business Value Aspects.

## Continuous Improvement (Six Sigma)

This Maturity Element addresses the Continuous Improvement of every relevant process through statistical process control. There are many incarnations of statistical process control but Six Sigma is called out here as the gauge because it is the predominant model used in the majority of Fortune 500 companies today. Six Sigma uses measurement and metrics to refine a process with the ultimate goal of driving out defects, variability, and reducing cycle times. The end result product or service provides evidence of the improvement through increased value and/or a higher margin. Six Sigma requires an adoption of its principles and methods as a company-wide culture, embedded as habit, and demonstrated as discipline. You start out unaware with no real knowledge, then advance to white belt, then green, and finally to black belt.

Remember that to one extent or another, the minute you start recording metrics for anything about your business with the intent of driving those metrics toward a goal, you are in fact utilizing statistical process control. Six Sigma is just statistical process control defined and refined to a point where it is a simple science within the reach of everyone who cares to learn it. It is the higher and more advanced (mature) next level of what many of you are already doing now. Here too you are free to replace the words Six Sigma with Continuous Improvement if it helps you to better comprehend this concept and construct.

Level 1 = Six Sigma Initial – Six Sig-Wuh? – The concept of controlling the production or delivery processes to continuously improve them is common knowledge but is not recognized as an entire philosophy that can drive value and profit relative to this business Value Aspect.

Level 2 = Six Sigma Aware – We've done the math and Six Sigma is the answer! – We recognize the importance of what Six Sigma will do for us and we know we need to adopt a philosophy of controlling processes in this business Value Aspect just as in any other.

Level 3 = Six Sigma Defined – We're actively adopting the concepts as white belts – We have a fledgling system in place and we largely utilize the resources provided by management to drive our maturing Six Sigma methodology relative to this business Value Aspect.

Level 4 = Six Sigma Managed – We have color belts and we know how to use them – Leadership lives up to the accountability assigned by management and we do our part to drive progress and solidify the Six Sigma philosophy relative to this business Value Aspect.

Level 5 = Six Sigma Optimized – We have black belts and Six Sigma is what we do – We fully participate in the organization's mature and robust Six Sigma system and strive for continuous improvement relative to this business Value Aspect.

## Continuous Refinement (Lean)

This Maturity Element addresses Continuous Refinement, the relentless pursuit of creating the highest value products and services by focusing on the reduction or elimination of waste in all aspects of the business. There are many incarnations of production waste management that consider the expenditure of resources in any way other than the direct creation of value of the end product or service to be wasteful. The modern version of Lean is called out here as the gauge because it is the predominant model used in the majority of Fortune 500 companies today. The Lean philosophy is to either stop or to not start doing anything that does not directly add value to what the customer is willing to pay for. It requires an adoption of the Lean principles and methods as company-wide culture, embedded as habit and demonstrated as discipline.

Similar to the relationship of Six Sigma to a fledgling process control system, Lean (to one extent or another) is likely already embedded in many of your systems and processes. Many of your people already think in Lean terms such as, "Why do that thing if it's not going to add value and it will just take more time?" Lean is also ultimately a refinement methodology for process control that has been defined and refined to the point where it is a simple science within the reach of everyone who cares to learn it. It, too, is the higher and more advanced (mature) next level of what many of you are already doing now. As with Six Sigma above, you are free to replace the word Lean with Continuous Refinement if it helps you to better comprehend this concept and construct.

Level 1 = Lean Initial – We like our steak lean! – The concept of expending no more resources than required to produce the desired results (products or services) is common knowledge but it's not recognized as an entire philosophy that can drive value and profit relative to this business Value Aspect.

Level 2 = Lean Aware – Lean methods would be very good for our health! – We recognize the importance of what Lean will do for us and we know we need to adopt a philosophy of managing waste in this business Value Aspect just as in any other.

Level 3 = Lean Defined – We're building out our Lean toolbox – We have a fledgling system in place and we largely utilize the resources provided by management to drive our maturing Lean methodology relative to this business Value Aspect.

Level 4 = Lean Managed – We have a toolbox and we know how to use it – Leadership lives up to the accountability assigned by management and we do our part to drive progress and solidify the Lean philosophy relative to this business Value Aspect.

Level 5 = Lean Optimized – We think Lean, we are Lean – We fully participate in the organization's mature and robust Lean system and strive for Continuous Refinement relative to this business Value Aspect.

## Finding Your Business Maturity Index

To utilize the BMI for your own organization you simply need to run through the process outlined above with respects to your organization. Do not be intimidated by terms you may have never considered to be relevant to small business such as Lean or Six Sigma. If they intimidate you, replace them with what they represent—Continuous Improvement and Continuous Refinement. Regardless of what you label them, these are valid indicators of any size organization. Also, do not be concerned where you are on the BMI relative to the top of the scale or relative to other organizations. As was indicated in Chapter 5 when I introduced the BMI as a tool, the vast majority of organizations will be crowded down at or near Level 1 with less and less organizations at each successive Level above (see Figure 9-4).

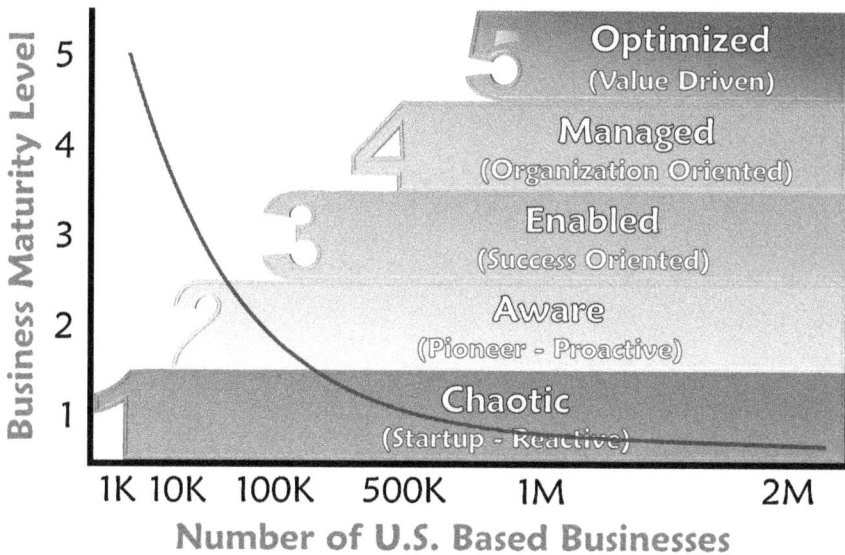

*Figure 9-4. Business Maturity Distribution*

There are very few Level 5 organizations in the entire world relative to Levels 4, 3, 2, and 1. It is a natural relationship but it is also an entirely unrestricted opportunity. Any organization can choose to be Level 5 and there is no barrier to attaining it. This opportunity by itself is a potential for significant competitive advantage. It's all in how you choose to define and run your business. If you have designed your Pyramid of Purpose and Value to address the continued cultivation of the Success Elements required for getting to the next level, you will in fact one day get to where you are going. Remember that being a Fortune 500 company or even a Fortune 100 company does not automatically grant Level 5 status. Nothing about your annual revenue should restrict you from becoming a Level 5 organization either.

To this point you have been given all the tools you will need to define, analyze, refine, and even gauge your business blueprint for success and gauge your business maturity. There is one final tool to cover. Although it was already introduced in Chapter 5, it will be completely detailed over the next two chapters. This final tool will allow you to actually drive the progress of the organization by continuously and incrementally improving every Value Aspect of the business while cultivating each Success Element. It will allow you to logically execute on your business Roadmap and Strategy as planned.

*More progress results from the violent execution of an imperfect plan than the perfection of a plan to violently execute.*

– Hubert Humphrey

# 10.0

## AGILE EXECUTION

For small and medium-sized organizations, when it comes to the cultivation of a business roadmap and strategy and the systematic execution on that strategy, the available tools and methods are sorely lacking in many ways. In this book, I have identified some excellent tools that have been around for a long time that will help you define, measure, and refine your processes, systems, and operations. But for this purpose, you need a tool that will allow you to take in the bigger picture that is the entire organization with all that is intertwined inside and outside of the organization. You need a tool that allows you to cultivate your business roadmap and execute on strategy as if it were a detailed, ongoing living project. You need a tool that will allow you to collaborate with anyone inside or outside the organization which can help you move forward, mature, and get you to the next level.

My innovation for the practice of business strategy cultivation and execution is to infuse and leverage the Agile Project Methodology. The Agile Project Methodology (or just Agile) at its simplest means continuous improvement realized through frequent releases (iterations) of the new version of this thing being working on, in collaboration with the entire team. For your business roadmap and strategy, the new release (iteration) is the new Version or next level results of your continuous improvement in any aspect of your business. Thus, Business Strategy meets Agile Execution.

For my own purposes, I chose to call this innovation Business Agile Strategy Execution or simply BASE. I have chosen this name because, as you may recall from Chapter 1, it fits nicely into place at the ground level of my Pyramid of Purpose and Value as the BASE of the pyramid. As discussed in Chapter 1, you design your pyramid from the top down with each level having the requirement that it must support all the levels above it. And the BASE is in fact the ground level where the rubber hits the road and all the real work is done. This is where we haul in the sheets and harness the wind that will get us to where we are going.

As you systematically cultivate your roadmap and execute on strategy, leveraging the Agile Methodology, you continuously and incrementally move your business closer and closer to the next level. Setting aside how I have chosen to implement these agile execution methods into my view of a complete business model and into my coaching system, the Agile Project Methodology is the most logical and concise way to bring together everything I have covered in this book.

I do believe that there is a paradigm shift on its way about how small and medium-sized businesses execute on business strategy. I know that business coaches, peer groups, and business improvement groups are going to adopt and master this methodology. No other tool can offer the potential for continuous improvement and systematically driving your business strategy as this one. This tool is the right size for small and medium-sized businesses and it does not have any special requirements for implementation.

I have spent the majority of this book presenting long-standing, proven concepts for managing your business and discussing how to apply them to drive the different aspects of your business to the next level. In this chapter and the one following, I will present the most advanced concepts and also the most powerful tool for driving your overall business roadmap and strategy. If you are not overly technical, the contents of these two chapters may seem too deep to deal with or too complex to be usable by you. Even if you are technical minded, this chapter may intimidate you early on.

Regardless of which camp you are in, you should read these two chapters for whatever level of understanding you can glean from them, even if you must read them twice through. I say this for two important reasons. First, you may recognize that many entrepreneurs and business owners are actually already utilizing some of the most important concepts of agile in how they cultivate their business roadmap and execute on strategy. I believe this will become evident as you read on. And second, if you understand this concept of leveraging Agile Execution to drive Business Strategy, you will have the most powerful tool there is for taking your business to the next level. Period.

As a lead-in to the next chapter and the main subject at hand—

Business Strategy Meets Agile Execution—I need to address a few things such as defining Agile, the basics of Agile Project Methodology versus Waterfall Project Methodology, and why one must choose Agile over Waterfall. I will first provide a clear definition of Agile and its unique terminology before comparing it to the alternative option for project management, the Waterfall Methodology. I will also provide a sufficiently detailed example of Agile Methodology before the comparison.

The upcoming discussion is in no way intended to be a comprehensive detail of the two methodologies; as such, I have provided no more detail than I believe is necessary to clearly see the difference between the two and to further the main subject of this chapter. I will also not be providing a definition of a Project or detailing the Waterfall Methodology as I believe they are simple enough concepts and I consider them to be basic knowledge for anyone who owns or manages a business.

## Agile Defined

Note: If you are a high level Agile wizard, please don't get stuck on the simple, distilled definition I choose to present here. If you truly understand Agile, you should understand the intent and the need to keep it simple and understandable. Fortunately for me no one owns Agile, which means its core framework and methods can be applied in any way one sees fit. I will show specifically how I choose to apply it in the next chapter.

First let's look at and define some unique terminology used in Agile. For a more detailed definition, you may want to refer to the Glossary in this book.

Issue: The technical name given to the individual things that need to be worked on, completed, or implemented. There are many common types of Issues, such as Problems, Feature Requests, Bugs to work out, Revisions to be made, and general To-do items. When breaking down the work, it is easier to simply call them all "Issues" and when you do need to look closer or group things, you can see they may be Bugs, Features, Revisions, etc.

User Story: The less technical name given to the individual things that need to be worked on, completed, or implemented, except that the narrative of the Issue is expressed from the end user perspective—e.g. As a [end user /customer role], I would like [the desire] so that [reasoning]. When Issues are represented in this fashion, it encourages the team to think of the work from the end user or customer perspective.

Project Backlog: Informally referred to as simply the Backlog, this is an accumulation of uncompleted work (Issues) that need to be dealt with. I often refer to the Backlog as the Laundry List of things to do.

Sprint: The group effort of the people involved in a project to further the focused development of the project in some measurable way within a reasonable amount of time. A sprint is planned and directed through collaboration. It is closely tracked to ensure progress and to see that no one gets or remains stuck on any issue.

Sprint Backlog: You may be able to figure this one out; simply put, it is the Backlog of the things the Sprint is focusing efforts on right now. You have the big Laundry List for the overall project, but you have picked out a select group of Issues to focus on which is then called your Sprint Backlog.

Iteration: Traditionally refers to a new Version of a piece of computer hardware or software. For our purposes, it will also refer to a new Version of some Aspect of your business, or maybe a new Version of your entire business. The word Release is often used synonymously, e.g. there is a new Release of the program you use.

Scrum: I have saved the hardest one for last, and this will be overly simplified for true Scrum Masters out there in the world. The Scrum can be seen as the project management mechanism. Everyone is constantly collaborating on the project, and the Scrum team (usually daily) sees to it that the current Sprint in progress remains focused on the common goal. They make changes as needed to ensure the Sprint completes the Sprint Backlog on time, the Iteration is completed, and the new Version is released.

## Agile In Action

Now to provide that detailed example and to keep it simple, I will use the most common example of agile methodology available today—the smartphone. Someone comes up with the idea for a new phone and decides to put a hefty computer chip into this new device. Then they need an operating system (software to run on the phone), so a project begins to build the new software. They list all the basics they need to make this thing work and along the way, they are collecting lots of ideas for cool features, formally called Issues. This then is the initial Project Backlog. Next, they start to sort through and prioritize all these Issues needing to be worked on. The Issues are grouped together into what are known as Sprints. Think of Sprints as prioritized grouping of Issues.

One Sprint contains all the tasks that must be completed just for this new phone to be able to make and receive a call. Another Sprint contains all the cool features that will drive potential customers to want to own one of these phones. And still another Sprint contains features that will be a little harder to implement but certainly should be included some day. The Sprint Planning produces the first few Sprints to create a working phone and make users want to own one.

The Scrum team begins working through the first Sprint Backlog that has all of the things required to get this phone to work. They have a reasonable deadline and they have daily or weekly Scrum meetings to make sure they are on task and on time. At or near the deadline they release the Cool Phone Version 0.9. Yea! Now they start to work on the next Sprint Backlog that adds all those cool features which will make potential customers want one of these phones. Our heroic team works through the current Sprint to complete the list of features by the determined deadline, and now they reveal the Cool Phone Version 1.0. Woohoo! We are taking this thing to market!

Once available to the public, the customer buys the Cool Phone Version 1.0 because they must own one now! They turn on the Cool Phone and start using it. All is well until they find a bug with how the phone auto dials random people when they put in into their pocket. The customer logs onto the manufacturer's website and reports a bug about how this phone is behaving. The bug reported is considered a User Story as it represents an end user (and customer) request. The project team adds this new Issue (Bug) to the Project Backlog and they rate it as important. During the next Sprint Planning, the team reviews all Issues and User Stories and decides it would be good for the end users (and the manufacturer's reputation) to make sure this Issue (Bug) gets fixed soon, so they put it into the upcoming Sprint Backlog.

The team goes to work as the whole Agile Project Lifecycle repeats and when the Sprint is completed, the new version of the Cool Phone

Version 1.1 is released. The customer gets a message on their phone saying, "There is an update to your phone. It will add these cool features and it will fix these bugs. Please tap here to update now." The customer taps to receive the update, the new version is installed, the phone reboots, and the phone no longer experiences problems with pocket dialing. As time goes on, more updates are built and released in the same manner. This then is agile in a nutshell.

Agile methods are referred to as an iterative and incremental method of creating products and services where the design and build activities are highly flexible and interactive. Project requirements and solutions evolve through collaboration of everyone relevant to the ultimate end product or service and goals. It is an adaptive and evolutionary development that relies heavily on continuous improvement and provides the lowest possible time to release usable solutions.

## Agile Versus Waterfall

The waterfall model is historically a sequential design process dating back fifty plus years. It received its name because of the way the phases of the model cascade downward. Originating in the manufacturing and construction industry during a time when highly structured environments were not particularly forgiving of change requests, the waterfall model was the most logical choice. It received its name from the simple downward flow of the project lifecycle. The waterfall model depends on a perfect understanding of the product requirements at the outset and minimal errors executing each phase with little tolerance for changes to the original requirements.

The Waterfall Project Lifecycle is as follows:
- Requirements are drawn up for the big concept.
- The Design feasibility and mock-up are completed.
- Construction begins and resources are allocated and scheduled.
- Verification is made to ensure the Concept and Goals have been met.
- The Maintenance of this new thing begins.

The waterfall methodology was perfect for big, long-term projects like building skyscrapers, bridges, and airplanes and it is a sequential approach (see Figure 10-1). Notice that if you were to make a major change in the Requirements, you have no choice but to stop nearly everything and (as the saying goes) go back to the drawing board. You would Redesign and Restart Implementation, sometimes scrapping everything to that point.

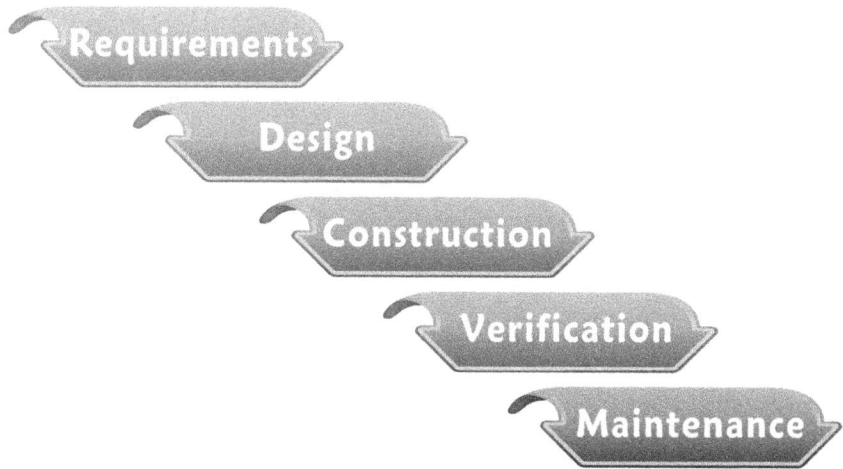

*Figure 10-1. Waterfall Methodology*

Waterfall Project Lifecycle Summary: Best suited for medium to large projects that can (and should) be clearly defined before production starts, and the end results are not likely to change significantly, e.g. a complete network migration of your business network to new hardware. For those qualified to do this kind of work, most aspects of the project involve simply performing routines that have been done many times before with a few refinements or changes. There are finite requirements for Time, Energy, and Money.

When the concept of software development was born, there were no other feasible project models to adopt except the long-standing waterfall method. When applied to the dynamic software development process, the waterfall method was immediately revealed as too rigid and non-receptive to change. It would also be discovered as we approached the 21st century that the waterfall method did not lend itself well to collaboration, and thus Agile was born.

The Agile Project lifecycle is an adaptive cycle that is incremental, iterative, and collaborative. This means that it looks to release new or improved usable products and services more frequently and on a regular basis based on the input from everyone involved, from the stakeholders to the end user (see Figure 10-2).

The Agile Project Lifecycle is as follows:
- Requirements are drawn up for the big concept (Project Backlog).
- The Sprint Planning begins and the Project Backlog is broken down into Sprint Backlogs.
- The first Sprint Backlog is selected.
- The first Sprint begins.
- The first Iteration/Version of the Package is released.
- The entire lifecycle repeats and the Package is continuously and incrementally improved.

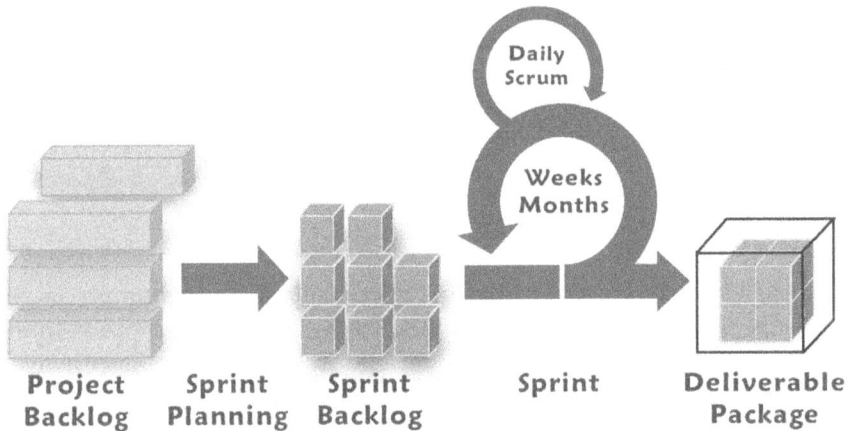

*Figure 10-2. Agile Project Lifecycle*

Agile Project Lifecycle Summary: Suited for small to large projects that cannot (or should not) be completely defined before getting started and are, by their nature, going to be changing fast and frequently, e.g. software applications, dynamically changing products and services, or even business strategy. Most aspects of the project involve detailed work that may require continuous collaboration with end users, benefactors, or stakeholders to develop the near and far future requirements. The project has an undetermined completion date, therefore there are near infinite requirements for Time, Energy, and Money.

## Why Agile?

Looking back at the example, you should recognize that unlike the Waterfall Methodology, if you need to change something major in an Agile Project, you can slip it into the next Sprint Backlog and put a higher priority on it and it will then be implemented ASAP. For example, in the initial Sprint that released the New Phone Version 0.9, any big changes to the requirements can be implemented quickly and without waiting for a complete redesign, because we're not building this entire thing and then taking it out to fly. We can take a look at the early release product or service and make critical adjustments before they are cast in stone or we've committed to full production. This compares to the Design feasibility phase of waterfall, however with waterfall, nothing happens until you have committed to the design completely. Which means that by the time you figure out this thing is not going to work or some major changes are required, you are essentially going to do the equivalent of trying to stop a freight train.

In addition, the maintenance is more than just maintenance; it is continuous improvement resulting from collaboration with everyone who helps build this thing through sales, distribution, and marketing and on to those who use it. Because Agile is also a Collaborative model, everyone involved is continuously communicating and sharing ideas and talking about making this thing better. It is expected that the end user or benefactor of this project is included in the collaboration; hence why in today's world, you can go to a manufacturer's website and report a bug or request a feature. The power of collaboration also means that when the end user or benefactors are included, you end up building something that is significantly closer to what they actually want, not just what you believe you understood they wanted.

To be clear, I do not intend to propose that the project of getting your business to the next level is a small project. It most certainly is not. However, it can be managed significantly better using agile methods because it really is a truly long-term project that requires continuous improvement, frequent iterations requiring dynamic resource availability, and open collaboration with everyone involved. That is the very definition of Agile. I should fairly note that you could also try to run the network migration I mentioned earlier in the Waterfall Project Lifecycle Summary as an agile project. And although it would benefit from the mindset and intent, oddly enough the planning and running of this type of project would still, by its nature, end up being more Waterfall than Agile.

Until now, Agile has been most commonly associated with software. It is now being leveraged effectively for non-software products, services, and project management. The agile methods have strong links to Lean and Six Sigma, all of which represent high efficiency and granular, measurable progress. You see it every day now, most prominently in your cell phone, desktop, laptop, and just about anything that has software or firmware. As in the previous example, you have surely witnessed Agile methodology on your handheld device. Not so noticeable is the manifestation of Agile in hardware as well. Take a closer look at replacement parts for newer devices and you will see that you are always getting the latest version of that device when the old one breaks.

Assuming what I have presented to this point is understood even to a basic level, if you match up the requirements for how best to define your business roadmap, execute on strategy, and drive your business to the next level with the most suitable and feature-rich project management methodology options available, Agile is the answer. I believe there is a direct correlation at all the right intersects between Business Strategy and Agile Execution—Continuous collaboration across teams and with everyone involved, dynamically changing goals and objectives for your business Value Aspects, and progressive strategies that can be driven effectively toward continuous incremental progress.

*Strategy without Tactics is the slowest route to victory. Tactics without Strategy is the noise before defeat.*

– Sun Tzu

# 11.0

## BUSINESS STRATEGY MEETS AGILE EXECUTION

When it comes to your long-term Business Roadmap and Strategy, you must endear to concepts such as the Way of the Turtle, as introduced in Chapter 1. I need to impart another concept to bind to, one constructed by author Jim Collins in his book *Great By Choice*. The concept Collins formulated and introduced is known simply as The 20 Mile March.

The 20 Mile March uses the example of contrasting strategies employed by the explorers Roald Amundsen and Robert Falcon Scott in their endeavor to be the first to reach the South Pole. Each explorer had his own team and his own unique plan. Both teams endured much of the same weather, hazards, issues, and adversities, but Amundsen's team managed to avoid the most perilous of these—not by luck but by strategy. Amundsen's team reached the pole first and on the exact day he planned while Scott's team arrived over a month later.

Collins points out that there were many success elements in Amundsen's favor, but among the most significant are: Amundsen had the discipline to maintain consistent progress by pressing forward through bad weather and holding the team back in good weather; Amundsen's strategy dictated the team was to make 15 to 20 miles a day—good, bad, or indifferent; And even when Amundsen's team suggested they could make better time in good weather, he said no.

Amundsen said no because he had carefully planned for everything he could anticipate or imagine, and his strategy for success relied on consistent progress while carefully managing resources and risk. Scott, on the other hand, would run his team to exhaustion in good weather to make up for bad runs in bad weather. Scott's team consistently faced life-threatening adversities and issues which largely resulted from his chosen tactics. Collins notes one clarifying fact: Scott's team faced only 6 days of gale force winds and traveled on none of them, while Amundsen's team faced 15 days of gale force winds and traveled on 8 of them.

I have introduced Collins' narrative because it provides the most realistic example of real-world continuous incremental progress but with a significantly higher cost of failure. With regards to the roadmap and strategy, small and medium-sized businesses don't always have the time, energy, inclination, or money to do as they wish at the speed they desire. And depending on the goal, it's also not always advisable even if they do have all of these resources. Organizations must also manage risk in all the forms it presents itself—change or challenge. The work efforts required to succeed with the business strategy must be broken down into logical, right-sized pieces. From there, these pieces must be grouped together into bundles the organization can manage and reasonably expect to accomplish given the current resources, within the organization's tolerance for risk and within a reasonable timeframe. By doing this, businesses can make continuous incremental progress and create measurable successes in getting to the next level. This is your business roadmap. This is what you would build upon, and then as the saying goes, rinse and repeat. This is your 20 mile march, it is the way of the turtle, and as I will show you in this chapter, it is the very essence of Business Agile Strategy Execution.

It should be crystal clear by now that the most successful entrepreneurs and businesses owners work from a concise, well-defined roadmap and strategy for their organization. The size and complexity of your business roadmap and strategy will always be directly proportional to the size of the organization you are building. When your organization is small and fledgling, the roadmap and strategy is likely quite simple but no less significant to you than the behemoth roadmap and strategy of the largest organization you can imagine. The process I am about to step through will help you get to the next level regardless of the size of your organization.

What this chapter intends to show you is the general process and flow of defining your business roadmap and strategy and how to systematically execute on that strategy. Everything I have presented to this point in the book should help you perform your own complete business analysis or collaborate with outside resources to have it completed. Regardless of whether you are starting up a new business, turning one around, or just trying to get to the next level, the distillation of that complete business analysis will result in the laundry list I have referred to so many times. It is the itemized list of issues, tasks, and to-dos to implement, upgrade, replace, archive, or fix for each of the Value Aspects of your business as you build or renovate your Pyramid of Purpose and Value and get to the next level

This chapter will provide some insight into how to sort, organize, evaluate, and assign risk to the big laundry list. It will provide guidance on defining the finite list of specific objectives and initiatives that make up the business roadmap and strategy. With the help of the Balanced Scorecard it will show you how to define metrics for gauging progress of objectives and your success. But most important, it will show you how to execute on your strategy with continuous incremental progress.

The formulation of complex business strategy involves both science and skill. Formulation of strategy is, in fact, the formulation of a hypothesis—Based on everything we know, if we do these things, we firmly believe that we will be successful at this endeavor. The science of strategy formulation is represented by critical thinking, and the phases of critical thinking are deeply embedded in the entire process. If you look closely at the Critical Thinking tool as described in Chapter 3 and compare it to the scientific method employed by the field of natural sciences, you should see the similarities and recognize that critical thinking is, for all intents and purposes, a scientific method itself (see Figure 11-1).

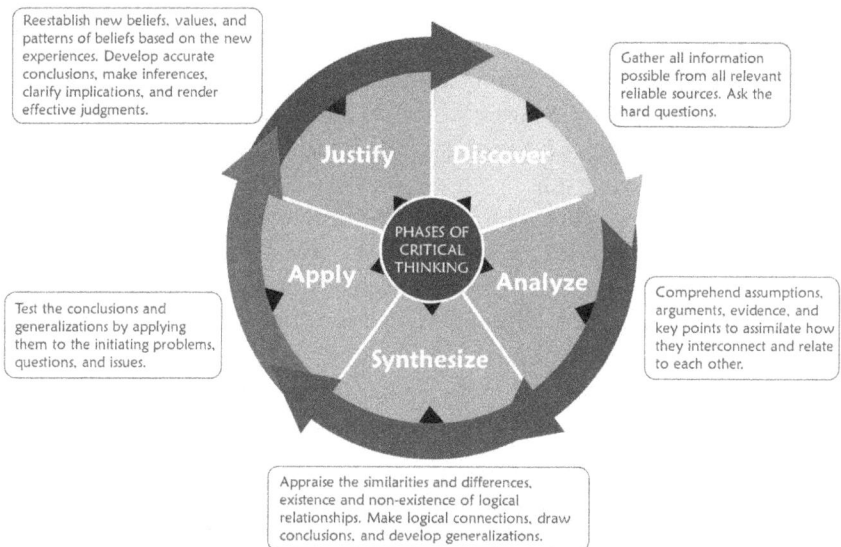

Reestablish new beliefs, values, and patterns of beliefs based on the new experiences. Develop accurate conclusions, make inferences, clarify implications, and render effective judgments.

Gather all information possible from all relevant reliable sources. Ask the hard questions.

**Justify**      **Discover**

PHASES OF CRITICAL THINKING

**Apply**      **Analyze**

**Synthesize**

Test the conclusions and generalizations by applying them to the initiating problems, questions, and issues.

Comprehend assumptions, arguments, evidence, and key points to assimilate how they interconnect and relate to each other.

Appraise the similarities and differences, existence and non-existence of logical relationships. Make logical connections, draw conclusions, and develop generalizations.

*Figure 11-1. Phases of Critical Thinking*

The skill of strategy formulation is represented by the human intellect and experience necessary to properly apply the scientific method—the critical thinking. Skill is only ever attained through study and practice. The point is that I can show you how to use the tools at hand, order and organize information, and adhere to constraints and requirements, but the skill—the human intellect and experience—must be applied by those who have a stake in the organization and the endeavor. This requires that they study the tools presented in this book, practice their use, and get connected with the right resources if they need help with applying these tools and methods.

Skill is required in the formulation of the assumptions and conclusions, interpretation of relationships, and overall hypothesis formulation that becomes the strategy. Even the decisions of what priorities are attached to objectives and which objectives are selected for execution (leaving others to wait or even be culled), and being able then to see how these objectives will lead to the desired outcomes, requires a certain level of skill. Science and the scientific process can only guide. As the narrative of the business roadmap and strategy formulation progresses, I will indicate where the science gives way to the skill.

Now to show you how Business Agile Strategy Execution works. The entire discussion on BASE relies on content from the Case Study and Example in the next chapter; as such, I recommend reviewing that chapter in its entirety for familiarity. It is also assumed you read and understand the previous chapter on Agile Execution. Using The Goober Group Case Study and Example, I will walk through the process of:

- Breaking down the business SWOT Analysis including stakeholder concerns, internal and external requirements, and inputs into a logically sorted and organized list of Issues, Tasks, and To-dos.
- Formulating the Solutions Recommendations for the each of the resulting SWOT Issues, Tasks, and To-dos.
- Formulating the overall business strategy by identifying the objectives which, if attained, will result in increased stakeholder and customer value.
- Laying out the business roadmap by identifying the order in which objectives will be executed on, how they will be measured, and the targets.
- Sorting and organizing the workload of the roadmap and strategy into the manageable-sized initiatives which must be executed on to attain the objectives and show results.

- Applying the agile methodology in order to execute on this big, beautiful comprehensive strategy that has been put together and—within the organization's constraints of time, energy, inclination, and money—move forward along the roadmap to success.

Along the way, I will show you how to employ several of the tools covered in earlier chapters, including Strategy Maps, the Balanced Scorecard, and of course the Agile Methodology.

When applying the agile methodology to the business roadmap and strategy, there must be a direct (or as close as possible to direct) correlation of the elements of agile to the roadmap and strategy. The terminology correlation is simple and is as follows:

| Roadmap and Strategy | Agile Methodology |
|---|---|
| Strategy | Project |
| Roadmap | Roadmap |
| Objective or Initiative | Landmark, Iteration, or Version |
| Business Analysis | Project Necessity Assessment |
| Solutions Recommendation | Project Scope and Description |
| Strategy Formulation | Project Planning |
| Objective Planning | Roadmap Planning |
| Initiative Planning | Sprint Planning |
| Issues, Tasks, and To-dos | Issues or User Stories |
| Workload | Backlog |
| Team | Scrum |
| Focused Work Assignment | Sprint |

For the narrative, I will tack on the agile terminology when appropriate with the intention of helping to solidify the correlation between Roadmap and Strategy and Agile Methodology. The primary terminology used, however, will always be that of the Roadmap and Strategy.

## Business SWOT Analysis

Relative to the agile methodology, the direct correlation of performing a complete business analysis is the project necessity assessment. It is the needs justification for expending time, energy, and money to accomplish something.

The process of breaking down the many and varied reports, analyses, and inputs of a business analysis can be difficult depending on the size of the operation, but if approached systematically with the right tools it can be accomplished with some semblance of order. The tools at hand are the SWOT Analysis and the Critical Thinking process with a supporting role from the ten business Value Aspects.

The starting point is the subject of study and concern—the example company, The Goober Group, a minority-owned small business operating in the Computer Related Services industry. The owner, Fiona Flattes, came to a crossroads in that she made a decision to get her business to the next level, knowing fully that she needed a solid business roadmap and strategy to do so.

The first step then was to gather information, and thus a complete business analysis was called for. What is specifically called for in any complete business analysis will be determined by the type of business being evaluated, although most of what is called for is common to any type of business. The prescribed formula for The Goober Group was a series of questionnaires for owners and employees and several sub-analyses including Competitive Forces Analysis, Generic Strategies Analysis, and a Target Market Analysis. It also required numerous supporting documents including a recent Feasibility Study, Business Plan, Financial Statements, and a complete Core Competency Matrix for the organization. Please refer to the Situation Analysis subsection of Chapter 12 for additional narrative and examples of questionnaire responses.

It is important to note that the level of detail in the data collected will directly translate (to the extent possible) into solid assumptions, requirements, relationships, conclusions, and generalizations in the next step of the Business Analysis. Consider the old computing term GiGo—Garbage in, Garbage out. Proceeding without or settling for less than accurate data could in fact cost the business dearly in time, energy, and money spent on a wholly immature strategy.

The discovery process must ask the right questions somewhere along the way that will illicit the responses necessary to identify all of the following for the endeavor:
- Requirements – such as how Esteban, Fiona's husband, must exit the business.
- Constraints – such as Fiona is not willing to borrow money to advance the business.

- Limits – such as the bulk of the organizational revamp must be completed by end of year 2017.
- Expectations – such as the establishment of a significant competitive advantage as an outcome.
- Apprehensions – such as the concern over letting perfectly good clients go just because they don't fit in "The Box".

Failure to identify these important inputs represents a failure in the discovery process itself or the administration of the discovery.

At this point we (Fiona and I) had all the inputs from the discovery phase, including the subjective and objective outputs of questionnaires and sub-analyses such as the Competitive Forces Analysis and the Porter's Generic Strategies Analysis. There was also the input and available information provided from the required supporting documentation. The next step was to begin a series of SWOT Analysis meetings where we would systematically boil everything down to a finite list of Strengths, Weaknesses, Opportunities, and Threats. To keep things simple, they were categorized according to the ten business Value Aspects.

This phase calls for the formulation of assumptions, development of dependencies, evaluation of evidence, and identification of key points. This phase relies on the actual human intellect to assimilate the information presented and the comprehension of how everything interconnects and relates. Some examples are:
- Assumptions – such as The Goober Group is moving to a Managed Service Provider (MSP) model based on Fiona's interest and intent for the business.
- Development of dependencies – such as any planned marketing efforts and expectations cannot be properly executed on unless the right person is found to be the Marketing Manager.
- Evaluation of evidence – such as the outputs of the Competitive Forces Analysis and Generic Strategies Analysis.
- Identification of key points – such as recognizing the many pointers to the Core Competencies of the organization need to be a major focus in order for any strategy to be successful.
- Interconnections and relationships – such as the matchups of high potential in the vertical market and the existing competencies of the organization. Another would be in recognizing the many Weaknesses of the organization being linked to a single individual.

This phase is the simple distillation of inputs and information into a finite list of Issues, Tasks, and To-dos, or for the sake of Agile, User Stories. This is the big laundry list of Strengths, Weaknesses, Opportunities, and Threats of the organization that must be addressed in one fashion or another, at one time or another if they intend to get to the next level. Please refer to the Strengths–Weaknesses–Opportunities–Threats Analysis discussion and examples in the Situation Analysis subsection of Chapter 12.

## Solutions Recommendation

Relative to the agile methodology, the direct correlation of the solutions recommendation is the definition of the project scope and description. Here, the breadth and extent of the project is defined, and that which specifically should be accomplished if the project moves forward is put into words.

The formulation of a Solutions Recommendation intends to adequately identify the drivers of value creation and outcomes that are the perceived value. Each SWOT, each Issue, each User Story must be addressed by deciding how best to deal with it. The next logical step is to begin a series of Solutions Recommendations meetings where each issue in the SWOT is systematically addressed. The output and end result is a series of consolidated "Do this to remedy that" statements. The end result business Solutions Recommendation as a whole will in turn be the input to the strategy formulation process. The process of formulating solutions is where a certain amount of skill is required and hopefully supplied by those closest to the endeavor.

Throughout the formulation process, the appraisal of similarities and differences, existence or non-existence of logical relationships, and development of conclusions and generalizations is subject to many influences, most of which can be known, listed, and thereby appropriately considered.

The list of influences most relevant to the formulation of a Solutions Recommendation is as follows:
- Matching and Converting Forces and Factors – One of the core precepts of a SWOT Analysis which intends to help associate and merge similar or closely related Opportunities with Strengths, Threats with Weaknesses, and the possibility of simply negating Threats or Weaknesses in some way or

another.

- Value Chain – The consideration of how what you do will translate into value somewhere in the value chain for both the customer and the organization.
- Value Aspects – The appropriate consideration of keeping all the Value Aspects of the organization progressing in maturity together.
- Refinement or Improvement (Lean and Six Sigma) – The ever-present litmus test that requires anything you spend time, energy, effort, or money on must be either refining the process or product (Leaning it out) or improving the process or product (Six Sigma).

Each SWOT item was evaluated and, where appropriate, paired or grouped with another SWOT item. Some Strengths were matched with Opportunities and in some cases, Weaknesses with Opportunities. Please refer to the Solution Recommendation subsection of Chapter 12 for additional narrative and clear examples of the Solutions Recommendation for The Goober Group.

Now that there are specific solutions formulated for each of the SWOT, the "laundry list" effectively graduates to become the Workload of the organization, required to be systematically addressed in order to get to the next level. For the sake of Agile, this is the Project Backlog. Workload implies that desired results will be attained in exchange for efforts. Although there is a valid Workload, it is not tied to creating value for the organization or the customer. And there is still no plan or strategy for how specifically it will be accomplished effectively and efficiently.

This then presents the biggest pitfall for many organizations. All too often, a business performs their own or calls for an outside SWOT Analysis, and once they have it in their hands, they go about working on the proposed solutions without really putting together a strategy. If you look closely at the example Solutions Recommendations in Chapter 12, you may think that it represents a basic but valid strategy on its own. It does not. Each valid SWOT Issue, Task, To-do, and proposed solution in the Workload must be translated into a coherent objective or initiative within a planned strategy for creating value for the organization or for the customer.

# Strategy Formulation

Relative to the agile methodology, the direct correlation of strategy formulation is the formal project planning. Here, the actual project(s) must be laid out that will accomplish all that is intended. As in project planning, it is sometimes advantageous to break the work down into multiple small projects (multiple strategies) in order to allow work to progress along parallel paths. The next step then would be conducting a series of meetings, all focusing on the actual Strategy Formulation using the Solutions Recommendations as input.

In the Strategy Formulation process, the intention is to translate the Solutions Recommendations into the actual Objectives for each of the specific perspectives of the organization. These will be the desired Outcomes (Value) for the Finance and Customer perspectives or the necessary Drivers (of Value) for the Internal and Learning and Growth perspectives of the Balanced Scorecard. The end result Business Strategy(ies) will be what the organization must execute on in order to get to the next level.

Here, as in the formulation of Solutions Recommendations, appraising of similarities and differences, identifying the existence or non-existence of logical relationships, and the development of conclusions and generalizations repeats but with consideration of different primary influences and with different expectations for outputs. In the Solutions Recommendation stage, the outputs were just that—recommendations for solutions to issues. In this stage, the outputs expected are the specific objectives that will result in value for the organization's stakeholders and customers or will help create that value. As in the Solutions Recommendation stage, the many influences can be known, listed, and therefore appropriately considered.

The list of influences most relevant to Objective and Strategy Formulation is as follows:
- Finance, Customer, Internal, and Learning and Growth Perspectives of the organization – The four perspectives of the Balanced Scorecard and the Strategy Map which represent the desired Outcomes (Finance and Customer) that the necessary Drivers of results (Internal and Learning and Growth) must be aligned with the organization's Vision and Mission and in balance in order for the business strategy to be considered valid and viable.
- Balance of Growth and Productivity Strategies – Relevant

axioms imposed by the Balanced Scorecard and Strategy Map that require a healthy organization to always have a balance between the Productivity Strategy (sell more) and the Growth Strategy (spend less).

- Time, Energy, Inclination, and Money – The general requirement that each and every item on the SWOT list must be considered against. What are the time constraints, requirements, etc.? What energy is required, do we have enough people to pull this off? Do we have the inclination to even care if this gets done? And the most important, can we fund this?
- Risk of Time, Energy, Inclination, and Money – The ultimate question of the actual risk to resources and efforts.
- Value Aspects – The appropriate consideration of continued performance in each of the Value Aspects of the organization.

The first step in strategy formulation is to identify what solutions could be translated into objectives that would lead to a desirable Outcome (value) in either the Financial or Customer perspectives of the Balanced Scorecard (see Figure 11-2).

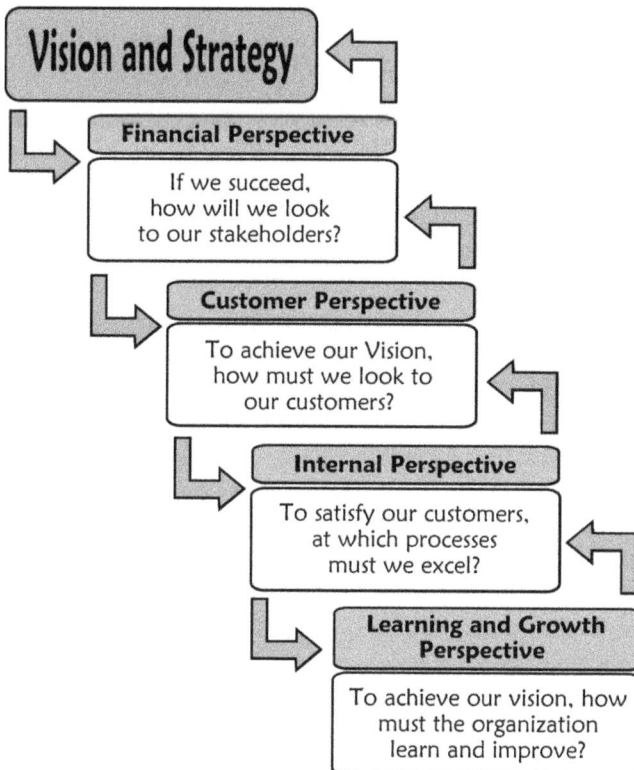

**Vision and Strategy**

**Financial Perspective**
If we succeed, how will we look to our stakeholders?

**Customer Perspective**
To achieve our Vision, how must we look to our customers?

**Internal Perspective**
To satisfy our customers, at which processes must we excel?

**Learning and Growth Perspective**
To achieve our vision, how must the organization learn and improve?

*Figure 11-2. Balanced Scorecard*

Any strategy must begin with the end result of value for the organization and the customer as the focal point. The next step is to identify what solutions could be translated into objectives for the Internal and Learning and Growth perspectives of the Balanced Scorecard that would support the Finance and Customer perspectives. These supporting objectives represent the Drivers of value. The process of objective identification and translation proceed until all Solutions Recommendations have been addressed. Please refer to the Solution Implementation subsection of Chapter 12 for additional narrative and clear examples of the strategies formulated for The Goober Group.

Nowhere in the process of Strategy Formulation is skill relied upon more than in the step of translating Solutions Recommendations into effective objectives. As mentioned previously, the skill, the human intellect, and experience must be applied by those who have a stake in the organization and the endeavor. The proper translation of Solutions Recommendations into effective objectives requires the complete understanding of the business, inside and out. It also requires a complete understanding of the tools used. This is the stage where an organization must seek outside help or support if it does not possess the skill of strategy formulation, at least until it becomes a core competency. And with study and practice, it can.

In the process of defining strategies, the generic Strategy Map and generic complementary Strategic Themes presented in Chapter 5 must be studied and considered closely. Recall that each of the generic strategy themes intends to focus the objectives of the Internal perspective on specific processes. In the evaluation of the Solutions Recommendation for The Goober Group, it became apparent early on that there would need to be multiple strategies formulated. As objectives were identified and properly placed into the Balanced Scorecard, it became apparent that there was a need for four distinct strategies, each with specific Outcomes and specific Drivers.

The first official strategy was Organization Realignment, a non-generic, short-term strategy in which the theme was to get the organization on the right track. At its core were the objectives to define what the new business would look like and to get cash flow straightened out. It was an abnormally short-term strategy to get the ship pointed in the right direction, as it were. The remaining three strategies each had a generic theme and were selected specifically because of how each coincided with the specific intended solutions recommendations.

By adopting individual themes for the strategies, each could progress, change, and succeed independent of the others. This in turn allowed The Goober Group to deal with conflicting priorities of short-term growth, long-term growth, and profitability while appropriately focusing on different Internal perspective processes. For the remainder of the BASE walk–through, the focus will be on the fourth (long-term) strategy for The Goober Group. This strategy was formulated with the generic theme to Build The Franchise and it was intended to take them through the upcoming fiscal year 2017. To this point, their Balanced Scorecard has only the selected objectives populated (see Figure 11-3).

| Theme: Build The Franchise | | | | |
|---|---|---|---|---|
| **Balanced Scorecard** | | | | |
| Perspective | Objective | Measure | Target | Initiative |
| FINANCIAL | • Increase Recurring Revenue<br>• Increase Per Client Revenue | • | • | • |
| CUSTOMER | • Be the Complete IT Solution<br>• Refocus Existing Clients to the MSP Offering<br>• Attract New Clients in Vertical<br>• Reduce Average Ticket Age<br>• Reduce Average Time on Ticket<br>• % Unscheduled Downtime | • | • | • |
| INTERNAL | • Partner with Vendors for MDF<br>• Increase Project Efficiency<br>• Fine-tune PSA and RMM for MSP<br>• Lower Ave. # Outstanding Issues<br>• Manage Service Delivery Backlog Hours | • | • | • |
| LEARNING AND GROWTH | • Establish ITIL Certification<br>• Establish HIPAA Compliance<br>• Establish EMR and Scan Systems as a Core Competency<br>• Get Everyone On Board<br>• Team Informed and Aligned | • | • | • |

*Figure 11-3. Build The Franchise Balanced Scorecard Objectives*

Only with all the objectives of the strategy in place for each of the four perspectives can the Strategy Map be designed. The Strategy Map intends to help tell the compelling story by presenting the very clear and enticing picture. The Strategy Map is the linking of objectives to show how they support the objectives above. The narrative of the strategy that has been formulated should closely describe the Strategy

Map as it flows from the bottom upward. There are two references for the narrative on the Strategy Map presented in Figure 11-4 which should be reviewed in sequential order: The first is The Strategy Narrative subsection of the Roadmap & Strategy section in Chapter 8. The second is the Build the Franchise subsection of the Solution Implementation section in Chapter 12.

| Theme: Build The Franchise | | | | | |
|---|---|---|---|---|---|
| **Strategy Map** | | **Balanced Scorecard** | | | |
| Perspective | | Objective | Measure | Target | Initiative |
| **FINANCIAL** | Increase Recurring Revenue / Increase Per Client Revenue | • Increase Recurring Revenue<br>• Increase Per Client Revenue | • | • | • |
| **CUSTOMER** | Complete IT Solution / Refocus Clients to MSP / Attract New Clients in Vertical / Reduce Ticket Age / Reduce Time on Ticket / % Unscheduled Downtime | • Be the Complete IT Solution<br>• Refocus Existing Clients to the MSP Offering<br>• Attract New Clients in Vertical<br>• Reduce Average Ticket Age<br>• Reduce Average Time on Ticket<br>• % Unscheduled Downtime | • | • | • |
| **INTERNAL** | Partner with Vendors / Increase Project Efficiency / Fine-tune PSA and RMM / Lower Outstanding Issues / Manage SD Backlog Hours | • Partner with Vendors for MDF<br>• Increase Project Efficiency<br>• Fine-tune PSA and RMM for MSP<br>• Lower Ave. # Outstanding Issues<br>• Service Delivery Backlog Hours | • | • | • |
| **LEARNING AND GROWTH** | ITIL Certification / HIPAA Compliance / EMR and Scan Systems as a Core Competency / Everyone On Board / Team Aligned | • Establish ITIL Certification<br>• Establish HIPAA Compliance<br>• Establish EMR and Scan Systems as a Core Competency<br>• Get Everyone On Board<br>• Team Informed and Aligned | • | • | • |

*Figure 11-4. Strategy Map and Balanced Scorecard Objectives*

## Objective Planning

Relative to the agile methodology, the direct correlation of Objective Planning is the Roadmap Planning. With the Strategy Map in place, sharing the strategy it represents is significantly easier and it will be even clearer with the addition of a well-laid-out Roadmap. Here is where you would actually plan and lay out the order of initiation and completion of the previously translated objectives of the project. It is in this stage that the actual initiatives that will accomplish the objectives will be formulated. Before this stage is complete, the measures, targets, and major initiatives for each strategy objective will be defined. This stage initiates yet another series of meetings focusing finally on the actual roadmap for the organization's progress. A requirement for success is of course to call in specific team members to help define initiatives that concern their roles, responsibilities, and departments.

The breakdown of objectives into initiatives and the definition of the initiatives should at this point be more formality than laborious task. There is a clear path from the initial SWOT Analysis (Issues, Tasks, To-dos, User story) to the Solution Recommendation ("Do this to remedy that" statement) to the Strategy for success (Objectives). In reality, at every stage and in every step along the way, initiatives are being identified and formulated. At this stage it is simply a matter of formally drawing the line from objective backwards to the solution(s) to be implemented which will attain that objective. The critical elements to be determined at this stage will be the actual measures of progress for the objectives and the associated targets which will show that the desired outcomes are being attained. Following are some objective and initiative examples from the Build The Franchise strategy.

There are two objectives initiated in the first of the four strategies and continued throughout each. They are the objectives to get the Team Informed and Aligned and Get Everyone On Board. These objectives will be attained by having a quarterly company retreat to share and discuss strategy and by initiating weekly standup meetings to maintain the focus and drive. These are measured by the Percent of Employees Aware of the strategy for the quarter and Percent of Employees at the Weekly Standup meetings, respectively. These objectives must be met in the first quarter of the year to set everything up for success.

One Learning and Growth objective is to Establish HIPAA Compliance. This objective is one of several that supports specific objectives for the Internal perspective. The objective calls for a multi-phase initiative to get the entire team trained. The first phase, HIPAA Compliance Phase I, focuses on the top level engineers and it is called out for this calendar year. This implies not only that there will be additional phases of the initiative to train the remaining team members, but also that the objective they intend to accomplish will most certainly be part of future strategies. The measure for this objective is Percent of the entire Team Trained with a target of 100%. Because HIPAA compliance is an external requirement imposed by the government, it must have a high priority. This requirement is the reason for the first phase having a targeted completion in or by the second quarter of the year. Note that this is an example of a multi-phase initiative that supports a single long-term objective.

An objective that was a bit more intricate and required a bit more planning was the Be the Complete IT Solution objective. In the strategy formulation, we decided that The Goober Group had to educate the customer on the need for regular Technology Roadmap meetings to help advance their IT infrastructure. These Technology Roadmaps represented not only significant value for the client—because their systems can be managed more efficiently—but also a significant opportunity for The Goober Group to sell more future project work. It became apparent that as the Client Roadmaps initiative matured and the clients became more receptive, the objective being achieved would actually mature as well. In the early phase of the initiative the objective was just to Build Brand Awareness (see the Customer perspective of the Organizational Realignment strategy). Then the objective became to Build Strategic Partnerships (see the Customer perspective of the Achieve Operational Excellence and Increase Customer Value strategies). And finally, in the Build The Franchise strategy, the initiative was at its most mature when the objective became Be the Complete IT Solution. Note that this is an example of a multi-phase initiative that supports several successive short-term objectives.

With the initiatives identified and largely formulated and the appropriate measures and targets defined for each objective, both the Balanced Scorecard and the Roadmap are now complete. For presentation and execution purposes, the Strategy Map is stripped off of the Balanced Scorecard (see Figure 11-5) and paired with the Roadmap (see Figure 11-6).

## Theme: Build The Franchise

### Balanced Scorecard

| Perspective | Objective | Measure | Target | Initiative |
|---|---|---|---|---|
| FINANCIAL | • Increase Recurring Revenue | • % of Total Revenue | • 80% | • See Client Refocus Below |
|  | • Increase Per Client Revenue | • Ave. Revenue Per Seat | • $4,500 | • See Client Roadmap Below |
| CUSTOMER | • Be the Complete IT Solution | • % Project Ownership | • 100% | • Client Roadmaps Phase III |
|  | • Refocus Existing Clients to the MSP Offering | • % Converted | • 100% | • Operation Client Focus |
|  | • Attract New Clients in Vertical | • # Assessment Requests | • 3/Mo. | • Marketing 2.0 WIIFM |
|  | • Reduce Average Ticket Age | • # of Days Old | • < 45 | • Ticket Targeting |
|  | • Reduce Average Time on Ticket | • # Minutes Per Issue | • < 50 | • Escalation Process |
|  | • % Unscheduled Downtime | • Average % Downtime | • < 0.10% | • Op. Goober Care Phase II |
| INTERNAL | • Partner with Vendors for MDF | • % Marketing Budget | • 5% | • Lunch & Learns |
|  | • Increase Project Efficiency | • % Budgeted Time | • < 100% | • Op. Agile Project Phase III |
|  | • Fine-tune PSA and RMM for MSP | • Valid MSP Reports | • 100% | • Op. Goober Care Phase II |
|  | • Lower Ave. # Outstanding Issues | • Ticket Count | • < 250 | • Agile Service Delivery Phase II |
|  | • Manage Service Delivery Backlog Hours | • # Days Backlogged Projects & Service | • < 5 | • Agile Service Delivery Phase II |
| LEARNING AND GROWTH | • Establish ITIL Certification | • % Team Trained | • 100% | • ITIL Certification Phase 1 |
|  | • Establish HIPAA Compliance | • % Team Trained | • 100% | • HIPAA Compliance Phase 1 |
|  | • Establish EMR and Scan Systems as a Core Competency | • % Team Trained | • 100% | • Final Friday Training |
|  | • Get Everyone On Board | • % Employees Aware | • 100% | • Q4 2016 Company Retreat |
|  | • Team Informed and Aligned | • % Employees @ % Standups | • 100% | • Weekly Standups |

*Figure 11-5. Balanced Scorecard for The Goober Group*

Notice that the Roadmap is a culmination of the most important objectives and initiatives that drive the success of the organization— not from the perspective of Finance, Customer, Internal, or Leaning and Growth, but rather from a perspective of continuous incremental improvement. The Balanced Scorecard, however, is from the four perspectives that represent a solid and well–laid-out strategy for success. The Roadmap (and Strategy Map) shows you where you are, where you are going, and how you will get there. The balanced scorecard keeps you on focus and measures your progress.

The final elements to be determined and assigned, before execution can begin on the roadmap and strategy, are the solidified timelines, deadlines, budget, and resources required for each initiative. This will be completed in the next stage, Initiative Planning, in addition to the finalization of the initiatives. Finalizing the initiatives requires breaking initiatives into logical phases when necessary. Note that if in the process of finalizing the initiatives, if any initiative changes significantly or cannot be completed within the expected and anticipated timeframe initially speculated, the Roadmap and possible one or more Strategy may need to be modified accordingly.

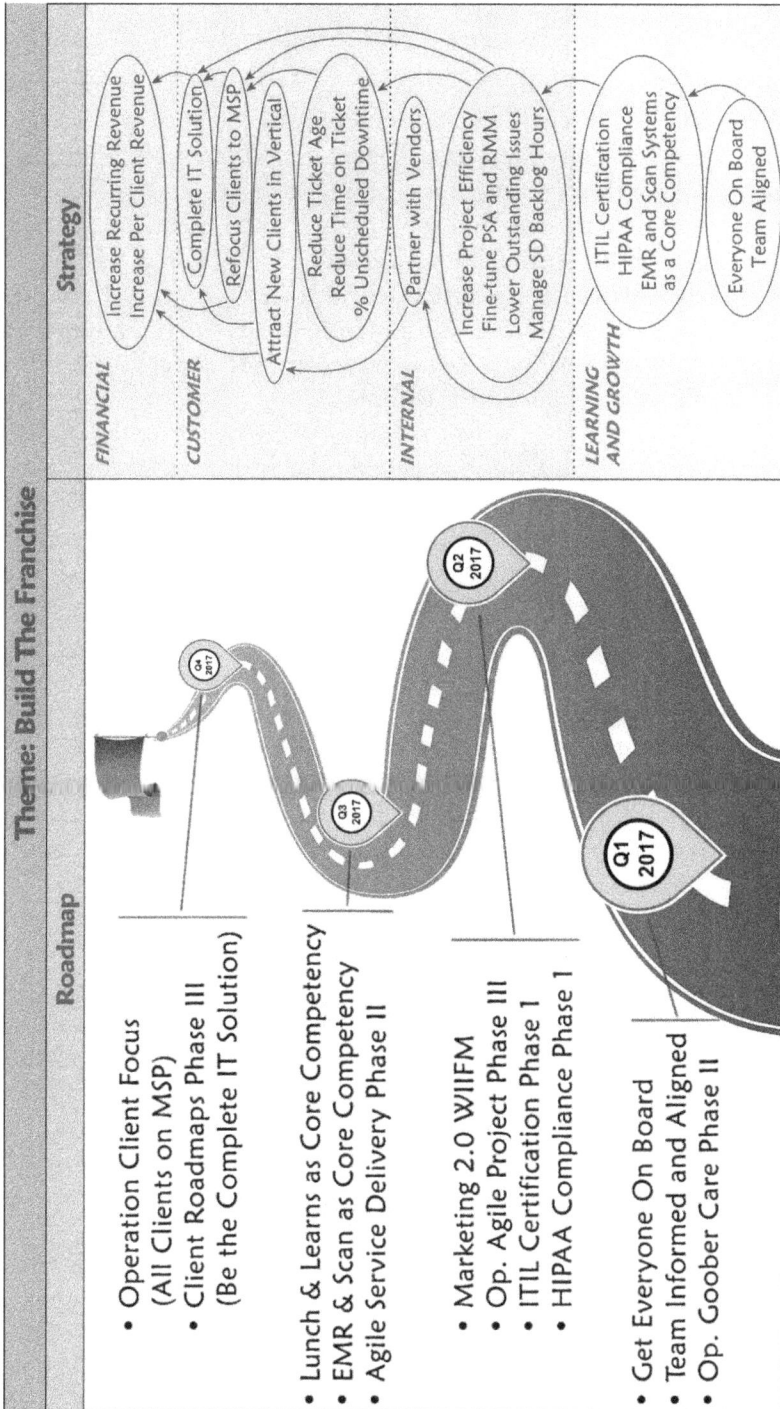

*Figure 11-6. Roadmap & Strategy for The Goober Group*

## Initiative Planning

With the finalization of the Balanced Scorecard and the Roadmap, these next two stages are where the actual efforts to execute on the strategy begin. They are also where the Agile Methodology really begins to shine and show through. What is required at this particular stage is the solidification of initiatives and their phases where necessary, followed by the assignment of timelines, deadlines, budget, and resources to each initiative. This stage is the assignment of work to be focused on and the delegation of responsibility in order to get the Initiatives rolling as planned. Relative to the agile methodology, the direct correlation of Initiative Planning is the Sprint Planning.

Recall from the discussion on Agile that the Sprint is a chunk of work selected form the project backlog that can effectively be implemented and executed on by the team (Scrum) within a reasonable amount of time. In software development, the Sprint is usually two to four weeks and the implementation is not actually fully planned until the Sprint planning meeting.

In Business Agile Strategy Execution, each objective, initiative, or phase of an initiative is for all intents and purposes each their own pre-planned Sprint. Each is a bite size amount of work (Issues, Tasks, To-dos, and User Stories) that an individual or team can reasonably be expected to accomplish or resolve within the Sprints timeframe. In BASE, the default Sprint timeframe is the business quarter. The business quarter was set as the default because we run our business and gauge its success from quarter to quarter. The strategy and the accompanying Balanced Scorecard used to measure progress along that time increment are also formulated. The final planning for each objective, initiative, or phase of an initiative is largely completed here in this stage when the size of the initiative is verified and all initiatives are assigned timelines, deadlines, budgets, and resources. Final implementation tactics will be formulated by the individual or team once the individual or team picks up the Sprint and begins working on it.

Based on the time, energy, and money of any given team or the organization overall, there is only so much of the workload that can realistically be completed in any given business quarter. As was covered in Chapter 8 in the Resources section, the capability and potential of any individual or team can be calculated. When it comes to setting aside a slice of time for an individual or team to work on the initiatives of the business strategy, you will find that unless the work of the initiative is directly in line with the day-to-day efforts of the individual or team, you must actually allocate a slice of their time to work on the business, not in the business.

For example, if the initiative is Marketing 2.0 and the tasks are all about designing the marketing materials and rolling out the advertising, these are all in line with the day-to-day roles and responsibilities of that individual and team. But if the initiative is Operation Agile Project Phase I, an engineer and possibly a manager must set aside time to define and document the new project process from top to bottom and test it out. This represents a measurable slice of time each week that these resources must be allocated to these tasks. What is required is that many individuals and team members must specifically set aside time each week, based on their assigned workload of initiatives, to work on their piece of the business strategy. They must be authorized and they must be trained to set aside time each week for contributing their efforts toward the organization getting to the next level. It must become a habit for everyone in the organization. Because of its importance, I will touch on this a bit more in the next section, Executing on Strategy.

Another consideration in a small organization is that it is most common for a single individual to be filling multiple roles. The owner is also the lead cook or lead engineer. The marketing gets assigned to the one person who seems to have an idea of what is required in addition to their regular duties as office manager, and so on. In these smaller organizations, the term "team" is used loosely because although there is one full-time employee who is assigned to a particular team, there are either no other actual members of the team or, if there are, they are only providing a supporting role when time allows. This means that it's easier said than done to just assign all the strategy workload related to a given business function to an individual with reasonable expectations of it being completed along any timeline.

The keys to success in Initiative Planning is that when finalizing any initiative, greatest consideration must be given to right-sizing the chunks of workload or backlog based on the organization, team, or individual capability and potential that a given team or individual can effectively execute on in the current or upcoming business quarter. An example of this would be that the Operation Agile Project initiative was planned to take nearly a year to complete and therefore required being broken into phases in order to create measurable success each quarter/Sprint cycle.

To this point, assuming finances are allocated and assuming the initiatives have been properly right-sized or phased, the last tasks are to set out timelines and deadlines and then assign the work. The finances required to support any given objective or initiative should already have been properly budgeted for in previous quarters. If not, and if absolutely necessary in the short term, they will need to be allocated through capital expenditure when the time comes.

Setting timelines and deadlines is accomplished by synchronizing the roadmap and objectives with the capacity and the capability of the organization. Assigning the work is simply the task of designating ownership of objectives and initiatives (Sprints) to individuals or teams. Once ownership is assigned, each team (Scrum) plans the final implementation tactics. Individual Issues, Tasks, and To-dos from across all initiatives and objectives that are either scheduled to begin in this business quarter or are highest priority are assigned to individuals with expectations of performance. Of course when the "team" is an individual, the final implementation tactics planning and assignment steps are usually pretty short.

Following is an example of the first few initiatives that have been completely planned out for The Goober Group's long-term strategy, Build The Franchise (see Figure 11-7).

| Initiative / Sprint | Begin (start) | End (due) | Issues – Tasks – To-Dos – User Stories | Est. Time | % Done | Status | Assigned To |
|---|---|---|---|---|---|---|---|
| **Q4 2016 Company Retreat** Expected completion 12/31/2016 | 12/16/2016 | 12/17/2016 | Reveal the fully completed Pyramid of Purpose and Value | 2 hours | 100% | Good | The Goober Group |
| | 12/16/2016 | 12/17/2016 | Discuss the details of the upcoming year's business strategy | 3 hours | 100% | Good | The Goober Group |
| **Operation Goober Care Phase II** Expected completion 03/31/2017 | 01/02/2017 | 03/31/2017 | Get accurate measurement of client system downtime and log it | 23 hours | 0% | Good | Sid Malhotra |
| | 01/02/2017 | 02/10/2017 | Complete the fine-tuning of the PSA for MSP | 6 hours | 0% | Good | Willie Gilligan |
| | 01/02/2017 | 02/10/2017 | Complete the fine-tuning of the RMM for MSP | 10 hours | 0% | Good | Waldo Nova |
| | 02/13/2017 | 03/31/2017 | Document the flow of an issue through the Service Delivery system | 15 hours | 0% | Good | Spencer Vork |
| | 02/13/2017 | 03/03/2017 | Define specific communications paths for the Service Delivery system | 4 hours | 0% | Good | Jimmie Sanchez |
| **Marketing 2.0 WIIFM** Expected completion 06/30/2017 | 04/03/2017 | 04/28/2017 | Create web pages for Free Assessments: Security, Network, Backup, Antivirus | 15 hours | 0% | Good | Lester A. Tackett / Marketing |
| | 04/03/2017 | 04/28/2017 | Design campaign for informing the clients about the Goober Care™ Value Proposition | 10 hours | 0% | Good | Pippa Watson / Office Manager |
| | 04/03/2017 | 04/28/2017 | Define the 7 Touches for customers responding to ads and marketing | 15 hours | 0% | Good | Gil McQueen / Sales |
| | 04/03/2017 | 04/28/2017 | Design the campaign graphics for social and email campaigns that show the brand | 25 hours | 0% | Good | Lester A. Tackett / Marketing |
| | 05/01/2017 | 06/30/2017 | Execute and track the marketing campaign to get new leads from Free Assessments | 40 hours | 0% | Good | Lester A. Tackett / Marketing |
| **Operation Agile Project Phase III** Expected completion 06/30/2017 | 04/01/2017 | 06/30/2017 | Project phase oversight and feedback in near real-time to evaluate process | 12 hours | 0% | Good | Service Management |
| | 04/01/2017 | 06/30/2017 | Process retrospective reviews and process adjustment meetings | 10 hours | 0% | Good | Service Management |
| **ITIL Certification Phase I** Expected completion 06/30/2017 | 04/01/2017 | 06/30/2017 | Obtain initial ITIL Foundation Certification for top level engineer | 100 hours | 0% | Good | Sparky Martin |
| **HIPAA Compliance Phase I** Expected completion 06/30/2017 | 04/01/2017 | 06/30/2017 | Attain initial HIPAA compliance for top level engineers through external training | 30 hours | 0% | Good | Zhi Nguyen |

*Figure 11-7. Strategy Initiatives Planning*

At this stage, the Balanced Scorecard Perspective is not indicated anywhere on the Strategy Initiative Planning sheet and neither are the objectives these initiatives intend to accomplish. Neither are the objective measures and targets. This is simply because the need for the efforts and work has already been justified, and as the timelines for the initiatives support the roadmap and strategy, it serves no purpose to indicate them on the sheet.

It is now only a matter of organizing the efforts and executing on the initiatives as planned utilizing the Resources at hand. The Balanced Scorecard is how you track your overall progress and Performance Measures toward success relative to the objectives that have been laid out. The Roadmap and Strategy are what you follow specifically to accomplish your success. This Initiative Planning is the Business Agile Strategy Execution in action. Refer back to the lower segment of the pyramid and you will see this relationship (Resources-Performance Measures-Roadmap & Strategy) laid out as the Blueprint for Success.

If the Initiative Planning sheet were completed for the entire year, you would see that each employee, regardless of team association, has their name on multiple initiatives. It is common and in most cases required that each person be working multiple initiatives in parallel. It is even more so required when there are multiple active strategies in play. This is, by the way, why the use of an Agile project board is highly recommended when your strategies begin to get intricate and are required when they become complex. Also remember that the overall workload from the backlog of all strategies in play that is put onto any one individual cannot exceed their capacity or capability. And if they are in multiple roles in the organization or their primary day-to-day duties are not in line with the work efforts required to accomplish the initiatives, their capacity or capability is a fraction of their total available.

If the objective, initiatives, and Sprints cannot be accomplished within the Sprint timeframe given the resources available, they must be re-planned as soon as possible. Attempting to force higher yields of work than should reasonably be expected will result in outright failure to complete the work required or mediocrity in the end results. Considering how much time, energy, and effort have likely been put into the long-term roadmap and strategy to this point, it would be foolish to allow failure for such reasons or to settle for mediocrity for any reason.

# Executing on Strategy

Now it is finally time to haul in the sheets and harness the wind that will get you to where you are going. You have painted the enticing picture and told the very compelling story. Everyone is on board and aligned. Now comes the time for discipline and execution. Discipline to hold the course and put forth the energy required to get to the next level. Execution must become a habit and it must be on focus. With the well-laid-out strategy and the planning of every initiative that will drive the outcomes you desire, you now have a roadmap and strategy for success.

To execute most effectively the organization must set aside time to get to the next level. Everyone in the organization must be authorized to do their part without need for reaffirmation or permission. For individuals and teams whose primary roles are very clear, such as Marketing and Sales, their work efforts toward the strategy and toward getting to the next level are pretty clear. Their efforts will constitute the bulk of their everyday work or can easily be slipstreamed into the day-to-day activities. But if they cannot be slipstreamed due to the workload already on that person or team, a concession must be made. This is also the case for individuals and teams whose roles are not so cut and dried, such as Service Delivery, Finance, or Human Resources. These roles, departments, or teams must be given authorization to set aside an appropriate slice of time each week to put forth the efforts required to execute on the strategy and help get the organization to the next level. A best practice is to set aside a day of the week and a block of time that is of sufficient size to make useful and measurable progress. And when that day and time comes along, the individual or team must be relieved of all duties, to the extent possible, in order to accomplish their contribution to the organization's strategy for success.

Before you get too excited about your efforts and your progress, you must also take in the bigger picture. Take note that there are initiatives still in play from the previous quarters that must continue to be worked. There are also initiatives for coming quarters that can be started early if resources allow. Looking over the entire strategy, the entire project, ideally work can be accomplished on these initiatives in parallel as time and resources allow. Each initiative can be advanced in its own way, continuously and incrementally to the next level. But this is only possible if you manage everything correctly.

And what if you have overestimated the time, energy, inclination, and resources of the team or the organization overall? What if the workload of the day-to-day operations of the business is significantly affecting their ability to accomplish the strategy work assigned? If you have overestimated your productivity capability or underestimated the complexity or work required, you must adjust the initiatives, objectives, timelines, deadlines, and resources accordingly. What has been designed here is a full-blown project for systematically executing on strategy with specific expectations for results. And as such, the project must be managed with the results it intends to accomplish always in mind.

This is where Agile shines the brightest. Every week at the standup (Sprint) meetings (for teams or for the entire organizations), there must be discussion on how the business strategy project efforts are going. In sailing, if we are off course, we adjust our tiller or we trim our sails or both to keep on course. In the weekly standup meetings, there must be quality communications and the end result must be definitive action items that will keep the project on course. Notice that because you have small iterations planned for short-term successes, you can actually make many minor adjustments to timelines, deadlines, issues, tasks, to-dos, and even priorities, all without toppling the entire Strategy Map. Because you are running an agile project, you can be much more dynamic in how you execute on your business strategy. And if need be, you can redesign many aspects of the strategy, again without significantly changing the overall Roadmap or Strategy Map. And that is Business Agile Strategy Execution!

At the end of every Sprint cycle (business quarter), you will have a Sprint review and retrospective just as you would with any project. In the Sprint review, you would ask questions such as: How did that go? Did we take too big of a bite out of the backlog? Did we try to accomplish too much relative to the available time, energy, inclination, and resources? If the answer is yes, then you back off on the size of the initiatives or phases, or you take smaller bites out of the backlog. If the answer is no, you go the other way to potentially get a little more done each quarter.

Remember that you are trying to attain smaller, short bursts of progress each month and each quarter to get solidly to the next level, not a giant big catharsis-type birthing of a jump. For most small and medium-sized businesses, attempting these large jumps isn't usually realistic or practical anyway. With BASE, you have built a system that lends itself to continuous incremental progress in getting each of the Value Aspects of your business to the next level following a well-managed and measurable process. This is again why agile is the right answer. By applying the agile project process to business strategy and executing on it for the long-term, best interest of the company, you have s blueprint for success.

I have one final note about execution and progress before I move on. If in any given week you or the team or the entire organization just did not have time to get anything done, you should not and cannot get discouraged. This big, beautiful picture you have for this endeavor is no longer stuck in your head, it has been put down on paper. It is a well-laid-out roadmap and strategy for getting the organization to the next level. With it in writing, it can be shared with a business partner, your advisers, your coach, and with anybody you like. It is now officially bigger than you and if everyone is on board, you are also not alone in making this thing come true. Most importantly, even if you are not meeting your timelines and your deadlines, when you or anyone on the team does take time or make time to work on the business instead of in the business, they can pick up where they left off and keep rolling.

The processes laid out in this book lend themselves to being dynamic (agile) in not only the formulation and execution of strategy but also the reformulation of strategy. If the strategy gets too far off course, it is easy enough to correct at any level. Once you have mastered these tools and methods, you will find you can formulate and execute on strategy better than the vast majority of entrepreneurs. And that in itself is a competitive advantage.

## Using an Agile Project Board

There is no better way to develop and execute on an agile business strategy than to utilize an agile project collaboration program or simply an agile project board. In fact, a detailed agile business roadmap and strategy requires a tool capable of actually driving the progress. Simple spreadsheets and documents will not drive your business roadmap and strategy progress, they will only help you track it.

An agile project board drives success because:
- It allows you to plan and track all aspects of your business roadmap and strategy in one place.
- It is an automated system with workflows and reminders.
- Objectives, initiatives, and issues have timelines, deadlines, estimated times to completion, and current status.
- Time and effort can be tracked incrementally across all

objectives and all teams.

- It provides metrics for the most important progress elements.
- It allows for the frequent small changes that may need to be made in the roadmap and strategy in an agile way.
- It can present your objectives, initiatives, and issues in different graphical representations that help everyone understand the big picture.
- Teams and organizations can collaborate from anywhere in the world on the shared strategy.
- Robust features support the collaboration such as discussion forums, document libraries, activity logs, and news updates.
- You can show others the detailed plans you have for your future business in many different ways.

Because of how important the use of an agile project board is to intricate and complex business strategy execution, I have developed a customized agile collaboration portal for use in my coaching and consulting program. Over the years, it has been customized specifically to support my Business Agile Strategy Execution model. It is well beyond the scope of this book to detail the agile project board and its features, but it is certainly within the scope to show clear examples of The Goober Group's strategy in action. The remainder of this chapter is screen shots from my Getting To The Next Level agile collaboration portal of The Goober Group business strategy. Look to the figure titles for Figures 11-8 to 11-15 for a description of each screen shot and agile project board feature being presented. Many agile project portals have common features and although not all are customized for business strategy, they will work just fine.

When it comes time to put what you have learned in this book to work, I implore you to find the right support tools to plan and execute your business roadmap and strategy. The Goober Group roadmap and strategy example in this book is representative of an intricate strategy. It is not, however, a complex strategy. You certainly can develop and execute an intricate strategy without the use of an agile project board, but I suspect you will have some trouble. If you have a truly complex strategy, you may not do very well without one.

You can get a closer look at how The Goober Group strategy is laid out and how a robust agile project board should look by surfing to my Getting To The Next Level (GTTNL) project site at gttnl.com and following the demo link. When the time does come that you do decide to look into an agile project board, please look to the back of this book for a special offer. There is a discount code that will allow you to utilize my customized agile project collaboration portal for up to one full year at a fifty percent saving. I have included this offer because I want you to succeed in your endeavors, and what better way than to make the most powerful tangible tool available to you.

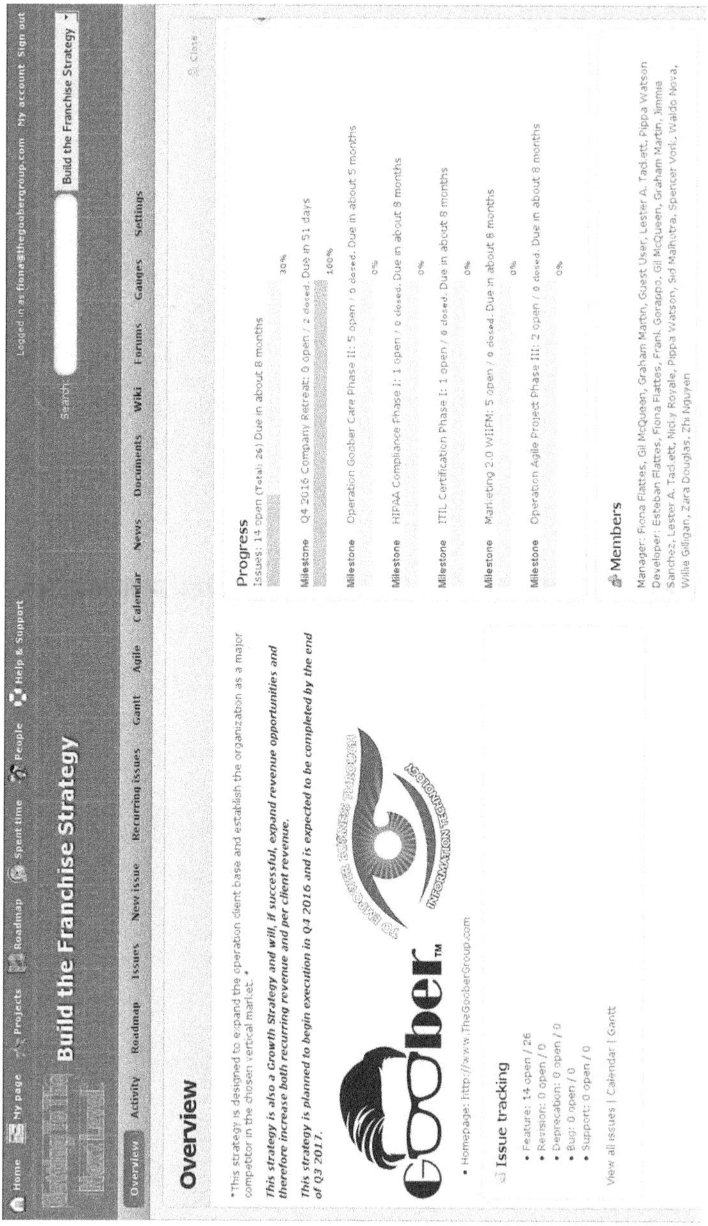

*Figure 11-8. Agile Project Board–The Business Strategy Overview*

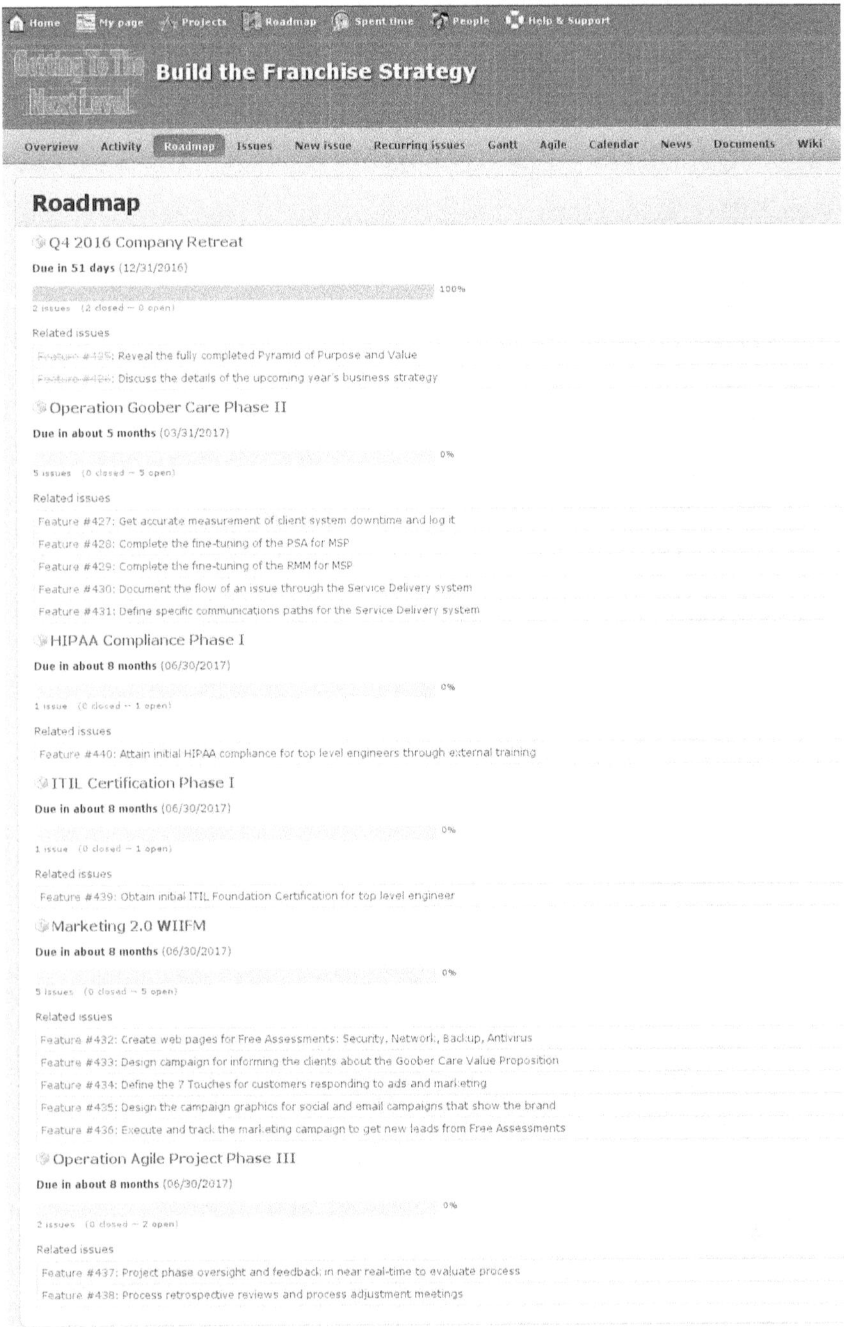

*Figure 11-9. Agile Project Board–The Business Strategy Roadmap*

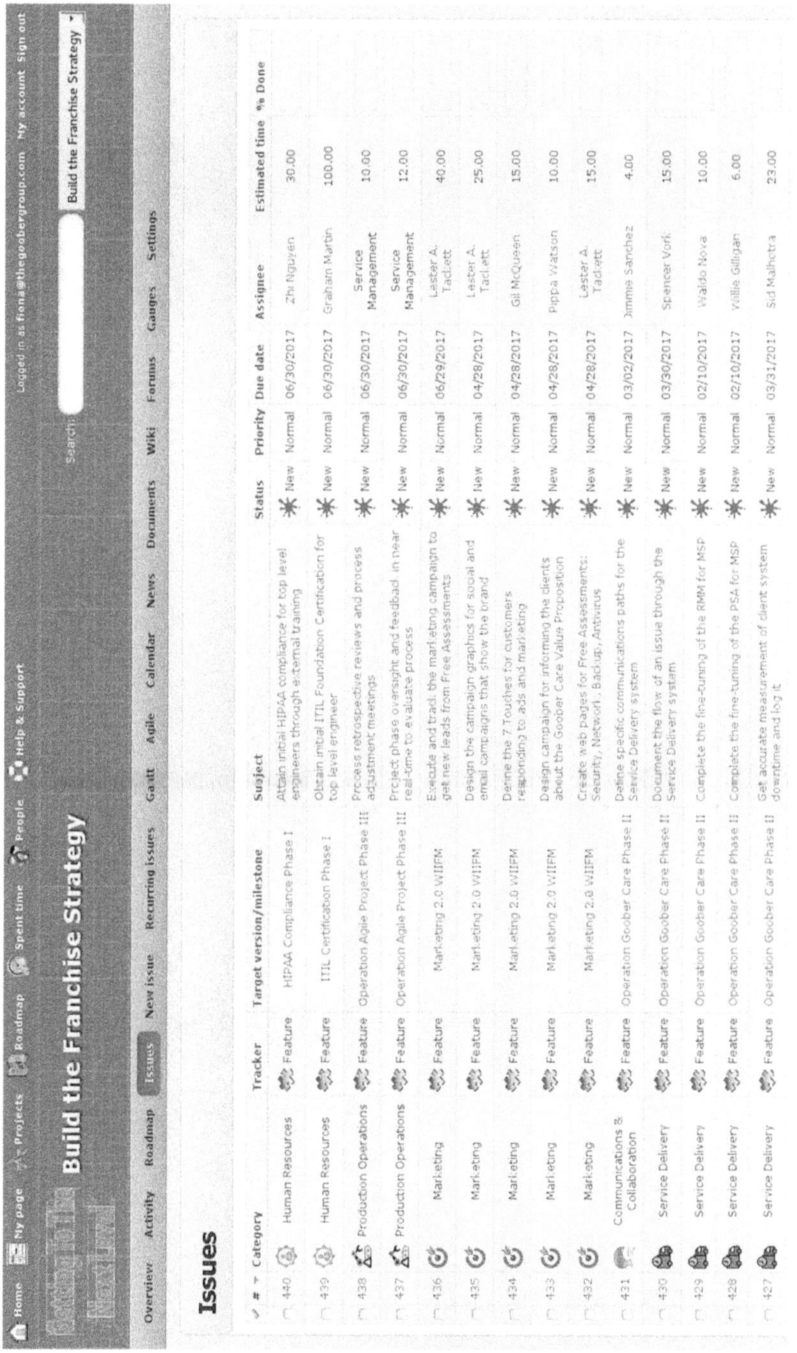

*Figure 11-10. Agile Project Board–The Issues (Laundry) List*

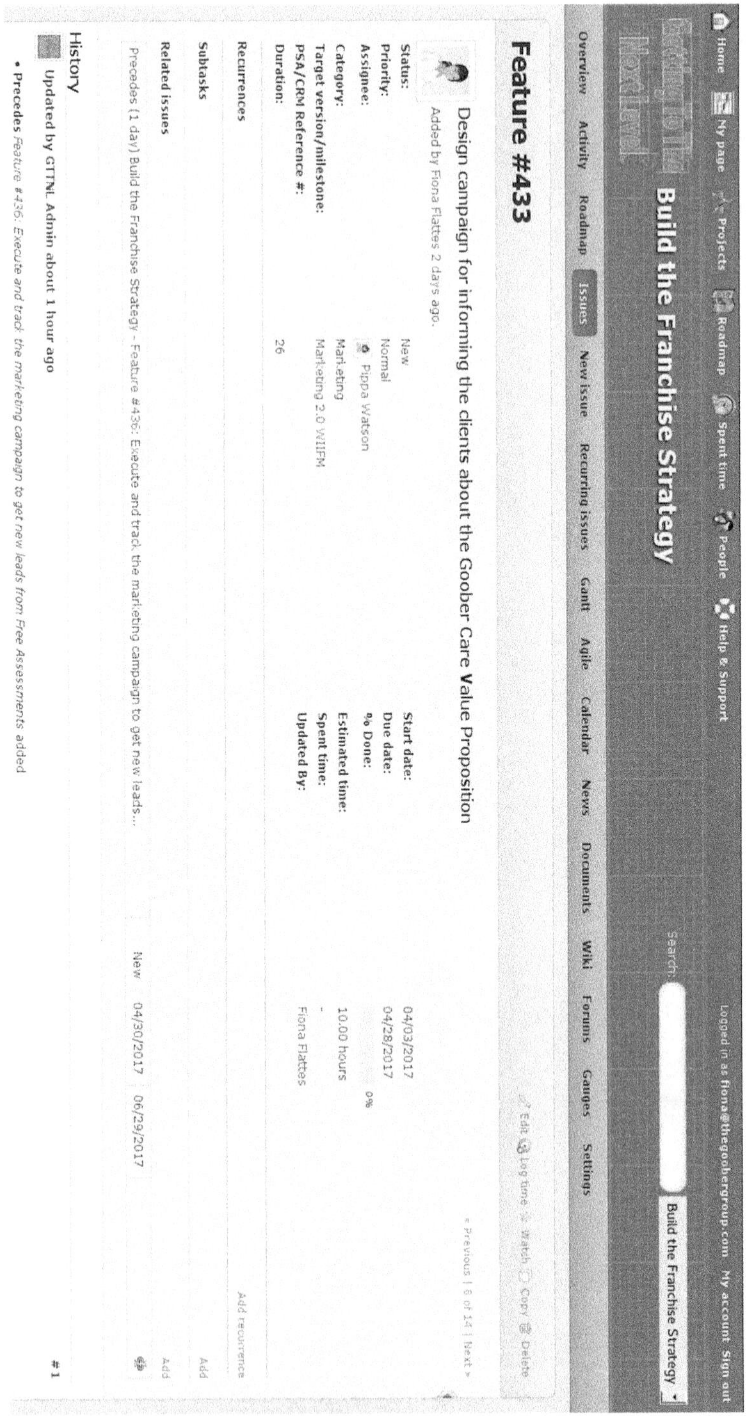
Home
My page
Projects
Roadmap
Spent time
People
Help & Support
Logged in as fiona@thegoobergroup.com
My account
Sign out
Build the Franchise Strategy
Search:
Build the Franchise Strategy
Overview
Activity
Roadmap
Issues
New issue
Recurring issues
Gantt
Agile
Calendar
News
Documents
Wiki
Forums
Gauges
Settings
Feature #433
Edit
Log time
Watch
Copy
Delete
« Previous | 6 of 14 | Next »
Design campaign for informing the clients about the Goober Care Value Proposition
Added by Fiona Flattes 2 days ago.
Status: New
Priority: Normal
Assignee: Pippa Watson
Category: Marketing
Target version/milestone: Marketing 2.0 WIIFM
PSA/CRM Reference #:
Duration: 26
Start date: 04/03/2017
Due date: 04/28/2017
% Done: 0%
Estimated time: 10.00 hours
Spent time: -
Updated By: Fiona Flattes
Recurrences
Add recurrence
Subtasks
Add
Related issues
Add
Precedes (1 day) Build the Franchise Strategy - Feature #436: Execute and track the marketing campaign to get new leads...
New
04/30/2017
06/29/2017
History
Updated by GTTNL Admin about 1 hour ago
#1
Precedes Feature #436: Execute and track the marketing campaign to get new leads from Free Assessments added

*Figure 11-11. Agile Project Board–The Issue Details*

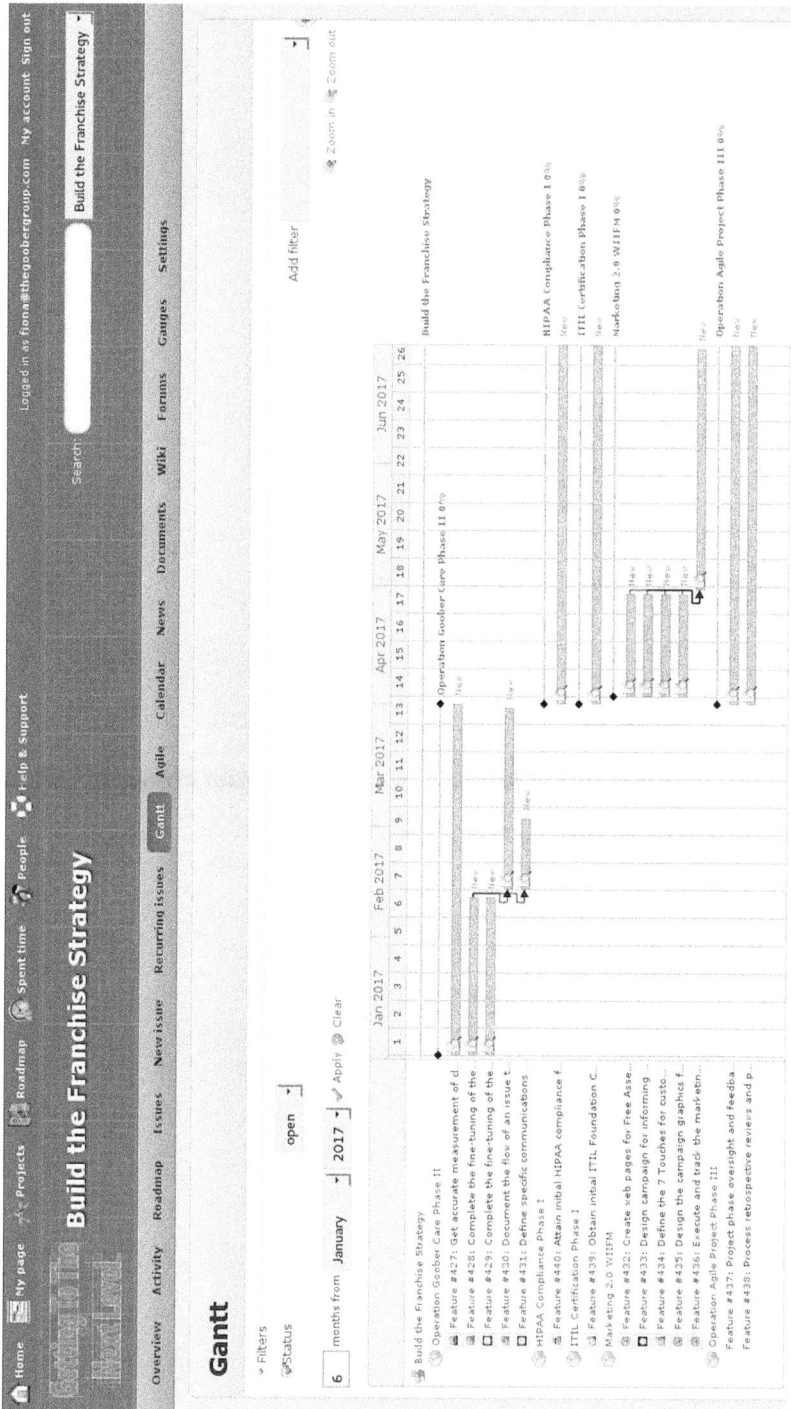

*Figure 11-12. Agile Project Board–Gantt Chart*

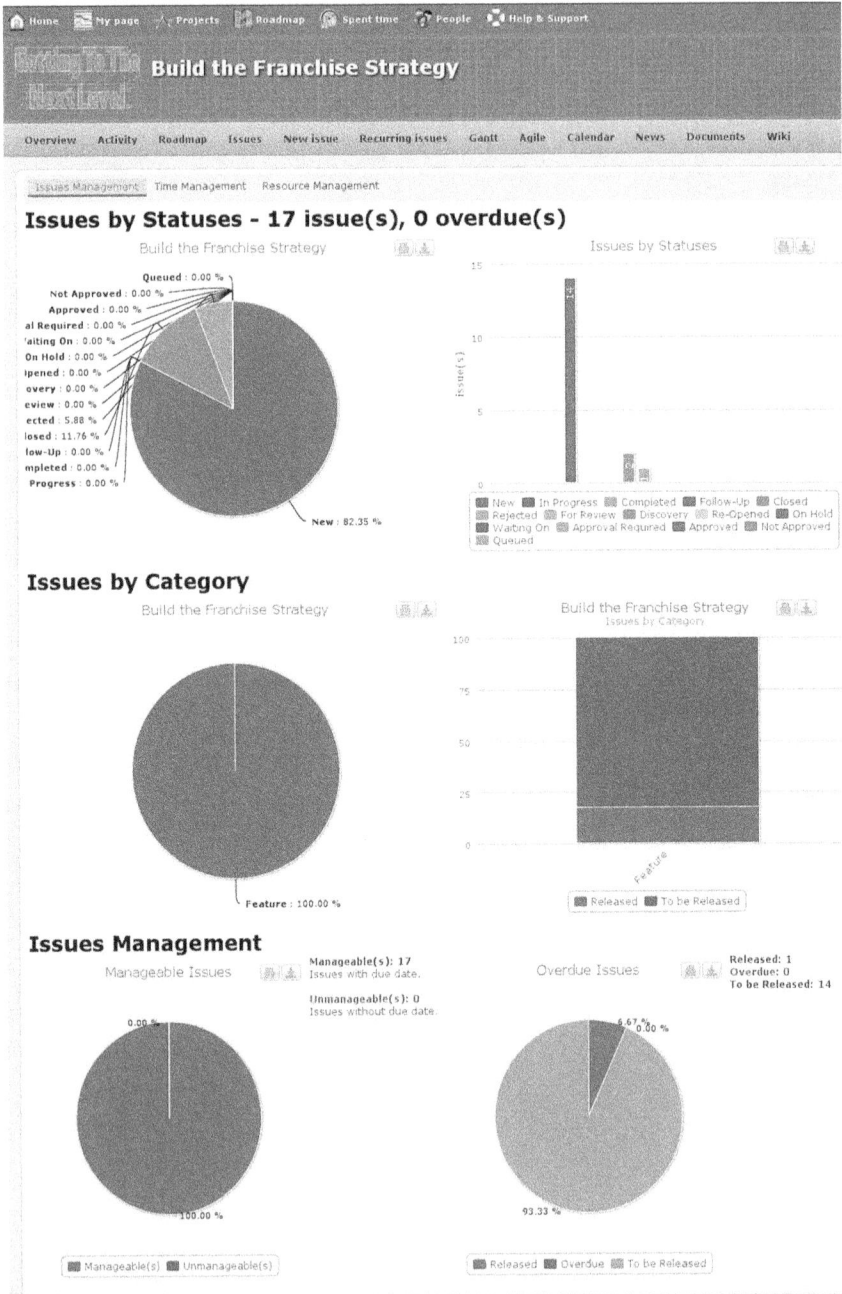

*Figure 11-13. Agile Project Board–Issues Management*

*Figure 11-14. Agile Project Board–Resource Management*

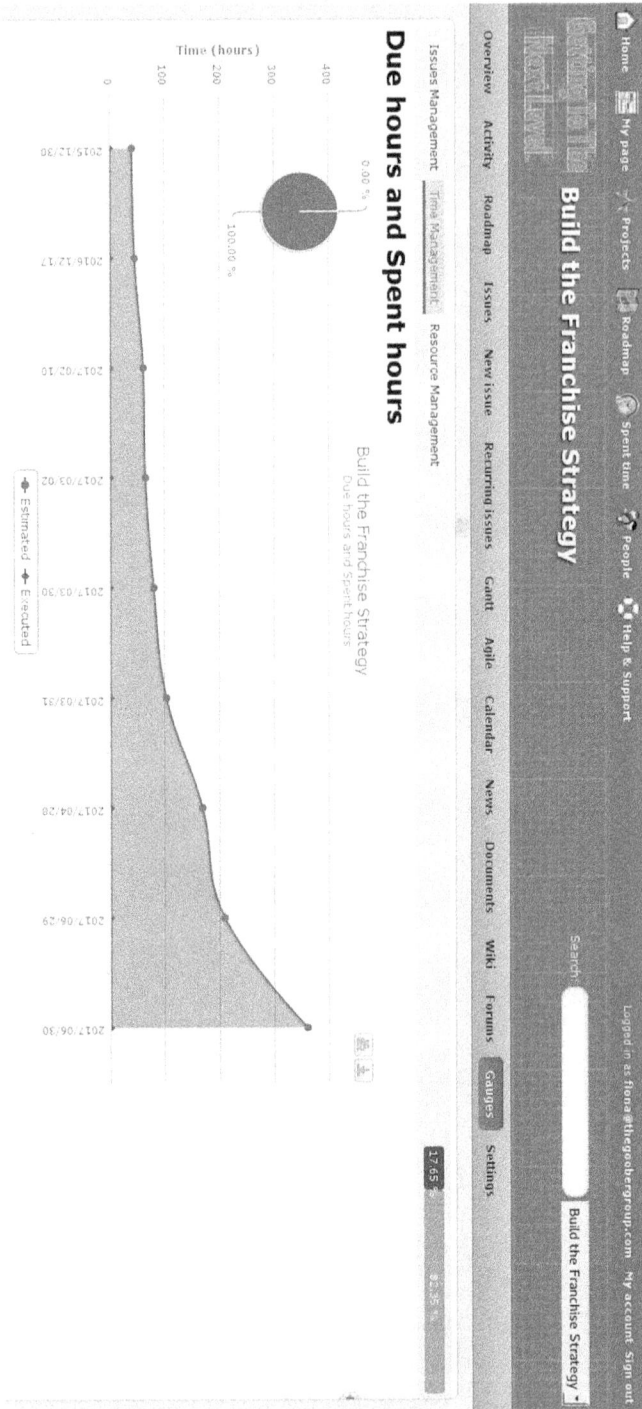

*Figure 11-15. Agile Project Board–Time Management*

*Whenever an individual or a business decides that success has been attained, progress stops.*

– Thomas J. Watson

# 12.0

## CASE STUDY & EXAMPLE

The case study presented here serves several purposes. First, it demonstrates how an organization can be broken down using some of the tools discussed in the tools chapters (see Chapters 3-5). Second, it offers an excellent model to use when showing you how to design your business from the top down using the Pyramid of Purpose and Value (see Chapters 6-8). Third, it provides an example to use when showing you how to build your business from the ground up using Business Agile Strategy Execution (see Chapter 11). And finally, because it is contrived from real life stories of entrepreneurs and businesses all over the world, I believe it provides a solid hero's story where you can hopefully see yourself in the lead role.

Example isn't another way to teach, it is the only way to teach. That being said, don't get too caught up in the details but instead focus on the journey. The details of the case study are only taken to the level necessary to get the main talking points and ideas in this book across to the reader and to support the chapters that rely on this example. Most of the supporting surveys, questionnaires, documents, external analyses, and reports that are required for a complete real-life case study are not included here as including all that content would easily push this chapter to several hundred pages. Throughout this case study you will see many select excerpts of these documents or brief references to them versus full versions as necessary to support the narrative and the intent. You will also recognize that this entire example is conveyed with a narrative style of writing versus a strict case-in-point style.

The following case study is based on a completely fictitious example company, The Goober Group, which operates in the Information Technology (IT) industry. IT refers to the information a business creates and uses, the computers and networks they employ to manage and use the information, and all the hardware and software related to these computers and networks. As previously mentioned, everything about The Goober Group, including the people, places, and scenarios, has been fabricated specifically for the purpose of creating a concise case study example for this book.

The study incorporates many real-life issues, some of which I have personally encountered and some of which have been shared with me, but all of which have been obscured enough so as to protect possible connections to any real-life scenarios. And even if someone were to claim they recognize a given scenario, the fact is they all are so common in small and medium-sized organizations within the Information Technology industry, it would be the equivalent of saying, "That's the exact same cold I had once too."

## Executive Summary

The Goober Group is a minority-owned small business operating in the Computer Related Services industry. After many years of being in operation and following the economic downturn, the owner found herself facing several issues that together are keeping the business from getting to the next level. The business is suffering from a lack of cash flow due to loose financial policies and practices. There are key roles being filled by individuals who are not properly qualified or experienced while other key roles are either undefined or are not staffed at all.

The line of products and services being offered is too wide to allow the focus required to obtain a competitive advantage in any meaningful way. The tools being used to deliver products and services are disparate and ineffectively tuned to the point that Service Delivery and therefore customer satisfaction are suffering for it. Further, performance measures cannot be obtained due to the lack of proper tracking of time spent on service delivery and projects.

Major considerations include the fact that the owner's spouse needs to move on to his own chosen career instead of settling for a role in this business which he is not trained nor qualified in. Expenses are growing out of control and cannot be allowed to continue. The business has no clear shared vision and mission to bind them together, and even if they did there is no clear direction for the business and no roadmap or strategy for success. There is a significant risk of losing quality talent if the organization as a whole does not get turned around and pointed in the right direction soon, a point beyond which recovery could take many years.

There are market opportunities available that, if capitalized upon, will catapult this organization well over the million dollar mark and establish them as a market leader. If the right strategies are formulated and executed upon, the organization could unify its solutions and tools, align its talent, and be poised to act on the market opportunities presented. The most crucial and significant changes required can be effected within a single calendar year. The following year would be the time to solidify internal processes and allow the business to grow homogenously. In the third full year, the business could begin to grow at a rate of no less than 30% annually provided they can find the quality talent to service the new clientele.

## The Problem Statement

The Goober Group, located in the South Florida region of the U.S., is a minority-owned and operated IT support services business that was launched nearly ten years ago in 2006. The owner, Fiona Flattes, struck out on her own after having spent more than twenty years working in the industry for other IT support service providers. She received her Bachelor of Science degree in Information Technology and worked as a medical receptionist while attending college. She believed an IT service provider should do more than just provide good technical service, it should also help the client grow their organization's IT infrastructure in anticipation of the client's business needs. This is something she witnessed little of in the organizations she had worked for to this point. Within a few short years she grew The Goober Group to just over $500K annual revenue and a handful of talented and like-minded people.

Fiona always ensured her team and her company had the right connections to necessary resources by identifying and maintaining memberships in specific organizations relevant to The Goober Group's industry and, where applicable, the businesses in their target market. She insisted all service team members maintain certain industry certifications from vendors and partners so as to keep themselves as individuals and the company as a whole reliable and recognizable as quality service providers. When she believed the timing was right, Fiona invested heavily into industry-specific tools that, if mastered, would position The Goober Group as an industry leader in their area and for their target market.

The Goober Group had never put together a proper marketing campaign and relied heavily on word of mouth and referrals for new business. They did receive many new client referrals because The Goober Group, as a small cohesive team, did in fact provide great technical support for their customers and their customers spoke well of them. As they received referrals they took on the new clients regardless of the size of the client organization or the size of their IT budget. The Goober Group began to learn the new tools intended to help them grow their business and manage their service delivery. This allowed them to maintain their excellent customer service even though the number of users and machines being managed was ever increasing.

As the effects of the U.S. housing crisis and impending economic downturn began to be felt in 2009, Fiona's business began to shrink, as did nearly every other business across the globe. It dropped back to just over half of its highest ever position and she was forced to lay off several highly talented people who had been with her for many years. During the downturn, The Goober Group witnessed a massive increase in freelance IT service providers coming into the market, representing cheap competition for their clients' business. They also witnessed many client businesses cutting back significantly on IT services needs and projects. Fiona saw firsthand what happens to a business when cash flow dries up. The number of competitors in their area and potential customers diminished greatly between 2009 and 2011, mostly due to lack of business, stiffer competition, and insufficient reserves to weather the storm.

Fiona nearly lost her business as clients bargained for lower rates and faster service. At this point in time there were only three people left in the business. With low cash flow, no cash reserves, and a massive backlog of work required just to keep existing clients, there was no time to attain a higher mastery of these tools let alone leverage them. She found herself unable to fully leverage the industry-specific tools that she believed would allow The Goober Group to more easily deliver better and faster services to more clients.

Fortunately, as the economy recovered so did Fiona's business, and she quickly regained her position and hired new people. Her husband Esteban Flattes is a certified public accountant who had been laid off during the worst of the crisis years. Esteban came on board The Goober Group to provide support for whatever they needed, starting with the bookkeeping and payroll. As the business grew, Esteban's role quickly expanded to include office manager and marketing manager. Currently, Esteban is hoping to get back to his chosen career as there are many opportunities awaiting him. Unfortunately, The Goober Group desperately needed him to continue to fill the role he had been molded into.

Fiona hired a salesperson in anticipation of the needs that would be created through the company's first ever full-fledged marketing campaign. Her goal was to expand the business through a coherent marketing of their signature Managed Services offerings to local businesses. As her husband began to attempt designing the marketing strategy, the salesperson sat patiently at his desk waiting for something to do. The salesperson did not seem to be exceptionally motivated to even do simple (easy) sales by writing up and selling much needed project work to existing customers.

Esteban Flattes was up against more than just the fact he was not actually a marketing manager by career or trade. He had been charged with designing a real marketing plan but was running into roadblocks at every turn. The Goober Group had not been doing even the basic marketing such as social media and monthly newsletters. They also had not developed the channels of communications with their vendors and partners that would allow them to tap into marketing materials and funds from those vendors and partners. And lastly, Esteban was having trouble understanding exactly what to market or advertise because he really didn't understand what The Goober Group offered for services.

Although Fiona had managed to keep her business alive through the economic downturn and brought it to a new height, she still had many problems with the organization that she knew were keeping her from getting to the next level. A recent and primary concern was that The Goober Group showed a total revenue of over $900K for the previous 12 months rolling, but even though revenue and net new business (new clients) were increasing, expenses were rapidly growing out of control. At this point her cash reserves were beginning to dwindle. Fiona came to the realization that she could not utilize her salesperson because she could not market. She could not market because she had not clearly defined her products and services. Further, even if Fiona did define, market, and sell a concise list of products and services, she had unresolved operations and service issues that would keep her from delivering the quality she intended and her clients deserved.

Fiona had been trying to build The Goober Group as an IT Managed Service Provider (MSP) but their business model and service offerings were not aligned with the intended model. Managed Services is a proactive method of managing IT services. It stands opposite the Break-Fix Service model which is reactive in nature. In Break-Fix Services, you call the service provider with a problem, it gets fixed, and you get billed accordingly. Work is typically handled on a first come, first served basis with the one who screams the loudest getting priority. The Managed Services model means the service provider manages and takes care of everything in your IT system and you are billed a flat fee per month. Everything is managed in priority order based on how widely the issue affects the systems being managed. While Fiona and her service team understood that Managed Services is not only their preferred method but also the most efficient method, they had never properly built out service offerings around that model. The Goober Group had been offering Break-Fix Services and trying to deliver Managed Services.

In my initial interview with Fiona, she told me she wanted to "take The Goober Group from being IT Schmos to MSP Pros," and she stated it again in her questionnaire response. What she meant was that she believed they were holding themselves back at amateur levels due to immaturity in many of the aspects of their business which were not being properly cultivated. She also knew that with the right strategy, she could in fact get this business to the next level. Everything about the industry and market climate looked favorable for The Goober Group. My recommendation to Fiona was that they did in fact need to reaffirm the design of the endeavor—her business—from the top down and then go about revamping it from the bottom up. I suspected there were several more issues involved that would need to be discovered and remedied. She agreed and we immediately began a complete business SWOT Analysis, including personal profiles on each team member.

## Situation Analysis

### Introduction
The complete business SWOT Analysis of The Goober Group began early in the final quarter of 2015, and the formulation of the roadmap and strategy was completed by the end of that quarter. In light of certain issues discovered during the analysis and based on their impact to the business, certain strategies were formulated and actions taken before the business analysis was completed for the best interest of the organization. These strategies and actions will be covered in detail in the Solutions Recommendation and Solutions Implementation sections.

The SWOT Analysis performed consisted of:
- DiSC profile for each member of the organization
- Situational Questionnaire for each member of the organization (including the principals)
- Business Profile Questionnaire for the principal(s)
- Porter's Five Competitive Forces Analysis
- Porter's Generic Strategies Analysis

The SWOT Analysis called for the following supporting documentation:
- Most recent Feasibility Study
- Most recent Business Plan
- All Financial Statements for the current and previous year
- Product and Service Line Card
- A recent Target Market Analysis
- Employee roster, resumes, and rap sheets
- Core Competency Matrix
- Copy of all client Service Agreements
- List of common service rates
- Client roster including effective hourly rate
- Calculated Fully Burden Cost of Labor

The SWOT Analysis resulted in the following report:
- Business Solutions Recommendation

The Questionnaires, Five Forces Analysis, Generic Strategies Analysis, and all Supporting Documentation served as a vehicle for discovery. They helped with understanding the culture, sentiment, bias, and pains of the organization. Evaluation of all these inputs resulted in the all-encompassing and fully comprehensive SWOT Analysis presented at the end of this section. The SWOT is, for all practical purposes, the complete laundry list of Strengths, Weaknesses, Opportunities, and Threats of the organization that must be addressed in one fashion or another at one time or another in order to get to the next level.


## Employee Roster

| Name | Role | Years |
|---|---|---|
| Fiona Flattes | Owner/Entrepreneur | 10 |
| | Programmer | |
| | Engineer | |
| Esteban Flattes | Bookkeeper | 4 |
| | Marketing Manager | |
| | Office Manager | |
| Calvin Green | Sales Manager | 1 |
| Graham "Sparky" Martin | Service Manager | 8 |
| | Project Manager | |
| | Service Coordinator | |
| Benjamin "Ben" Hawkins | Lead Engineer | 7 |
| Zhi Nguyen | Engineer | 5 |
| William "Willie" Gilligan | Engineer | 3 |
| Sidharth "Sid" Malhotra | Field Technician | 3 |
| Waldo Nova | Field Technician | 2 |
| Spencer "Spork" Vork | Field Technician | 4 |
| Nicholas "Nicky" Royale | Help Desk Tech | 1 |
| Frank "Speed Bump" Gorappo | Help Desk Tech | 6 |
| James "Jimmie" Sanchez | Receptionist | 2 |

*Total Employees – 13*
*Total Service Delivery Team – 10*


## Relevant Situational Questionnaire Responses

*Notes: The questions and answers noted here are only a select few of the nearly one hundred questions on the Situational Questionnaire completed by each person in the organization.*

Q: What is the company Vision Statement?

A: Only Fiona Flattes responded with correct or near-correct statements.

"To empower business through Information Technology."

Q: What is the company Mission Statement?

A: Only Fiona Flattes, Graham Martin, and Benjamin Hawkins responded with correct or near-correct statements.

"Our mission is to enable your company to focus on its core business and operate smoothly because we focus on the technology as our core business."

Q: What are the stated company Values?

A: All guessed except Fiona Flattes who indicated she had not specifically defined any specific company values but suggested several on the fly.

"Integrity, Knowledge, Experience, and Collaboration."

Q: Describe the company culture, if possible?

A: Fiona Flattes – The Goober Group has a culture that is relaxed by default. Day-to-day operations are not micromanaged unless some problem results in scrutiny of a particular process, behavior, or individual. The employees all have good intentions and there are usually no bad attitudes, but sometimes we do not hold strictly to procedures or fully deliver best practices, especially when under stress. The employees lack a concrete set of expectations that they would be judged by on a regular basis, which might improve the consistency of performance.

A: Esteban Flattes – We have a friendly yet very result-driven culture.

A: Benjamin Hawkins – Adaptability and quick reactions to the changing market, competition, and external environment; entrepreneurship-type attitude.

A: All others responded with some form of "Talented, driven, dedicated team players in a family environment."

Q: Do you feel or see that this company is growing?

A: All responded "Yes" followed by concerns of various pain points mostly related to quality of work product and response time to clients' needs. Most cited the need for more quality technical support talent or the need for more sales people.

Q: If this company is to grow, what are the biggest issue(s) it faces?

A: Fiona Flattes – Structured and documented standards, procedures, and processes.

A: Esteban Flattes – We are not focused on what we sell or deliver.

A: Being able to handle more clients. (5 responses)

Q: Are there solutions that don't work or are troublesome?

A: We cannot get any useful reports out of our ticketing system because we do not track all work and time. (4 responses – all management)

A: We sell too many brands of products to have any consistency in configuration. (7 responses)
Q: Does your team or the company have a formal written Project Process?
A: Yes. (3 responses)
A: No. (4 responses)
A: I don't know. (6 responses)
Q: Does your team or the company in general have any problems breaking projects down into measureable size tasks?
A: Yes. (6 responses)
A: No. (0 responses)
A: I don't know. (7 responses)
Q: Does your team or the company in general have any problems recognizing when the project is off course or out of scope?
A: Yes. (6 responses)
A: No. (0 responses)
A: I don't know. (7 responses)
Q: Does your team or the company usually lose money or make money on projects?
A: Make money. (1 response)
A: Lose money. (6 responses)
A: I don't know. (6 responses)
Q: Does the team or the company have a problem with Sales or Marketing selling projects outside the skill set of what the team can do?
A: All responded "Yes" except Calvin Green (Sales Manager).


## Relevant Business Profile Questionnaire Responses

*Note: These questions were only asked of Fiona Flattes as the President and sole principal of the organization. The questions and answers noted here are only a select few of the more than fifty questions on the Business Profile Questionnaire.*

Q: Who is your target market?
A: We really don't have a specific target market. Ever since the recession we've taken any client we can get. Lately we've been trying to stay away from really small businesses. They seem to pay slowly, they don't use a lot of hours, and they never want to sign any agreements. We do not do residential services except for when it is the owner of a business and they need us to work on their home computers.
Q: What are your current operating metrics, and what drivers are set to push performance in finance, marketing, sales, production, service, etc.?

A: We don't have any except for our ticket count and our service board backlog. We try to keep the ticket count and backlog down and we try to operate financially in the black. We keep a backlog of work so we know how each week will look and it helps with planning service and projects. I keep thinking I need to get some goals set but I don't feel we have a plan to make it actually happen.

Q: Select all items that are a current, recent, or upcoming concern.

*Note: All items listed below were checked.*

- Our engineers are still not working in real-time and we're losing hours.
- Our clients all have different net terms and most don't pay as agreed.
- We need to develop sales and marketing but don't know where to start.
- Engineers do things differently for each client. We lack important standards.
- Our CRM and RMM could be doing so much more. We need to tune them up.
- We have clients who don't respect our employees or what we do for them.

Q: What does this company represent to you in your life? i.e. Is it your life's work and you intend to pass it on to your children? Do you intend to work in it forever? Do you intend to grow it to a certain size and then sell it off?

A: I intend to grow it and have the employees become the owners with myself on the board of directors, and eventually my shares will feed my retirement fund. Then I will go travel.

Q: What would you like to do with the company short-term (3 months – 1 year) and medium-term (1 – 5 years)?

A: Short-term, I would like to start tracking all work time, solidify some standards, and get our project process figured out. I would like to become more elite in what we offer and who we offer it to, that is, to carve out a specific client type that we can serve best. Long-term, I would like to increase recurring revenue from managed services and actually start putting some real money away for the future of the company and for my retirement. I think we have great potential but we lack guidance and execution, especially on the marketing. I want to take The Goober Group from being IT Schmos to MSP Pros.


## Strengths–Weaknesses–Opportunities–Threats Analysis

All of the relevant forces the organization is experiencing or expects to experience which must be addressed are culminated here. Each of the ten business Value Aspects is represented and each indicates the relevant Strengths, Weaknesses, Opportunities, and Threats that have been identified. Some entries may include supporting narrative as necessary.

*Note: This is an extremely stripped-down version of a complete SWOT. Attempting to present a complete SWOT would detract from the intended message.*

## Communications & Collaboration

- Strengths
  - o The organization has great potential and seeding of its culture. The key people and those with the most history in the organization have quite the same mindset as to how the company should present itself and behave.
  - o The organization has good knowledge management and collaboration systems in place and has above-average competency (for the size of organization) in creating and managing content. This represents a significant advantage in that it directly translates into usable skills for helping clients manage their systems and learn to collaborate effectively.
- Weaknesses
  - o The organization's Vision, Mission, and Values are not widely disseminated and therefore cannot help bind the team and gel the culture. Without them it will be harder as the business grows to have any new people feel like they belong to something bigger than themselves rather than just having a place to work.
  - o Although there are good systems in place for knowledge management and collaboration, there are key documents missing which requires the organization to rely on common knowledge for key elements of both. If something were to happen to certain key people (if they leave for example), the organization, knowledge management system, and collaboration system could be rendered nearly useless.
- Opportunities
  - o No significant or relevant Opportunities identified.
- Threats
  - o No significant or relevant Threats identified.

## Finance & Accounting

- Strengths

- o The business has zero debt plus excellent credit. This allows great agility in deciding which direction the organization should go and how to get there.
- o High liquidity of financial assets also translates directly into agility and options.
- Weaknesses
  - o Labor costs are above expected levels due to an inordinate pay for the lead engineer, Benjamin Hawkins. His pay has apparently been increasing regularly because every time the owners go on vacation, he feels he is left behind to "babysit" and ends up holding them up for more money. This is in addition to a sweetheart deal he negotiated when he came on board seven years ago. He was given a higher pay because he brought some existing clients with him. These same clients have long since left the care of The Goober Group, but as a deal is a deal, his pay has remained at the negotiated level. In addition, Benjamin refuses to meet training requirements for maintaining his Microsoft certifications, a key component in the value proposition the organization offers. Benjamin's salary and benefits package is equal to Fiona's, but based on his current skill set and experience, it should be approximately $25K annually lower than it is.
  - o There are no clearly defined goals for increasing revenue and specifically recurring revenue. The organization cannot increase profit or grow if there are no specific goals to drive marketing and sales.
  - o There are no clearly defined goals for managing expenses and costs of goods sold, and there is no formal budget for the coming year, only projections of what will be spent based on past history. There are no specific large draws on finances to speak directly to, but there must always be some oversight, checks, and balances in place.
  - o There are no defined penalties or percent fee for accounts in arrears and no process for applying them. There must always be a cost for borrowing money and an associated cost for paying late—it incentivizes prompt payment.
- Opportunities
  - o With excellent credit and a solid position, several banks and investors are actively seeking to provide funding for the next venture. If the strategy requires funding, it is estimated that up to $1M could be accessed depending on the amount of collateral available to Fiona and the strength

of the business plan.

- Threats
  - o Too many clients are not paying on time. A/R is > 30% out more than 45 days. This item affects Finance but is a Weakness of the Sales process and policies.
  - o Hardware and software are being ordered before clients actually pay for them. The Goober Group is in effect acting as the bank for the clients. This significantly hinders cash flow and is not a good business practice for an organization of this maturity.

## Human Resources

- Strengths
  - o The organization has a fantastic process for finding, acquiring, training, and cultivating quality talent. Provided it is used correctly, it will certainly continue to allow The Goober Group to bring on the best talent available.
- Weaknesses
  - o The Sales Manager role is improperly filled. Calvin Green is a very nice person, but he does not understand this industry and he is not gaining any understanding as time goes on. He admittedly feels out of sorts. He indicated he took the job because he needed the work, really likes Esteban and Fiona, and truly believed he could get the hang of it. Fiona indicated she had in fact been "sold" on Calvin and his skills by Calvin himself. He is actively looking for work on LinkedIn and he even asked me for an introduction to another client of mine in the area. This role must be filled with the right person or NO ONE.
  - o There is a genuine need to replace Esteban in as short of time possible for more than the obvious reasons. He is being pressed into the additional roles of Marketing Manager and Office Manager and he is not performing the marketing role in any beneficial way. His desire to strike back out into his chosen field creates a significant stress on the relationship of the owners and is a detriment to the culture of the organization. I know both Fiona and Esteban realize this, but it must be indicated here for the purpose of ensuring it is resolved in the process of strategy formation.
- Opportunities
  - o The receptionist, James Sanchez, has some low-level skills

in computers and over the past two years, he has acquired a broad understanding of the work The Goober Group does. He also has a desire to quit this job because he is falling asleep at his desk most of the time. He is supposed to be backing up Esteban on marketing but since Esteban has no idea what he really should be doing, nor the time to do it, James is significantly underutilized. James has the DiSC profile of a service coordinator, as well as the intellect and above all the interest. Since this is a role that needs to be filled, he could easily be shifted into it.

- Threats
  - The local IT service provider Invasive IT is constantly calling The Goober Group's engineers and attempting to lure them away. The owner is an ex-employee who took several clients with him (scalped) when he became disgruntled and left in 2009. Everyone here knows him and none of the team seem to be at all interested in jumping ship, mostly due to the good culture and environment here. However, he will continue to be a threat as a disrupter and will pick off young inexperienced hires if they are not educated and taken care of here.


## Marketing

- Strengths
  - The organization has an important differentiation potential due to its Core Competencies in both ITIL certification and HIPAA Compliance. Leveraging these in new redefined service offerings can present a significant competitive advantage depending on the target market. These competencies should help define the ideal target market.
  - The Core Competencies across the team related to Electronic Medical Records and digital cardiology scan management solutions, in addition to other healthcare related lines of business applications, presents a significant competitive advantage potential. These competencies should help define the ideal target market.
  - The business has the revenue to create an appropriate budget to support an aggressive and sustained advertising and marketing campaign.
  - The business has a well-designed website and appropriate sample (attraction) offerings to use for day-to-day basic

marketing.
- Weaknesses
  - o The services offered by The Goober Group are too wide and varied to allow focus of value. The initial question presented in challenge to the list of offerings is "Why would I sign up for a recurring monthly fee when I don't believe I will use that much IT service? Why not just pay as I go?" The offerings are no different than the large majority of other IT service providers who are targeting much of the same clients as The Goober Group.
  - o There is no set product line card of products sold and serviced by The Goober Group. The customer is dictating the products to buy and they are not always business class. There are multiple issues here. First, there is no consistency in product configuration because there are so many brands being sold. Second, selling non-business class equipment to the client and then being expected to maintain them to the level required for this level of service is actually costing the organization time and money. There must me a reasonable set of products and solutions that are business class to offer to the clients.
  - o There is no qualified or dedicated person to do marketing. Esteban is talented but is not versed in any way required to effectively do marketing. Left to their own devices The Goober Group has managed to put a warm body in the role part-time, but this function is so critical to driving new business that there must be either a full-time in-house or an outsourced solution for marketing.
- Opportunities
  - o The market studies accessed indicate IT spending is seen as much more important in Medical, Legal, and Financial businesses. This is believed to be due to government regulations and requirements coupled with the higher risk of downtime and data loss in light of recent global infiltrations and attacks.
  - o The study of The Goober Group's Core Competencies and Fiona's interests for the business direction reveal an opportunity to move into a vertical market focused on the medical industry, specifically Cardiology practices.
  - o Strategic partnering with select vendors who are offering Marketing Development Funds and even willing to allow The Goober Group to present content at their events can be a significant advantage as The Goober Group has Core

Competency knowledge to share. All the marketing around these events alone can generate a measurable amount of free advertising for The Goober Group and immeasurable fodder for social media and a regular client newsletter.

- Threats
  - o There are numerous new IT service providers moving into the market and most are presenting offerings at lower prices than The Goober Group for what appears to be effectively the same services.
  - o There is a significant threat by one local IT service provider (Invasive IT) who is consolidating many smaller organizations (under $1M) in an effort to grow revenue and market share. This organization is believed to be stalled due to moving too fast, and their reputation indicates they are low cost and low value. They do not pose a significant threat, but their marketing and sales tactics will require The Goober Group to have a clear differentiation in products and services.
  - o There is a growing threat from new entrants to the market by print service providers. There is a push to move into the Managed IT Service arena as a way to grow market and revenue. It is believed that it will take several years for these companies to mature enough to compete for more intricate projects, but they do pose an immediate threat to helpdesk, field service, and bench tech services.

## Organization Infrastructure

- Strengths
  - o All business Operating Systems are virtual and The Goober Group owns only the end-user computers and the small amount of supporting network equipment. This is a great benefit in that it allows anyone to work from anywhere and still have access to all resources. This is also beneficial in that it allows the organization to scale as needed very quickly.
- Weaknesses
  - o Not all of the selected solutions for the organization's Operating Systems are on the same outsourced infrastructure. The collaboration servers are housed with one cloud service provider while the user and data servers are on another. The Goober Group has assembled all the right tools and solutions to run the business and has built out

the needed systems, but several critical systems are housed on different vendor platforms. It is highly recommended that if an organization is using one vendor for services such as virtual servers, they should have all of their servers on that same service unless there is a compelling reason not to do so. By utilizing one cloud solution provider for all virtual servers it creates consistency in resources and allows the organization to tap into one unified service system when it is needed. This has come about as the organization has grown because there is no set standard for resource utilization.

- Opportunities
  - o There is a potential opportunity to decrease infrastructure costs and obtain a higher level of Core Competency across the organization, in addition to negating the previously mentioned weakness. By unifying solutions for virtual servers to The Goober Group's preferred cloud services provider, all engineers and techs will be deepening their knowledge of the single solution to the benefit of the organization and the clients. Mastery of the single solution represents a significant competitive advantage and increased customer value.
- Threats
  - o No significant or relevant Threats identified.


## Procurement & Logistics

- Strengths
  - o The product identification and selection solution is well integrated to the quoting and invoicing system. Leveraging this for product ordering by select authorized team members as a process will significantly reduce errors and speed up delivery times.
- Weaknesses
  - o Techs and engineers are spending an inordinate amount of time running parts and supplies to customer offices. When the bench tech has completed work or when the customer needs something repaired, the Field Engineers or an available Help Desk tech runs the parts or equipment to or from the client offices. As The Goober Group does not charge for travel time, this practice actually creates an unregulated cost center for the service delivery department.
- Opportunities

o Selecting specific vendors and specific brands for product offerings of major hardware and software can help establish a higher standard of quality in products and value for the customer. It will also allow The Goober Group to increase the strength of specific Core Competencies related to these products. Selecting the best-of-breed brands can represent a competitive advantage. The selection of the preferred provider of these brands should be a practice in pitting vendors against each other for the best pricing and delivery.

- Threats
  o No significant or relevant Threats identified.

## Production Operations
- Strengths
  o The Goober Group appears to have all the right tools available, having tapped into the entire stack of solutions offered by the Ticketing System and Remote Monitoring and Maintenance vendor SolarWinds MSP. Continuing to train and leverage these tools will continually increase the Core Competency and efficiency of the team.
- Weaknesses
  o There is no set project process and the project manager has no training in running projects. Projects are not being scoped and defined properly and the timelines, deadlines, and time required are being consistently misquoted, resulting in loss of time, energy, and good faith with clients. Most of the real-time loss is in not recognizing when things come up that are not part of the project (scope creep). This Weakness has come about as Fiona has trusted the service manager, Graham Martin, to manage projects but failed to require that he obtain some formal training. His team management skills suffice for service delivery in general but projects seem to be just a little more complex than he currently understands. I believe he simply needs proper education and guidance and he will do fantastic.
  o The service ticket management system is not fully tuned. Additionally, there is a lack of a set flow of a ticket through the service process, and communications with clients are sporadic and incoherent. There must be a specific thread of communication woven as a client issue progresses through the system. This is also affecting projects in that

there is no set project process and as such, no set project communications protocol.

- Opportunities
  o No significant or relevant Opportunities identified.
- Threats
  o No significant or relevant Threats identified.

## Research & Development

- Strengths
  o The organization has some very talented people with exceptional knowledge of ITIL and extensive experience with IT Managed Services. This presents a potential to create very specialized and differentiated value propositions for the target market. It will be one of the deciding factors in the roadmap and strategy to be developed.
- Weaknesses
  o There is no Cloud Solution offering being developed. This has been identified as a critical requirement in order to be a relevant Managed Service Provider. The Goober Group seems to have all the pieces, they simply have not performed the design and documentation of what the solution will look like. This SWOT item could be assigned to Marketing as a Weakness, however Marketing only establishes that there should be a solution. It will remain here as it is for R&D to first innovate the product life cycle to present to Marketing.
- Opportunities
  o There are numerous specific training and certification opportunities that can be tapped into through memberships in certain industry associations, some of which The Goober Group is already in association with. By endearing to these memberships and programs, The Goober Group could significantly elevate the standings of all the talent in the organization which in turn gives significant strength to the value proposition being offered.
- Threats
  o No significant or relevant Threats identified.

## Sales

- Strengths
  o No significant or relevant Strengths identified.

- Weaknesses
  - o Those who are doing Sales are not filtering clients to verify they are actually the target clients The Goober Group is after or if they are even a good fit for the organization. This is a mindset brought on by the economic downturn, perpetuated by a lazy sales person, and neglected by upper management. The organization must stop this type of selling and it must remedy the problem clients it currently has found itself to be stuck with.
- Opportunities
  - o No significant or relevant Opportunities identified. *Note that Sales opportunities will need to be reviewed once the sales role is properly defined and filled, the products and services defined, and the target markets are refined.*
- Threats
  - o No significant or relevant Threats identified.


**Service Delivery**
- Strengths
  - o No significant or relevant Strengths identified.
- Weaknesses
  - o Engineers and technicians are not working and tracking time in real-time and they are not following the set (although scant) processes for the flow of a ticket through the service delivery system. The amount of time missing from the day of each tech or engineer is unknown but estimated at over 45% (time not tracked). At a rate of $150 per hour for the standard service rate, this amounts to approximately $150/hr. x 8 service delivery personnel capable of creating billable hours x (45 hours per week's potential x 45%) = $24,300 per week. This is nearly $100,000 of either revenue for the organization or value to the customer that is unaccounted for. This alone has the potential to more than double the revenue of the organization if managed correctly. The actual results will only be verifiable once the entire team is 100% working in real-time.
  - o There are no metrics driving service delivery. There is a backlog report indicating what work is in the pipe but there are no set goals to help set expectations and measure progress. Even with the lack of certain workflows and processes, some goals can be set, sought, and monitored. Items like: maximum ticket count that triggers all hands

working late or on a Saturday, average time on tickets to manage runaway work, and individual and team efficiency metrics. These will be easier to manage once processes are refined and propped up, but many can be initiated immediately.

- Opportunities
  - o   No significant or relevant Opportunities identified.
- Threats
  - o   No significant or relevant Threats identified.


## Summary

My overall opinion of The Goober Group is that it is well-prepped for expansion and success in the coming years if the opportunities are doggedly pursued and its critical weaknesses addressed quickly and without prejudice. In reviewing the SWOT list, it becomes apparent that a majority of issues can in fact be corrected by creating or revising internal processes. However, there are certain weaknesses that are significant and must be addressed immediately. A major point to be made is that the team feels they belong and they like their jobs, the company, and their supervisors, and that certainly means a great deal to an organization trying to get to the next level.

The most powerful factor in any organization's success is the quality talent—the human factor. It is obvious that The Goober Group does not have all the right people in all the right places. It is imperative that Esteban be replaced in any fashion possible as soon as possible for everyone's benefit. In addition, I'm certain it could go without saying that the scenario The Goober Group finds itself in regarding the performance and compensation of the lead engineer, Benjamin Hawkins, is a huge weakness. This will not be easily resolved but it must be at the top of the list of changes that absolutely must come about soon. These two challenges have far-reaching implications in the organizational culture and in financial perspectives and as such must be well planned.

There is nothing about the current scenario for The Goober Group that is dire or that cannot be remedied relatively quickly through a well-laid-out roadmap and strategy for the business. With a clearly defined and aligned strategy, every Value Aspect of the organization will come in line and begin to mature. It will require commitment and execution on everyone's part but I believe this will not be the hardest journey the organization has ever been through.

## Solution Recommendation

There are issues that must be addressed immediately and issues that can be resolved over time. Below is the laundry list of changes to be effected. These must of course be translated into coherent strategies that can be shared with the organization and effectively executed upon. The list is presented in somewhat priority order, however the actual strategy planning will determine the most effective and beneficial order. Every item on this list will need to be directly tied to a positive benefit to the Financial or Customer Perspective of the organization.

Relevant Changes to Come About:
- The organization should pursue a course that matches the desires of Fiona and the strengths of the organization. This means moving toward being a top level Managed Service Provider focused on the Medical Industry, potentially Cardiology services.
- The organization must define itself using the Pyramid of Purpose and Value so that there is a clear Culture, Compass, and Roadmap for the business. This includes defining the finite MSP Value Proposition and a decidedly vertical Target Market.
- There must be a solid budget formulated for the coming two years so the business knows what it will cost to get to the next level.
- Accounts Receivable must be brought in line immediately with zero tolerance to reduce financial risk. This will also help the cash flow of the organization, an important factor in executing the future strategies.
- The business must stop loaning money to the clients in the form of extended credit for products and services. All equipment must be paid for when ordered and projects must have down payments.
- Once the MSP Value Proposition is defined, all existing clients must be moved to that model as fast as possible. The organization cannot effectively offer two primary services, and it is advantageous to the recurring revenue to move to the MSP model.
- The Goober Group must find a full-time Office Manager to replace Esteban as soon as possible. This person will not need to be an accountant but will need basic bookkeeping skills.
- Payroll should be outsourced for efficiency.
- The Goober Group must find a qualified Marketing Manager and then shortly thereafter, find a qualified Sales Manager. The

organization will not get to the next level without them.

- The role of Service Coordinator should be defined, and it appears James Sanchez is a perfect candidate to take on the role. This will alleviate a lot of disorganization in the service delivery and increase the utilization of Mr. Sanchez.
- The PSA and RMM tools must be tuned properly in order to have a smooth Service Delivery system. It is currently costing time and holds customer satisfaction down.
- To provide a high quality Managed Services offering, the Service Delivery team must learn to work and track time in real-time. The required reports for a well-managed MSP rely on this data and it must be accurate.
- A Project Process must be defined, documented, and followed to stop losing money on every project. It will require time to implement and acquire competency but it is imperative to offering a complete MSP solution of high customer value.
- The Cloud Computing Solution employed by The Goober Group for internal use and presented to the clients should be consolidated into one single solution from a single vendor, if possible. The extent to which it is unified will directly strengthen the ability for The Goober Group to manage and sell the solution at higher profits with lower overhead.
- Standards and Procedures must be unified across the organization by the addition of a few simple documents.
- The Goober Group must identify its Core Competencies so it knows where it must learn and grow in order to meet the demands of the customers and be competitive.
- There must be quarterly employee evaluations in order to help the team members learn and grow with the organization according to the needs of the business and the clients.
- Specific certifications, compliances, and competencies provided externally to the organization (ITIL, HIPAA, etc.) must be acquired in order to create a competitive advantage and to support the desired Value Proposition of the organization.
- The techs and engineers must stop being equipment couriers for the customer. A reliable and reputable courier should be retained to shuttle equipment to and from client offices. It will significantly increase utilization of the team.

All recommended changes should be sorted, prioritized, and organized into specific strategies so that the organization may effectively execute each strategy to success and then move to the next. The mindset and therefore the primary objectives of each strategy should be focused on the ultimate goals not the minutia. This means following a basic Balanced Scorecard approach of identifying the desired outcomes of the organization's Financial and Customer Perspectives and then devising the Internal Processes and Learning and Growth Perspective initiatives that will drive those outcomes.

### Long-term Business Roadmap

Four distinct strategies should be developed which should be launched simultaneously and executed on sequentially over the next fiscal year. Together, these represent the immediate short-term Business Roadmap (see Figure 12-1). Note that each individual strategy, once solidified, will have its own detailed roadmap as depicted in Figure 8-4 from Chapter 8. Tracking of the goals and the progress for each strategy would be performed using individual Balanced Scorecards. Each strategy should have a specific theme and be designed to achieve different organizational objectives, all while addressing relevant SWOT issues. These suggested strategies are derived using Kaplan and Norton's generic Strategy Themes and Map template. The recommended strategies are:

- Organization Realignment – A short-term Productivity strategy designed to Improve Cost Structure.
- Achieve Operational Excellence – A short-term Productivity strategy to Increase Asset Utilization.
- Increase Customer Value – A medium-term Revenue Growth Strategy to Enhance Customer Value.
- Build the Franchise – A long-term Revenue Growth Strategy to Expand Revenue Opportunities.

It should be noted that this recommended long-term roadmap and these strategies are to be developed with the intention of getting the business on track and focused in the short-term. They would not and are not expected to take the business beyond the coming fiscal year. An entire new roadmap and set of stratagems based on the success of these stratagems and the future needs of the organization must be formulated. The Goober Group would still need to begin formulating these new longer-term plans no later than Q3 of the coming fiscal year. For example, once the initial strategy to Achieve Operational Excellence is completed, it is recommended that a reevaluation of relevant Value Aspects of the business be performed, a new strategy to Improve Operational Excellence devised, and the Business Roadmap extended. There should always be a pursuit of continuous incremental improvement.

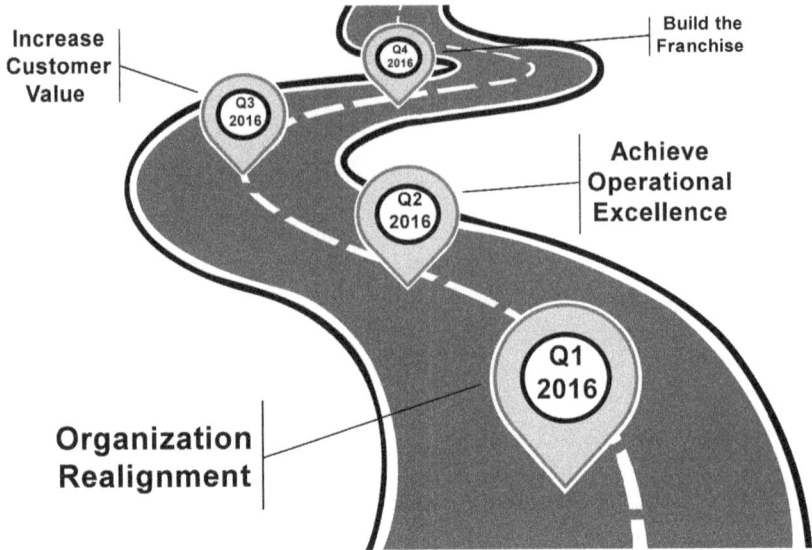

*Figure 12-1. The Goober Group 2016 Roadmap*

## Summary

The recommended roadmap and strategy, if executed in a timely fashion, will position The Goober Group in a specific vertical market with excellent opportunities for growth within as little time as possible. Building on the existing Core Competencies by pursuing the outlined learning and growth initiatives will help establish a competitive advantage in the selected vertical market. Refining the internal processes of the organization and solidifying the Value Proposition will help them establish a significant competitive advantage.

The early alignment of everyone on the team with the vision, mission, and values of the organization is crucial. Continued conversations about every aspect of the business roadmap and strategy will ensure everyone knows their piece of the success. Training plans are rigorous but must be met for the business to get to the next level as planned. The Goober Group seems to be a dedicated and fully capable team, so there shouldn't be any issues with meeting the goals as long as management provides the required support.

With the refined Value Proposition, The Goober Group should have no problems attracting the kind of clients they are targeting, provided they maintain a high level of customer intimacy. This means engagement, partnership, service, and care. They must also promote and protect The Goober Group brand.

Balanced Scorecards should be meticulously maintained and shared so everyone can see the progress and move toward shared success. If the objectives, metrics, or initiatives need to be adjusted or revised, they should be done as swiftly as possible as soon as it is recognized that there is a problem, provided there is in fact a problem. It is also true that if the metrics set out are too lenient or low, they should be raised appropriately, not for yield but for steady progress.

## Solution Implementation

### Assumptions

Based on Fiona's vision, mission, and values statements, her stated desires for what she would like The Goober Group to become, and Porter's Generic Strategies Analysis, it was decided that the overall business strategy would be a Differentiation Focused strategy. Norton and Kaplan, the developers of the Strategy Map, call this a Customer Intimacy Strategy. To be successful it requires that the primary focus for the Customer Perspective of the Balanced Scorecard always be on Relationship and Brand. Although initial short-term strategies may have themes that do not directly translate to Customer Intimacy, all long-term strategies will.

Based on the products and services The Goober Group has innovated, and also taking into account their core competencies, all market analyses indicated that the greatest potential for a competitive advantage is to focus on a single vertical market with only Managed Services offerings. Specifically, they should be most successful by focusing broadly on the medical industry and narrowly on Cardiology offices and Cardiology scan centers. This will require the complete conversion or abandonment of clients who are only consuming break-fix services.

It is assumed that Esteban Flattes will begin a job search in earnest immediately with the intention of leaving the organization no later than the end of Q1 2016. This helps establish a timeline and deadline for certain initiatives. It is also assumed that the sales person, Calvin Green, will be fired or laid off immediately. Calvin is neither participating in nor contributing to the organization and he represents more risk than reward. There is no severance package due or expected and the recoup of his salary will help fund the endeavors at hand.

## Dependencies

These strategies rely heavily on the ability for Fiona and The Goober Group to execute as planned in a timely fashion. Failure to do so will result in a significant loss of time, momentum, and opportunity. Each strategy seeks to create specific financial strength that in turn funds future strategies. For example, failure to get Accounts Receivable in line by the end of the first quarter of 2016 will mean there may be insufficient funds to hire a marketing manager in Q2.

The ability to execute these proposed strategies and the success of those strategies depends heavily on revenue and cash flow. It has been discussed with Fiona and Esteban and has been decided that if revenue is required, three possibilities exist that will be pursued as needed. In order of execution if required, they are:

A)   Esteban's salary will be reduced, even to zero if necessary.

B)   Fiona will take advantage of a Business Line of Credit or Loan.

C)   Fiona will take a salary cut to the extent possible.

## Stratagems in General

Following are each of the strategies that has been laid out, including brief narratives of what they intend to accomplish relative to the SWOT. Each strategy is presented as a Strategy Map, including the corresponding Balanced Scorecard used to measure progress and track success. Look to the narrative for indications of priority, urgency, intended order of implementation, and supporting explanation, as necessary. Look to the Balanced Scorecard for the specifics of the objectives, measures, targets, and initiatives relative to the four Business Perspectives. There won't always be a direct one-to-one correlation of strategy objectives or initiatives to SWOT elements, however each relevant element of the SWOT has been addressed somewhere within the four strategy themes.

## Organization Realignment Strategy

The initial strategy, planned to begin execution in Q1 2016, is presented in Figure 12-2 and is expected to be completed by the end of that quarter. The theme for this strategy is Organization Realignment. The strategy is designed to prepare the organization for subsequent strategies and initiatives to come in future quarters. This strategy is a Productivity Strategy that will, if successful, improve the cost structure by increasing cash flow and decreasing expenses.

**Theme: Organization Realignment**

| Perspective | Strategy Map | Objective | Measure | Target | Initiative |
|---|---|---|---|---|---|
| FINANCIAL | Increase Cash Flow | Increase Cash Flow | % A/R > 30 Days | < 5% | See A/R Efforts Below |
| | Decrease Expenses | Decrease Expenses | % of Revenue | 50% | Build Out the 2016-17 Budget |
| CUSTOMER | Show Shared Values | Show Shared Values | # of Clients Aware | 100% | Communications Campaign |
| | Build Brand Awareness | Build Brand Awareness | # of Clients Aware | 100% | Client Roadmaps Phase I |
| | Better Ship & Handle Logistics | Better Ship & Handle Logistics | # of Clients Aware | 100% | Courier Intro & Best Practice |
| INTERNAL | Reduce A/R Risk | Reduce A/R Risk through Policy | # of Clients Aligned | 100% | A/R Inline Campaign |
| | Reduce Proj Pymt Lag Time | Reduce Project Payment Lag Time | # of Clients Aligned | 100% | Project Payment Campaign |
| | Reduce Equip Pymt Lag Time | Reduce Equip Payment Lag Time | # of Clients Aligned | 100% | Product Payment Campaign |
| | Payroll Process Efficiency | Improve Payroll Process Efficiency | % Complete | 100% | Implement Payroll Service |
| | Get Courier Service | Get Courier Service to Increase Tech and Engineer Efficiency | % Complete | 100% | Implement Courier Service |
| LEARNING AND GROWTH | Office Mngr. Competency | Solidify Office Mngr. Competency | % Complete | 100% | Recruit Office Manager |
| | Improve Service Logistics | Improve Service Logistics | % Complete | 100% | Create Service Coord. Role |
| | Identify Core Competencies | Identify Core Competencies | % Complete | 100% | The Core Competency Matrix |
| | Unify Standards & Procedures | Unify Company Standards and Procedures | % Complete | 100% | Implement the Standards and Procedures Seed Document |
| | Organization Defined | Define the Organization | | | Build the Pyramid of Purpose and Value |
| | Everyone On Board | Get Everyone On Board (Tell the compelling story) | % Employees Aware | 100% | Q1 2016 Company Retreat |
| | Team Aligned | Team Informed and Aligned | % Empl. @ Standups | 100% | Weekly Standups |

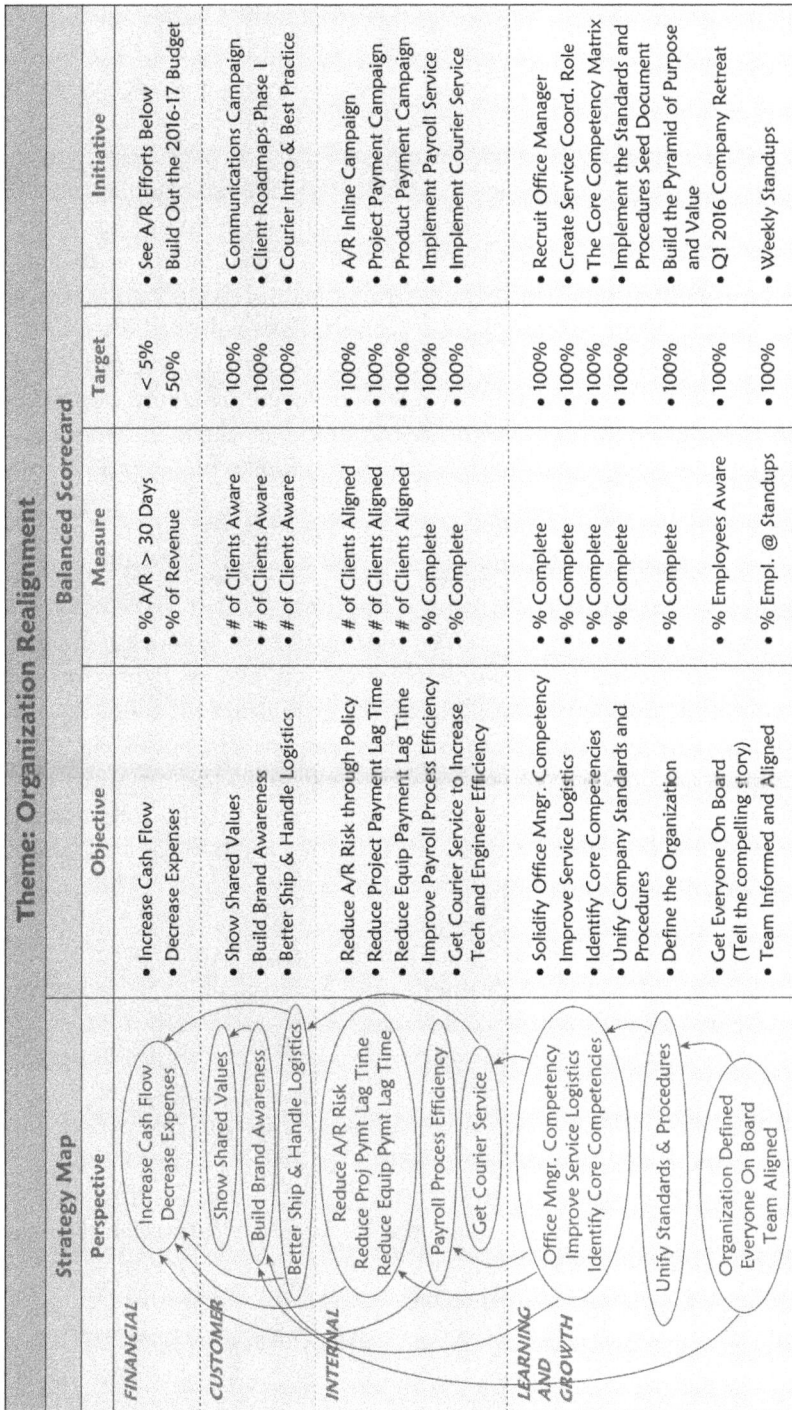

*Figure 12-2. Organization Realignment Strategy Map and Balanced Scorecard*

The organization must start by getting finances in order starting with a solid budget for the coming fiscal year and beyond. There will be policies put into place to govern how payments and receivables are managed. First, the A/R policy will be established followed by an aggressive initiative to bring all accounts currently in arrears up to date within 90 days. Next, a policy will be put in place requiring all products be paid for when the customer orders them. And finally, a policy will be implemented requiring a 50% down payment when a project is signed and requiring the remainder due according to landmarks and completion of the project. These two initiatives will stop the company from effectively being the bank for the client and will significantly improve cash reserves and cash flow. There will be a communications campaign around each new policy to help the client understand the organization's position, how the changes will take place, and how they (clients) are affected.

The organization must build the Pyramid of Purpose and Value from top to bottom so that it is clear what The Goober Group's desired culture is, where its compass is pointing, and what its roadmap for success looks like. Once completed, there will be a quarterly retreat to share and discuss everything about the pyramid with the employees, including the Strategy Maps, so they can all see and share in the blueprint for success. There will be weekly standup meetings for all teams or groups to ensure crystal clear focus on the initiatives and priorities of the week, month, and quarter relative to the Balanced Scorecards.

To replace Esteban as soon as possible, the search for a qualified office manager will begin immediately. Additionally, a payroll service will be vetted to assume those responsibilities from Esteban. To improve service logistics and service delivery overall, a role for Service Coordinator (SC) will be created and the receptionist, James Sanchez, will shift into that position. His reception duties will be absorbed into the SC role.

As a requirement for completing the Pyramid of Purpose and Value, a Core Competency Matrix must be completed. It will reveal where The Goober Group must focus recruitment and training efforts, and it will guide future learning and growth for everyone in the organization.

A master Standards and Procedures document must be created to tie together the disparate information and knowledge systems. Along with its implementation will come the requirement for continued synchronization of all organizational content for optimal utilization.

The initiative Client Roadmaps Phase I will be launched to begin building the reestablished Goober Group brand with the client base. The client must be made aware of the need for regular Technology Roadmap meetings and the value of a Technology Roadmap specific to their systems. It will help The Goober Group begin to show their expertise and their understanding of the client systems. It will also prepare both The Goober Group and the client for upcoming stratagems.

A continued communications campaign will be initiated to inform the client base of The Goober Group's refined vision, mission, and values. In addition, it will inform the clients of changes being made in The Goober Group and how these changes translate into improved customer value. This will include the move to solid Technology Roadmaps and changes to the service delivery process.

To improve the logistics of moving products and equipment and to significantly improve the efficiency of techs and engineers, The Goober Group will vet and employ a courier service to do the majority of pickup and delivery of equipment. There will be a specific communications campaign initiative for informing and training the team and the client.

### Achieve Operational Excellence Strategy

The second strategy, planned to begin execution in Q2 2016, is presented in Figure 12-3 and is expected to be completed by the end of that quarter. The theme for this strategy is Achieve Operational Excellence. The strategy is designed to trim down the operations as much as possible in as short of a timeframe as possible in preparation for subsequent strategies and initiatives of future quarters. This strategy is also a Productivity Strategy and, if successful, will increase asset utilization by increasing labor yield, decreasing labor expenses, and increasing the effective hourly rate of each client.

## Theme: Achieve Operational Excellence

| Strategy Map | Perspective | Objective | Balanced Scorecard Measure | Target | Initiative |
|---|---|---|---|---|---|
| **FINANCIAL** — Increase Labor Yield; Decrease Labor Expenses; Increase Effective Hourly Rate | FINANCIAL | • Increase Labor Yield | • % Team Efficiency | • 65% | |
| | | • Decrease Labor Expenses | • % of Revenue | • 55% | |
| | | • Increase Effective Hourly Rate | • % Eff. Hourly Rate | • 80% of Rack | • See Internal Process Efforts Below |
| **CUSTOMER** — Build Strategic Partnerships; Reduce Ticket Age; Reduce Time on Ticket | CUSTOMER | • Build Strategic Partnerships | • # Clients w/Full Map | • 100% | • Client Roadmaps Phase II |
| | | • Reduce Average Ticket Age | • # of Days Old | • < 45 | • Ticket Targeting |
| | | • Reduce Average Time on Ticket | • # Minutes Per Issue | • < 50 | • Escalation & BP Processes |
| **INTERNAL** — Core Comp + Employee BSC; Fine-tune PSA & RMM; Consolidate Int Cloud Solution; Implement Project Process | INTERNAL | • Core Competency Coupled with Employee Balanced Scorecards | • # Employees Aligned | • 100% | • Quarterly Employee Evaluations |
| | | • Consolidate Internal Cloud Solution | • % Completed | • 100% | • Op. Goober Cloud Phase I |
| | | • Implement the Project Process | • % Completed | • 100% | • Op. Agile Project Phase I |
| | | • Fine-tune PSA and RMM for Issues Flow & Communications | • Focused Customer Service Delivery Polls | • 5 of 5 | • Agile Service Delivery Phase I |
| **LEARNING AND GROWTH** — Establish Marketing Competency; Work & Track in Real-time; Define Project Process; CompTIA MS Trustmark; Everyone On Board; Team Aligned | LEARNING AND GROWTH | • Establish Marketing Competency | • % Complete | • 100% | • Recruit Marketing Manager |
| | | • Working and Tracking Time in Real-time Training | • % Time Track/Day | • 100% | • MSP Pro Academy Course |
| | | • Define the Project Process | • % Complete | • 100% | • Op. Agile Project Phase I |
| | | • Obtain CompTIA Managed Services Trustmark | • % Complete | • 100% | • Operation Trustmark |
| | | • Get Everyone On Board | • % Employees Aware | • 100% | • Q2 2016 Company Retreat |
| | | • Team Informed and Aligned | • % Employees @ % Standups | • 100% | • Weekly Standups |

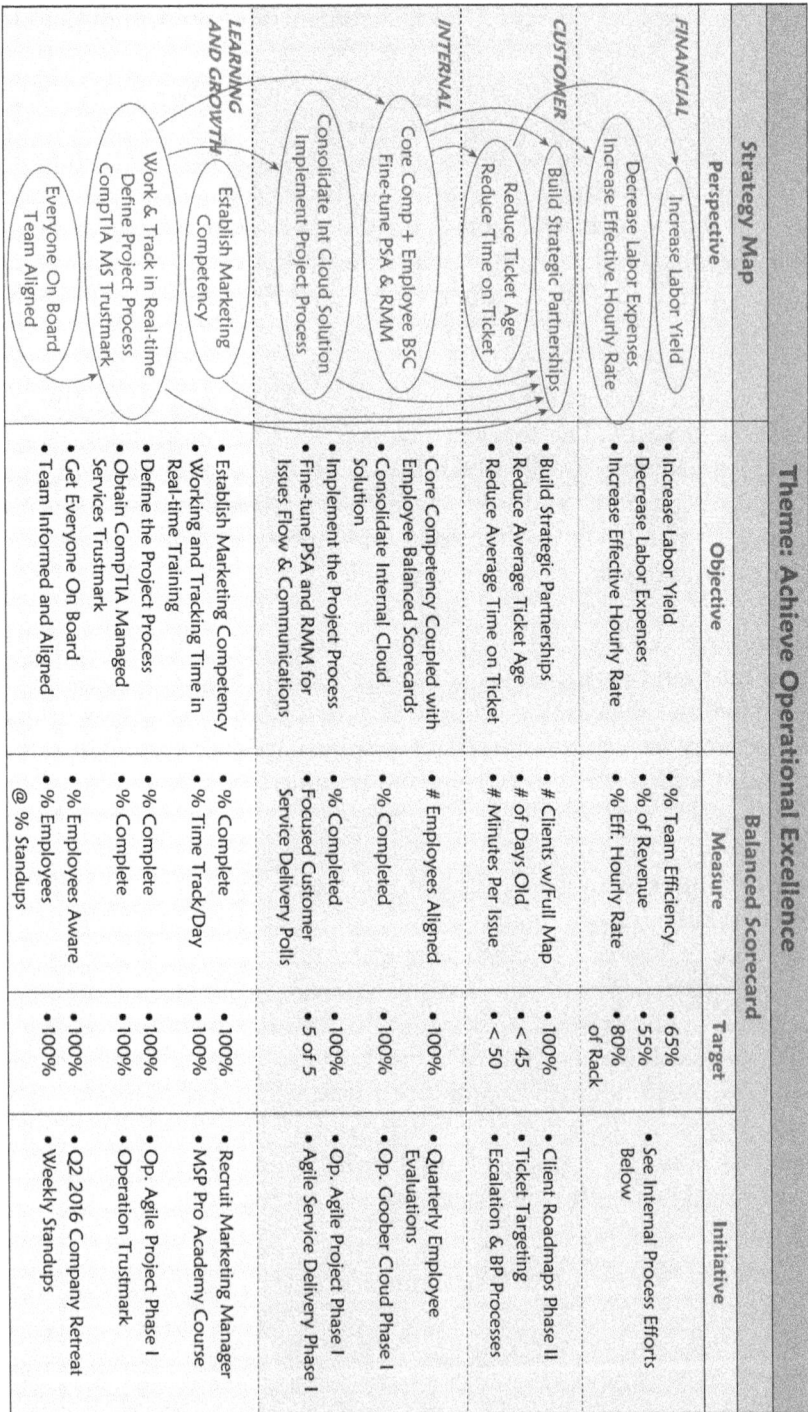

*Figure 12-3. Achieve Operational Excellence Strategy Map and Balanced Scorecard*

A relentless internal campaign must be employed to align the entire organization with the newly completed Pyramid of Purpose and Value and especially the Business Roadmap & Strategy. The initiation of this strategy should begin at the quarterly retreat and continue in the weekly standup meetings. Again, with the intent of ensuring all teams or groups have a crystal clear focus on the initiatives and priorities of the week, month, and quarter relative to the active Balanced Scorecards.

With a completed Core Competency Matrix, the alignment of The Goober Group's quality talent with the Learning and Growth needs of the organization can be effected through quarterly employee evaluations. In effect, there will be a Balanced Scorecard for each employee.

The most important initiative for this strategy is to get everyone on the Service Delivery team to work and track time in real-time or as close to it as possible. Each member will complete the required Working and Tracking Time in Real-Time course offered by the MSP Pro Academy. Additional courses will be taken by the Service Coordinator, as needed. The clarity of where time is going for each team member will represent the single largest recovery of revenue for the organization or value for the client possible. This initiative is the primary driver of the increased labor yield and increased effective hourly rate objectives. There is no initiative in any of the four strategies that will have as important or significant of an impact as this one.

In preparation for moving to a pure MSP model and to fully leverage the PSA and RMM solutions stack, these tools must be tuned properly. This will start with an initiative to streamline the flow of issues through the system and all communications related to that flow.

Between the Working in Real-time and the PSA and RMM tuning initiatives, The Goober Group should be able to immediately begin tracking the average time on tickets and age of tickets. Old tickets should be targeted for resolution to reduce the lingering of issues. Time on tickets should be scrutinized to identify the most effective threshold for escalation. Both of these metrics represent low-hanging fruit in the form of improved customer service that has value to the client in addition to the time and revenue benefits.

The Goober Group must acquire a tangible competency in marketing and as such will begin searching for a Marketing Manager. This will fulfil an important requirement for getting the organization to the next level and, if successful in this quarter, it will allow for proper execution of marketing strategies in the next quarter.

The first step in establishing an externally recognized competency is to acquire the CompTIA Operation Trustmark. This competency will help boost brand recognition for The Goober Group and create marketing fodder. It also establishes a strategic partner in CompTIA.

To get projects under control and in line, a formal project process will be established. Once established and documented, an initiative to get each open project aligned to the new process will be in order. If properly aligned, project efficiency will begin to increase significantly within a few business quarters.

There is an initiative to consolidate the organization's internal cloud solution to a single strategic partner, if and where possible. The benefits include the ability to provide a more clarified solution offering to clients, systematized and consistent training of The Goober Group talent, decreased costs, and a higher level of response from the vendor partner due to an elevated engagement level.

The Goober Group will begin to create Strategic Partnerships with the clients by building out their individual Technology Roadmaps for the clients' systems. This is phase II of the Client Roadmap initiative. By helping to plan and budget for the changes that will help the client get their IT to the next level, The Goober Group can also begin to estimate future backlog of work.

## Increase Customer Value Strategy

The third strategy, planned to begin execution in Q3 2016, is presented in Figure 12-4 and is expected to be completed by the end of the second quarter of 2017. The theme for this strategy is Increase Customer Value. The strategy is primarily designed to refocus the organization and the client base on the newly designed MSP Value Proposition and narrowed product line. This strategy is a Growth Strategy and will, if successful, result in a strengthened bottom line—primarily in recurring revenue—with a measurable rise in hardware and software sales.

**Theme: Increase Customer Value**

| Strategy Map | | Balanced Scorecard | | | |
|---|---|---|---|---|---|
| Perspective | Objective | Measure | Target | Initiative | |
| **FINANCIAL**<br>Increase Cash Flow<br>Decrease Expenses | • Increase Recurring Revenue<br>• Focus on Line Card Products | • % of Total Revenue<br>• % HW & SW Sales | • 60%<br>• ↑ 25% | • See Client Refocus Below<br>• See Product Line Below | |
| **CUSTOMER**<br>Refocus Clients to MSP<br>Build Strategic Partnerships<br>Get Marketing Moving<br>Reduce Ticket Age<br>Reduce Time on Ticket | • Refocus Existing Clients to the MSP Offering<br>• Build Strategic Partnerships<br>• Get Marketing Moving<br>• Reduce Average Ticket Age<br>• Reduce Average Time on Ticket | • % Converted<br>• # Clients w/Full Map<br>• % People Engaged<br>• # of Days Old<br>• # Minutes Per Issue | • 100%<br>• 100%<br>• > 30%<br>• < 45<br>• < 50 | • Operation Client Focus<br>• Client Roadmaps Phase II<br>• Marketing 1.0 The Basics<br>• Ticket Targeting<br>• Escalation Process | |
| **INTERNAL**<br>Define Ideal Client<br>Solidify the Product Line<br>Identify Strategic Vendors<br>Define MSP Offerings<br>Fine-tune the Project Process<br>Define Cloud Solution Offerings | • Define the Ideal Client<br>• Solidify the Product Line and Identify Strategic Vendors<br>• Define Managed Services Offerings<br>• Fine-tune the Project Process<br>• Define Cloud Solution Offerings | • % Defined<br>• % Completed<br>• % Completed<br>• % On New Process<br>• % Completed | • 100%<br>• 100%<br>• 100%<br>• 100%<br>• 100% | • Build "The Box"<br>• Operation Product Line<br>• Op. Goober Care Phase I<br>• Op. Agile Project Phase II<br>• Op. Goober Cloud Phase II | |
| **LEARNING AND GROWTH**<br>Sales Competency<br>Product Line Training<br>MSP Offerings Training<br>Cloud Solutions Training<br>Everyone On Board<br>Team Aligned | • Establish Sales Competency<br>• Product Line Training<br>• MSP Offerings Training<br>• Cloud Solutions Training<br>• Get Everyone On Board<br>• Team Informed and Aligned | • % Complete<br>• % Employees Trained<br>• % Employees Trained<br>• % Employees Trained<br>• % Employees Aware<br>• % Employees @ % Standups | • 100%<br>• 100%<br>• 100%<br>• 100%<br>• 100%<br>• 100% | • Recruit Sales Manager<br>• Final Friday Training<br>• Final Friday Training<br>• Final Friday Training<br>• Q3 2016 Company Retreat<br>• Weekly Standups | |

*Figure 12-4. Increase Customer Value Strategy Map and Balanced Scorecard*

The internal campaign to align the entire organization with the Pyramid of Purpose and Value will continue. At the quarterly retreat, the primary discussion must focus on the new Value Proposition, Goober Care™, being released this quarter and the efforts to move all existing clients to those services. Extensive training will be required on everyone's part, and weekly standups will keep everyone focused on the initiatives and priorities of the week, month, and quarter relative to the active Balanced Scorecards. Daily and weekly reminders to work and track time in real-time must be maintained.

The first initiatives will be to solidify the actual Goober Care™ MSP offerings and build out the agreements and pricing. The training for these offering will start immediately upon completion of the agreements. Internal training will ensure organizational competency in delivering these services. Client awareness training will take place in (or in conjunction with) the Technology Roadmap meetings.

The second initiative will be to solidify the intended product offerings by identifying and initiating strategic partnerships. Once established, the internal training for these solutions will begin. Internal and client training will be the same as with the MSP initiative.

The Goober Group will need to define the Ideal Client—"The Box". This will help determine to what extent the organization will attempt to covert an existing client to the new Value Proposition. It will also help determine if potential new clients are a match for The Goober Group.

Once the MSP agreements are completed, the initiative to refocus existing clients to the new offerings will begin. The largest revenue clients should be converted first unless there is a compelling reason to wait. This is the primary driver of the increased recurring revenue objective.

Basic marketing will be initiated with a focus on building the brand through recognition. This will include social media, blogging, newsletter, postcards, and so on.

The Goober Group must acquire a tangible competency in sales and as such will begin searching for a Sales Manager. This will fulfill an important requirement for getting the organization to the next level and, if successful in this year, will allow for proper execution of sales strategies in the coming quarter.

Efforts initiated in the previous quarters will continue or advance including the Client Roadmaps, Ticket Targeting, and Escalation Process. Operation Goober Cloud will advance to phase II where the solution offering will be defined. Immediately following the solidification, training for the new offering will begin. Operation Agile Project Process will also advance to phase II where the fine-tuning of the process will take place. Training for the new Project Process will not be necessary for managers as they are the ones who will be defining the process. For engineers and techs, the training will be on the job.

## Build the Franchise Strategy

The fourth strategy, planned to be introduced in Q4 of 2016 and begin execution in Q1 2017, is presented in Figure 12-5 and is expected to be completed by the end of Q4 2017. The theme for this strategy is Build the Franchise. The strategy is designed to expand the operation's client base and establish the organization as a major competitor in the chosen vertical market. This strategy is also a Growth Strategy and will, if successful, expand revenue opportunities and thereby increase both recurring revenue and per-client revenue.

**Theme: Build The Franchise**

| Strategy Map | Perspective | Objective | Measure | Target | Initiative |
|---|---|---|---|---|---|
| Increase Recurring Revenue; Increase Per Client Revenue | FINANCIAL | • Increase Recurring Revenue | • % of Total Revenue | • 80% | • See Client Refocus Below |
| | | • Increase Per Client Revenue | • Ave. Revenue Per Seat | • $4,500 | • See Client Roadmap Below |
| Complete IT Solution; Refocus Clients to MSP; Attract New Clients in Vertical; Reduce Ticket Age; Reduce Time on Ticket; % Unscheduled Downtime | CUSTOMER | • Be the Complete IT Solution | • % Project Ownership | • 100% | • Client Roadmaps Phase III |
| | | • Refocus Existing Clients to the MSP Offering | • % Converted | • 100% | • Operation Client Focus |
| | | • Attract New Clients in Vertical | • # Assessment Requests | • 3/Mo. | • Marketing 2.0 WIIFM |
| | | • Reduce Average Ticket Age | • # of Days Old | • < 45 | • Ticket Targeting |
| | | • Reduce Average Time on Ticket | • # Minutes Per Issue | • < 50 | • Escalation Process |
| | | • % Unscheduled Downtime | • Average % Downtime | • < 0.10% | • Op. Goober Care Phase II |
| Partner with Vendors; Increase Project Efficiency; Fine-tune PSA and RMM; Lower Outstanding Issues; Manage SD Backlog Hours | INTERNAL | • Partner with Vendors for MDF | • % Marketing Budget | • 5% | • Lunch & Learns |
| | | • Increase Project Efficiency | • % Budgeted Time | • < 100% | • Op. Agile Project Phase III |
| | | • Fine-tune PSA and RMM for MSP | • Valid MSP Reports | • 100% | • Op. Goober Care Phase II |
| | | • Lower Ave. # Outstanding Issues | • Ticket Count | • < 250 | • Agile Service Delivery Phase II |
| | | • Service Delivery Backlog Hours | • # Hours Backlogged Projects & Service | • < 5 | • Agile Service Delivery Phase II |
| ITIL Certification; HIPAA Compliance; EMR and Scan Systems as a Core Competency; Everyone On Board; Team Aligned | LEARNING AND GROWTH | • Establish ITIL Certification | • % Team Trained | • 100% | • ITIL Certification Phase 1 |
| | | • Establish HIPAA Compliance | • % Team Trained | • 100% | • HIPAA Compliance Phase 1 |
| | | • Establish EMR and Scan Systems as a Core Competency | • % Team Trained | • 100% | • Final Friday Training |
| | | • Get Everyone On Board | • % Employees Aware | • 100% | • Q4 2016 Company Retreat |
| | | • Team Informed and Aligned | • % Employees @ % Standups | • 100% | • Weekly Standups |

*Figure 12-5. Build the Franchise Strategy Map and Balanced Scorecard*

The internal campaign to align the entire organization with the Pyramid of Purpose and Value will continue. At the quarterly retreat, the primary discussion must focus on the new Strategy Map as it will be the theme for the entire next twelve months. The organization will now be moving into more steady daily processes and routines including training initiatives. New external training initiatives will be introduced, and the weekly standups must keep everyone focused on the initiatives and priorities of the week, month, and quarter relative to the active Balanced Scorecards.

The first initiative executed on must be Operation Goober Care phase II. It will fine-tune the primary tools used to deliver the Managed Services offering and will enable the accurate reports used to show the value of the MSP offering. This includes the measurement of unscheduled client system downtime. The unscheduled downtime metric is the most prominent for the value proposition being offered. It must be met or exceeded for The Goober Group to establish and maintain their significant competitive advantage.

Operation Client Focus, if still incomplete, must be completed by the end of the quarter/year. All existing clients must be on Managed Services or off the client list.

Operation Agile Project will advance to phase III where efficiency will be driven to a minimum of 100%. This efficiency level represents the expected minimum level of efficiency for projects, and attaining it will show that The Goober Group can in fact consistently execute on profitable projects.

The Client Roadmap initiative will move into phase III where the focus will be on demonstrating to the clients through Technology Roadmaps that The Goober Group has their entire IT system strategy and projects mapped out for the foreseeable future. This will allow The Goober Group to sell deep into the existing client base for projects and the required hardware and software. The success of this initiative is imperative to becoming the leading provider for IT services in this vertical market.

Marketing will launch its initiative to inform potential new clients about The Goober Group's offerings, competency, and track record. The lead offerings will be the Security, Antivirus, Backup, and Network assessments. This initiative represents the first real push of marketing and will help establish baselines in response to advertising.

The Agile Service delivery initiative will advance to phase II where two new metrics will begin being tracked: Outstanding Ticket Count and Total Hours Backlogged. These internal metrics will help gauge team potential and establish labor requirements based on workload.

The initiative to begin presenting Lunch and Learns will be launched with the initial intent of developing the process of tapping into vendor and strategic partner marketing funds. All media surrounding the events will also help establish brand recognition and present a positive image of The Goober Group.

Efforts initiated in the previous quarters will continue or advance including the Ticket Targeting and Escalation Process. New multiphase initiatives for training on important core competency skills will be initiated. Some internal training efforts will include establishing the EMR and Scan Systems as core competencies. External training efforts will include establishing ITIL Certification and HIPAA Compliance. These efforts will take several months to complete for the entire team.

## Discussion and Retrospective

The presentation of the Roadmap and Strategy to The Goober Group team went very well and was received with measurable excitement. There were some skeptics of the roadmap, indicating concerns that the timeline was too aggressive for the organization to meet. Others were concerned with how the changes would be received by the existing customer base. All prerequisites were met including laying off the Sales Manager and preparing a two-year financial budget.

Late in the first quarter, the lead engineer, Benjamin Hawkins, who seemed to have been coming along fine (although reluctantly) with working and tracking time in real-time, seemed to give up on the entire effort. He had already been lagging behind the rest of the team in completing his timecard daily as required, and he was very resistant to allowing the Service Manager and Service Coordinator to be involved in his schedule and work flow. When he was called on by Fiona to explain his actions, he actually stated, "This is oppressive to make me work like this. I just want to take care of the clients." He eventually quit without notice.

Zhi Nguyen moved into the Lead Engineer role which turned out to be an excellent fit. He proved to be a natural at project management and is a great mentor. There was a controlled scramble to fill an engineer role, and luckily a talented young woman named Zara Douglas came on board. In the end, there were minimal disruptions to service and the overall team efficiency actually took an uptick in short order.

Client communications about changes and effects were executed exceptionally well throughout the year. With the addition of a new Office Manager, Pippa Watson, early in Q1, internal communications and collaboration became a part of the company culture. Pippa ramped up quickly and ended up managing all the initiatives for A/R, product, and project policy changes. Certain clients were extremely put off but it turned out those who made the most noise didn't fit in the "The Box" and were gone by the third quarter of the year.

By the third quarter, cash flow and revenue had responded as expected and within targeted metrics. Labor yield exceeded expectations and targets, largely due to the fact that the targets were underestimating the true team potential. Only after Service Delivery Backlogs were tracking accurately did it become apparent that the team potential was nearly 7% higher than estimated.

The Effective Hourly Rate of clients also exceeded expectations and targets. This was due in large part to the fact that the Managed Services offering was received well by existing clients who were perfect matches for the model. With finely-tuned PSA and RMM tools and the entire team tracking time in real-time, Service Delivery was able to manage work more effectively than ever.

The new Sales Manager, Gil McQueen, and the Marketing Manager, Lester A. Tackett, have proven that they are the right fit for the organization and do in fact have the skills required to help take this business to the next level. The marketing efforts moved along faster than planned and Gil designed the Sales Process in his first week. The problem came about that The Goober Group was faced with more new clients than they could onboard effectively or could service.

To help alleviate the problem of having too many clients, efforts to refocus all existing clients onto the Managed Services offering was modified. It was decided that a rigorous cross-check would be performed to see if clients actually met the requirements of The Goober Group's ideal client. Those who did not were not offered the Managed Services offering but were instead directed to a smaller local service company which was more aligned with their business model.

The end result was that the average size of client and number of seats went up, which was one of the intended long-term results of the defined strategies.

In retrospect, the overall stratagem ended up being highly aggressive and did indeed create a significant amount of pressure on the organization as a whole and on certain individuals. It should also be mentioned that to this point, the stratagem has been executed on in an extraordinary fashion with stellar results. Although Fiona and her team were given several chances to redefine the timelines and ease the pressure, there was a genuinely resounding call to keep moving forward as planned. Everyone seemed to be well-aligned and focused on the end results. They all truly believed in the compass direction of the business and they all are truly endeared to the culture Fiona has seeded. The Goober Group is truly getting to the next level and now has the added responsibility of maintaining what they have attained. They do in fact have great successes to build upon.

*Twenty years from now you will be more disappointed by the things that you didn't do than by the ones you did do. So throw off the bowlines. Sail away from the safe harbor. Catch the trade winds in your sails. Explore. Dream. Discover.*

– H. Jackson Brown, Jr.

# 13.0

## The Next Level

To this point, I have covered everything related to defining your business identity and building out your Pyramid of Purpose and Value, including the tools for analyzing and refining your business. I have even detailed a few specific super tools that help you drive your Business Roadmap and Strategy (BASE) and measure the maturity of your organization (BMI). Before I close this chapter and the book, there are a few more important aspects of your business and your personal life that need to be touched on.

Some of these final subjects are the ever-present variables you must always have in your line of sight and must consider when you come to turning points along your roadmap to success. These include subjects like Refining Your Business Identity, Growing Your Operation, Finance and Private Equity, The End Game, Mergers and Acquisitions, and Business Valuation. Some of these subjects are about long-term strategic positions that you must have clearly defined for the best interest of the stakeholders and principals of the organization. These include Legal Representation, Business Insurance, and Protecting Your Business. And last are a few comments on Engaging a Business Coach or Mentor and getting involved in Mastermind, Peer, and Business Groups.

### Refining Your Business Identity

There is an old saying that you must change to remain the same. In the fast-paced world we live and do business in, this has never been truer. If you are an entrepreneur, you know that in today's economy, you either move to a business model that works or your business dies quickly. The pace of change in technology is accelerating, and businesses need an operating model that allows them to thrive. I believe you should be willing to do whatever it takes to keep your business running healthy and sustainably for the ultimate purpose of attaining the shared vision. But I also believe you should not be hasty in any way about how you approach the decision to change significantly.

The natural progression of refining your business identity should be that you follow the simple methods of critical thinking and logic that have been laid out in this book. You should leverage the tools presented here as intended when it is prudent to do so. You should rely on your circle of council and your business sense and if you are concerned, you should reach out further for help. If you have the right people on board and you perform regular checks on your metrics and goals, there is only so far you can get off course. If a market change calls for a new study, do it and do it fast. Then make roadmap and strategy adjustments as dictated. If a crucial talent leaves the organization, you go straight to your Core Competency Matrix and start analyzing the potential effects and strategizing for how you will negate them or cure them.

The most natural refinement of your business identity will come from the organized repetitive cycles you go through in the normal course of business. Weekly scrum meetings, monthly sales and market reviews, monthly finance meetings, quarterly talent assessments, and quarterly strategy sessions. The concept of continuous incremental improvement applies to your business identity and your Pyramid of Purpose and Value as it does to anything else in your business.

With the tools and methods presented in *Getting To The Next Level*, you have the power to steer your organization in any direction you like. If the time comes when you decide any element, aspect, or dimension of your business no longer holds true to the shared vision, you now have the tools to redefine the entire endeavor. You can make it happen in months or in days; it all depends on your time, energy, money, and inclination. You are empowered to create success.

## Growing Your Operation

With rare exception, every organization that learns to run a healthy and sustainable business finds new opportunity to grow the business and is sometimes put under heavy influence to do so. Planned growth of the organization should in fact be part of the long-term plan and strategy of the business. For example, adding talented employees as new clients are added in order to maintain customer satisfaction and meet production, or taking on clients that have been beating down your door as the talent pool expands.

Outside of the planned roadmap and strategy and natural growth, there will be opportunities that come in the form of unexpected increased desire for your products and services, market expansion, competition shrinkage, technological innovation, and a myriad of other possibilities. The heavy influence beyond those things planned for in the roadmap and strategy will usually come in the form of stakeholders seeing a steady if not increasing revenue stream and recognizing the potential for simply turning the wheel faster to increase that flow.

However these opportunities and influences come about, you must still have plans for growing homogeneously and strategically versus explosively. I'm not saying you can't go stratospheric if the time is right, but hear me when I say that it is not sustainable unless it is controlled flight. By all means do not miss a real opportunity, but also do not set the entire organization and everything you have worked so hard to accomplish up for undue risk. If you are prudent, you will know when it's time to take advantage of the opportunity or if you will give in to the influence and how to plan your strategy accordingly.

If the opportunity comes, you must decide how it best fits into the long-term best interest of the organization. You must assess the risk and you must manage that risk because your entire business could be at stake. You have the tools and you have the guidance. Do not let the lack of your use of these resources be your excuse for growing too fast when you should be holding back. I have personally seen organizations push to expand right as the 2008 economic downturn began full swing. Their complete disregard—not lack of knowledge mind you, but disregard—for the true economic situation was veiled by nothing less than their greed for higher returns and more revenue. A thousand other companies never made it through that downturn for the same or similar reasons. Bigger organizations that understood the implications simply cut new product lines and dropped advertising campaigns. Many even shrank the organization a little knowing it was the wise thing to do to protect the future of the organization as a whole.

All of my warnings and concerns aside and provided you have done your homework, when the right opportunity does come along or you have reached the specific point in your roadmap and strategy to execute, you should be fully prepared. If financing is required and your plan and strategy is slow and methodical, you are much more likely to get those who are most reputable with the lowest interest rates to back your advance. If you have prepared your Feasibility Study, Market Analysis, and Business Plan, you will be ready to move smoothly and safely into the opportunity. I would never recommend taking out a loan or getting a line of credit you do not need, but when the time comes, it is the right thing to do. It is a natural and expected function of getting to the next level.

## Financing and Private Equity

When it comes time to acquire financing or private equity, you must carefully consider what you're doing. If you are a sole proprietor or the principal of a small organization putting up collateral for a loan or line of credit, you are effectively gambling on your venture. My advice is that you had better be certain within reason that you will be able to manage the money as planned and get the results you are after. This is where the entire discussion of the Oakland Athletics baseball team and the Way of the Turtle come into play. If you have done the math and you're playing the odds, you have the highest reasonable expectation of success. If you leverage beyond those odds, you are taking on increased risk and you must fully understand the implications.

There is a frequent question I hear from entrepreneurs regarding banks and lending for their small business ventures. They will ask why the bank refuses them. The bank has told them they cannot lend them any money because the entrepreneur does not have any money saved away in the bank, they do not have any retained earnings in the company, and they have no equity anywhere to be found. The entrepreneur cannot understand this and they say, "This is stupid! If I had all this cash, equity, and savings, I wouldn't need a loan in the first place. I need money to run or even save my business right now." This is exactly the reason they will not lend them money.

A bank is not going to loan you money to run your business or bail out your sinking ship. That's what friends and relatives do, maybe. The bank, however, may be glad to help a viable, healthy, and stable business with retained earnings and value to get to the next level. The business of a bank is to repeatedly lend money to viable lenders in exchange for a nice return on their investment. They will do business with people who can pay them back and will be there tomorrow when the business day starts. Think about the continued message woven throughout this book—you're building a viable, healthy, and sustainable business. This and only this type of business will have any chance of receiving funding from a bank when they need it most.

Venture capital is different than banks in that there is a higher tolerance by the lender for risk. It still does not mean you can just go put your hand out and get cash, far from it. This is also, however, where much larger amounts of funding can come from provided you have painted a very nice picture and have told a very compelling story. The venture capitalist is actually looking for the higher risk opportunities, but you need to know that with higher risk come higher rates of interest and returns on the investment. A venture capital lender may actually want a piece of the pie as it were—some recurring revenue or even a share of the business. Make sure you fully understand what you are committing to and be sure you consult a lawyer beforehand.

What's interesting in the world economy is that bank loans and venture capital are free flowing when the economy is up and tight when it's down. The reason is simple: The odds are good that in an up economy, businesses in general are healthier than in a down economy. The risk of loss due to non-repayment can be spread over many loans in many industries and many sectors. When the economy is down, the odds of profit and growth are down. The risk cannot be spread out as far and therefore is much higher in general for the lenders.

Consider all of the risk factors before you look for money outside of your organization. The strongest organizations only fund from outside when they absolutely do not need the money but want the access to it. The best example is a simple business line of credit. The business can get rates so low, it is ridiculous not to use the money whenever they need it to fund hiring a new employee, purchasing tools and additional raw materials, etc. My personal recommendation is to have enough retained earnings and cash on hand that you do not need to borrow unless you are making a major move. You can put the business money into funds and other financial instruments that will pay your business returns while it's sitting there.

## The End Game

Many people find a real contradiction between building a business around a shared Vision and simultaneously planning the end game for the endeavor or venture. It's really not that contradictory if you keep the right perspective of the two concepts. The Vision is the guiding light or idea that gives people that warm feeling that they belong to and are working toward a worthy cause of some kind, and hopefully they are. The end game is a responsible plan for how you as the individual or the principals as a group will go their separate ways at some point in the future, if that is in the plans.

Remember that the business Vision is supposed to be clear, resilient, and long term, and is usually expected to outlive those who conceived of and birthed it. The end game is the carefully laid plans for how to proceed at certain turning points along the roadmap to success of the endeavor or venture. It is also the specific plans for how to proceed if faced with the failure of the endeavor or venture. When you began designing your pyramid, you were expected to formulate the big picture that you could share which showed how the world would look if you succeed at your venture. When you go to the bottom level, you were also instructed to plan the end game or at least the contingencies that indicate a stopping point.

The hardest thing to do is plan for failure but in a real business, it is actually irresponsible not to. If you ever meet anyone who tells you with regards to their business venture, "I never gave failure a thought," or, "Failure was not an option," that's very brave and gallant, but this person either isn't telling the entire story or they aren't really all that sharp. I say they're not telling the entire story because even those who claim to be so brave as to venture millions on a single fragile deal have, at the very least, reconciled in their minds that they are willing to accept the consequences of complete burn down failure and loss of everything involved. And that in itself is an end game, just not one I recommend as a regular and standard business strategy.

The end game can be as simple as seeing the business through to a nice stepping off point for you and what you bring to the table. Many sharp entrepreneurs get things going and then sell their great idea off to those who have the resources to take it to the next level. Many others have plans of building a solid business that will one day be a large corporation capable of handling the largest share of the world market they operate in—read Amazon, Google, and Oracle. And then there are those things in life and in the world that just "happen", causing the end of the endeavor or the venture or at least bringing it to a crossroads.

When things just "happen" it means there is little or no time to execute an end game strategy. Aside from a death of a principal of the organization, it also means someone didn't have a weather eye on the horizon watching for storm signs. Your choices at this late stage are usually about how best to gather provisions and abandon the sinking ship. When crossroads are met, it indicates you have been prudent and if you are reading the signs right, you at least have choices about whether to batten down the hatches or set sails and run from the storm.

When things "happen" that take down your business, nearly every one of them can be traced back to mistakes or weaknesses in either the business roadmap and strategy or the execution of it. I don't mean to be insensitive, but at this point it's often best to cut your losses, learn your lessons, and get on with the next big thing. At least in the crossroads scenario, you have time and space to execute the end game plan if that is the choice. It allows you to feel you have some choice in your fate, including the orderly disassembly of the business for the best interest of all involved. It's not pretty, but it's the right thing to do.

Either of the scenarios presented require that you face the immutable truth about the true state of your business. You must employ zero based thinking. Ask the simple question: knowing what I know now, would I get involved in this venture? Is my business still valid and feasible? If the answer is no, either figure out how to fix it or get out now. Do not drive the business into the ground and burn bridges with quality talent, valuable partnerships, and potential supporters of future ventures. Too many failing businesses flounder here, waiting for who knows what to come along and change the winds or the tides. It is irresponsible and a waste of good talent, resources, and money.

As for how the Vision of the organization can be held up as valid while the owners and principals are planning on selling this business the minute they reach sixty or the business value reaches X million, that is indeed a valid concern. I would offer up that if the Vision is well-laid-out, it actually should be able to stand on its own for many years to come regardless of who owns the organization or who is running it. The Vision is still what drove this endeavor to this point and if maintained and upheld, if the levels of the pyramid below it are maintained, it will also get it to the next level.

If you recall, an important component of your Business Plan is the exit strategy, or end game. For the purposes of the Business Plan, you must be able to explain what your exit strategy is whether it is relative to the success of the endeavor or the contingency of failure. Your investors will want to know what the signals of success are and what actions will be taken for exiting the venture. Likewise, they will also want to know what compelling signs will indicate failure and what actions will be taken to preserve capital and possibly even recapture capital. Recapturing capital means selling off components of the business or wholesaling resources used for production in an attempt to reduce the losses realized by the investors.

## Business Valuation

Every business needs to know and track its value, the estimate of economic value of an owner's interest in a business. A publicly traded company must by law and regulation update this information frequently, but the private company is not required to do so. However it certainly should do so on a regular basis. There may come a time when the owner(s) or principals of the organization feel the need to change things up as discussed in the previous section. One principal may want out or may even want to shut everyone else out. There may be a desire to sell outright or be acquired.

You should always be tracking the value of the business for your own purposes, but when the time comes for money to change hands, you must be able to come to a reasonable determination of the price you are willing to pay or receive to effect the exchange. You may certainly be capable of determining the value of the business on your own for general purposes, but what I present here is a bit of logic to help you understand why you should not do so if the purpose is to sell the business.

When money actually changes hands, you will be engaging in a legally binding transaction that has potentially far reaching implications. Assuming everyone involved has performed their due diligence and is proceeding under the proper financial and legal guidance, there is likely going to be many caveats and stipulations about the deliverables and the payment. If you have done the basic math and you believe you have everything in order, you could be either undervaluing your business or setting yourself up for clawbacks in payments or down right loss of future payments. Everybody wants to be on the high side of the deal, nobody wants to be on the downside. But those that find themselves on the downside quickly look for any possibility of getting at least back to even if not a little ahead as planned, and that often means legal action and legal action means money being burned at ridiculous rates.

I do have one more important reason for having the valuation performed by an outside entity on a regular basis. As I will be discussing shortly, you must have a consideration for everyone involved as principals of the organization in case of unforeseen circumstances. If, for example, you have a spouse and something happens to you, a regular valuation of the business will go a long way toward helping that person to be properly compensated for the business if they choose to sell it off or sell off your share. It would be an established record from an outside party indicating the value of the business at regular intervals. This alone may help prevent opportunistic people from taking advantage of those who have already lost something much more precious and valuable than the business. They should not have to also lose any chance of rightful compensation for that individual's life work.

## Mergers and Acquisitions

The acquisition of other businesses is one of the fastest ways to grow your organization and fuel the Core Competencies, Human Element, Market Share, and Revenue. Merging with another organization is often the best way to couple your big idea with a bigger rocket. You must know what you're in for before you embark on either journey. If you are selling your idea off, you must know that just like in the movies, no matter what your paperwork or spoken deal says, you no longer get to have a significant effect on the outcome of this thing. And often the idea is not what the acquiring company is after. It's a nice bonus, but if it's not the crown jewel of the deal for the acquiring organization, it may be mothballed or just die a slow death due to lack of resources and funding. And if you are trying to couple your Vision to a bigger rocket, acquisition is not for you. The Vision of your organization will be a nice sentiment, but if the organization that is buying you up or out is at all stable, they likely have a nice shiny Vision statement of their own written on a plaque on their office wall.

You might also think it's a pretty simple thing to acquire and merge, but I've seen smooth, small mergers of small companies—one of just over $1M revenue and just over a handful of people, and the other just under $1M and just under a hand full of people—take over a year to be completely settled. The acquiring owner successfully negotiated the deal in less than ninety days including due diligence, financial scrutiny, and legal documents. Nearly a year later, their Compass is fixed and the Strategy for Success is well-laid-out, but their Culture (the top of the pyramid) is still shaky because of the Human Element and the buy-in of the shared Vision. I must also mention that most of the strategic planning for the near and far future of the company came to a near complete halt. This means that, while stable and sound, the current Strategy for Success is not adapting and is not being fed the proper resources to drive it forward. Nice ship, nice sails, nice crew, but nobody at the tiller to steer to the wind.

The intention was to meld the two companies together to make one nice big family with a larger customer base, more resources, and of course the combined revenue of both. The biggest problem was (and almost always is) that the most crucial elements of the organization— the Human Element, the quality talent—did not grow up in the acquiring company and do not have the same endearment to the new leader as to the old. They never had a real choice in buying in to the Vision and getting on board or walking away. This means that when it comes time to adopt the new processes, methods, and leadership, there is not only the natural and normal kind of resistance to change, there is also a real emotional resistance.

Knowing this emotional resistance exists and mastering change management can help significantly. However, the reality is that in a small organization, it is highly likely that within one or two years you are going to lose every employee from the acquired organization. And it's not really about you, it's simply because you are not the captain those people signed up to crew for and your enticing picture and compelling story are not what got them excited. Before you attempt a merger you must be fully prepared for this, and it is also true that if presented well, they may just completely fall in love with your story and shared Vision one day along the way.

My final words on Mergers and Acquisitions (M&A) is that you must get outside help before you attempt this for at least the first one if not the first several. I have seen sharp people come up fairly short on both sides of these kinds of deals. Engage a business coach or mentor who knows about these things, and if it's a big enough deal, engage a firm that handles M&A. They will not be cheap but they have experience that can save you thousands if not millions depending on the size of the deal. They can make sure you have the right Arbitration, Separation, Performance, and other clauses and stipulations that are often overlooked or not even thought of.

## Protecting Your Business Legacy

The task of protecting a business is not as simple as it may have been in the past, and if the venture is paying off it can actually become pretty complicated. There are the simple things you should know about such as liability insurance, business interruption or continuity insurance, and errors and omissions coverage. It's beyond the scope of this text and outside of my personal expertise to attempt anything more than a basic description of theses coverages. Because it is in fact a complicated subject best addressed by a registered agent, I am going to leave it to them and only speak to the needs or requirements for these protections. If your business is worth running, it is worth protecting it properly from the forces that can work against it.

Liability insurance is usually where it all starts and if you are running a business, it is almost always required by your landlord before you can take possession of the office or plant space. It is intended that it will protect you and your landlord when someone slips on a banana peel or walks into a glass door. But it should also protect you from those who claim they slipped on a banana peel or walked into a glass door.

Now let's say your business is hit by a meteor or some other such flying object gone off course. Business continuity coverage is intended to help you to spin up your business one block down the street from the big hole in the ground that used to be your business. It intends to provide you with the tools, operating systems, and necessities to get your business back up and rolling in as little time as possible. Of course how this manifests itself is significantly different for different businesses. If you run a plywood manufacturing plant, it will take a bit of coordination, timing, and a lot of work to get this all back up and rolling. If you are running a tech company where nearly everyone is consistently out visiting clients or is able to work from anyplace where there is an internet connection and a computer, you are going to be back up and running in no time. What matters is having the coverage to allow this to happen versus finding out the cost of spinning all of this up on short notice using your precious cash reserves.

Errors and omissions coverage is intended to protect you from mistakes that may happen in the normal line of doing business. For example, let's say you handle computer network maintenance and in the course of the day, you receive notification that a server went offline. If your tech looks at the error and, in attempting to correct it, loses important and valuable data that cannot be recovered or recreated, you might be sued. This coverage also helps when it comes to writing contracts and agreements. The application process for this is pretty extensive and you should answer everything completely and honestly. I point this out because ironically, if you ever make a claim, the insuring agency will scrutinize your actions to validate that you were operating within the confines you stated that you would be. If you stated that in your mechanic shop you never work on cars more expensive than $100,000 and you blow up the engine on a Lamborghini worth $1.2M, let's just say that you will come to the crossroads of your end game scenario.

Now for one of those things that is easy to understand but actually difficult to protect and recover. Today we have this wonderful thing called the internet, and within the internet we have these nice social systems being built. Whether you know it or not and whether you believe it or not, you have an online reputation, as does your business, as do the people who work in your business. So do your competitors, partners, and clients. To the point, you must protect your online reputation and, to the extent possible, that of your business.

I don't know if there is currently any kind of insurance for this, but I have no doubt that one day it will exist. Unfortunately, the remedy will likely be limited to remuneration for your trouble and funding for legal actions intending to force retractions or corrections to posted information. What you need to know is that the rules of the internet are that once it's out there, you can't take it back and you can't undo it. It never really goes away and someone will show up with it one day. Think of it like a face tattoo. You can get it removed and have a pretty noticeable scar or cover it up, but there it is, forever.

The last subject in this section is one of grave consideration but it is necessary for the protection of the business's legacy. It is common sense to have a trustworthy lawyer on hand to look over agreements and other legally binding documents, but at some point you must also have a working relationship with a probate lawyer. Probate is the process of validating someone's will after they have passed. It puts everything on hold until the cause of death is determined and everyone has their say in challenging the will. A probate lawyer is a type of licensed attorney authorized to do business within a given state who is experienced at advising representatives and beneficiaries of an estate on how best to settle all of the final affairs of a deceased person.

Why am I bringing this grim subject up? Because unfortunately, I've had extensive firsthand experience. I have seen several companies go through the horribly draining process of dealing with the passing of a principal of the company and all that it entails. And not once did things go as planned when the principal passed. Having an ongoing relationship and regular conversations with a probate lawyer means that if something happens, that person or firm has some knowledge of your dreams and aspirations for this venture you are in. They can provide you with invaluable advice about what you need to have in place beyond insurance policies and a will. It also means there is a chance, just a chance that the business can live through the ordeal. It may be that the endgame plan is to sell off the business or dismantle it, but even then the probate lawyer will have some direction on how to proceed.

Don't leave these things to chance if you love your business, this thing you're building. I'm sorry to say insurance is expensive and for the most part, I feel it is a predatory industry. I'm sorry to say lawyers are expensive and for the most part, I think they have built their own self-perpetuating industry. All of that aside, think about everything I have presented. You are building something you want to last and something that is bigger than just you. You need to protect it from everything that is foreseeable and everything that is not. This means having the right people in your circle of council, including lawyers and insurance agents.

## Engaging a Business Coach or Mentor

Consider the true power and value of engaging a business coach or at least taking on a business mentor. If you and your business are ready, engaging with a business coach or mentor can truly propel you or your business not only to the next level, but far beyond. But you and your business must absolutely be ready and receptive for it to be of any use. Many people believe that the only time they need to engage a business coach is when their business is in trouble or already failing. While that certainly is a critical time to engage a business coach, the most successful business owners and managers believe strongly in an ongoing relationship with a coach that they know, like, and trust. Many of the most successful people in the world will tell you that they have engaged coaches of different disciplines, throughout their lives, depending on what specifically they were trying to accomplish. What these highly successful people have learned is the power of business coaching and the value of having educated and experienced advice at their fingertips when they need it most.

Your business is really no different than a team that has set their sights on the gold medal. If you want the gold, if you want a shot at the top spot in your market, then somewhere along the way you will need to engage someone who can see your vision and knows how to turn it into success. Good coaches know how turn vision into success, for themselves and for others. They love to use and share that ability and passion with others to build cohesive and effective teams. Great coaches can show you how to create success as a habit. They will teach you how to not only create success, but also how to recognize and be ready for the opportunities that lead to this top level success I'm speaking of.

If the time comes, the moment you recognize your need for help in getting to the next level is when you should act on it. Don't wait. You will have a smaller hump to get over in the long run, and it could save you countless hours of frustration. Remember that this endeavor you are engaged in is not just about this one leg of the race and tomorrow. It's about every leg you need to sail, tomorrow and the next day, as well as the ultimate destination. I will tell you that as an entrepreneur and business coach, I not only have a business mentor of my own, I also have a Taekwondo Master to guide my physical discipline, a mastermind group to collaborate with, and a close circle of council to consult. I would never be as successful as I am without each and every one of them.

## Mastermind, Peer, and Business Groups

These groups could have been listed in the Tools chapters but I believe they are more appropriately mentioned here. There are groups in nearly every industry that promote networking and collaboration for almost anyone in the value chain of a given market. They may be simple user groups, associations, or even affiliations focused on PESTEL concerns. The groups that I want to highlight are the Mastermind Group, Peer Group, and the Business Group. Each is unique in what they offer, how they are operated, and their purpose.

The power of each of these groups comes from how we can gain knowledge and insight from the different approaches offered by the other members. Getting involved in any one of these groups means you are connecting with people who are likely experiencing exactly the same problems you are. These groups can help in building partnerships with people and companies who may or may not be in the same industry. These partnerships can be crucial to the success of a small business trying to get to the next level. You can think of each of these three groups almost as stepping stones in the maturity of your organization. I'll explain as we move along.

## Mastermind Groups

The concept of the mastermind group was formally introduced by Napoleon Hill almost 100 years ago, and today it is still considered one of the most powerful entrepreneurial tools known in business. In his timeless classic *Think and Grow Rich*, Napoleon Hill describes the mastermind principle as "The coordination of knowledge and effort of two or more people, who work toward a definite purpose, in the spirit of harmony." He also states, "No two minds ever come together without thereby creating a third, invisible intangible force, which may be likened to a third mind."

You may already have experienced the power of a mastermind group without realizing it. The best example would be a time when you were deep in conversation with a small group of sharp individuals and suddenly found yourself internally invigorated with new and different ideas, maybe even solutions to things you had been pondering for months. This is the power of a mastermind group.

A mastermind group can consist of people from the same industry and sector or from diverse industries and sectors. Sometimes it is most beneficial to meld with those from the same industry or sector. Every entrepreneur should be involved in at least one organized mastermind group no matter how mature their organization is. Seek out mastermind groups now to tap into the invaluable insight and feedback on important strategy and planning for your endeavor.

Mastermind groups should be free and easy to find or put together but unfortunately, it is common to find a cost of admission or dues depending on who's running the groups. The cost should not be prohibitive even for small companies.

## Peer Groups

Traditionally, a peer group (or Peer Advisory Group) is a collection of small business owners or entrepreneurs from different industries or sectors that get together on a regular basis to compare metrics and scorecards, share best practices, and offer each other support in attaining their respective goals. These groups can also be from the same industry or sector but if they are, great care is taken to ensure there are no direct competitors in the group.

Every organization should seek out industry specific networking groups, even if only for the purpose of knowing who is in their industry and market and to establish connections and partnerships. But you must seek out peer groups when your organization has matured enough to have established (or is sincerely ready to begin establishing) tangible metrics for measuring your success.

Peer groups are about the metrics and holding each other accountable. They will usually have an inherent Mastermind component as a benefit of participation, but it is not the driving purpose of the group. Peer Groups will almost always have an associated cost and should be strictly guided by the organization that coordinates them. The cost is almost always prohibitive for smaller companies, but there will be a time when the value meets or exceeds the cost. You must see it as a necessary and crucial cost once you reach the point I indicated earlier.

## Business Groups

The formal business group is actually a combination of the mastermind group and the peer group, but it usually offers much more. Most business groups are tied to the offerings of the organization that coordinates them or their partners and affiliates. You can gain access to significant savings in many of the most important solutions for your business and gain access to resources not offered outside of the group.

Business groups will always have a significant cost associated with them and strict requirements for participation and membership. Seek out business groups when it makes sense for the organization to commit to the growth potential that can come from this membership. Organizations that have not solidified their pyramid down to the BASE will not be ready to capitalize on and gain the greatest benefits from this membership. Conversely, when your organization is ready and the group is the right group, it can significantly change the business for the better.

## Summary

However you approach them, don't ever let membership in any of these groups interfere, hinder, or change your plans too much. Seek advice and give it all the consideration it is due, but hold true to your vision. If a group does not fit your style, culture, compass, ethics, or any other coveted value, move on and find another. There are plenty to choose from.

# Getting Everyone on Board

Over the years I have developed what I call the checklist for Getting Everyone On Board. When it comes time for pinning the big plan up on the wall and getting everyone on the team to buy in, these are the criteria required for success. Consider it the ideal motivational snippets that will help you get everyone aligned and in tune with what is about to happen. Now of course you can just call the shots and tell everyone what is and is not going to happen, but a motivational presentation followed by specific affirmation points somehow produces much better results.

By going through this process, it means that as you move along and come across roadblocks or issues, you can have conversations that are not necessarily about the roadmap and strategy under way but more about how the organization is proceeding under the assumptions concluded to in the roll-out meeting. You can specifically talk about where the breakdown is occurring. Is this person no longer willing to be receptive to the new changes we are implementing? If not, why, and how do we remedy this? Is the team not willing to participate in the larger discussions because someone is shutting them down at every turn? If so, who's doing the rock throwing and how do we remedy it? These affirmations are presented here and should be delivered in first person.

### #1  Be flexible wherever ethically possible but do no harm!
If we are going to get to the next level, we will all find times when we need to be flexible about how we do some things. But nothing about our game plan and strategy should be given such great importance or value as to supplant the values of the company and the client. We're not out to gain the system and we're not out to screw anyone over or damage anything.

### #2  Be open and receptive to the new changes
Everyone knows that for a new idea to take hold, you have to be open to the new vision of this "thing". And for it to grow and thrive, you have to be willing to allow these changes that are required to happen.

### #3 Be a champion of this new thing the company has adopted

We create our own success. No big new thing worth achieving truly comes easy. They need people to get behind them as champions and push them across the finish line. And sometimes, even carry them.

### #4 Participate, encourage, and engage in open dialogue

When there are discussions around the new plan and strategy, be involved at any level you think will be of value. Encourage your teammates to do so as well. It's called crowdsourcing of ideas or an Idea Mill, and it only works if there's a crowd. And don't undervalue your (or anyone else's) opinion. If you are on the team, your participation is expected and without it, the team may be missing balance or valuable perspective.

### #5 Provide useful, positive input without reserve

If you have ideas and input and you firmly believe you are presenting things that will put energy into the mix (not suck it out), don't hold back. Even if it is struck down or set aside. Remember that Thomas Edison said he made at least a thousand attempts at creating his light bulb before he found the right filament material, environment, and settings. And I'm not saying you can't have negative input, but do have great reserve with it.

### #6 Throw Darts not Rocks

When you do have input that may hinder, slow, or even stop progress, be sure you are very specific about the issues and problems you are pointing out. Don't just lob big rocks into the road for the team to have to move, break up, or roll out of the way. It's not productive and it's not useful.

### #7 As we implement things, realize we must stop doing one thing to be able to start doing another

In nearly any machine, system, or process, you have no choice but to pull out the old thing before you can install the new thing. So it also goes with habits and time. You have to stop the old way to make room in your mind, day, and process for this new thing. You won't be successful any other way.

### #8 Do not settle for mediocrity!

As the author and speaker Jim Collins states in his book *Good to Great*, "Good is the enemy of great." If you settle for mediocrity, that is exactly what you will have.

### #9  You must be able to call anyone on anything

The most productive and powerful teams know that you have to be able to call anyone on anything. Challenging ideas and creating the dialogue that brings about the refinement of your strategy is essential to success in any endeavor. Without it, there is no check and balance for this big fantastic thing you are trying to build or attain.

### #10  Don't take it personally, it's not about you!

This one applies to everyone in the organization from the top to the bottom. From the owner on down to the managers and the production floor. As we move forward and implement these new things and roll out our strategy, you are bound to experience something that rubs you the wrong way or even feels like it's personal. As long as your boss has not specifically tagged you as a problem child, you have to realize it's not about you. When you are building or implementing something or just trying to get to the next level, you have to remember that we are a team and everyone on it has a stake in the success. So when someone bugs you about a timeline, deadline, or the quality of the thing, you have to realize it's usually not about you. It's about this thing we are trying to do. And the only way it will be successful is if we keep on track with our roadmap and strategy. And that includes timelines, deadlines, quality standards, and performance indicators.

## Continuous Incremental Improvement

My most clarifying statement when it comes to the current stage of any business endeavor is as follows: Getting to the next level requires that the leaders of the organization recognize when this thing they have built has become bigger than the sum of its parts. From then on, the vision, mission, and planning of its future can no longer be maintained solely in their minds. It must be set out on paper for everyone to see, understand, and champion. Only then can the company begin to move to the next level.

With your Pyramid of Purpose and Value complete, you may strike out to find financial backing and other resources to get this project rolling. You may even break ground and start building the business as you are searching for capital. We know that this latter scenario is closer to reality as many if not most businesses have hung out the shingle and opened the doors (pyramid half built) before they even realize they need a complete plan and strategy. And too many of them continue to operate with full knowledge that a plan and strategy should exist, believing they don't really need one. But if and when those blocks of an incomplete or poorly built pyramid begin tumbling down, it's a sure sign they should go back to the drawing board.

Together, the levels of the pyramid form a feasible, healthy, well-balanced organization stack and interlock to represent and convey everything about the organization's Culture, Compass, and Blueprint for Success. The actions required to repair or renovate your pyramid are very similar to those required to build one in the first place. You utilize specific tools from your toolbox with specific intent based on what you are trying to accomplish. If an organization finds its pyramid is starting to lean, so to speak, or that one level or another is not supporting those above it as designed, it may be that you need to perform some maintenance. You can evaluate and adjust or correct anything about any level of the organization necessary to bring it to full upright structural integrity.

Of course, you should always move slowly, carefully, and diligently when changing any level of the pyramid. But with the top levels—Vision, Mission, Values, and the Human Element, i.e. the Culture segment—you must always use extreme caution because of what these levels represent, the core of the organization. You could actually change everything below the Culture segment and never affect those top levels. But if you change as much as one critical element of the top level, it permeates down through every level all the way to the BASE. Changes at the top have the potential to topple the pyramid faster than structural failure at the bottom.

Changes to the Compass and Blueprint for Success segment should not be knee-jerk or drastic unless those rapid changes are actually triggers or contingencies planned into the roadmap and strategy. This assumes that these planned triggers or changes are reliant on some evaluation such as a risk assessment, market change requiring new analysis, or changes in PESTEL forces, to name a few. The prudent sailor holds course even through the storm when they know their course is true and correct, even if the compass tells them they are off. If you follow a solid repetitive process for strategy planning and execute methodically, you will never be very far off course.

If you're doing it right, you are running the execution of your business roadmap and strategy like an ongoing project with a life of its own. You are holding frequent retrospective meetings to discuss completed phases of the roadmap. You are holding regular strategy meetings to measure your progress and success, and you are adjusting accordingly. You should look at the project just as you would any other, driving out rework and duplicate work and striving for repeatability and reproducibility in the processes you use to execute. You should strive for continuous incremental improvement through ownership of process and through execution on strategy as planned.

## Discipline and Execution

Discipline and execution are required core competencies of a successful organization and of every individual in that organization. The ability to move with all necessary diligence on the plans that have been laid out requires discipline and execution. These are the powerful Drivers that make every bit of difference in which businesses will and will not get to the next level. But discipline and execution are only effective if those who must act are properly trained and practiced in these skills.

Unfortunately, I've seen many organizations that have laid out grand plans but fail to execute, for whatever reasons. Or they simply lack the discipline to stay focused on the long-term business roadmap and strategy. These companies end up stagnating at the lower levels of business maturity and spend quite a bit of time reworking strategies that repeatedly become outdated due to lack of execution. I do consider discipline and execution to be a significant source of competitive advantage and I guarantee the lack of it is a source of competitive disadvantage.

I must also clarify the necessity of discipline and execution when faced with adverse scenarios. As a core internal competency, a business owner must also always be able to recognize the true gravity of a situation that they find themselves in, recognize when they're in it, and act on it accordingly without hesitation. This is actually easier to do than it sounds, provided you do not let the sentiment of optimism cloud your judgment. Admittedly, this is a learned skill but nonetheless a learnable skill. If you look at the last critical situation you were in, at the end, didn't you eventually just do what needed to be done? And was it not exactly what should have been done at the beginning of the scenario?

A perfect example is General Motors during the economic downturn of 2008. They had been losing money and churning out quarterly reports which showed signs of doom if a course correction was not made soon. When it came to be that the leading automobile manufacturer in the world was taken over by the U.S. government, consider what happened in very short order. The U.S. government thinned General Motors out, leaned them up, and shed the companies that weren't making any money. The next thing you knew, General Motors was turned around, had repaid the bail-out funding with interest, and they were back in the game, ready to continue to compete at the top level.

I don't care to get into discussions about whether it was right or wrong to bail them out or how it came to be or even the fallout from and opinions on the outcome. The simple fact is had those that were running General Motors not been overly optimistic and had they taken stock of the true gravity of their situation, they themselves could have taken the exact same actions and avoided bankruptcy and loss of brand. My personal belief is that they did not possess the discipline to hold to the prescribed strategy called out in the plans. I guarantee a systematic plan to cut losses and dismantle no-performing business units existed. If they recognized it, they simply failed to execute.

For the majority of small businesses there are no bailouts, and missing the signs and failure to act when they are seen most assuredly means the complete loss of the business. Failure to recognize the true gravity of the situation when things are going sideways or down may be the leading reason that less than one in five small businesses ever make it to their fifth anniversary. Taking action is the sole determinant of the outcome that you have a choice in. Fail to act and you are at the will of the elements, but act and you may very well be able to influence your own fate. We know that success is determined by our actions but for some reason, we do not so readily acknowledge the same relationship of failure and inaction.

There is a saying that no one plans to fail, they simply fail to plan. If you follow through and built out your Pyramid of Purpose and Value, including the Roadmap and Strategy, you will have made solid plans for success. And you should also have defined contingencies for failure. At this point, the only thing that counts is the discipline to stay focused on the roadmap and the ability to execute on strategy, including contingencies if the situation arises.

Discipline and execution are in the DNA of next-level companies as a result of the Culture and, more specifically, the Human Element. When these skills are honed sharp, they effectively become a super power. But like any super power, discipline and execution aren't worth much if they don't get used. Exercise your super power regularly and rely on it to get to the next level. It means you will also be able to tap into it when you are faced with the next game-changing scenario. Again, this is in fact the super power that makes every bit of difference in which businesses will and will not get to the next level.

## Putting It All Together

Regardless of whether you are just getting started in business or trying to get to the next level, you need a solid blueprint for success. What I have presented here in these chapters is much more than just the blueprint—it is the mindset and the methods to go along with it. If you follow what I have laid out, hold true to your culture and your compass, and follow through on your blueprint for success, I firmly believe that you will be successful in all your endeavors. You will create a sustainable, significant competitive advantage. You will be a leader in your market and your industry, and you will be at the top of both.

Transform your dreams and vision into the clear and enticing pictures and the compelling story that attract quality talent into your organization and strong backers for your venture. Design your pyramid from the top down and build it from the bottom up. Share your vision. Put it on the wall and point to it and tell stories about it. Tell everyone you know what you are building and what you are out to accomplish. Seek out the best talent you can and create a culture they can thrive in. Determine your compass direction, draw up the roadmap and strategy, and then set sail. Get up every day and in at least some small way, move your organization and your business one step closer to your goals and one step higher toward the next level. Do not settle for mediocrity in anything you do or you will have exactly what you settled for—mediocrity.

Believe in your own vision enough that all negatives will be outweighed by the desire to see this thing come true. If you do, it will drive you to do and accomplish whatever is necessary. Run your business as if it's going to be taken over if you don't do it right, and prepare for the next economic downturn or catastrophic event to the best of your ability. Build your pyramid and your business strong enough to withstand the drawdowns to finances and resources when competition gets rough or during the next economic downturn. Build strong relationships, partnerships, and circle of council so you have safety nets and other support structures for when things get rough. And if the time comes, reach out for help from whomever can truly help you because nothing less than your entire business could be at stake.

Trust that the long play is the best for building a solid, sustainable business and trust that playing the smart odds in your strategy will consistently yield solid gains. I'm not saying you should not take any chances, but I am saying that staying on the solid side of the odds is the smarter side of risk. And always consider what is truly at risk. Swinging for the fences is for Cinderella story seekers. Base hits are for those who want consistently high scores and wins. They have the long-term goal solidly in mind and the success that comes with it solidly in hand. Homeruns will come along naturally.

Endear to the Way of The Turtle and the Twenty Mile March because they are what truly make millionaires and legends. Even if your plan is to exit out, merge, or be acquired, what you instill as a habit in the organization may live on after you are gone as retained business value. But of greater importance is how it adds to your track record as a consistent producer of results, attributed to your mastery of calculated and managed risk. This speaks for your integrity, reliability, and character.

Make success a habit by adopting the execution mentality and allowing it to soak into your DNA. Build your integrity to be as solid as you want your Pyramid of Purpose and Value and the organization it represents to be. Learn to execute like clockwork on your goals, objectives, and strategy. This alone—learning to create success as a habit—could be the most powerful fuel for stratospheric success as you work on getting to the next level.

Remember that the road to the top is a road of continuous incremental improvement and progress. Getting to the next level and building a sustainable business that is competing at the top of the market requires nothing less than everything you've got. Don't hold back and don't give in. I will say it again, this journey is not for the faint of heart, but we know that fortune favors the brave. I believe you will be successful at everything you set your focus on. So be brave, focus on your vision, and get started on getting to the next level.

Good luck in all your endeavors!

# Glossary

ACCOUNTING – system that provides quantitative information about the finances of a person or business entity. Includes recording, measuring, and describing financial information.

ACCOUNTS PAYABLE – list of debts currently owed by a person or business. These are debts incurred mainly for the purchase of services, inventory, and supplies.

ACCOUNTS RECEIVABLE – list of money owed on current accounts to a CREDITOR, which is kept in the normal course of the creditor's business and represents unsettled claims and transactions.

ACCRUAL BASED ACCOUNTING – accounting method whereby income and expense items are included in taxable income or expense as they are earned or incurred, even though they may not yet have been received or actually paid in cash.

ACQUISITION – one company taking over controlling interest in another company.

AGILE METHODOLOGY – a principal of continuous improvement and frequent iterations or releases used most commonly in software development but also easily adapted to production operations and even business strategy execution.

ANSOFF MATRIX – matrix portraying the relationship of the product and target markets relative to the four most common growth strategies: Market Penetration, Product Development, Market Development, Diversification.

ARCHIVE IN PLACE – to abandon the use of while leaving in place.

ASSETS – anything owned that has value; any interest in REAL PROPERTY or PERSONAL PROPERTY that can be used for payment of debts.

BACKLOG – value of unfilled orders placed with a manufacturing company. Whether the firm's backlog is rising or falling is a clue to its future sales and earnings.

BALANCE SHEET – financial statement that gives an accounting picture of property owned by a company and of claims against the property on a specific date. The left (debit) side of a balance sheet states assets; the right (credit) side shows liabilities and owners' equity. The two sides must be equal (balance). The balance sheet is like a snapshot of the position of an individual or business at one point in time.

BALANCE SHEET PROJECTIONS – the extrapolation of date in the BALANCE SHEET for the purposes of estimating the future landscape of the organizations finances.

BALANCED SCORECARD – a tool to help management focus on a coherent set of near-term performance measures derived from the company's vision and strategy that if accomplished would help differentiate the organization from its competition while creating great customer value and shareholder profit.

BARRIERS TO ENTRY – conditions making entry into certain businesses extremely difficult. These include high funding requirements, high technological or trade learning curves, unknown or little known business practices, tightly controlled markets, stringent licensing procedures, the need for highly skilled or trained employees, long lead times, and specially designed facilities.

BENCHMARK – a study to compare actual performance to a standard of typical competence. Standard unit for the basis of comparison; universal unit that is identified with sufficient detail so that other similar classifications can be compared as being above, below, or comparable to the benchmark standard.

BEST PRACTICE – successful standard operating procedures for a given business type. Consultants observe and evaluate various firms and gather information on what works. They then offer their conclusions on the best practices for the given industry to another client.

BLUEPRINT – photographic print where lines and solid shapes are developed in white on specially prepared blue paper for the purpose of showing how something (such as a building) will be made.

BLUEPRINT FOR SUCCESS – the design indicating how one intends to create success.

BOWMAN'S STRATEGY CLOCK – model of corporate strategy

that extends Michael Porter's three Generic Strategic positions to eight ordered around a circle thus representing the dial face of a clock. It intends to represent the most common cost and perceived value combinations an organization can choose to use including the likelihood of success for each strategy.

BRAND – identifying mark, symbol, word(s), or combination of same that separate one company's product or services from another.

BRAND NAME – that part of a BRAND, TRADEMARK, or service mark that can be spoken, as distinguished from an identifying symbol. A brand name may consist of a word, letter, or group of words or letters.

BRAND RECOGNITION (BRAND IMAGE) – qualities that consumers associate with a specific BRAND, expressed in terms of human behavior and desires, but that also relate to price, quality, and situational use of the brand. For example: A brand such as Mercedes-Benz will conjure up a strong public image because of its sensory and physical characteristics as well as its price. This image is not inherent in the brand name but is created through advertising.

BREAK-EVEN ANALYSIS – financial analysis that identifies the point at which expenses equal gross revenue for a zero net difference. For example, if a mailing costs $100 and each item generates $5 in revenue, the break-even point is at 20 items sold. A profit will be made on items sold in excess of 20. A loss will result on sales under 20. The break-even point may be analyzed in terms of units, as above, or dollars.

BUDGET – estimate of revenue and expenditure for a specified period. Of the many kinds of budgets, a CASH BUDGET shows cash flow, an expense budget shows projected expenditures, and a CAPITAL BUDGET shows anticipated capital outlays. The term refers to a preliminary financial plan. In a balanced budget, revenues equal expenditures.

BUSINESS AGILE STRATEGY EXECUTION (BASE) – the synergetic combination of Business Strategy with Agile Execution. The results of which is a systematic method for defining and refining the organization ROADMAP AND STRATEGY to realizing continuous improvement in any aspect of the organization through frequent iterations of the specific aspects being focused on.

BUSINESS GROUP – select business owners and principals who meet regularly to discuss their performance metrics, share knowledge, network and participate in mastermind sessions. A combination of MASTERMIND and PEER GROUPS.

BUSINESS IDENTITY – a depiction of an organization through sharing of its business CULTURE, COMPASS, ROADMAP AND STRATEGY. Often portrayed using the Pyramid of Purpose and Value.

BUSINESS MATURITY INDEX (BMI) – a grading system for an organization to gauge its overall business maturity. It can be used for internal purposes or for comparison to other organizations.

BUSINESS MODEL – structure of a particular business in terms of how it functions. Its purpose is central to its structure.

BUSINESS PLAN – document that organizes a business concept, including marketing and management strategies and financial projections.

BUSINESS RESOURCES – the resources that a business must put into place if they are to pursue a chosen business strategy. BUSINESS RESOURCES can usefully be grouped under several categories: Financial, Human and Physical.

BUSINESS ROADMAP – a time-based plan that defines where a business is, where it wants to go, and how to get it there which usually indicating landmarks along the path to success.

BUSINESS STRATEGY – a term to describe the policies, processes, and procedures employed to help a company operate according to its vision and mission statement in order to achieve its goals.

BUSINESS VALUATION – a process and a set of procedures used to estimate the economic value of an owner's interest in a business.

CALL TO ACTION – an instruction to the audience to provoke an immediate response.

CAPABILITY MATURITY MODEL – a methodology used to develop and refine processes. It is a five-level evolutionary path of increasingly organized and systematically mature processes. It was originally developed at Carnegie Mellon University.

CAPITAL – finance: money and other property of a corporation or other enterprise used in transacting its business. Economics: factories, machines, and other human-made inputs into the production process.

CAPITAL EXPENDITURE (CAPEX) – the expenses related

to acquiring or upgrade fixed or physical assets such as production equipment or OPERATING SYSTEMS.

CASH BASED ACCOUNTING – used by most individual taxpayers. The cash method recognizes income and deductions when money is received or paid.

CASH FLOW PROJECTIONS – finance: analysis of all the changes that affect the cash account during an accounting period. Cash flow from OPERATIONS is one factor in a breakdown, usually shown as sources of cash and uses of cash.

CASH FLOW STATEMENT – statement showing how much cash is generated from a company's core products or services.

CERTIFIED PUBLIC ACCOUNTANT (CPA) – a designation given by the American Institute of Certified Public Accountants to anyone who have passed the exam and meet the work experience requirements.

CHANNEL VALUE – the value realized through STRATEGIC PARTNERSHIPS with other organizations that have aligned interests in business purpose.

CHART OF ACCOUNTS – organized list of the names and numbers of all accounts in the GENERAL LEDGER.

CIRCLE OF COUNCIL – people in your life you know and trust enough to provide you with honest and useful feedback and advice.

COACHING – the activities of teaching and training individuals or teams with the intention of helping their performance while provide direction.

COLLABORATION – to work with another person or group in order to achieve or do something.

COLLATERAL – the property offered as security, usually as an inducement to another party, to lend money or extend credit.

COMMUNICATIONS & COLLABORATION – the VALUE ASPECT of your business focused primarily on functions and activities related to Communications & Collaboration throughout the organization. One of the ten VALUE ASPECTS.

COMPANY – group of people organized to perform an activity, business, or industrial enterprise. see ORGANIZATION.

COMPASS – device that is used to find direction by means of a needle that always points north: something that helps a person make choices about what is right, effective, etc.

COMPETITION – rivalry in the marketplace. Goods and services will be bought from those who, in the view of buyers, provide "the most for the money." Hence competition will tend to reward the more efficient producers and/or suppliers and so lead the economy toward efficient use of resources.

COMPETITIVE ADVANTAGE – measure of an organization's product or service distinctiveness in a given market. see CORE COMPETENCE and SIGNIFICANT COMPETITIVE ADVANTAGE.

CONTINUOUS IMPROVEMENT – the core element of the Japanese philosophy known as Kaizen for improvement of working practices, personal efficiency, etc. The fourth of the five BMI SUCCESS ELEMENTS.

CONTINUOUS INCREMENTAL IMPROVEMENT – as in CONTINUOUS IMPROVEMENT but includes an element of AGILE METHEDOLOGY in which frequent iterations are a cornerstone. The intention is to realizing progress in small increments for best utilization.

CONTINUOUS REFINEMENT – the relentless pursuit of creating the highest value products and services by focusing on the reduction or elimination of waste in all aspects of the business. The fifth of the five BMI SUCCESS ELEMENTS.

CONTROLLING – measure assuring conformity with an organization's policies, procedures, or standards, as in quality control.

COORDINATING – the process of organizing people or groups so that they work together properly and well.

COPYRIGHT – protection by statute or by the common law, giving artists and authors exclusive right to publish their works or to determine who may so publish.

CORE COMPETENCY – distinctive employee, product, or service capability leading to a long-term organizational advantage. see COMPETITIVE ADVANTAGE.

COST BENEFIT ANALYSIS – analysis method of measuring the benefits expected from a decision, calculating the cost of the decision, and then determining whether the benefits outweigh the costs.

Corporations use this method in deciding whether to buy a piece of equipment, and the government uses it in determining whether government programs are achieving their goals or proposed programs are worthwhile.

COST OF GOODS (COGS) – figure representing the cost of buying raw materials and producing finished goods. Included are direct factory labor and certain overhead.

CRITICAL THINKING – the objective analysis and evaluation of an issue in order to form a judgment.

CULTURE – way of thinking, behaving, or working that exists in a place or organization (such as a business).

CURRENT ASSETS – cash, accounts receivable, inventory, and other assets that are likely to be converted into cash, sold, exchanged, or expensed in the normal course of business, usually within a year.

CURRENT LIABILITIES – debt incurred by the reporting entity as part of normal operations and that is expected to be repaid during the following 12 months. Examples are ACCOUNTS PAYABLE, short-term loans, and that portion of long-term loans due in one year.

CUSTOMER – buyer of a product or service.

CUSTOMER RELATIONSHIP MANAGEMENT (CRM) – the management of communications and interaction with potential and current customers. It involves technology that helps organize and automate the marketing and sales processes and often integrates with customer service, and technical support systems.

DEBT FINANCING – raising capital through borrowing as with the sale of bonds; contrast with EQUITY FINANCING, which is raising capital through the sale of an ownership portion (stock).

DEMOGRAPHICS – population statistics with regard to socioeconomic factors such as age, income, sex, occupation, education, family size, and the like. Advertisers often define their TARGET MARKET in terms of demographics; thus, demographics are a very important aspect of media planning in matching the media with the market. Each demographic category is broken down (by the various research companies) according to its characteristics.

DEPRECIATION – accounting: deduction allowed a taxpayer, representing a reasonable allowance for the exhaustion of property used in a trade or business, or property held for the production of income. Economics: loss in the value of an asset, whether due to physical changes, obsolescence, or factors outside the asset.

DISCIPLINE – pertaining to training that corrects, molds, or perfects the mental faculties or moral character.

DISTRIBUTION CHANNEL – set of institutions that perform all the activities required to move a product and its title from production to consumption.

DISTRIBUTION MODEL – management's plan for moving products to intermediaries and final customers.

DOWN STREAM VALUE – flow of corporate activity from parent to subsidiary which has perceived value by the end consumer.

DRIVES – the forces that give shape or impulse to factors that drive the business cycle - the ideas that have driven history. The cause component of Cause and Effect. see OUTCOME.

DUPLICATE WORK – to work on something that someone else is also working on with no expectation that it will yield any greater or repeated benefits. The wasted effort of perform or attempting to perform a task that has either already been completed or that would represent an unnecessary duplication in the efforts.

EBITDA – Earnings Before Interest, Taxes, Depreciation, and Amortization, calculated by taking OPERATING INCOME and adding back depreciation and/or amortization. Often used for corporate valuation purposes by applying a multiple derived from comparable companies that sold. EBITDA is often appropriate when depreciation or amortization of intangible assets deduced under GAAP overstates the economic decline in value of those assets.

END GAME – the strategically planned last moves for an organization including contingencies for exhaustion of funds, loss of market, loss of resources, desire to move on to next thing, and so on.

ENDEAVOR – to seriously or continually try to do (something).

ENROLLED AGENT (EA) – a federally-authorized tax practitioner who has technical expertise in the field of taxation and who is empowered by the U.S. Department of the Treasury to represent taxpayers before all administrative levels (examination, collection, and appeals) of the Internal Revenue Service.

EQUITY – In general: (1) residual ownership or (2) fairness.

Accounting: paid-in capital plus retained earnings. Banking: difference between the amount for which a property could be sold and the claims held against it.

EQUITY FINANCING – raising money by selling part of the ownership, such as stock in a corporation, in contrast with debt financing.

EXECUTION – a systematic process of rigorously discussing how's and what's, questioning, tenaciously following through and ensuring accountability.

EXPENSES – the costs chargeable against revenue for a specific period.

FEASIBILITY STUDY – determination of the likelihood that a proposed product or development will fulfill the objectives of a particular investor.

FINANCE – the way in which money is used and handled; especially the way in which large amounts of money are used and handled by governments and companies.

FINANCE & ACCOUNTING – the VALUE ASPECT of your business focused primarily on functions and activities related to Finance & Accounting throughout the organization. One of the ten VALUE ASPECTS.

FINANCIAL ACCOUNTING – accounting system that provides BALANCE SHEET and INCOME STATEMENT results.

FINANCIAL INSTRUMENT – tradable assets of any kind. Including cash, evidence of an ownership interest in an entity, a contractual right to receive or deliver cash, or other financial instruments.

FINANCIAL STATEMENTS – written record of the financial status of an individual, association, or business organization. The financial statement includes a BALANCE SHEET and an INCOME STATEMENT (or operating statement or profit and loss statement) and may also include a statement of changes in WORKING CAPITAL, NET WORTH, and CASH FLOW.

FINANCING – the act or process or an instance of raising or providing funds.

FIRM – general term for a business, corporation, partnership, or proprietorship. Legally, however, firm refers only to a non-incorporated business. see ORGANIZATION; COMPANY.

FIXED ASSETS (sometimes called LONG-TERM ASSETS) – in accounting, property used for production of goods and services, such as plant and machinery, buildings, land, and mineral resources. see CURRENT ASSET; INTANGIBLE ASSET.

FIXED COSTS – cost that remains constant regardless of sales volume. Fixed costs include salaries of executives, interest expense, rent, depreciation, and insurance expenses. They contrast with variable costs (direct labor, materials costs) and semi variable costs, which vary, but not necessarily in direct relation to sales.

FORECASTING – estimating future trends. Stock market forecasters try to predict the direction of the stock market by relying on technical data of trading activity and fundamental statistics on the direction of the economy. Economic forecasters try to foretell the strength of the economy, often by utilizing complex ECONOMETRIC models as tools to make specific predictions of future levels of inflation, interest rates, and employment.

GAP ANALYSIS – the comparison of actual performance to desired performance with the intention of identifying strategy to obtain the full potential of performance. In a situational GAP ANALYSIS it refers to identifying how to get to the end result from the starting or current position.

GENERAL LEDGER – formal ledger containing all the financial statement accounts of a business. It contains offsetting debit and credit accounts. Certain accounts in the general ledger, termed control accounts, summarize the details booked on separate subsidiary ledgers.

GENERALLY ACCEPTED ACCOUNTING PRINCIPLES (GAAP) – conventions, rules, and procedures that define accepted accounting practice, including broad guidelines as well as detailed procedures. see FINANCIAL ACCOUNTING STANDARDS BOARD (FASB).

GETTING TO THE NEXT LEVEL – strategically planned success in which the individual, team, or organization rely on the internal culture to move in the direction their compass points and continuously and incrementally improve their position by systematically executing on their blueprint for success.

GOAL – individual or organizational objective target to be achieved within a particular time period. An organizational goal, for example, may be to become number one in market share of a particular product within the following year.

GOST STRATEGY PLANNING – method of planning strategy in which the specific Goals, Objectives, Strategies, and Tactics are identified and placed in the correct order.

GROSS MARGIN – see GROSS PROFIT.

GROSS PROFIT – difference between revenue (sales) and the cost of goods sold. The gross profit as a percentage of revenue is termed the gross profit margin. Gross profit is different from NET PROFIT, which is gross profit net of other income or expenses, interest expense, and taxes.

GROSS REVENUE or GROSS SALES – total sales at invoice values, not reduced by customer discounts, returns, or allowances or other adjustments.

HUMAN ELEMENT – the actuator, custodian, and perpetuator of the organization's CULTURE. It is the single most powerful determinant of success for a healthy and viable business. Only with a healthy company CULTURE can an organization truly focus on next level innovation.

HUMAN RESOURCE MANAGEMENT – term that is replacing personnel management and implying that personnel managers should not merely handle recruitment, pay, and discharging, but should maximize the use of an organization's human resources.

HUMAN RESOURCES – personnel pool available to an organization. The most important resources in any organization are its HUMAN ELEMENT which is managed through the HUMAN RESORUCES function. One of the ten VALUE ASPECTS.

IDEAL CUSTOMER – the specific traits of the ideal customer aside from the demographics that make them part of your target market. Traits such as; pays on time, likes our organization, treats our people well, etc.

INBOUND LOGISTICS – comprehensive plan for scheduling the receipt of required supplies and materials at destinations as needed.

INCOME PROJECTIONS – the extrapolation of date in the INCOME STATEMENT and BALANCE SHEET for the purposes of estimating the future landscape of the organizations finances.

INCOME STATEMENT – financial statement that gives operating results, such as NET INCOME and loss and depreciation, for a specific period; also referred to as earnings report, operating statement, and profit-and-loss statement.

INFORMATION TECHNOLOGY – study or use of systems including computers and telecommunications for storing, retrieving, and sharing information.

INFORMATION TECHNOLOGY SERVICE MANAGEMENT – the activities that are directed by policies, organized and structured in standard processes and procedures that are performed by an organization to plan, design, deliver, operate and control information technology (IT).

INITIAL PUBLIC OFFERING (IPO) – corporation's first offering of stock to the public. see HOT ISSUE.

INNER FOCUS – the CULTURE and climate in the company (ORGANIZATION).

INNOVATION – use of a new product, service, or method in business practice immediately subsequent to its discovery.

INTANGIBLE ASSETS – right or nonphysical resource, including copyrights, patents, trademarks, goodwill, computer programs, capitalized advertising costs, organization costs, licenses, leases, franchises, exploration permits, and import and export permits.

INTELLECTUAL PROPERTY – any concept, idea, literary creation, computer program, or other artistic or creative work that is definable, measurable, and proprietary in nature.

INTERNATIONAL FINANCIAL REPORTING STANDARDS (IFRS) – standards and interpretations adopted by the INTERNATIONAL ACCOUNTING STANDARDS BOARD (IASB). The FINANCIAL ACCOUNTING STANDARDS BOARD (FASB) and IASB are committed to crafting one set of accounting standards to unify accounting standards worldwide, which in turn should improve comparability of financial statements across national jurisdictions.

INTERNATIONAL ORGANIZATION FOR STANDARDIZATION (ISO) – an independent, non-governmental international organization with a membership of 163 national standards bodies. Through its members, it brings together experts to share knowledge and develop voluntary, consensus-based, market relevant International Standards that support innovation and provide solutions to global challenges.

INVENTORY TURNOVER – ratio of annual sales to inventory, which shows how many times the inventory of a firm is sold and replaced during an accounting period.

ITERATION – process of repeating a particular action. A definite iteration occurs when the specified action will be repeated a fixed number of times. An independent iteration occurs if the repetitions stop when a particular condition is met, but the number of repetitions is not known in advance. Iteration can be the next version of the thing being focused on for advancement.

KNOWLEDGE MANAGEMENT – in general: the creation, maintenance, and dissemination of Explicit and Tacit knowledge within the organization and when necessary, outside the organization. As a SUCCESS ELEMENT it gauges the ability of the organization to implement and adopt KNOWLEDGE MANAGEMENT as a superior CORE COMPETENCY. The second of the five BMI SUCCESS ELEMENTS.

LEADERSHIP AND STAFFING – the SUCCESS ELEMENT that gauges the maturity of the organizations ability to adopt the organization MISSION, VISION, CULTURE, and COMPASS from the top down. The first of the five BMI SUCCESS ELEMENTS.

LEADING INDICATORS – economic statistics that often change direction before the general economy changes. Stock market indexes are considered leading indicators, as stock indexes often decline before the economy declines and improve before the general economy recovers from a recession. Leading economic indicators therefore help predict the future economy. Contrast with COINCIDENT INDICATORS, LAGGING INDICATORS.

LIQUIDITY – ability of an individual or company to convert assets into cash or cash equivalents without significant loss. Investments in money market funds and listed stocks are much more liquid than investments in real estate, for instance.

LOGISTICS – comprehensive plan for scheduling the receipt and delivery of required supplies and materials at destinations as needed.

MACRO ENVIRONMENT – contextual level of the business environment. Totality of national and international institutional forces acting upon societies and organizations; dynamics of environmental interaction on a global scale.

MANAGEMENT – combined fields of policy and administration and the people who provide the decisions and supervision necessary to implement the owners' business objectives and achieve stability and growth.

MARGIN – the difference between the total value and the collective cost of performing the value activity.

MARGIN OF PROFIT – relationship of gross profits to net sales. Returns and allowances are subtracted from gross sales to arrive at net sales. Cost of goods sold is subtracted from net sales to arrive at gross profit. Gross profit is divided by net sales to get the profit margin, which is sometimes called the gross margin. The result is a ratio, and the term is also written as margin of profit ratio.

MARKET LIFE CYCLE – the natural progression of a product through a sequence of stages from introduction to growth, maturity, and decline.

MARKET RESEARCH – the action or activity of gathering information about consumers' needs and preferences.

MARKET SEGMENTATION – the process of dividing a broad target market into subsets of consumers, businesses, or countries that has, or is perceived to have, common needs, interests, and priorities.

MARKET SHARE – the portion of all the TOTAL AVAILABLE MARKET (TAM) that can be considered won or controlled by a particular company or product.

MARKETING – process associated with promoting for sale goods or services. One of the ten VALUE ASPECTS.

MARKETING STRATEGY – plan for promoting products and services.

MASTERMIND GROUP – group of like-minded entrepreneurs who meet regularly to share, lean on each other, give and get advice, and tackle complex problems.

MATERIAL – goods used in the manufacturing process. see DIRECT MATERIAL.

MCKINSEY 7S FRAMEWORK – a framework that allows an organization to develop core competencies and capabilities of the individual and the organization in a way that is in balance with both the hard and soft elements of the business.

MERGER – classified as a type A reorganization, in which one corporation absorbs the corporate structure of another, resulting in liquidation of the acquired enterprise.

MESO ENVIRONMENT – transactional level of the business environment. Includes customers, suppliers, partners and competitors.

MICRO ENVIRONMENT – organizational level of the business environment. Includes the ten business VALUE ASPECTS and pertains to all levels of the Pyramid of Purpose and Value.

MISSION – definition of a corporation's vision and values, often printed on plaques and wallet cards, posted on its WEB SITE, and otherwise publicized.

NET INCOME – sum remaining after all expenses have been met or deducted; synonymous with net earnings and with NET PROFIT or NET LOSS (depending on whether the figure is positive or negative.

NET LOSS – negative figure remaining after all relevant deductions have been made from the gross amount.

NET PROFIT – positive figure remaining after all relevant deductions have been made from the gross amount.

NET WORTH – the amount by which the fair market value of all assets exceeds liabilities. see EQUITY.

NON-OPERATING EXPENSE – the expenses associated with the production of product or delivery of services such as machine electricity and the labor to run the machines.

NON-OPERATING INCOME – income from sources other than the day-to-day operations of the business such as interest income or rent received from other business properties.

OBJECTIVE – ultimate goal or target of an individual's or a group's efforts and strategy, as in final objective.

OCCUPATIONAL SAFETY AND HEALTH ADMINISTRATION (OSHA) – office that administers and enforces the federal Occupational Safety and Health Act, regulating safety and health in the workplace.

OPERATING EXPENSE – see OPERATING EXPENDITURE.

OPERATING INCOME – see REVENUE.

OPERATING SYSTEMS – refers to the Business Operating Systems (BOS) as the organization wide collection of systems (hardware, firmware, software, cognitive) and their accompanying principals, processes, procedures, and practices. This is not to be confused with the simple software that is run by a computer to enables human interaction and perform work.

OPERATION EXPENDITURE (OPEX) – the expenses associated with the day-to-day activities of the business (not production) such as payroll, sales commissions, benefits, rent, taxes, fees or advertising costs, etc.

ORGANIZATION – structure of roles and responsibilities functioning to accomplish predetermined objectives. Organizations have grown tremendously in size in the twentieth century and are found in all parts of the private and public sectors.

ORGANIZATION INFRASTRUCTURE – the layout or framework of supporting functions required to run and manage the business model. This will include technology concerns such as computer networks and OPERATING SYSTEMS for planning, finance, accounting, legal, regulation, and quality. One of the ten VALUE ASPECTS.

ORGANIZING – to arrange by systematic planning and united effort.

OTHER FOCUS – competitive landscape we (the ORGANIZATION) are in.

OUTBOUND LOGISTICS – comprehensive plan for scheduling the delivery of required supplies and materials at destinations as needed.

OUTCOME – the way a thing turns out; a consequence. The desired result of efforts. The effect component of Cause and Effect. see DRIVERS.

OUTER FOCUS – the larger realities that shape the environment the outfit (ORGANIZATION) operates in.

PARTNERSHIP – organization of two or more persons who pool some or all of their money, abilities, and skill in a business and divide profit or loss in predetermined proportions.

PATENT – making exclusive or proprietary claims or pretensions.

PDCA (PLAN-DO-CHECK-ACT) – a four-step iterative method used for the control and continual improvement of processes, procedures, or products.

PERFORMANCE MEASURES – the information collected that is related to the exhibited performance of individuals, group, teams, systems, component, or the organization overall.

PESTEL ANALYSIS – tool used to analyze macro-environmental factors that may impact an organization.

PLANNING – function of organizing a sequence of predetermined actions to complete future organizational objectives.

PORTER'S FIVE COMPETITIVE FORCES – a framework used to analyze the level of competition within an industry during business strategy development.

PORTER'S GENERIC STRATEGIES – Cost Leadership, Product Differentiation, and Market Focus are the three generic business strategies that can result in a solid COMPETITIVE ADVANTAGE for any business.

PRIMARY ACTIVITIES – the activities related directly to the creation of the product or delivery of the service including the after sale assistance or after service support.

PRIMARY TARGET MARKET – the segment of your selected MARKET your organization believes has the greatest potential for unit sales.

PRIVATE EQUITY – a source of investment capital from high net worth individuals and institutions for the purpose of investing and acquiring equity ownership in companies.

PROCEDURE – a series of actions that are done in a certain way or order. An established or accepted way of doing something.

PROCESS – a series of actions that produce something or that lead to a particular result.

PROCESS CONTROL – the continuous monitoring, analyzing and adjustment of a system with the intention of maintaining the system output within a specific desired range.

PROCUREMENT – acquisition of goods (materials, parts, supplies, equipment) required to carry on an enterprise. Procurement expenses can be a major cost of doing business.

PROCUREMENT & LOGISTICS – the VALUE ASPECT of your business focused primarily on functions and activities related to Procurement & Logistics throughout the organization. One of the ten

VALUE ASPECTS.

PRODUCING – to compose, create, or bring out by intellectual or physical effort.

PRODUCT – output or end result of production process. For example, automobiles are a product of the automobile companies.

PRODUCT DEVELOPMENT PROCESS – stages of introducing a new product or service concept and managing its development until it actually comes to market. The stages include analyzing the market, targeting potential buyers, understanding the productive capacity of the organization, developing a product to fit the market needs, distributing it to the marketplace, and analyzing customer feedback.

PRODUCT LIFE CYCLE ANALYSIS – the technique used to assess impacts associated with all the stages of the product's life, from first release to finish.

PRODUCTION – formal activity that adds value to goods and services, including creation, transport, and warehousing until used. Production is an organized process with specific goals.

PRODUCTION OPERATIONS (OPERATIONS) – activities associated with the actual creation of the product or service being offered. This would include machines, OPERATING SYSTEMS, production, testing, and facility management. One of the ten VALUE ASPECTS.

PROFIT – positive difference that results from selling products and services for more than the cost of producing these goods.

PROFIT AND LOSS STATEMENT – see INCOME STATEMENT.

PROFIT MARGIN – see MARGIN OF PROFIT.

PROPRIETARY TECHNOLOGY – owned by a particular person. In TRADE SECRETS law, proprietary property is information or knowledge in which the person developing it has ownership rights. Such rights are usually protected by contract and have not been the subject of a PATENT application.

PROTOCOL – formal diplomatic rules of etiquette. A system of rules that explain the correct conduct and procedures to be followed in formal situations.

PSYCHOGRAPHICS – determining market segmentation based on consumer psychological profiles. The two general areas include how the consumer views himself or herself in relation to the rest of the world and income characteristics.

PURCHASING – to buy (property, goods, etc.): to get (something) by paying money for it. The business functions of managing purchases within the organization.

PYRAMID OF PURPOSE AND VALUE – a simple framework for lying out and graphically depicting an organization's structure, strategy, and business identity. It is the representation of our organizations Micro Environment and everything within it.

QUALIFICATION – a special skill or type of experience or knowledge that makes someone suitable to do a particular job or activity.

REGULATION – rules used to carry out a law; act of administering a law. Many government agencies prepare regulations to administer a law.

REPEATABILITY – an ability to say, do, create, or accomplish something again.

REPRODUCIBILITY – an ability to say, do, create, or accomplish something that is exactly the same as or very similar to the original or previous.

RESEARCH & DEVELOPMENT (R&D) – scientific and marketing evolution of a new product or service. Once such a product has been created in a laboratory or other research setting, marketing specialists attempt to define the market for the product. Steps are then taken to manufacture the product to meet the needs of the market. One of the ten VALUE ASPECTS.

RESOURCES – human, financial, physical, and knowledge factors that provide a firm the means to perform its business processes.

RETAINED EARNINGS – NET PROFITS accumulated in a business after dividends are paid; also called undistributed profits or earned surplus. Retained earnings are distinguished from contributed capital.

RETROSPECTIVE – relating to or being a study that starts with the present condition and collects data about the past history to explain the present condition with the intention of improving the processes having been executed.

RETURN ON INVESTMENT (ROI) – amount, expressed as a

percentage, earned on a company's total capital—its common and preferred stock EQUITY plus its long-term funded debt—calculated by dividing total capital into earnings before interest, taxes, and dividends.

REVENUE – amount received. It generally denotes a GROSS figure, such as sales from a business, taxes collected by a government, or an amount received for performing a service.

REWORK – to work again on something that has already been worked but with successful results. The effort of perform a task successfully because the first attempt was performed unsuccessfully.

ROADMAP AND STRATEGY – the specific future plans, goals, metrics, and cross functional alignment employed by the organization to create success. The third of the five BMI SUCCESS ELEMENTS.

RULE BASED MANAGEMENT – management practices that focus both the major strategic and everyday operating decisions of the organization on decision tree created by successive levels of management.

SALES – in general: any exchange of goods or services for money. Finance: revenue received in exchange for goods and services recorded for a given accounting period, either on a CASH BASIS (as received) or on an ACCRUAL BASIS (as earned). One of the ten VALUE ASPECTS.

SALES STRATEGY – the specific plan to entice customers to purchase your value proposition (products and services).

SCRUM – an agile term referring to multiple small teams working in an intensive and interdependent manner. The term comes from the game of Rugby (scrummage) and refers to the formation the team uses to restart play after an event that causes play to stop.

SEED CAPITAL – see SEED MONEY.

SEED MONEY – venture capitalist's first contribution toward the financing or capital requirements of a start-up business. see VENTURE CAPITAL.

SERVICE – work done by one person that benefits another.

SERVICE DELIVERY – the delivery, support, maintenance, or enhancement of the products and services include scheduling, communications, installation, training, repair, upgrades, and spare parts management. One of the ten VALUE ASPECTS.

SERVICEABLE AVAILABLE MARKET (SAM) – the part of the TOTAL AVAILABLE MARKET (TAM) that can actually be reached.

SIGNIFICANT COMPETITIVE ADVANTAGE – the scenario presented when the measure of an organization's product or service distinctiveness in a given market is significantly greater that a competition. Usually associated with complete or total dominance of a market or the possession of a nearly impossible to obtain or duplicate CORE COMPETENCY.

SMARTER – an acronym for a project or goal attainment process. SMARTER stands for: Specific, Measurable, Achievable, Relevant, Time-bound, Execution, Retrospective.

SOLE PROPRIETORSHIP – business or financial venture that is carried on by a single person and is not a TRUST or CORPORATION.

SPRINT – to run or go at top speed especially for a short distance. In AGILE METHODOLOGY it is the small group of work to be focused on for a short period of time with the intention of creating the next iteration or version.

START UP  new business venture. In VENTURE CAPITAL parlance, start-up is the earliest stage at which a venture capital investor or investment pool will provide funds to an enterprise, usually on the basis of a business plan detailing the background of the management group along with market and financial projections. see SEED MONEY.

STRATEGIC OBJECTIVE – long-term organizational goals that are derived from the Mission statement and Shared Vision to be used in driving the business ROADMAP AND STRATEGY.

STRATEGIC PARTNERSHIP – long-term association between two or more organizations, such as airlines, to share initiatives and resources for the purpose of gaining a mutual COMPETITIVE ADVANTAGE.

STRATEGIC PLANNING – management act of determining a firm's future environment and response to organizational challenges; crucial decisions determining the direction of a firm.

STRATEGY – management plan or method for completing objectives; plan of procedures to be implemented, to do something.

STRATEGY MAP – a graphical representation of the business Strategy showing the cause and effect logic connecting the desired

Outcomes with the Drivers that will lead to those Outcomes.

SUCCESS ELEMENTS – the five core competencies of an organization that apply to any of the ten VALUE ASPECTS that are so critical to the success of the organization as a whole that failure to cultivate and progress in any one area will actually block an organization from getting to the next level.

SUPPORTING ACTIVITY – activities that support the Primary Activities in that they provide the required resource management, technology, quality talent, and other organization wide functions.

SUSTAINABLE BUSINESS – business environment that does not overwhelm the ecosystem, allowing sufficient environmental resources to remain for future generations.

SWOT ANALYSIS – evaluation of a company's Strengths, Weaknesses, Opportunities, and Threats; often a component of strategic planning or a business plan.

SYSTEM – organization of functionally interactive units for the achievement of a common goal. All systems have inputs, outputs, and feedback, and maintain a basic level of equilibrium.

TACTIC – short-term method for resolving a particular problem. For example, a tactic for quickly increasing a product market share may be a television advertising blitz.

TARGET MARKET – group of persons for whom a firm creates and maintains a PRODUCT MIX that specifically fits the needs and preferences of that group.

TARGET MARKET ANALYSIS – the study of a market usually with the intention to discern very specific information that will help determine the attractiveness of that market for a specific industry.

TECHNOLOGY DEVELOPMENT – activities associated with research and development of new and existing products and services, innovations, and processes. This would include aspects of knowledge management, best practices, Core Competencies, and training.

TOTAL AVAILABLE MARKET (TAM) – the total size of the market available to an organization in an industry if there were no competition. see SERVICABLE AVAILABLE MARKET (SAM) and TARGET MARKET.

TRADEMARK – [superscript] ® ™ insignia or logo that distinguishes one maker's goods from all others; any mark, word, letter, number, design, picture, or combination thereof in any form that is adopted and used by a person to denominate goods that he makes, is affixed to the goods, and is neither a common nor generic name for the goods nor a picture of them, nor is merely descriptive of the goods. Protection from INFRINGEMENT upon a trademark is afforded by the common-law action for unfair competition.

TURNAROUND – favorable reversal in the fortunes of a company, a market, or the economy at large. Stock market investors speculating that a poorly performing company is about to show a marked improvement in earnings might profit handsomely from its turnaround.

UNITS (X) (WIDGETS) – any division of quantity accepted as a standard of measurement or of exchange. For example, in the commodities market, a unit of wheat is a bushel, a unit of coffee a pound, and a unit of shell eggs a dozen.

UPSTREAM VALUE – value added to products or services of vendors or partners that supply inputs to your process.

VALUE – worth of all the rights arising from ownership; quantity of one thing that will be given in exchange for another. A fair return or equivalent in goods, services, or money for something exchanged.

VALUE ASPECTS – the finite number of functions and activities that any business can be defined by, broken down into, and evaluated upon.

VALUE BASED MANAGEMENT – management practices that focus both the major strategic and everyday operating decisions of the organization the key drivers of value.

VALUE CHAIN – the concept that primary and supporting activities of an organization all can be mapped to the end result product or service value and therefore managed for optimal customer value and organization margin.

VALUE JUDGMENT – judgment reflecting values and opinions. A value judgment is a biased opinion.

VALUE PROPOSITION – the innovation of products or services intended to present the business, it products, or its services in an attractive way the potential target market customers.

VALUE SYSTEM – a set of consistent values endeared to and exhibited in the support of ethical or ideological integrity.

VALUES (CORE VALUES) – something (as a principle or quality) intrinsically valuable or desirable. The principals that support the organization or endeavors MISSION and VISION.

VARIABLE COSTS – cost that changes directly with the amount of production, such as direct material or direct labor needed to complete a product. see FIXED COST.

VENTURE (BUSINESS VENTURE) – a venture (business venture) is the launch of an organization for purpose and reasonable expectation of executing on a plan to create financial gain.

VENTURE CAPITAL – important source of financing for START-UP companies or others embarking on new or TURNAROUND ventures that entail some investment risk but offer the potential for above-average future profits; also called risk capital. Prominent among firms seeking venture capital are those classified as emerging growth or high technology companies.

VERTICAL INTEGRATION – a company's domination of a product by controlling all steps in the production process, from the extraction of raw materials through the manufacture and sale of the final product. For example, some oil companies explore, refine, and retail gasoline. Contrast with HORIZONTAL INTEGRATION.

VISION (SHARED VISION) – view of the future that can shape current management strategies. The robust and enticing picture that tells the compelling story that investors and entrepreneurs will buy into.

VOLATILITY – characterized by or subject to rapid or unexpected change e.g. a volatile market.

WATERFALL – the waterfall model is historically a sequential design process dating back fifty plus years. It received its name because of the way the phases of the model cascade downward.

WHOLESALER – middleman; person who buys large quantities of goods and resells to other distributors rather than to ultimate consumers.

WIDGET – symbolic gadget, used wherever a hypothetical product is needed to illustrate a manufacturing or selling concept. If you are a service based business time is your widget.

WORKING CAPITAL – funds invested in a company's cash, ACCOUNTS RECEIVABLE, inventory, and other current assets (gross working capital). It usually refers to net working capital, that is, current assets minus current liabilities.

ZERO BASED THINKING – a decision-making process requiring that one imagines themselves returning to the point before a particular decision was made or event took place. The subject then allows themselves to make the decisions with the current knowledge of the outcome. Ask the question: Knowing what I know now, would I...

# Bibliography

Agnes, Michael. *Webster's New World Dictionary*. New York, NY: Pocket Books, 2003.

*Ansof Matrix* Ansoff, Igor.: *Strategies for Diversification*, Harvard Business Review, Vol. 35 Issue 5,Sep-Oct 1957, pp. 113-124

Bossidy, Larry, Ram Charan, and Charles Burck. *Execution: The Discipline of Getting Things Done*. New York, NY: Crown Business, 2002.

Bowman, Cliff, and David Faulkner. *Competitive and Corporate Strategy*. London: Irwin, 1997.

Colbeck, P. J. *Information Technology Roadmap for Professional Service Firms*. Canton, MI: Perspective Shifts Press, 2006.

Collins, James C. *Good to Great: Why Some Companies Make the Leap ... and Others Don't*. New York, NY: HarperBusiness, 2001.

Collins, James C. *How the Mighty Fall: And Why Some Companies Never Give in*. New York, NY: HarperCollins Publishers, 2011.

Collins, James C., and Morten T. Hansen. *Great by Choice: Uncertainty, Chaos, and Luck: Why Some Thrive despite Them All*. New York, NY: HarperCollins Publishers, 2011.

Collins, James C., and Jerry I. Porras. *Built to Last: Successful Habits of Visionary Companies*. New York, NY: HarperBusiness, 2004.

Covey, Stephen R. *Principle-Centered Leadership*. New York, NY: Simon & Schuster, 1992.

Deming, W. Edwards. *Out of the Crisis*. Cambridge, MA: MIT Press, 2000.

*Dictionary of Business and Economic Terms (Barron's Business Dictionaries)*, Jack P. Ph.D., CPA Friedman, Kindle Edition - Sold by: Amazon Digital Services LLC

Drucker, Peter F. *The Effective Executive: The Definitive Guide to Getting the Right Things Done.* New York, NY: HarperBusiness, 2006.

Drucker, Peter F. *The Essential Drucker: The Best of Sixty Years of Peter Drucker's Essential Writings on Management.* New York, NY: HarperCollins, 2006.

Drucker, Peter F. *Innovation and Entrepreneurship: Practice and Principles.* New York, NY: Harper & Row, 1985.

Drucker, Peter F. *Management: Tasks, Responsibilities, Practices.* New York, NY: Harper & Row, 1974.

Drucker, Peter F. *The Practice of Management.* New York, NY: HarperBusiness, 2006.

Duhigg, Charles. *The Power of Habit: Why We Do What We Do in Life and Business.* New York, NY: Random House, 2012.

Dyer, Wayne W. *The Power of Intention: Learning to Co-create Your World Your Way.* Carlsbad, CA: Hay House, 2004.

Frankl, Viktor E. *Man's Search for Meaning.* Boston, MA: Beacon Press, 2006.

George, Michael L. *Lean Six Sigma for Service: How to Use Lean Speed and Six Sigma Quality to Improve Services and Transactions.* New York, NY: McGraw-Hill, 2003.

Gerber, Michael E. *The E-myth Revisited: Why Most Small Businesses Don't Work and What to Do about It.* New York, NY: HarperBusiness, 2001.

Gittell, Jody Hoffer. *The Southwest Airlines Way: Using the Power of Relationships to Achieve High Performance.* New York, NY: McGraw-Hill, 2003.

Gladwell, Malcolm. *Blink: The Power of Thinking without Thinking.* New York, NY: Little, Brown and Company, 2005.

Gladwell, Malcolm. *Outliers: The Story of Success.* New York, NY: Little, Brown and Company, 2008.

Gladwell, Malcolm. *The Tipping Point: How Little Things Can Make a Big Difference.* Boston, MA: Little, Brown and Company, 2000.

Glaser, Edward M. *An Experiment in the Development of Critical Thinking.* New York, NY: AMS Press, 1972.

Goleman, Daniel. *Emotional Intelligence: Why It Can Matter More than IQ.*

New York, NY: Bantam Books, 2005.

Goleman, Daniel. *Focus: The Hidden Driver of Excellence*. New York, NY: HarperCollins Publishers, 2013.

Hill, Napoleon. *The Law of Success in Sixteen Lessons*. Blacksburg, VA: Wilder Publications, 2011.

Hill, Napoleon, and Arthur R. Pell. *Think and Grow Rich*. New York, NY: Jeremy P. Tarcher/Penguin, 2005.

Kaplan, Robert S., and David P. Norton. *The Balanced Scorecard: Translating Strategy into Action*. New York, NY: Harvard Business Review Press, 1996

Kaplan, Robert S., and David P. Norton. *Strategy Maps: Converting Intangible Assets into Tangible Outcomes*. Boston, MA: Harvard Business School Press, 2004.

Kaplan, Robert S., and David P. Norton. *The Strategy-focused Organization: How Balanced Scorecard Companies Thrive in the New Business Environment*. Boston, MA: Harvard Business School Press, 2001.

Liker, Jeffrey K., and Gary L. Convis. *The Toyota Way to Lean Leadership: Achieving and Sustaining Excellence through Leadership Development*. New York, NY: McGraw-Hill, 2011.

Marston, William Moulton. *Emotions of Normal People*. London: K. Paul, Trench, Trubner & Company, 1928.

McConnell, Ben, and Jackie Huba. *Creating Customer Evangelists: How Loyal Customers Become a Volunteer Sales Force*. Chicago, IL: Dearborn Trade Pub., 2003.

Peters, Thomas J. *Thriving on Chaos: Handbook for a Management Revolution*. New York, NY: Harper & Row, 1988.

Peters, Thomas J., and Robert H. Waterman, Jr. *In Search of Excellence: Lessons from America's Best-run Companies*. New York, NY: HarperBusiness, 2006.

Pink, Daniel H. *Drive: The Surprising Truth about What Motivates Us*. New York, NY: Riverhead Books, 2009.

Pink, Daniel H. *Free Agent Nation: The Future of Working for Yourself*. New York, NY: Warner Books, 2002.

Pink, Daniel H. *To Sell Is Human: The Surprising Truth about Moving Others*.

New York, NY: Riverhead Books, 2012.

Porter, Michael E. *Competitive Advantage: Creating and Sustaining Superior Performance*. New York, NY: Free Press, 1985.

Porter, Michael E. *Competitive Strategy: Techniques for Analyzing Industries and Competitors*. New York, NY: Free Press, 1980.

Reichheld, Frederick F., and Rob Markey. *The Ultimate Question 2.0: How Net Promoter Companies Thrive in a Customer-driven World*. Boston, MA: Harvard Business Press, 2011.

Schutz, Will. *The Human Element: Productivity, Self-esteem, and the Bottom Line*. San Francisco, CA: Jossey-Bass Publishers, 1994.

Shoffner, H. George., Susan Shelly, and Robert A. Cooke. *Finance for Nonfinancial Managers*. New York, NY: McGraw-Hill, 2011.

Sinek, Simon. *Start with Why: How Great Leaders Inspire Everyone to Take Action*. New York, NY: Portfolio, 2009.

Stratten, Scott. *UnMarketing: Stop Marketing. Start Engaging*. Hoboken, NJ: Wiley, 2012.

Tzu, Sun, Shawn Conners, and Lionel Giles. *The Art of War by Sun Tzu - Classic Edition*. El Paso, TX: El Paso Norte Press, 2009.

Walton, Sam, and John Huey. *Sam Walton, Made in America: My Story*. New York, NY: Doubleday, 1992.

Welch, Jack, and Suzy Welch. *The Real-Life MBA: The No-nonsense Guide to Winning the Game, Building a Team and Growing Your Career*. New York, NY: HarperCollins, 2015.

# INDEX

www.ingramcontent.com/pod-product-compliance
Lightning Source LLC
Chambersburg PA
CBHW031407180326
41458CB00043B/6645/J